ALLEGORY

ALLEGORY

THE DYNAMICS OF
AN ANCIENT AND MEDIEVAL TECHNIQUE

JON WHITMAN

HARVARD UNIVERSITY PRESS
CAMBRIDGE, MASSACHUSETTS
1987

Library of Congress Cataloging-in-Publication Data
Whitman, Jon, 1949–
Allegory: the dynamics of an ancient and medieval
technique.
Includes index.
1. Allegory.   2. Literature, Medieval–History and
criticism.   3. Classical literature–History and
criticism.   I. Title.
PN56.A5W55 1986   809'.915   85-27261
ISBN 0-674-01645-9

To my parents

PREFACE

A study of allegory is liable to expose in more ways than one the tendencies of its subject. In my early research I sought to clarify certain principles which helped to organize allegorical writing in the Latin and vernacular traditions of the late Middle Ages. Allegory, however, has a way of showing how the attempt to specify such points of reference only produces new reference points for consideration. A number of allegorical developments which preceded the late medieval period increasingly seemed to me to require a close analysis of their own. My investigation of this ancient and early medieval material, scattered in a range of primary sources and treated in a variety of specialized studies, led to this book, which closes at the mid-twelfth century. The allegory discussed in the final chapter is not only a culmination of certain early allegorical procedures, but also an anticipation of changes to come.

The book was substantially completed in 1983, although I have made minor adjustments since that time. Studies published after 1983 are not cited. For reasons of economy two features of the original manuscript have been omitted from the published text. One is the bibliography. Although the notes direct attention to some useful resources for further research and to the main sources of my own indebtedness, they do not acknowledge all the valuable studies which have some bearing on the argument. The other change in format is the transliteration of Greek into English characters. Aside from special cases, like my transcription of Greek v outside certain diphthongs as English y, this is a straightforward exchange. The broader issue of how to treat originally Greek terms has its own complications, however, and in different contexts I present a word like *nous* in italics, roman type, quotation marks, or a variant spelling such as 'Noys,' the form used in this and most discussions for the character in the *Cosmographia*.

Whatever the inconsistencies in the 'letter' of this book, its spirit has been supported by people close to my work. For their stimulating teaching of medieval and Renaissance literature at different stages of my studies, I am grateful to Robert

Hanning, Edward Tayler, E. Talbot Donaldson, John Burrow, and Theodore Andersson. Among those who have encouraged my work are Karl-Ludwig Selig, Carl Hovde, Walter Jackson Bate, and Robert Kiely. I owe particular thanks to Pamela Gradon, who supervised the graduate program during which my study of allegory began, for her learning and thoughtfulness. Larry Benson, one of the readers of my dissertation, has repeatedly helped me to assess the direction of my research. The scholar and friend to whom I am most indebted in all my work is Morton Bloomfield, who supervised my dissertation and continues to share with me his spirit and wisdom.

Over the course of my research I received support from several other sources. My early work on allegory was assisted by a Kellett Fellowship from Columbia for study at Magdalen College, Oxford and by Lehman and Whiting Fellowships at Harvard. My later work was aided by research fellowships from the University of Virginia; a Sesquicentennial Associateship at its Center for Advanced Studies; an appointment as a Visiting Scholar at Harvard; a Fellowship for Independent Study and Research from the National Endowment for the Humanities; research support from Ben-Gurion University of the Negev; a grant from the Center for Absorption in Science, the Israeli Ministry of Immigrant Absorption; and a fellowship at the Institute for Advanced Studies of the Hebrew University of Jerusalem. At various stages of writing I received useful advice from readers of the work. My most profound debt of this kind is to Winthrop Wetherbee, for his acute analysis at crucial moments in the book's development. Others who made helpful suggestions include Barbara Nolan, Angus Fletcher, and the readers for Oxford University Press and Harvard University Press whose names are not known to me. My continuing indebtedness to other scholars is apparent throughout the text and notes. I am grateful to the editors at Oxford University Press and Harvard University Press, Kim Scott Walwyn and Margaretta Fulton, for their skillful guidance and patience during the preparation of the work for co-publication, and to Mary Worthington for her careful copy editing of the text. If I could have incorporated all the scholarly and technical suggestions I received, this would have been a better book; for any omissions and errors, I alone am responsible.

In the end, I am indebted to others whose thoughts I have unknowingly come to think are my own and, above all, to those whose influence upon this book is inseparable from their broader influence upon my life. The deepest of these abiding debts I owe to my parents, who have sustained and encouraged me in every way. Although I can never fully express to them the extent of my love and respect, perhaps the dedication to them of a book on allegory suggests in some limited way how they mean more to me than I can ever say.

J.W.

CONTENTS

ABBREVIATIONS

Abbreviations of other works are cited in the notes. In the case of any additional work by an author cited here according to name alone (e.g., Pépin, the abbreviation for *Mythe et allégorie*), at least part of the title of the different work accompanies the author's name in the citation (e.g., Pépin, *Théologie cosmique et théologie chrétienne*).

Series and Periodicals

AHDLMA: *Archives d'histoire doctrinale et littéraire du moyen âge*
Beiträge: *Beiträge zur Geschichte der Philosophie des Mittelalters*
CCSL: *Corpvs Christianorvm, Series Latina*
CSEL: *Corpus scriptorum ecclesiasticorum latinorum*
MGH: *Monumenta Germaniae Historica*
MP: *Modern Philology*
PG: *Patrologiae Cursus Completus, Series Graeca*
PL: *Patrologiae Cursus Completus, Series Latina*
PMLA: *Publications of the Modern Language Association*
StM: *Studi medievali*

Primary and Secondary Texts

Anticlaudianus: *Alain de Lille*: *Anticlaudianus,* ed. R. Bossuat (Paris, 1955)
Brinkmann: Hennig Brinkmann, *Mittelalterliche Hermeneutik* (Tübingen, 1980)
Buffière: Félix Buffière, *Les Mythes d'Homère et la pensée grecque* (Paris, 1956)
Chenu: M.-D. Chenu, *Nature, Man, and Society in the Twelfth Century,* tr. Jerome Taylor and L. K. Little (Chicago, 1968)
Cosm.: *Bernardus Silvestris*: *Cosmographia,* ed. Peter Dronke (Leiden, 1978), cited by section and line number in the case of verse passages, by section, paragraph, and line number in the case of prose passages
Cosm. (tr.): *The* Cosmographia *of Bernardus Silvestris,* tr. Winthrop Wetherbee (New York, 1973)
Coulter: James A. Coulter, *The Literary Microcosm: Theories of Interpretation of the Later Neoplatonists* (Leiden, 1976)
Courcelle, *Tradition*: Pierre Courcelle, *La Consolation de philosophie dans la tradition littéraire: antécédents et postérité de Boèce* (Paris, 1967)
Daniélou: Jean Daniélou, *From Shadows to Reality: Studies in the Biblical Typology of the Fathers,* tr. Wulstan Hibberd (London, 1960)

de Lubac: Henri de Lubac, *Exégèse médiévale: les quatre sens de l'Écriture*, 2 pts. in 4 vols. (Paris, 1959–64)

DPN: 'Alan of Lille, "De Planctu naturae," ' ed. N. M. Häring, *StM*, 3a ser., 19 (1978), 797–879

Dronke, 'L'amor': Peter Dronke, 'L'amor che move il sole e l'altre stelle,' *StM*, 3a ser., 6 (1965), 389–422

Dronke, *Fabula*: Peter Dronke, *Fabula: Explorations into the Uses of Myth in Medieval Platonism* (Leiden, 1974)

Grant: R. M. Grant, *The Letter and the Spirit* (London, 1957)

Gregory, *Anima*: Tullio Gregory, *Anima mundi: La filosofia di Guglielmo di Conches e la Scuola di Chartres* (Florence, 1955)

Gregory, 'L'idea': Tullio Gregory, 'L'idea di natura nella filosofia medievale prima dell'ingresso della fisica di Aristotele: il secolo xii,' in *La filosofia della natura nel Medioevo: Atti del Terzo Congresso Internazionale di Filosofia Medioevale, 1964* (Milan, 1966), pp. 27–65

Gregory, *Platonismo*: Tullio Gregory, *Platonismo medievale: studi e ricerche* (Rome, 1958)

Jauss, 'Entstehung': Hans Robert Jauss, 'Entstehung und Strukturwandel der allegorischen Dichtung,' in *Grundriss der romanischen Literaturen des Mittelalters* VI/1, ed. H. R. Jauss and Erich Köhler (Heidelberg, 1968), pp. 146–244

Jauss, 'Form': Hans Robert Jauss, 'Form und Auffassung der Allegorie in der Tradition der *Psychomachia* (von Prudentius zum ersten *Romanz de la Rose*),' in *Medium aevum vivum: Festschrift für Walther Bulst*, ed. H. R. Jauss and Dieter Schaller (Heidelberg, 1960), pp. 179–206

Jauss, 'Transformation': Hans Robert Jauss, 'La transformation de la forme allégorique entre 1180 et 1240: d'Alain de Lille à Guillaume de Lorris,' in *L'humanisme médiéval dans les littératures romanes du xiie au xive siècle*, ed. A. Fourrier (Paris, 1964), pp. 107–46

Krewitt: Ulrich Krewitt, *Metapher und tropische Rede in der Auffassung des Mittelalters*, Beihefte zum 'Mittellateinischen Jahrbuch,' 7 (Ratingen, 1971)

Lewis: C. S. Lewis, *The Allegory of Love* (Oxford, 1936)

Pépin: Jean Pépin, *Mythe et allégorie: les origines grecques et les contestations judéo-chrétiennes*, enlarged edition (Paris, 1976)

Smalley: Beryl Smalley, *The Study of the Bible in the Middle Ages* (New York, 1952)

Spicq: C. Spicq, *Esquisse d'une histoire de l'exégèse latine au moyen âge* (Paris, 1944)

Stock: Brian Stock, *Myth and Science in the Twelfth Century: A Study of Bernard Silvester* (Princeton, 1972)

SVF: *Stoicorum Veterum Fragmenta*, ed. Ioannes ab (Hans von) Arnim, 3 vols. (Leipzig, 1903–5), Index Volume by M. Adler (Leipzig, 1924)

Verbum et Signum: *Verbum et Signum*, ed. Hans Fromm, Wolfgang Harms, and Uwe Ruberg, 2 vols. (Munich, 1975)

Wetherbee: Winthrop Wetherbee, *Platonism and Poetry in the Twelfth Century: The Literary Influence of the School of Chartres* (Princeton, 1972)

Wolfson, *Philo*: Harry Austryn Wolfson, *Philo: Foundations of Religious Philosophy in Judaism, Christianity, and Islam*, 2 vols. (Cambridge, Mass., 1947)

Wolfson, *Fathers*: Harry Austryn Wolfson, *The Philosophy of the Church Fathers: Faith, Trinity, Incarnation*, 3rd edn. (Cambridge, Mass., 1970)

I THE ALLEGORICAL PROBLEM

It is fitting for us to accept the likely story in these matters
and not to search beyond it. (Plato, *Timaeus* 29D.)

From its beginnings, allegory has been known as an oblique
way of writing. Despite various attempts to explain it in its
literary form, it still conceals many of its secrets. Modern
readers, indeed, may be inclined to leave it to its own
mysterious ways. To us, obscurity is at best a sign of the
author's elusiveness, and at worst an indication of his bad
faith. In either case, it seems to be an obstacle between us and
the truth. Even our recent courtship with obscurity in the arts,
our 'modernism,' has wearied us, and we long for plain speech
and clear thought.

It is a sensible wish. In our concern for clarity, however, we
might remember that what we take to be our simplest expressions often conceal a multitude of obscurities. It is not only
that a single name can refer to many things, and a single thing
be called by many names. Since Babel, we have been ac-
customed to this confusion in our language. It is rather that our
very drive for clarity generates obscurity as a by-product. The
deeper we penetrate into the center of things, the more we
leave even our plainest language on the circumference. Those
'solid' objects all around us—they are really, so we are told,
swirling, dizzying movements of molecules in space, if only we
could see them with microscopic eyes. If we may borrow a
phrase from allegory, our language is constantly telling us that
something is what it is not.

There have been attempts, of course, some of them famous,
to remove these obscurities from our language and thought.
Perhaps the most successful approach to the problem, however,
has been to exploit it. For the fall from our pristine state of
language has not been a total loss. As a result of it, we have
constructed a most beautiful consolation for our exile, the
solace of fiction. All fiction—the very word confesses its exile
from the truth—tries to express a truth by departing from it in
some way. It may embellish its subject, rearrange it, or simply

verbalize it, but in every case, that ancient dislocation of words from their objects will keep the language at one remove from what it claims to present. Allegory is the extreme case of this divergence. It seems to refer to something in the fiction, but actually refers to something else in fact. Allegory turns its head in one direction, but turns its eyes in another. In the traditional formula, it says one thing, and means another.*

In its obliquity, allegorical writing thus exposes in an extreme way the foundation of fiction in general. The fact is sometimes ignored by those who concentrate upon other kinds of writing. Allegory, if we may use the expression, is outspokenly reticent, proclaiming that it has a secret, while other techniques tend to conceal the fact. From the beginning, the practitioners of allegory have claimed that it provides an initiation into a mystery. Whatever the value of that claim, perhaps the technique offers a kind of initiation into some of the mysteries of fiction itself.

If allegory intriguingly suggests its own promise, it also revealingly displays its own problems. The basis for the technique is obliquity—the separation between what a text says, the 'fiction,' and what it means, the 'truth.' This very obliquity, however, relies upon an assumed correspondence between the fiction and the truth. The apparent meaning, after all, only diverges from the actual one insofar as they are compared with each other. In these two conflicting demands—the divergence between the apparent and actual meanings, and yet the correspondence between them—it is possible to see both the birth and the death of allegorical writing. The more allegory exploits the divergence between corresponding levels of meaning, the less tenable the correspondence becomes. Alternatively, the more it closes ranks and emphasizes the correspondence, the less oblique, and thus the less allegorical, the divergence becomes. In this way, allegory tends to be at odds with itself, tending to undermine itself by the very process that sustains it. The degree to which such potential pressures become active in allegorical writing varies between texts, and at times allegory acquires forms which accommodate some of its internal tensions. Before any detailed treatment of specific cases and

* For a linguistic and conceptual overview of the word, with its changes in nuance and application, see Appendix I, 'On the History of the Term "Allegory."'

qualifications, though, it might be useful to look briefly at the problem in general.

There are two traditions of allegory, each attempting in its own oblique way to express the truth. One is the tradition of allegorical *interpretation*. Interpretive allegory claims to discover the truth hidden beneath a text. It begins in earnest in the sixth century BC, with the philosophic interpretation of Homer.[1] In all interpretive allegory, we can observe the pull between divergence and correspondence to which I have referred. As an example, we might take a text in which the figure of Athena descends from the skies and speaks to a man. Interpretive allegory would argue that this is just a fiction for the true meaning. Athena, so the interpretation would go, really corresponds to 'wisdom.' Once this correspondence is established, however, we can sustain it only by a series of divergences, or transfers, from the literal meaning of the text. For example, wisdom, unlike Athena, cannot 'descend.' The author must be saying obliquely that wisdom 'occurs' to a man, or perhaps, that the man becomes wise. Similarly, wisdom cannot 'speak.' The author must be saying obliquely that wisdom informs the man's thoughts. In this way, allegorical interpretation repeatedly departs from the apparent meaning of the text,

---

[1] On allegorical interpretation as a whole, the following studies are especially valuable. For ancient Greek and Roman exegesis, see Buffière; Pépin; the series of articles by J. Tate, 'The Beginnings of Greek Allegory,' *Classical Review*, 41 (1927), 214-15; 'Cornutus and the Poets,' *Classical Quarterly*, 23 (1929), 41-5; 'Plato and Allegorical Interpretation,' *Classical Quarterly*, 23 (1929), 142-54 and *Classical Quarterly*, 24 (1930), 1-10; 'On the History of Allegorism,' *Classical Quarterly*, 28 (1934), 105-14; and the study of late antique Neoplatonic interpretation by Coulter. On the transition between antique interpretive allegory and the early Jewish and Christian interpretation of the Bible, see Wolfson, *Philo*; *Fathers*; Grant; R. P. C. Hanson, *Allegory and Event: A Study of the Sources and Significance of Origen's Interpretation of Scripture* (Richmond, Va., 1959); and Philip Rollinson, *Classical Theories of Allegory and Christian Culture* (Pittsburgh, Pa., 1981). On the origins and techniques of Christian typology, see Erich Auerbach, 'Figura,' orig. pub. 1944, tr. Ralph Manheim in *Scenes from the Drama of European Literature* (1959; repr. Gloucester, Mass., 1973), pp. 11-76; the thematic studies of Daniélou; and the revaluation by A. C. Charity, *Events and their Afterlife: The Dialectics of Christian Typology in the Bible and Dante* (Cambridge, Mass., 1966). On medieval scriptural exegesis in general, see Spicq; Smalley; and the monumental study of de Lubac. On the broader range of hermeneutical activity in the Middle Ages, including the exegesis of figurative discourse at large, the natural world as a whole, and the conceptual format of secular and sacred texts, see Krewitt; *Verbum et Signum*; Brinkmann; and Judson Boyce Allen, *The Ethical Poetic of the Later Middle Ages: A decorum of convenient distinction* (Toronto, 1982). Other works esp. helpful on particular problems in allegorical interpretation will be cited later.

reinterpreting it in order to sustain a correspondence. Needless to say, this places great strain on the text, and as the divergences widen, the allegory is liable to break. Thus, if later we see this same Athena pulling a man's hair, or raging in battle against some opponent, it becomes increasingly difficult to sustain the correspondence between her and wisdom. Wisdom, after all, does not 'rage.' In such cases, we must admit that there is a literal element to Athena which cannot be allegorized. In short, our allegorical interpretation breaks down. We originally sustained it by a series of divergences, transferring fictional descriptions into actual meanings. Eventually, though, the divergences proliferate, and tend to undermine the original correspondence. On the other hand, had we simply confined the correspondence to the passage in which Athena speaks to a man, we would undermine our allegory from the other direction. By leaving the warlike Athena of the later passage to the literal level, we would be admitting that the allegory breaks down in that part of the text. In short, a narrow correspondence leaves no room to sustain an allegory, but a wide divergence destroys it as well. Whichever path allegorical interpretation chooses, it is potentially on a collision course with itself.

The same internal conflict affects the other tradition of allegory, the tradition of allegorical *composition*. Unlike the philosophic method of interpretive allegory, compositional allegory is essentially a grammatical or rhetorical technique. In its most striking form, it personifies abstract concepts and fashions a narrative around them.* Although personification develops episodically in classical literature, its first full-scale deployment occurs at the turn of the fourth and fifth centuries AD, with the *Psychomachia* of Prudentius.[2] In procedure,

---

* For a linguistic and conceptual overview of personification, see Appendix II, 'On the History of the Term "Personification." '

[2] On the broad tradition of personification, the following studies are particularly useful. For a survey of ancient and medieval developments, see Lewis, esp. pp. 44–111, an account that is still valuable, though it is significantly qualified by more recent scholarship and deeply revised in this book. For personification in Greek thought, see Karl Reinhardt, 'Personifikation und Allegorie,' an essay written in the late 1930s, but first published in *Vermächtnis der Antike: Gesammelte Essays zur Philosophie und Geschichtsschreibung*, ed. Carl Becker (Göttingen, 1960), pp. 7–40; T. B. L. Webster, 'Personification as a Mode of Greek Thought,' *Journal of the Warburg and Courtauld Institutes*, 17 (1954), 10–21; and Otto Seel, 'Antike und Frühchristliche Allegorik,' in

personification is virtually the inverse of allegorical interpretation. While interpretive allegory moves, for instance, from the fictional Athena to the underlying meaning of 'wisdom,' compositional allegory begins with 'wisdom' itself, and constructs a fiction around it.

Nevertheless, in personification too we can see that same pull between an initial correspondence and an increasing divergence. We begin, for example, with a correspondence between the actual meaning, the wisdom of a man, and our fictional character, the figure of 'Wisdom.' In fact, as long as we do not elaborate the figure of 'Wisdom' in any way, the correspondence is so strict that we can scarcely call it allegorical. 'Wisdom' itself refers directly to wisdom; it does not refer obliquely to something *else*. And allegory, after all, says one thing, but means another. In order to create an allegory, therefore, we must depart from this perfect correspondence.[3] For example, we might attribute to our fictional character a body, or a costume, or an action. In so doing, however, we begin that process of divergence from our original strict correspondence, a process which is liable to undermine the correspondence. Wisdom itself, after all, has no shape, no clothing, and no activity. The more personal attributes we give our personification,

---

Festschrift für Peter Metz (Berlin, 1965), pp. 11–45. For personification in Roman thought, see H. L. Axtell, *The Deification of Abstract Ideas in Roman Literature and Inscriptions,* Diss. Chicago 1907 (Chicago, 1907), and two overviews by L. R. Lind, 'Roman Religion and Ethical Thought: Abstraction and Personification,' *Classical Journal,* 69 (Dec. 1973-Jan. 1974), 108–19, and 'Primitivity and Roman Ideas: The Survivals,' *Latomus,* 35 (1976), 245–68. For the development of medieval personification and the emergence of the early vernacular tradition, see Jauss, 'Form'; 'Transformation'; 'Entstehung'; Richard Glasser, 'Abstractum agens und Allegorie im älteren Französisch,' *Zeitschrift für Romanische Philologie,* 69 (1953), 43–122; Charles Muscatine, 'The Emergence of Psychological Allegory in Old French Romance,' *PMLA* 68 (1953), 1160–82; and Marc-René Jung, *Études sur le poème allégorique en France au moyen âge* (Bern, 1971). For some general remarks on the medieval technique, see Rosemond Tuve, *Allegorical Imagery: Some Mediaeval Books and Their Posterity* (Princeton, 1966), and for the grammatical procedure itself, see Morton W. Bloomfield, 'A Grammatical Approach to Personification Allegory,' *MP* 60 (1963), 161–71. Other studies of the subject will be cited later.

[3] Such divergence, or transfer, has been recognized as a requirement for compositional allegory since the earliest discussions of the subject. See, e.g., Demetrius (dated between the third century BC and the first century AD; cf. App. I), *Demetrius On Style,* ed. and tr. W. Rhys Roberts (Cambridge, 1902), par. 100, p. 118; Cicero, *Orator,* ed. and tr. H. M. Hubbell (Cambridge, Mass., 1939), xxvii, 94; Quintilian, *Institutio Oratoria,* ed. and tr. H. E. Butler, 4 vols. (London, 1920–2), IX, ii, 46; and my broader discussion in App. I.

the more we turn it first into a mere character type of wisdom, and finally into a wise individual. The same dilemma that faces interpretive allegory thus confronts compositional allegory, too. A narrow correspondence between wisdom and the fictional character 'Wisdom' leaves no room for oblique, allegorical activity. But a wide divergence between the two eventually undermines the allegory, as well, by shifting it to the literal level of a wise individual. Whichever path compositional allegory chooses, it too is potentially on a collision course with itself.

While personification is the most striking kind of compositional allegory, it is not the only kind. Allegorical composition need not employ abstract characters at all.[4] We might express a

4 For some recent discussions of the range of allegorical composition, see Walter Benjamin, *Ursprung des deutschen Trauerspiels*, orig. pub. 1928, tr. John Osborne as *The Origin of German Tragic Drama* (London, 1977), 'Allegory and Trauerspiel,' pp. 159–235, on allegory's 'fragmentation' of the world, as 'ideas evaporate in images,' which in their very ruin point toward consolidation; Northrop Frye, *Anatomy of Criticism: Four Essays* (Princeton, 1957), pp. 89–92, 341–2, along with his more recent article, 'Allegory,' in the *Princeton Encyclopedia of Poetry and Poetics*, ed. Alex Preminger, enlarged edition (Princeton, 1974), on a 'sliding scale' between 'allegorical' and 'anti-allegorical' expression; Edwin Honig, *Dark Conceit: The Making of Allegory* (Providence, R. I., 1959), esp. pp. 113–45, on 'analogy, irony, and dialectic transfer'; Angus Fletcher, *Allegory: The Theory of a Symbolic Mode* (Ithaca, N. Y., 1964), esp. pp. 70–180, on the 'part-whole relationship,' and 'progress and battle' as principal kinds of action; Michael Murrin, *The Veil of Allegory: Some Notes toward a Theory of Allegorical Rhetoric in the English Renaissance* (Chicago, 1969), esp. pp. 54–74, 98–166, on 'value judgments' in the theory and practice of Renaissance allegory; Pamela Gradon, *Form and Style in Early English Literature* (London, 1971), 'The Allegorical Picture,' pp. 32–92, on diverse traditions in ancient and medieval allegory; Gay Clifford, *The Transformations of Allegory* (London, 1974), esp. pp. 1–35, 94–129, on the 'coherence' of allegory, and subversive tendencies since the Renaissance; Stephen A. Barney, *Allegories of History, Allegories of Love* (Hamden, Conn., 1979), on allegories of 'typology' and 'reification'; Maureen Quilligan, *The Language of Allegory* (Ithaca, N. Y., 1979), on polysemous narrative as a progressive commentary on its own ambiguity and certain challenges posed to allegorical writing since the seventeenth century by shifts in epistemological perspective; Paul de Man, *Allegories of Reading: Figural Language in Rousseau, Nietzsche Rilke, and Proust* (New Haven, 1979), on texts from the eighteenth century and later as 'allegorical' enactments of conflicting demands posed by their own rhetorical modes; Michael Murrin, *The Allegorical Epic* (Chicago, 1980), a 'companion volume' to his earlier work, on 'polyvalent' allegory and the manipulation of the marvelous in works of Virgil and major Italian and English Renaissance poets; and the collection of essays exploring different strategies of allegory from the Middle Ages to the modern period in *Allegory, Myth, and Symbol*, ed. Morton W. Bloomfield, Harvard English Studies, 9 (Cambridge, Mass., 1981). For an overview of some recent scholarship on medieval allegory, with a particular interest in twelfth-century composition and interpretation, see Christel Meier, 'Zum Problem der allegorischen Interpretation mittelalterlicher Dichtung,' *Beiträge zur Geschichte der Deutschen Sprache und Literatur*, 99, 2 (1977), 250–96. As these and other recent studies demonstrate, the Romantic distinction between

wise course of action, for example, not by exhibiting the prudent behavior of 'Wisdom,' but by describing the judicious navigation of a ship. This strategy exposes the first complication in non-personification allegory. In such narratives, the initial correspondence between meaning and expression is no longer so close as in the case of wisdom and 'Wisdom.' Despite this complication, the potential for allegory remains. For example, we might picture the forces of confusion as tempestuous seas, or call the rule of reason the rudder. Inevitably, even this kind of allegory is caught in the familiar predicament. On the one hand, in order to preserve the correspondence between sound thinking and thoughtful sailing, we must restrict the narrative to brief parallels, such as reason and the rudder—and even they may seem strained. On the other hand, should we seek to expand the narrative, we risk an increasing divergence from the story's original point. Thus, it will be hard to match the ship's gunwales with the configuration of wisdom. Even if we concentrate on parallels considered safe, such as confusion and tempest, the account is likely to slip into details appropriate only to one side. In effect, the allegory seems trapped between constraint and license: unable to lift its anchor, on the one hand, and liable to go adrift, on the other.[5]

'allegory' and 'symbol' is problematic; for some remarks on this question, see the discussion and refs. in Chs. III and IV and App. I. The issue of whether allegory is a 'mode,' a 'genre,' or a 'form' seems less helpful at this time than a close analysis of the dominant allegorical traditions themselves. Finally, while there are broad senses in which it can be claimed that all composition or interpretation is in some measure 'allegorical,' this view is liable to give an already distended word so wide an application as to compromise both its historical meaning and its analytic usefulness. The compositional tradition of allegory has a flexible but circumscribed position in the development of literary expression in general, just as the interpretive tradition of allegory has such a position in the development of critical commentary in general. All *allegory* is in some measure compositional or interpretive, but it would require a special plea to turn the species into the genus.

[5] The parallel between living and seafaring is one of the earliest examples of allegorical composition. In the form of the 'ship of state,' where the ship corresponds to the state, the storms to civil wars, the haven to peace, etc., it has a special place in allegorical practice and theory. Reinhardt, *Vermächtnis*, pp. 36–40, calls attention to the ancient 'ship of state' allegories of Alcaeus, Archilochus, and Theognis, and argues that 'the old poetry does not yet know the allegorical in its true sense.' The language, he writes, is too fixed to its subject, and has no choice ('keine Wahl') as to whether to express itself allegorically or not. He contrasts the 'hotter breath' ('seinen heisseren Atem') of such political warnings with Horace's imitation of Alcaeus' ship allegory in *Odes* I, 14, which is self-sufficient, pure ('autarken, reinen') in its allegorical presentation. This contrast has much in common with a distinction we shall

Such allegories, which do not employ abstract figures, vary in structure, consistency, and style. In them, though, as in all compositional allegory, the pull between correspondence and divergence sets the narrative at odds with itself. Personification, with its initial, perfect, doomed point of correspondence, preeminently dramatizes this problem, and it will be our central concern here.

The pull between the oblique and the direct, or between divergence and correspondence, is only the most general feature of interpretive and compositional allegory. It is not a 'model' explaining the whole complex development of the technique. On the contrary, both allegorical traditions develop quite diverse strategies over time which modify their internal conflicts. More importantly, as these two traditions increasingly influence each other, their strategies gradually interact and finally transform the original dilemma.

In a broad sense, the potential for such interaction is implicit from the start in allegorical writing. The more an author develops a concept like wisdom into a character, the more he implies at least a latent interpretive program. When Boethius introduces the figure of 'Philosophy' in his *Consolation*, he depicts her in conspicuously allusive (and torn) attire, as if to signal the demand for elucidation (and reintegration) that occupies the rest of the work. By the time the initiating figure turns into the character of 'Nature' in Alan of Lille's *Complaint*, such allegorical attire provides an elaborate cosmic agenda for the gradual self-revelation of the figure and the

see between the restrictive, objectifying tendency of early personification and the expansive, oblique detachment that later develops. On 'detachability' as a criterion of allegory, see Morton W. Bloomfield, 'Allegory as Interpretation,' *New Literary History*, 3 (1972), 310–11. Horace's poem was cited by Quintilian in his seminal discussion of allegory as a sustained series of metaphors ('continuatis translationibus'), *Inst. Orat.* VIII, vi, 44. In the English Renaissance, George Puttenham virtually translates Quintilian in arguing that '*Allegoria* is when we do speake in sense translative . . . as for example if we should call the common wealth, a shipe, the Prince a Pilot,' etc.; see Fletcher, *Allegory*, p. 77, n. 10. For recent treatments of Horace's ode, see Reinhart Hahn, *Die Allegorie in der antiken Rhetorik*, Diss. Tübingen 1967 (Tübingen, 1967), pp. 105–26. In the hands of the theorists, and most of the practitioners, the ship of state allegory remained rather wooden, betraying the allegorical dilemma. The broader comparison between the passage of life and the sea voyage has received more flexible and ingenious treatment from antiquity to the modern period; for some general bibliography, see the refs. in Dronke, *Fabula*, p. 94, n. 1.

delineation of human 'nature' itself.[6] In this respect, allegory tends to produce not only conflicting pressures between the figures of a narrative and the facts of analysis, but opportunities for adjustment, by playing its compositional and interpretive strains off each other.

The nature of such interplay, however, involves more than an intricate effort to cope with an internal dilemma. It depends upon deep philosophic and literary movements which develop in their own right and which transform the very tension between analysis and narrative that distinguishes both allegorical traditions. Already in antiquity, for example, Stoic interpreters are transfiguring the characters of mythology into the constituents of a dynamic physical continuum, a 'scientific' strategy that in turn promotes the flexible deployment of abstract forces themselves, from the interlocking agents of the cosmos to the interacting aspects of the soul.[7] In late antiquity Neoplatonic philosophers are attempting to relate the very nuances of a text to the different levels of the world, while compositional writers are seeking to maneuver their characters between different levels of action by exploiting the modulations of figurative language itself. In late antiquity and the early Middle Ages, Christian theologians are trying to incorporate the very sequence of the scriptural *historia* into the design of exegesis, thereby posing the compositional problem of enacting the order of the world by the progression of a plot. Such conceptual and imaginative movements not only enrich the interpretive and compositional traditions, but help to coordinate them with each other.

While this interaction develops over the broad course of allegorical writing, it reaches a critical stage, I believe, in the twelfth century. The decisive turning point in this movement is the *Cosmographia* of Bernard Silvestris, written near the midpoint of the century. In this text, the coordinating tendencies of earlier movements in antiquity and the Middle Ages begin to

[6] On such disclosing features in the clothing of these two characters, see Paul Piehler, *The Visionary Landscape* (London, 1971), pp. 39-40, 50-4. On some self-revealing tendencies in allegory at large, see the studies cited above in n. 4 of Fletcher, pp. 81-4, 120-35, 308-24; Barney, pp. 48-50, 97-101, 124-5; and Quilligan, pp. 51-64, 97-8, 224-78; cf. my discussion in later chapters.

[7] On these and other developments briefly anticipated here, see my detailed analysis and documentation in later chapters.

coalesce in a comprehensive, far-reaching design. A scientific account of the multiple dimensions of an historical process becomes inseparable from the poetic elaboration of modulating figures in a coherent sequence. At the same time, the two allegorical traditions themselves at last converge in a systematic form. Bernard *interprets* the story of creation by *creating* allegorical agents to act out the story; he thus radically integrates the act of interpretation with the act of personification. Although this strategy does not wholly resolve the internal dilemmas of the two allegorical traditions, it subtly plays their tensions off each other, producing an allegory at once conceptually controlled and imaginatively diversified. In the process, the work consolidates the internal dynamics of allegorical writing, stimulating the sophisticated allegorical movement of the late Middle Ages.

It should be stressed that these developments do not constitute a deliberate or steady 'evolution' toward a goal. It is true that allegory is a particularly self-conscious way of writing, and the very act of adopting it engages allegorists to different degrees in the formal problems of their own procedures and the interpretive and compositional traditions at large. This very engagement, however, develops only as such writers seek to articulate their own conceptual and imaginative concerns, thereby placing increasing demands upon the technique. These demands, in turn, constantly generate new formal problems in the act of modifying old ones. Allegory never produces a 'definitive,' much less a 'perfected,' text. It rather achieves various states of equilibrium, adjusting to uneven and overlapping pressures and constantly susceptible to disequilibrium and readjustment.

Even the most provisional analysis of this process would be impossible without the extensive scholarly research into specific aspects of allegory conducted during the past half century, and particularly during the past generation. With respect to the interpretive tradition, there are now broad surveys of ancient Greek and Roman exegesis; rich accounts of the exotic hermeneutical activity of late antiquity; systematic inquiries into scriptural exegesis of the ancient and early medieval periods; and book-length studies of imposing exegetes such as Origen, Augustine, Pseudo-Dionysius, and Eriugena. With respect to the compositional tradition, there are suggestive overviews of the beginnings of personification; useful discussions of the rhetorical theory of allegory; comparative analyses of the emergence of vernacular allegory; and book-length studies of central allegorists such as Prudentius, Martianus Capella, Boethius, and Bernard Silvestris himself. Beyond these specific investigations, there are numerous explorations of allegorical technique at large, most concentrating on texts written after the closing point of this study, the mid-twelfth century, but each providing valuable insights about the procedures of allegory as a whole.[8] Such continuing research testifies to the importance of the subject not only for the Middle Ages, but for the modern period itself.

While this book draws deeply upon these earlier works, it differs considerably from them in scope, orientation, and procedure. First, it is not a 'history' of allegory, although it analyzes texts in chronological sequence over the course of two millennia, from the *Iliad* to the *Cosmographia*. Too many problems remain unresolved in the current state of research to attempt such a survey, and even if a history were possible, it would be far too complex for a single volume. My analysis rather concentrates on certain works central to the allegorical tradition, offering a close reading of particularly revealing passages. While not itself a history, the study stresses the fact that allegory changes over time; it thus explores each text in its historical dimension, as a work with both a past and a future, fulfilling certain possibilities of the technique, only suggesting others. By turning to works from both the exegetical and poetic traditions of allegory at different stages of their development, the book aims to bring questions raised by studies of either tradition alone into a more direct engagement with each other. It would be possible to select other texts exhibiting other perspectives; the notes direct attention to a range of scholarly discussions which complement and sometimes qualify the arguments appearing here in compressed form. The analysis itself offers a framework in which to assess the conceptual and stylistic diversity of the technique.

Second, this book is not a 'theory' of allegory, although it repeatedly raises theoretical issues during the course of its

8 For these studies on the interpretive and compositional traditions and on allegorical technique as a whole, see the refs. above in nn. 1, 2, and 4, and the detailed bibliography and discussion in the following chapters.

analysis. As its title suggests, it concentrates rather on the actual practice of allegory, the internal operations which organize allegorical works. While it thus emphasizes the forces at work in particular texts, it argues that they participate in a continuous if variegated movement with its own broad coherence. By relating the analytic and narrative pressures within specific allegorical texts to the developing interplay between analysis and narrative in the interpretive and compositional traditions at large, the study suggests that the dynamics of each allegorical work are finally inseparable from the dynamics of allegorical writing as a whole.

Finally, even with respect to the passages upon which it concentrates, this book is not a study of all aspects of allegorical writing, although it frequently explores a range of procedural, thematic, and tonal issues. It is scarcely possible in one book even to mention all the important features of allegory; the detailed references in the notes provide an essential supplement to the discussion here and an explicit guide for further research. Limitations of space have also forced me to restrict my comments on later allegory to the briefest and most occasional points of reference; readers specializing in other periods will recognize many places where it would be possible to examine at length the later implications of early developments. The study itself concentrates on certain parallel changes within the emerging philosophic and literary traditions of allegory, with a particular interest in the kinds of interactions necessary to produce the rich strategies of personification which culminate in the *Cosmographia*.

At the same time, any analysis of such a process requires attention to a host of philosophic and literary texts related only in varying degrees to allegory itself. Sometimes the most revealing turns in allegorical strategy appear initially in works which are not themselves wholly allegorical in format. Thus, the exploration of the interpretive tradition here not only deals with specifically exegetical writing, but also draws at times upon works influencing its procedure: the philosophic critique, the religious polemic, the mystical treatise, the spiritual encyclopedia, the scientific commentary. Similarly, the exploration of the compositional tradition not only concentrates on personification allegory, but also draws at times upon works contributing to its development: the moral anecdote, the psychological essay, the mythological epic, the saint's life, the pastoral lyric. Each of these diverse forms has its own independent development; when my analysis turns to one of them, it is not to discuss its general relationship to allegory, but only to expose certain specific changes in allegorical technique. A comprehensive account would include not only extended analyses of the relationship between these kinds of writing and allegory as a whole, but also discussions of broader forms not examined here: architectural structures, iconographic designs, institutional patterns. It might please the allegorists in retrospect that an understanding of their technique implies an understanding of a whole world, but by the same token, that kind of knowledge must await the life to come.

At the same time, perhaps it is only right that a study of allegory should begin by acknowledging its own imperfections. By its very nature, allegory is the most elusive of techniques, constantly seeming to be other than what it is. It exhibits something of the perpetually fluctuating, uncertain status of the world it depicts. Such a fugitive world, as Plato argued, is not susceptible to definitive treatment, but only to provisional description—to an *eikos mythos*, a likely story. If allegorical writing constitutes that story, then any account of allegory—the story of a story, as it were—must be all the more provisional. At the same time, such an account may at least suggest something of the value of its subject. For allegory, which is always pointing toward a goal that lies beyond it, is forever having to come to terms with its own provisionality. In the process, it encourages its readers not only to aspire toward some world of perfect fulfillment, but to direct attention to the limited world of which they are part.

II *ANCIENT CONFIGURATIONS*

But clearly there is a first principle, and the causes of things are not infinite, either in sequence or in kind. (Aristotle, *Metaphysics* II, ii, 994a1–2.)

HOMERIC ORIGINS: GODDESS, MAN, PASSION

It is hardly possible to specify a first stage in the development of allegory. The allegorical impulse appears in an incipient form in our oldest philosophic and literary records, dispersed in a wide variety of contexts. Insofar as we can speak of a particular stimulus for its development in Greek and Roman antiquity, we must turn, with the ancients themselves, to the poetry of Homer. Although Homer himself writes no allegorical work, his twofold perspective of gods interacting with men promotes the earliest systematic tendencies of the two allegorical traditions —the one procedure seeking to analyze the constituents of the divine world, the other seeking to articulate the categories of the human one. These procedures gradually incorporate other tendencies, acquire their own momentum, and finally interact to produce a kind of composite realm of abstract figures, increasingly autonomous in their operation. Even while this conceptual movement passes beyond the designs of Homeric poetry itself, though, it keeps recalling the terms and contexts of that poetry, as if to redefine its own abstract formulations in relation to it. In this sense, Homer's work is both a revealing point of departure and a recurring point of reference for the early allegorical tradition.

If there is a central episode in this process, it is the primal event at the beginning of the *Iliad*, in which Achilles and Agamemnon quarrel, and Achilles considers for a moment whether or not to draw his sword and kill Agamemnon. The episode shows how the Homeric method constantly verges on allegory without quite slipping into it:

. . . And the anger (*akhos*) came to Peleus' son, and the heart within his shaggy breast pondered by halves,

whether he should draw from his side the sharp sword,
driving away the assembly, and kill the son of Atreus,
or whether he should check the anger (*kholon*) and restrain the
thymos.
While he was weighing these two courses in his mind and
thymos,
and was drawing the great sword from its scabbard, Athena
descended from the sky
· ·
She, standing behind Peleus' son, caught him by the fair hair,
appearing to him only; for none of the others saw her.
Achilles in amazement turned about, and straightway knew
Pallas Athena and her terrible eyes shining . . .

Athena, radiant in her divinity, explains that Hera has sent
her, and urges Achilles to stay his anger. Achilles responds:

'Goddess, it is necessary that I obey the word of you two
[Athena and Hera],
angry though I am in my *thymos*. For so it is better.
If any man obeys the gods, they listen well to him.'
He spoke, and held his heavy hand upon the silver sword hilt,
and thrust the great sword back into the scabbard, nor disobeyed
the word of Athena. And she went back to Olympus
to the palace of aegis-bearing Zeus with the other gods.

But Peleus' son once again with harsh words
spoke to the son of Atreus, and did not yet let go of the anger
(*kholoio*) . . .[1]

From the perspective of interpretive and compositional
allegory, we may divide this passage into two parts, one dealing
with the goddess Athena, the other dealing with the passion of
anger—with Achilles himself poised, as it were, between the
two forces. In the case of Athena, it must be admitted that our
original example of interpretive allegory was not, after all, entirely theoretical. Athena may have been affiliated particularly
with 'wisdom' even in Homer's day. Homer's later commentators, in any case, allegorized her as Wisdom itself.[2] In the *Iliad*,
though, it is plain that her correspondence with Wisdom is not

[1] See *Iliad* I, 188–224; for the Greek text, see *Homeri Opera*, ed. D. B. Monro and T.
W. Allen, 3rd edn., 2 vols. (Oxford, 1920). My translation is based in part on that of
Richmond Lattimore, *The Iliad of Homer* (Chicago, 1951).
[2] See Buffière, pp. 279–89, and Tate, 'Plato and Allegorical Interpretation' (1929),
143, nn. 4 and 13, and 'Cornutus and the Poets,' 43.

perfect. Homer's text diverges from this correspondence too widely to sustain the allegorical parallel for long. It is not only that Athena pulls Achilles' hair, an effective but perhaps not entirely *sagacious* way for Wisdom to attract Achilles' attention. With ingenuity, we might to be able to allegorize this away. It is rather that in Book V we shall see this same Athena, this allegorical candidate for Wisdom, preparing to go into battle, taking up the huge sword with which she slays fighting men 'against whom she is angry' (*hoisin kotessetai*, V, 747). Anger was precisely the quality that the Athena of Book I was supposed to have conquered in Achilles' heart; now she cannot even conquer it in her own. As if this were not enough, in Book XXII, in the famous duel between Hector and Achilles, Athena—whom we once thought might be Wisdom—deliberately deceives Hector, and hastens his death, so that Hector, in almost his last words, says that 'Athena cheated me' (*eme d' exapatēsen Athēnē*, XXII, 299)—hardly an appropriate thing for Wisdom to do. The fact, of course, is that Athena is too literal a goddess too often to be consistently 'something else,' the something else of allegory. Any sustained correspondence we try to establish between her and Wisdom must fail. Homer's text diverges too much from our allegorical interpretation to sustain the parallel.

When we consider the force of anger, on the other hand, and with it the possibility of personification, or compositional allegory, our allegorical designs collapse for the opposite reason. No longer is the text too expansive for the allegory; now it is too constrictive. At the start, it is true, an abstraction, anger (*akhos*), comes to Peleus' son, Achilles. If we were reading a medieval personification allegory, we might expect the next line to describe this anger, to point out his fierce expression and fiery eyes, at least to mention his furious words of wrath. The next line, however, does nothing of the kind. It does mention briefly what seems to be an internal division within Achilles, as 'the heart pondered by halves,' so there is still an opportunity for the abstraction of two impulses, each urging Achilles in the opposite direction. For all these promising beginnings, however, the personification never develops. It is rather the literal Achilles who takes over the action in the third line. The original text stresses the fact even more than our translation, as Homer twice inserts 'he' (*ho*) to designate the new subject of the foreground. The question is whether *he*, Achilles, should draw from his side the sword, whether *he* should kill the son of Atreus—or whether, on the other hand, he should check the anger and restrain the *thymos*, the faculty of emotion or enthusiasm. The conflict is not really between one part of Achilles and another part, but rather between Achilles himself and that alien force, 'anger.' Anger, in turn, does not rage against another abstraction, but against the literal Achilles. Modern readers may be tempted to push Homer's language beyond what it says, and imagine here the internal conflict of abstract forces. A long allegorical tradition, after all, stretches between Homer and us. We would not be the only ones so tempted. Alexander Pope, who wrote at a late stage in the development of that tradition, could hardly resist the temptation. When the man who imagined all those busy sylphs around Belinda's locks came to translate these lines, he peopled Homer's narrative with a pair of abstract counselors:

> Achilles heard, with Grief and Rage opprest,
> His heart swell'd high, and labour'd in his Breast.
> *Distracting Thoughts* by turns his Bosom *rul'd*,
> Now fir'd by *Wrath*, and now by *Reason* cool'd;
> *That prompts* his Hand to draw the deadly Sword,
> Force thro' the Greeks, and pierce their haughty Lord;
> *This whispers* soft his Vengeance to controul,
> And calm the rising Tempest of his Soul.

Torn between the beauties of Pope's translation and the integrity of Homer's text, here at least we must agree with Bentley's verdict: 'A very pretty poem, Mr. Pope; but you must not call it Homer.'[3]

Perhaps it will be argued that Homer's 'anger' does have its abstract counterpart after all: Athena, or 'wisdom.' Unfortunately, we have already seen the dangers of this interpretive procedure. Even ignoring them, we must admit that Athena does not directly confront her opposite number, 'anger,' but again, the literal Achilles himself. The truth is that, far from being a personification, in the end 'anger' loses the one activity

---

[3] For Pope's version, see *The Iliad of Homer*, tr. Alexander Pope, ed. Reuben A. Brower and W. H. Bond (New York, 1965), I, 251–8 (my italics). Bentley's precise words, incidentally, are a matter of dispute, but whatever the wording, his general sentiment remains the same.

which Homer almost attributed to it at the start. It was when anger came to Achilles that he considered whether to 'draw from his side the sharp sword' to kill the son of Atreus. At the close of the passage, Achilles chooses the opposite course of action and 'thrust the great sword back into the scabbard'—and yet, Homer explicitly tells us, he 'did *not* yet let go of the anger.' In short, Achilles has kept the abstraction while stripping it of the one activity proper to it. We are very far indeed from Pope's abstract 'Thoughts' which by turns 'rul'd' Achilles. In Homer, it is the person who acts, not the personification.

This tells us first, something about Homer, and second, something about personification. As for Homer, we are seeing here an example of that intervention by 'daemonic agents' which occurs throughout Homer's narrative. Anger is not really part of Achilles himself; it intrudes upon him, from the outside, as it were, just as does *atē* (moral blindness) or *menos* (physical strength) to other characters in the text. This kind of intervention does not exactly absolve Achilles of personal responsibility for his behavior; rather, the point is that Homer hardly conceives of responsibility without reference to such causal agents. Even the *thymos*, one of the organs of Homeric man, is something strangely independent of the man himself, so that in one breath, Homer can couple the anger that 'comes' to Achilles with the *thymos* that is presumably part of him: 'whether he should check the *anger* and restrain the *thymos*.' It is as if anger and *thymos* were their own realities, separate from the personality itself.[4]

Now we might think that this would facilitate anger's personification. After all, nothing could seem more made to order than an abstraction that has its own reality. But whatever else it is, allegory is *oblique* writing. While it involves a correspondence between what the text says and what it means, it requires a

---

[4] On 'daemonic agents' in Homer, see E. R. Dodds, *The Greeks and the Irrational* (Berkeley, 1951), pp. 1–18. On the independent force of the organs of Homeric man, see Bruno Snell, *The Discovery of the Mind*, tr. T. G. Rosenmeyer (Cambridge, Mass., 1953), p. 19: 'Homer is unable to say: "half-willing, half-unwilling;" instead he says: "he was willing, but his *thymos* was not". This does not reflect a contradiction within one and the same organ, but the contention between a man and one of his organs . . . As a result there is in Homer no genuine reflexion, no dialogue of the soul with itself.' On personal responsibility here, see Hugh Lloyd-Jones, *The Justice of Zeus* (Berkeley, 1971), pp. 10, 22–3.

divergence between these two levels, as well. And this is the problem with 'anger.' It is not anything 'else.' It is not the name we give to something that is really inside Achilles. It is not some fiction obliquely signifying an interior reality. It is too literal for that. Whereas earlier our allegorical interpretation broke down because there was too great a divergence between Athena and wisdom, here our allegorical composition breaks down because there is too strict a correspondence between the text and its actual meaning. Anger cannot act obliquely because it does not signify anything obliquely. It signifies only itself, and hence its only action is to cause anger. This straight-jacketing of a concept will limit Greek personification throughout its development, as we shall see. It is an aspect of the famous Greek concern for lucidity and precision, logical and taut expression, which sculpted their language, as well as their temples. Already in Homer there is a tendency to objectify, to fix things in objective states. The procedure has its own great beauties, of course, but one of them is not literary allegory. Here, the tendency to make 'anger' an object in its own right restricts any oblique signification it might otherwise have, and confines the text essentially to the literal, non-allegorical level.[5]

Nonetheless, the allegorical potential of Homer's work remains striking. In its own ways the *Iliad* itself suggests something of the reductionist process that later organizes the interpretive tradition and the expansionist process that later promotes the compositional one. It is not just that Homer occasionally reduces Athena, for example, to the role of 'rational counsel,' or that, conversely, he sometimes shows 'anger' overtaking a personality. It is that the very dynamics of his plot are sensitive to such tendencies, even if his poetic technique does not display them systematically. Thus, in the famous bed-chamber scene of Book III (ll. 380–448), the goddess Aphrodite turns into a kind of 'Vieille' figure and finally becomes almost the principle of sexual attraction itself—a *daimōn*, Homer explicitly calls her here[6]—in order to act as go-between for Paris and Helen. And as for the anger of Achilles,

[5] On the resistance of Homer's text to allegory, see Erich Auerbach, *Mimesis*, tr. Willard R. Trask (Princeton, 1953), pp. 6, 13–14.
[6] See *Iliad* III, 420; Coulter, p. 58, draws attention to the term.

it not only overcomes him, but reverberates until it fills the world, finally taking the ominous form of abstract 'Strife' at large (*Eris*). 'At first she rears up only a little,' comments Homer, 'but then she strides upon the earth with her head striking heaven' (IV, 440–5). This emerging personification is nearly a model of the story as a whole, and as we shall see, it is nearly a prophecy of the allegory to come. In Homer's poem, of course, such philosophic and literary nuances are still broadly diffused. But in a later, more self-conscious age, when analytic interpretation and abstract composition have developed in their own right, the two procedures will once again come together, this time with renewed force.

PRE-SOCRATIC GODS; PLATONIC SOUL

To see this process in its early stages, we might divide our investigation again according to the two allegorical traditions. Allegorical interpretation begins in earnest in the sixth century BC, with the philosophic interpretation of Homer. Interpreters like Theagenes of Rhegium, Anaxagoras, Metrodorus of Lampsacus, the sophist Prodicus, and others from the sixth to the fourth centuries BC had diverse motives for their commentaries. Some wished mainly to exemplify their own cosmological doctrines; others were concerned to defend the poets against charges of immorality. The effect of their practice, however, was the same: the poetic text turned into a mere fiction hiding underlying philosophic truths.[7]

The truths, whether physical or ethical in kind, were universal in scope. Thus, the battle of the gods in *Iliad*, Book XX, 'really' depicted the cosmic conflict of the four elements. Again, the goddess Athena 'really' signified the principle of reason; Aphrodite, desire; Ares, war. Similar strategies were applied to Hesiod's poetry. The literal meaning of the text was only a pleasant diversion, in both senses of that word. Through allegorical interpretation, however, it was possible to reduce these divergences to the philosophic core underlying them.

[7] On early Greek allegoresis, see Pépin, pp. 97–124, and Tate, 'Beginnings of Greek Allegory,' 214–15, and 'Plato and Allegorical Interpretation' (1930), 3–4, 10. On the philosophic displacement of the poetic text, see Tate, 'Plato and Allegorical Interpretation' (1929), 145, and Wolfson, *Philo*, Vol. I, pp. 138–9, 143.

These early procedures decisively affected the whole enterprise of later allegorical interpretation. For such exegetes, the
poetry of Homer and Hesiod signified the very principles of
the world. Their philosophic efforts, in fact, corresponded with
the development of ancient philosophy itself, considered by
both Greeks and Romans to be the study of such principles, the
causes (*aitiai*) and foundations (*arkhai*) of things. Plato, for
example, in the *Phaedo* and the *Republic*, called his Ideas *aitiai*,
the causes of things. Aristotle, defining knowledge in his
Posterior Analytics, declared that 'we only think that we know
something when we know its cause (*aitia*).' The Stoics made the
underlying principles of things (*arkhai*) central to their philosophic investigations. And when Cicero called wisdom 'the
knowledge of things human and divine, and of the causes
(*causarumque*) by which those things are controlled,' or when
Virgil celebrated the philosopher as 'felix, qui potuit rerum
cognoscere causas'—happy the one who has been able to know
the causes of things—each was affirming a fundamental
association between philosophy and the study of causes. This
basic association continued throughout antiquity and the
Middle Ages, despite other descriptions of the discipline, different approaches to the specific part of philosophy entrusted
with causal analysis, and deep controversies over the nature of
the causes themselves. Long before such systematic developments, though, in the early philosophic interpretation of
Homer and Hesiod, to philosophize a text meant to find not
only its underlying meanings, but the underlying principles of
the world.[8]

---

[8] On the correspondence between early Greek exegesis and philosophy, see, e.g.,
Tate, 'On the History of Allegorism,' 107, and Buffière, 3, 81, 131, 134, 140. For
Plato, see *Phaedo* 99B, 100C, and *Republic* 508E; see also *Timaeus* 68E; *Philebus* 30D;
Sophist 265C; Paul Shorey's note to the *Philebus* passage in *What Plato Said* (Chicago,
1933), p. 608; and G. M. A. Grube's distinction in *Plato's Thought* (London, 1935),
p. 302, n. 3. For Aristotle, see *Posterior Analytics*, ed. and tr. Hugh Tredennick
(Cambridge, Mass., 1966), II, xi, 94a20-1. For the Stoics, see David E. Hahm, *The
Origins of Stoic Cosmology* (Columbus, Ohio, 1977), pp. 29, 34, 43-4. For Cicero, see *De
Officiis*, ed. and tr. Walter Miller (London, 1913), II, ii, 5. For Virgil, see *Georgics* II,
490. For the association between philosophy and the study of causes in the Middle
Ages, see, e.g., Boethius, *De Consolatione Philosophiae* IV, pr. vi; John of Salisbury,
Metalogicon II, 1; IV, 16; Aquinas, *Com. In Metaph. Prooem.*; *In Metaph.* IV, lect. 1; *In I
Post. Anal.*, I, lect. 4; *Summa Contra Gentiles*, I, 1; *Summa Theologiae*, I, i, 6; and Boccaccio,
Genealogie Deorum Gentilium Libri, XIV, 4.

If we turn to the tradition of compositional allegory for a moment, we shall see a striking parallel with this philosophic technique of interpretive allegory. Personification, too, seeks to expose the underlying principles of events. Instead of saying that a man acts wisely, for example, personification specifies 'Wisdom' itself as the principle that causes the event. Instead of saying that a man falls in love, personification specifies 'Love' itself as the agent that precipitates his fall. That is, like interpretive allegory, personification tries to investigate the causes of things—a fact eventually suggested in medieval theories of language themselves. Only compositional allegory proceeds by inverting the procedure of interpretive allegory, which reduces the fictional details of a text to their underlying principles. Personification begins with the underlying core itself, and then elaborates it into a fiction. It is the grammatical counterpart of the philosophic study of causes.[9]

By its very nature, then, the literary tradition of allegory had the potential to complement the analytic one. Like the two halves of that split egg in Plato's *Symposium*, 'one was always looking for the other.' A potential consummation, however, is not an actual one, even if there are already certain common tendencies in the diverse poetic and philosophic movements of the sixth and fifth centuries BC to develop an underlying 'structure' for phenomena.[10] The first true personification allegory in the West, the 'Choice of Heracles' of the fifth-century BC sophist Prodicus, perhaps suggests something of the possibilities and limitations of such a strategy in its early figurative form. Heracles sits down in a quiet spot, perplexed as to which of two 'paths' he should take, one of 'virtue,' the other of 'vice.' Suddenly, two women approach him, the one comely and modest, the other painted up and 'having

[9] For some medieval approaches to the relation between figurative language and abstract causes, see Brinkmann, pp. 199-200. For a broad argument that literary discourse as a whole implies the 'hypothesizing functions' of philosophy and other disciplines, see Wesley Trimpi's valuable study, *Muses of One Mind* (Princeton, 1983), esp. pp. 25-79. From this perspective, it might be argued that personification radically articulates the 'literary hypothesis' by organizing the plot with characters which are themselves in one sense fundamental principles. The developing relation between literary and philosophic tendencies in allegorical writing, though, is a complex process with features of its own; see below.

[10] See Hermann Fränkel, *Early Greek Poetry and Philosophy*, tr. Moses Hadas and James Willis (New York, 1973), esp. pp. 285-6, 321-4, 422-9, 481-508.

shameless eyes.' Although the provocative figure of Vice rushes forward and promises Heracles the 'easy way' of sensual delights, it is the poised figure of Virtue, frankly expounding the difficulties and rewards of her way, who has the final word.[11]

Perhaps the most immediately revealing feature of this brief, limited vignette is that it considers Heracles, a man celebrated for his heroic exploits, not really from the outside, but almost from the inside, confronted by his own options. The general concern with an ethical, even an introspective side of Heracles is not unique to Prodicus; in different ways, it finds early lyric and dramatic expression in Pindar and Euripides, and already by the turn of the fifth and fourth centuries BC it takes interpretive form in the exegesis of Heracles' labors as the triumph of reason over passion—a moralization with a rich mythographic afterlife.[12] Such developments eventually produce a complex interplay between 'exterior' and 'interior' perspectives scarcely suggested in Prodicus' own sketch. Nonetheless, his work begins to diagram the process of deliberation itself,[13] thereby visualizing, if only in a preliminary way, the alternatives in a decisive moment of choice.

First, more programmatically than Homer's account of Achilles at a critical turning point, Prodicus' tale tends to translate an ethical condition into a physical configuration, making one dimension parallel to the other. The man is 'situated' not only morally, in a crisis, but topographically, at a crossroads—although at least in the reported version that has come down to us, each 'road' (*hodon*) is hardly more than a figure of speech, and Heracles himself considers his alternatives only in the vague but evocative setting of a 'stillness' or 'quiet place' (*hēsukhian*).[14] While the nuances are coordinated, they are not elaborately articulated.

[11] For the tale, told by Xenophon, see the *Memorabilia*, ed. and tr. E. Marchant (Cambridge, Mass., 1953), II, i, 21-33. Cf. Reinhardt, *Vermächtnis*, p. 13.

[12] For a survey, see G. Karl Galinsky, *The Herakles Theme* (Totowa, N. J., 1972), pp. 29-38, 56-73, on Pindar and Euripides; pp. 56, 106-7, 190-224, on moralization of the labors from antiquity to the Renaissance.

[13] See Galinsky, pp. 101-2, who also notes later adaptations of the work, pp. 103, 162, 198-9, 213-14.

[14] On the visualization of psychic experience in later allegory, see Piehler, *Visionary Landscape*, cited above in Ch. I, n. 6.

Second, the figures approaching Heracles are not actual daemons or gods, but animated categories of life, which simulate his possibility of moving in two directions by their own action of moving toward him. Opposed in demeanor as well as advice, the two figures even engage in incipient competition, as when Vice hastens to Heracles to make the first appeal, or Virtue finally directs part of her discourse to Vice herself (II, i, 23 and 30). Here is at least a suggestion of the struggle of Virtues and Vices that will eventually acquire intricate features of its own and finally pass into the *Psychomachia* and a variety of later artistic transfigurations.[15] It should be emphasized, however, that in Prodicus' account the struggle remains almost exclusively verbal, expressing the options and objectives of behavior; the speeches, still addressed largely to the man himself, exhibit more the arts of persuasion than the urgency of a soul in doubt.

Finally, the presentation of Heracles' choice has a conceptual transparency, an instructional clarity that abstracts a particular episode into a universal encounter.[16] At the same time, such transparency has its risks; 'Friends call me Happiness,' announces the figure with shameless eyes, 'but those who hate me nickname me Vice.' This is not to say that the self-betrayal of a vice or the self-assertion of a virtue cannot turn into a compelling strategy, but only that here the figures have not yet fully emerged from rhetorical flourishes into agents of interpretive force. Nor, for all their exhortations, do they genuinely 'interweave' in the 'maze' of human action, to quote a Renaissance adaptation of how two figures 'did contend / Which should have Hercules to friend'—although that adaptation seeks to transform, albeit with 'labor,' even the contrariety of Vice into the potentiality of Pleasure 'Reconciled to Virtue.'[17]

However suggestive the touches in Prodicus' story, the emergence of personification as a complex technique of explanatory power is finally inseparable from the deep philosophic analysis

---

[15] On such literary implications, see Seel, 'Antike und Frühchristliche Allegorik,' cited above in Ch. I, n. 2, pp. 21-2, 36-7, and my discussion below; on artistic transfigurations, see Erwin Panofsky, *Hercules am Scheidewege*, Studien der Bibliothek Warburg, Vol. 18 (Leipzig, 1930).

[16] See Seel, 'Antike und Frühchristliche Allegorik,' p. 22, on 'the *fabula docet*, the protreptic aim' of the tale.

[17] See Ben Jonson's masque, *Pleasure Reconciled to Virtue*, ll. 224-35, 292-311, in *Ben Jonson: The Complete Masques*, ed. Stephen Orgel (New Haven, Conn., 1969).

of the workings of the soul itself. Such investigations do not themselves display personification in imaginative terms, but they clarify the abstract elements and internal operations which contribute toward the development of the technique. The most important of these early investigations, which belongs to a generation somewhat later than that of Prodicus, is the work of Plato, and characteristically, Plato's overall tendencies are divided. As a famous philosophic opponent to exegetical allegory (and even at times to Homeric poetry itself), he reflects the uneasy relation between the interpretive and compositional traditions in the fourth century. At the same time, however, he also suggests, if only in an incipient form, that philosophic deployment of poetry for which his work as a whole is celebrated.

As in Homer, Plato's near-personification emerges from the need to specify the causes of human action. In his early work, Plato divides the personality into two parts, body and soul, the one mortal and subject to the passions, the other immortal and, in isolation, perfectly serene. The object of the philosopher, therefore, is to purge the soul of the 'folly of the body,' as Plato puts it in the *Phaedo*. This division, though, leads to an impossible dilemma: if the soul is directly opposed to the body and its passions, how can the philosopher have a *passionate* desire for truth, devoid as he is of all emotion?

The *Republic* attempts to solve this dilemma by considering the passions, along with the reason, to be part of one soul, which uses passionate energy on behalf of intellectual activity.[18] Plato thus abandons his old two-part model, and divides the soul into three parts, each the cause of a particular kind of action. One part is the principle of reason, *to logistikon*. Another is the principle of appetite or desire, *to epithymētikon*. Between these two, as it were, is the principle of emotion, anger, or high spirit, the *thymos*. In several respects, this is no longer the *thymos* that Homer's Achilles had to restrain while checking his anger, as if it and anger were independent of Achilles himself. Aside from Homer's other differences in orientation, he had not really divided up the personality into parts, but had rather placed

---

[18] On this strategy, see Grube, *Plato's Thought*, p. 129; Dodds, *Greeks and the Irrational*, p. 213. The *Republic*'s approach has political and ethical motives and implications, as well; cf. F. M. Cornford, 'Psychology and Social Structure in the *Republic* of Plato,' *The Classical Quarterly*, 4 (1912), 246-65, and R. Hackforth, 'The Modification of Plan in Plato's *Republic*,' *The Classical Quarterly*, 7 (1913), 265-72.

what seemed to be a part of Achilles *alongside* him. In the end, therefore, it was Achilles who determined the outcome, not some personification. Even the rather different figures impinging upon Heracles tended more to be courses of conduct for the man himself to consider than the constituent forces of his choice. Plato, by contrast, divides up the whole personality, without remainder, as it were. He thus establishes a separate foreground for the conceptual principles of desire, anger, and reason, leaving the literal 'man' obliquely in the background. Here at last we shall be able to watch abstract concepts struggle with each other on their own ground, without the intrusion of the literal level.

At least, so we hope. For when we reach the critical moment when Plato describes how the philosopher harnesses his passions to his reason, we have the uneasy feeling that some literal presence behind us is really controlling the action:

And do we not often observe, when *desires* (*epithymiai*) constrain a man contrary to the *reason* (*ton logismon*), that *he* (*hauton*) reviles himself and is *angry* (*thymoumenon*) with that within him which constrains him; and that as it were in a faction of two parties the *anger* (*ton thymon*) of such a man becomes (*gignomenon*) the ally of the *reason*? But its (*auton*) making common cause with the *desires* against the reason, when reason specifies not to do so—that, I think, is the kind of thing you would not say you ever observed in yourself, nor, I think, in anyone else, either.[19]

As usual, Plato's text is deceptively lucid, and seems to explain succinctly that wise action arises from the alliance of *thymos* or anger with reason. Delighted as we are by the clarity of his account, we might almost overlook the fact that Plato really postpones the explanation for the alliance. If I may put it this way, he omits the *reason* for *thymos'* alliance with reason. Plato's whole analysis, after all, depends on the exhaustive division of the human personality into three quite distinct parts: desire, *thymos*, and reason. By definition, therefore, *thymos* has no

---

[19] *Republic* IV, 440AB. My translation is based in part on Paul Shorey's revised edition (Cambridge, Mass., 1937). Here again we must not push the original text beyond what it says. The phrase I have translated as 'when reason specifies not to do so' (*hairountos logou mē dein*), Shorey translates as: 'when reason whispers low, "Thou must not."' It is the same impulse that led Pope to translate the Homeric passage as 'This whispers soft his Vengeance to controul, / And calm the rising Tempest of his Soul.'

reason of its own. Here, however, it seems to act as if it already has a reason for helping the rational principle. Later Plato says it helps reason 'by nature' (*physei*, 441A), even while he distinguishes it from reason. This, obviously, begs the question. In fact, the question arises whichever direction Plato turns. On the one hand, 'anger' cannot act in a 'reasonable' way without an internal 'reason'; on the other hand, neither can 'reason' properly be 'angry' with desire, since 'anger' is a separate part of the soul. Plato's only escape is the literal 'man' to which he reverts.

Once again, the original text expresses this shift even more than our translation. It is that very one (*hauton*), 'he,' the man himself, who 'reviles' himself and is 'angry' with the desires, not the concepts which were supposed to act out the drama. As for the *thymos*, it mysteriously 'becomes' (*gignomenon*) the ally of the man's reason.[20] The concord of the soul's three parts presupposes a harmony that none of the parts can provide. Such an appeal to factors beyond the internal model recurs in a different form in the *Timaeus*, with its endless cycle of antecedent causes accounting for psychic harmony or disharmony, and in Plato's last dialogue, the *Laws*, with its admission that the reason 'needs helpers,' and its eventual, poignant appeal to that generality, 'man.' Indeed, wherever Plato seriously confronts this dilemma, his model, with its allegorical potential, tends to break down.[21]

In one sense, this breakdown in the *Republic* results from the same straightjacketing of a concept that restricted Homer to the

[20] Plato's very language tends to confuse the agency of the *thymos* with that of the man himself. The series of accusatives in indirect discourse (*tina, hauton, thymon, auton*)—now referring to the 'man,' now referring to the *thymos*—somewhat obscures the agent supposed to be responsible for making the alliance. The subject keeps alternating in the passage that follows, and Shorey requires three different notes to specify who, in his view, is the actor (see n. c on p. 400, nn. b and c on p. 402). As for the view expressed in n. b on p. 402 that '*thymos* is plainly the subject,' whatever the subject is, it is not *plainly* so, in view of the *tis*, the man, who opens the sentence. In such language, a 'part' of the personality keeps slipping into the personality itself. Since composing this analysis, I have noticed similar concerns about the philosophic issue in R. C. Cross and A. D. Woozley, *Plato's 'Republic': A Philosophical Commentary* (London, 1964), pp. 124, 128-30.

[21] See *Timaeus* 82-90, with the controversy on determinism in A. E. Taylor, *A Commentary on Plato's Timaeus* (Oxford, 1928), pp. 18-19, 612-15, and F. M. Cornford, *Plato's Cosmology* (London, 1937), pp. 340-9. Cf. the 'good breeding' of the white horse in the famous model of the soul in *Phaedrus* 246, 253-4, and see *Republic* 441E. For *Laws* 644CD, see the edition of R. G. Bury, 2 vols. (Cambridge, Mass., 1926).

literal level in his treatment of the *thymos*. As in Homer, Plato's *thymos* cannot do anything outside its strict definition. In order to ally itself convincingly with reason, the *thymos* would need to change, to develop, to welcome reason—in short, to diverge from its strict definition. That is, it would have to change here from an abstract concept into a personification. Plato's concepts, however, remain distinctly separate from each other —'an alien thing against an alien,' he calls them (*allo on allō*, 440A; cf. also 441C). It is in the absence of such flexibility —such obliquity, to use a term from allegory—that Plato reintroduces the 'individual' himself.

We should not judge Plato, of course, on the basis of whether or not he succeeds in being allegorical. As in Homer, the literality and surface hardness of the description has its own beauty and its own immense historical interest. The whole point of Plato's tripartite division, however, is to probe beneath the surface, to explain the sources of human action. In order to show such causes interacting on their own level, Plato comes to the verge of personification. He exposes the explanatory potential of personification, even if he does not himself fulfill it.

In a deeper sense, Plato's keen analysis of the personality here suggests philosophic changes which are profoundly enriching the Homeric problem. On a personal level, his account poses the dilemma of the 'true' self, whose very nature is rationally to ascend yet whose condition in this life consists of impulses at odds with each other.[22] This is a problem we shall see given new structural and conceptual treatment by the late antique Neoplatonists, with their allegory of the soul ascending to a higher order only by completing the process of descending to a lower one. Indeed, the division of the personality here raises the elusive question of what constitutes the irreducible 'individual,' an issue that increasingly preoccupies the allegorical treatment of the personality from late antiquity to the Middle Ages. On a more general level, Plato's tendency to revert to factors 'behind' his abstract causes suggests the notorious problem of the 'third man' that comes so to haunt his Ideas. This is an issue given new articulation by the Neoplatonists of the twelfth century, with their allegory of cosmic and psychic agents actually controlled by a divine source.

[22] See W. K. C. Guthrie, 'Plato's Views on the Nature of the Soul,' in *Recherches sur la tradition platonicienne* (Geneva, 1957), pp. 3–22.

In the broadest sense, though, Plato's problematic model
—which scarcely formulates the elements of the whole before
displaying the need to pass beyond them—dramatically exposes
the central linguistic and philosophic dilemma we have seen
from the start. The more we try to clarify, to penetrate into the
center of things, the more we leave our old language on the circumference. The attempt to specify causes will always feed on
itself and render the old model obsolete.

In this respect, even when the model changes, the dilemma
remains. Aristotle, for example, divides the soul not into three
parts, but into two: rational and irrational. Then he subdivides
the irrational side into the vegetative principle, which is
responsible for growth, and the spirited principle, which is
responsible for appetite and desire.[23] By treating the spirited
element of the soul as a subdivision of the irrational side,
however, Aristotle separates the spirited element from the
rational one, and thereby risks that same divorce of passion
from reason which the early Plato faced in the *Phaedo*. Accordingly, Aristotle subtly shifts the irrational side of the soul
toward rationality:

Thus it appears that the *irrational* side of the soul has two parts. The
one is vegetative and has no share in reason at all. The other is the
seat of the appetites and of desire in general and *partakes of reason insofar as it listens to reason and obeys it* . . .

Such concessions obviously place unbearable strains on the
original model, and the master of classification is forced to alter
his division in the space of a paragraph. Having just said
that the irrational side of the soul has two parts, Aristotle now
confesses:

But if it is necessary to say that the appetitive part, too, has reason,
then the *rational* side of the soul also has two parts. The one part has

---

[23] Plato himself seems to have tended toward this division in his late work, as if to
avoid the limits of his three-part model. See D. A. Rees, 'Bipartition of the Soul in the
Early Academy,' *The Journal of Hellenic Studies*, 77 (1957), 112–18, and later studies
cited by W. W. Fortenbaugh, *Aristotle on Emotion* (New York, 1975), p. 23, n. 1, along
with his discussion, pp. 23–44. For Aristotle's changing approaches to bipartition, see
D. A. Rees, 'Theories of the Soul in the Early Aristotle,' in *Aristotle and Plato in the Mid-
Fourth Century*, ed. I. Düring and G. E. L. Owen (Göteborg, 1960), pp. 197–9; Irving
Block, 'The Order of Aristotle's Psychological Writings,' *American Journal of Philology*,
82 (1961), 50–77; Charles Lefèvre, *Sur l'évolution d'Aristote en psychologie* (Louvain,
1972), pp. 225–30; and Fortenbaugh, pp. 26–30.

reason in the strict sense and in itself; *the other has reason in the sense that it listens to reason as one listens to a father.*

At this point, Aristotle leaves the discussion, qualifications trailing behind him, and allegory peeking out of the ruins of his conceptual framework: 'It listens to reason as one listens to a father.'[24]

While personification has not truly emerged in these passages, they remain valuable in assessing both the nature and the history of compositional allegory. It is no longer possible to argue, for example, that the divided will, or *bellum intestinum*, is effectively the discovery of the first century AD, or that from this division personification follows.[25] As for the first claim, the

[24] For suggestions of this last phrase, see Plato's *Republic* IV, 440D, 441A, and *Timaeus* 70A; cf. *Nicomachean Ethics* III, xii, 1119b11–15, and *Eudemian Ethics* II, i, 1219b27–31. My translation of this elusive passage from the *Nicomachean Ethics* I, xiii, 1102b28–1103a4 is based on the translations of W. D. Ross in *The Basic Works of Aristotle* (New York, 1941), ed. Richard McKeon; H. Rackham, *The Nicomachean Ethics* (Cambridge, Mass., 1934); and Martin Ostwald, *Nicomachean Ethics* (New York, 1962). The word *logos*, translated here as 'reason,' does not mean the faculty of reasoning itself; cf. John Burnet (ed.), *The Ethics of Aristotle* (London, 1900), pp. 35, 58, and H. H. Joachim, *The Nicomachean Ethics*, ed. D. A. Rees (Oxford, 1951), pp. 51, 61–2. Nevertheless, it remains necessary to clarify how one element of the soul possesses the rational principle that belongs properly to another element. For the play on *logos* in this passage, see J. A. Stewart, *Notes on the Nicomachean Ethics* (Oxford, 1892), Vol. I, pp. 166–7; Burnet, *Ethics*, p. 61; Rackham, *Nicomachean Ethics*, pp. 66–7, n. a.; and R. Gauthier and J. Jolif, *L'Éthique à Nicomaque*, 2nd edn. (Louvain, 1970), II, i, 97–8. The *double entendre* points up the dilemma as much as it resolves it. The first *kai* of 1103a2 may mean that we are to retain the twofold division of the irrational side even while we divide the rational side into two. Alternatively, it may refer, as in 1102b29, to the general, twofold division of the whole soul into irrational and rational sides. In either case, though, the question of how appetite acquires 'reason' remains. The view that Aristotle attributes a 'cognitive' component to emotion by definition, thus making it capable of reasonable behavior, has been argued by W. W. Fortenbaugh, *Aristotle on Emotion*, cited above in n. 23, esp. pp. 11–17, 35, 70–9, 84–7, 90–1. Cf. also his 'Aristotle's *Rhetoric* on Emotions,' orig. pub. 1970, now reprinted in *Articles on Aristotle: 4. Psychology and Aesthetics*, ed. Jonathan Barnes, Malcolm Schofield, and Richard Sorabji (London, 1979), pp. 133–53. Both the inherence and the propriety of 'cognition' in the emotion itself are doubtful, however. See the reviews of Fortenbaugh's book by J. Dybikowski, in *Philosophical Quarterly*, 26 (1976), 102–3, and A. C. Lloyd, in *Archiv für Geschichte der Philosophie*, 58 (1976), 268–71. In the end, even the philosophic champion of change and habituation can scarcely accommodate desire with reason without appealing to figurative language—or shifting to the literal level of 'man.' Cf. Aristotle's famous description of intelligent choice (*proairesis*), *Nicomachean Ethics* VI, ii, 1139b4–5, ed. Rackham, translation based on David Ross, *Aristotle*, 5th edn. (London, 1949), p. 199: 'Hence choice is either *desireful reason* or *reasonable desire*, and such an origin of action is a *man*.' (*dio ē orektikos nous hē proairesis ē orexis dianoētikē, kai [hē] toiautē arkhē anthrōpos.*)

[25] Cf. Lewis, pp. 60–1, on the first century AD: 'the men of that age, if they had not discovered the moral conflict, had at least discovered in it a new importance. They

bellum intestinum here appears quite plainly in the fourth century BC. Most of *Republic* IV, in fact, likens civil harmony and discord to personal harmony and discord (435 f.), and three times Plato explicitly treats the parts of the soul as 'factions' in an internal civil war (440B, 440E, and 444B). As for the second claim, while the divided will may be one of the necessary conditions for the personification of the soul, it is clear that something beyond this division is necessary for such personification to develop. The forces of the personality need not only to be divided, but to be fully abstracted, removed to their own level of discourse, and capable of diverging from their strict definitions. There is a third lesson, too, in the emerging personifications of these philosophers. While the grammatical tradition of compositional allegory is inverse in procedure to the philosophic tradition of interpretive allegory, and while each tradition has its own development, it is impossible to treat them in isolation from each other.[26] Philosophy and exegesis, by specifying underlying principles or causes, may expose the basis for personification allegory and hasten its development. To appreciate the role of philosophy in this advance, however, we must first return to that other tradition of allegory, philosophic interpretation in its own right.

STOIC COSMOLOGY: *PHYSIS* AND *MYTHOS*

While a rich variety of exegetical strategies develops during the last centuries BC, it is in the Stoic interpretation of Homer's and Hesiod's gods that the reductive tendency of exegesis finally converges with a systematic, radical approach to philosophy and language as a whole.[27] The program of the Stoa is not susceptible to simple paraphrase. During the long evolution of Stoic thought, there are changes in emphasis and doctrine, and the existing source material is fragmentary and dispersed in conflicting contexts. Here it is particularly fortunate, then, that our study seeks not to trace a history, but to expose certain

were vividly aware, as the Greeks had not been, of the divided will, the *bellum intestinum*.' Lewis does, however, acknowledge 'other, subsidiary, causes.'

[26] Cf. Lewis, p. 48, n. 2: 'my subject is secular and creative allegory, not religious and exegetical allegory.'

[27] For an overview of interpretive approaches during this period, see Pépin, pp. 125–72.

significant strategies. As examples, we might concentrate on two interpretive texts, one reflecting views established by the great third-century BC founders of the Stoa, Zeno, Cleanthes, and Chrysippus, the other displaying critical shifts in orientation as Stoicism becomes increasingly diffused in the first century AD.

The first of these texts is a Stoic account of the Greek pantheon, reported by one of our more reliable doxographers, Diogenes Laertius. God, according to the Stoics, is,

as it were, the father (*patera*) of all, both in general and in that particular part of him pervading (*diēkon dia*) all things, and which is called by many names according to its powers. They give him the name Dia, through whom (*di' hon*) are all things; Zeus (*Zēna*), insofar as he is the cause of life (*zēn aitios*) or pervades life (*dia tou zēn kekhōrēken*); Athena, because of the extension (*diatasin*) of his ruling part (*hēgemonikou*) to the aether; Hera, because of his suffusion of the air (*aera*); Hephaestus, because of his spreading to the craftsmanlike fire (*tekhnikon pyr*); Poseidon, because of his saturation of the water; and Demeter, because of his permeation of the earth. Similarly, they have given him his other names, by fastening on some particular attribute.[28]

In this striking reduction of mythology to physical principles, nearly every term reflects the Stoic exegetical strategy at large. 'Father' (*patera*), for example, indicates more than a general notion that God originates the universe and presides over it. In the Stoic view, God creates the world by an unmistakably biological process, a view expressed more elaborately in the famous description (possibly Zeno's) of God as a seed-principle, or seminal reason (*spermatikon logon*), left behind in the wet (*hygrō*), giving birth (*apogennan*) to the elements (*DL* VII, 136), or in Chrysippus' notorious allegorization of the lovemaking of Zeus and Hera as the infusion of such spermatic principles into matter (*SVF* II, 1071–4). This particular act of exegesis Chrysippus apparently performed with such panache that no witness will divulge the sensational details. For his part, Diogenes refuses to 'soil his lips' with the story (*DL* VII, 187–8).

---

[28] My translation from Diogenes' *Lives of Eminent Philosophers*, hereafter *DL*, VII, 147, is based on the edition of R. D. Hicks, 2 vols. (London, 1925).

At the same time, this vivid biological process differs both from a primitive vitalism and from the kind of mythological generation described by Hesiod. Far more methodically than the pre-Socratics, the Stoics transform the notion of a world 'full of gods' from a mythological to a cosmological principle, by animating the very operation of nature. The gods lose their personalities in the interests of science, but bequeath to the world that survives them their personal energy and dynamism. This is no tentative, apologetic interpretive program, as in early exegesis. In the Stoic agenda, *mythos* turns systematically into *physis*. [29]

Such a radical strategy finely accommodates the Stoic notion of the dynamic continuum, in which, as the Stoics suggest, God is no more separate from matter than the vibration is separate from the chord of a lyre. But it also tends to break down the allegorical distinction between the cause of a phenomenon and the phenomenon itself. Diogenes' account dramatizes this levelling effect by its fourfold exploitation of the form *dia* ('through'), as if to drive the divine 'through and through' each physical particle, and by its revealing oscillation between Zeus as 'cause' of life (*zēn aitios*) and Zeus 'pervading' life (*dia tou zēn kekhorēken*). A single source of energy flows through a host of particular effects. [30]

This notion of a fluid continuum has extreme consequences for allegorical interpretation; it tends to homogenize the

[29] For the application of Thales' celebrated phrase to the Stoic program, see Plutarch in *SVF* II, 1049. The Stoic adaptation of biological principles to physics has been increasingly documented since the fundamental research of Friedrich Solmsen and S. Samburaky a generation ago. The most comprehensive treatment is by Hahm, *Origins of Stoic Cosmology*, cited above in n. 8, hereafter Hahm, esp. pp. 45–8, 60–6, 75–6, 140–6, 159–60, 168–9, 173–4, 194–5, 200, 209–11. The specific derivations and reconstructions claimed in this and other recent works on Stoic physics remain controversial. While drawing deeply upon such research, neither here nor elsewhere does my overall argument depend on the acceptance of these specific theoretical claims. I am grateful to Professor Marcia L. Colish for generous bibliographical suggestions on the Stoic tradition.

[30] The classic discussion of the dynamic continuum is in S. Samburaky, *Physics of the Stoics* (London, 1959), pp. 1–48, now refined, e.g., by the studies cited below. On the inseparability of God and matter, see, for example, *SVF* I, 88; II, 313, 526–8, 1022, 1034–5, 1041, 1047; and the discussions of Max Pohlenz, *Die Stoa: Geschichte einer geistigen Bewegung*, 4th edn. (Göttingen, 1970), pp. 65–9; Hahm, pp. 3–4, 9–12, 29–34, 59–60; and Robert B. Todd, 'Monism and Immanence: The Foundations of Stoic Physics,' in *The Stoics*, ed. John M. Rist (Berkeley, 1978), pp. 137–60. On the etymologies, see below.

diverse figures of a text. As differentiations in the Stoic cosmos are but degrees of 'tension' (*tonos*) in an all-pervading force, so Athena in Diogenes' account is but Zeus' 'extension' (*diatasin*) into the aether—an aether revealingly associated by Chrysippus at one point (*SVF* II, 1076) with Zeus himself, at another point (*SVF* II, 1078) with Rhea. Indeed, the fluidity of the process finally implies the redundancy of all such figures. As Chrysippus notes (*SVF* II, 604), in the periodic world conflagration (*ekpyrōsis*) the one surviving god is Zeus, who consumes all, only to generate anew an identical cosmos with an identical fate. Such is the apocalyptic conclusion of that continuous, pulsating process of expansion and contraction which pervades a cosmos in a state of 'tension.'[31]

These passages display two related perspectives which will need to be refined in later exegesis. First, the conflation of narrative elements in Stoic interpretation corresponds to the redundancy of historical action in the Stoics' cyclical cosmology; story and history are eternally returning to the same point. A stronger sense of temporal progress, on both the narrative and physical planes, will be essential to sustained allegory. Second, the effort to mesh together different narrative figures, whether within a single mythology or between divergent systems, as in the association of aether with both Homer's Zeus and Hesiod's Rhea, needs to acquire a greater sensitivity to narrative context. This sensitivity will develop slowly even in Christian exegesis. In any case, it is no longer adequate to conceive the Stoic enterprise as a passage from mythology to monotheism.[32] More radically, it is a physics, dynamically exploiting a mythology.

[31] On the reductive treatment of the text, see Alain Le Boulluec, 'L'Allégorie chez les Stoïciens,' *Poétique*, 23 (1975), 301-21. On 'tension,' see Samburdky, *Physics of the Stoics*, pp. 30, 36, 43, 81-8, 114, and Hahm, pp. 153-4, 166-73, 183, n. 78, 244-5. On the gods as components of the whole, see, e.g., the celebrated claims in Cicero's *De Natura Deorum*, hereafter *ND*, I, xv, 40 and II, xxviii, 71; the passage from Athenagoras quoted by A. C. Pearson, *The Fragments of Zeno and Chrysippus* (1891; repr. New York, 1973), pp. 93-4 (broken off in *SVF* II, 1027); and the remarks of Buffière, pp. 151-4. On cyclical recurrence and change, see Gerhart B. Ladner, *The Idea of Reform* (1959; repr. with Addenda, New York, 1967).

[32] Cf. Lewis, p. 57: 'The twilight of the gods . . . represents, in fact, the *modus vivendi* between monotheism and mythology.' On the Stoics' relation to popular religion, see Pohlenz, *Die Stoa*, pp. 96-8, and Myrto Dragona-Monachou, *The Stoic Arguments for the Existence and the Providence of the Gods* (Athens, 1976), pp. 25-6.

In this lies its promise for later allegory. Thus, the Stoic principle of expansive/contractive 'tension,' along with related cyclical conceptions in antiquity, entails a *Götterdämmerung* with far-reaching imaginative repercussions. Whether or not the *Cosmographia* actually envisages recurring world cycles, it brilliantly transforms the notion of simultaneous centrifugal and centripetal tendencies in the cosmos—at once elaborating and conflating the cosmic figures of its plot, as we shall see, in a complex movement toward both the circumference of the universe and its center. Further, the close Stoic link between cosmic and personal life, reflected here in Diogenes' reference to Zeus' 'ruling part,' the *hēgemonikon* (the Stoic command center of the soul, located in the heart), popularizes along with its Platonic counterpart the parallel between macrocosm and microcosm crucial to the development of later medieval allegory; there is a human dimension in the very 'pulse' of this animated universe. Indeed, in a very diffused form the general vision recurs long after the Middle Ages, as when a later Romantic is haunted by certain 'centripetal and centrifugal forces,' by the telltale 'swelling' and 'subsiding' of the whole universe 'at every throb of the Heart Divine.' 'And now—this Heart Divine,' continues Poe, 'what is it? *It is our own.*' Or at least, in the more restrained medieval version, it ought to be.[33]

Perhaps the most striking example of the allegorical limits and possibilities of Stoic physics is the interpretation in Diogenes' account of Hephaestus as 'craftsmanlike fire' (*tekhnikon pyr*)—a fire 'going on its way to genesis,' in the rest of the celebrated Stoic definition. Applied by the Stoics to both God and Nature, this definition, like the notion of a divine seed-principle, still too closely conflates divine cause with natural phenomenon to allow one figure to diverge from the other. Later, though, when a host of Neoplatonic and astrological commentaries make crucial distinctions in the causal

[33] On the relation between the expansive/contractive Stoic cosmos and the *Cosmographia*—a relation deeply qualified, as we shall see, by the quite different Neoplatonic vision of cosmic 'procession' and 'return'—see Chs. IV and VI, below. For the important Stoic contribution to the macrocosm/microcosm tradition, see Hahm, pp. 45–8, 60–78, 136–74, 200–12. Among many overviews of the tradition, see esp. the recent discussion of Brinkmann, pp. 52–73 ('Die Welt und der Mensch'), with extensive bibliography. For the quotation from Poe's extraordinary *Eureka*, see *The Works of Edgar Allen Poe*, ed. Edmund Clarence Stedman and George Edward Woodberry, Vol. IX (Chicago, 1895), pp. 130, 133–4.

meaning of 'craftsmanlike,' this animating *ignis artifex* finally emerges from God as a radiant 'Nature' in her own right.[34] Similarly, in its psychic role as the 'fiery pneuma' (*pneuma enthermon*) driving human life, the Stoic fire is the single agent of both spiritual and sexual activity. Only when the later allegorization of Hephaestus (or Vulcan) plays these generative and regenerative functions off each other, along with Vulcan's (and the fire's) third dimension, craftsmanship, does the allegory of human *ingenium* systematically develop, leading at last to the *Complaint of Nature*. In the end, by turning mythology into cosmology, the Stoics bring the early exegesis of Homer and Hesiod to its logical conclusion. But they also thereby radicalize the ancient tendency to undermine and displace the poetry itself. Full-fledged allegory finally requires a physics that deploys, rather than simply exploits, a poetics.[35]

There is a final strategy informing Diogenes' account that exemplifies the Stoics' relation to later allegory: the etymological approach to meaning. Long before the Stoics, of course, philosophers had associated such words as Zeus (acc. *Zēna*) and life (*zēn*), or Hera and air (*aēr*), to explain the 'true meaning' of certain gods.[36] The Stoics, however, intensify the

---

[34] For both God and Nature as 'craftsmanlike fire,' see the references in Hahm, p. 212, n. 1. On the passage of this consolidating principle into imaginative discourse, see Michael Lapidge, 'A Stoic Metaphor in Late Latin Poetry: the Binding of the Cosmos,' *Latomus*, 39 (1980), 817-37. On the *ignis artifex* and the transition from World Soul to Nature, see *The* Didascalicon *of Hugh of St. Victor*, tr. Jerome Taylor (New York, 1961), I, 10 and n. 71; the critical documentation in Gregory, *Anima*, pp. 123-246; *Platonismo*, pp. 122-50; 'L'idea,' pp. 42-51; and Ch. V, below.

[35] On 'fiery pneuma,' see Hahm, pp. 68, 70, 159-62. For the broad tradition of generative and regenerative fire and the influential role of the Stoics, see Carl-Martin Edsman, *Ignis Divinus: le feu comme moyen de rajeunissement et d'immortalité: contes légendes mythes et rites*, Publications of the New Society of Letters at Lund, 34 (Lund, 1949), esp. pp. 200-3. On the medieval Vulcan and *ingenium*, see Wetherbee, esp. pp. 95, 115-22, 128-32, 136-7, 181-5, 198-210, 221-2, 232-6; for the broader tradition of the 'Genius' figure with which such developments interact, see Jane Chance Nitzsche, *The Genius Figure in Antiquity and the Middle Ages* (New York, 1975).

[36] For 'Etymology as a Category of Thought,' see Ernst Robert Curtius, *European Literature and the Latin Middle Ages*, tr. Willard R. Trask (New York, 1953), pp. 495-500. For the ancient exegetical use of the technique, see Buffière, pp. 60-5. For precedents regarding the associations here with Zeus and Hera, see Heraclitus, cited in Tate, 'On the History of Allegorism,' 106, and Plato's *Cratylus* 396AB, 404C. For the exploitation of etymology as an exegetical strategy in the Middle Ages, see Roswitha Klinck, *Die lateinische Etymologie des Mittelalters* (Munich, 1970), qualified by Klaus Grubmüller, 'Etymologie als Schlüssel zur Welt? Bemerkungen zur Sprachtheorie des Mittelalters,' in *Verbum et Signum*, Vol. I, pp. 209-30.

procedure in two ways. First, they apply it to virtually the whole pantheon, treating the names and attributes of the gods as linguistic deviations from physical principles, 'causas,' as Cicero's *De Natura Deorum* puts it. In this sense, all of mythic narrative constitutes for the Stoics a single, modulating voice, like the single, vibrating chord of the cosmic lyre. Second, and more broadly, the Stoics treat this ambiguity in poetic texts as only one testimony to the widespread divergence of human language from its natural foundation. 'Omne verbum ambiguum natura esse,' declares Chrysippus, where the very word 'natura' displays the point: words are ambiguous by their own nature, and ambiguous with respect to Nature itself.[37]

Broadly speaking, the Stoics thus expose that pervasive duality in language which will later inspire systematic allegory. Even their limited linguistic speculations about the relation between 'derivative' and 'fundamental' terms such as 'just' and 'justice,' for example, have substantial allegorical potential. Thus, Langland will make the distinction between 'merciful' and 'mercy' an element in his allegorical plot, and Spenser will make the variation between the adjective and the noun a measure, as it were, of the distance between an imperfect knight and personified perfection: 'You shamefast are,' Sir Guyon is informed as he meets a blushing damsel at the House of Alma, 'but *Shamefastnesse* it selfe is shee.'[38] As with their treatment of the names of the gods, though, the Stoics aim

---

[37] For the broad Stoic critique on the 'causas' of the gods' names, see, e.g., *ND* II, xxiv–xxviii, 63–71, III, xxiv, 62–3, and Pépin, pp. 125–31. For the polyvalence of mythic discourse and human language in general, see Le Boulluec, 'L'Allégorie chez les Stoïciens,' esp. 312–21, who specifically discusses the Chrysippus quotation (*SVF* II, 152). For some philosophical problems in the Stoic grammatical program, see Andreas Graeser, 'The Stoic Theory of Meaning,' in *The Stoics*, ed. Rist, pp. 97–9.

[38] For the Stoic approach to 'just' and 'justice,' see Michael Frede, 'Principles of Stoic Grammar,' in *The Stoics*, ed. Rist, pp. 68–70. On 'merciful' and 'mercy' in Langland's *Piers Plowman*, see, e.g., the B-text, ed. George Kane and E. Talbot Donaldson (London, 1975), ii, 31–2 and xvii, 229–34; cf. the elaborate allegory of adjective and substantive in the C-text, iv, 335–409, with the comments of A. G. Mitchell, 'Lady Meed and the Art of *Piers Plowman*,' orig. pub. 1956; repr. in *Style and Symbolism in* Piers Plowman, ed. Robert J. Blanch (Knoxville, Tenn., 1969), pp. 184–6, and John A. Alford, 'The Grammatical Metaphor: A Survey of Its Use in the Middle Ages,' *Speculum*, 57 (1982), esp. 754–9. For the passage from Spenser's *Faerie Queene* II, ix, 43, see the edition of A. C. Hamilton (London, 1977). For the adjective/noun relation here, see Isabel G. MacCaffrey, *Spenser's Allegory: The Anatomy of Imagination* (Princeton, 1976), pp. 82–3; cf. pp. 100, 169–70, 221, 283. For variants on this strategy in *Pilgrim's Progress*, see the valuable analysis of Quilligan, *Language of Allegory*, cited above in Ch. I, n. 4, pp. 127–31.

less to manipulate such disparities than to conflate words with their 'actual' meanings. As a result, they tend to atomize and finally to dissipate the elements of language. Before sustained interpretive allegory can develop, it needs somehow to reconcile its analytic demands with a sense of the coherence and continuity of a text on its own plane. In a word, exegesis needs to give imaginative discourse not only a physics, but a logic of its own.

This kind of sensitivity increasingly develops by the turn of the first centuries BC and AD, as Stoicism passes broadly into a host of philosophic strategies, circulating widely and qualifying each other. To appreciate the exegetical effects of this process, we may turn to the extraordinary *Homeric Problems*, written in the first century AD by a certain Heraclitus—not the ancient 'obscure one' who helped to inspire the Stoa, but one who claimed to remove obscurities from Homer's text. Had Homer not written allegorically, Heraclitus declares at the start of his treatise, he would be guilty of irreverence to the gods. Accordingly, when Heraclitus comes to the troubling passage in Book V of the *Iliad*, in which Diomedes wounds a god, Ares, he hastens to explain:

Ares is nothing other than *war*. He takes his name from *arē*, which signifies 'harm.' This becomes clear to us from reading that he is 'furious, born of evil, shifting sides' (*Iliad* V, 831). These epithets suit *war* more than a god. For all *warriors* are filled with fury. In their murder of opponents, they boil over with frenzy. . . .

It is very credible that Ares is wounded by Diomedes in no other part but 'the hindmost part of the *flank*' (*Iliad* V, 857). For Diomedes, slipping easily into the *flank* of the *enemy front*, which was not completely guarded, put the foreigners to flight. . . .

Thus we have shown by manifest proofs in each case that it was not Ares who was wounded by Diomedes, but *war*.[39]

Granted, the liabilities in Heraclitus' interpretation are plain. In his effort to reduce Homer's gods to their underlying meanings, Heraclitus reduces the text to a disjointed series of physical effects. First, we learn by etymology that 'Ares' really means war itself. To sustain the correspondence, Heraclitus

---

[39] See *Héraclite: Allégories d'Homère*, ed. and tr. Félix Buffière (Paris, 1962), ch. 31, pp. 37–8; my translation.

then shifts Ares' fury from *war* in general to the actual *warriors*, 'filled with fury.' Then, the 'flank' of war itself becomes the flank of a particular *army*. The reductive effort finally betrays itself in the claim that Ares' wound must be the wound of war itself—as if even that generality, war, were a physical object. The result of these shifts is virtually to decimate the text —rather than Ares—parcelling it out into various material effects. In his fragmentation, Heraclitus ignores the fact that a few lines later, Ares—supposedly war itself—leaves the battlefield, but the war, as Homer explicitly tells us, still rages on. Whatever the logic of Heraclitus' philosophy as he proceeds to the next episode, Homer's internal logic seems left far behind.

At the same time, Heraclitus' enthusiasm has its intriguing side. Thus, when he reaches the scandalous reference in the *Odyssey* to Hephaestus catching Ares and Aphrodite in the act of adultery, he seems to expand and contract the story rhetorically in accordance with his diverse (not traditionally 'Stoic') interpretations—one interpretation stressing the generative effect of the lovers, the other stressing the refining power of the smith. When treating Ares and Aphrodite as the Empedoclean opposites of 'Discord' and 'Love' producing the world, Heraclitus introduces (from non-Homeric sources) their child *Harmonia*, who issues forth according to the 'harmonious' (*harmosthentos*) concordance of the whole. It is as if the process of genesis promoted the introduction of this figure, whose very name gives abstract expression to the attributes of an 'harmonious' world. By contrast, when stressing the controlling craftsmanship of Hephaestus the smith, Heraclitus reduces the name of the goddess of love (*Aphroditē*) to an adjective, the 'lovely (*epaphroditō*) craft' of Hephaestus, as if to subordinate her grammatically, as well as conceptually, to her master. Whereas once, in the generative process, an attribute seemed to be expressed by means of an independent figure, now, conversely, in the refining process, an independent figure seems to be compressed into an attribute. Though Heraclitus produces these brief, isolated nuances almost in spite of himself, at such moments he nearly differentiates his interpretation by modulating his composition.[40] It remains a long way, of course, to that cosmic smith

---

[40] See ch. 69, pp. 73–5; cf. ch. 43, pp. 52–3, and Buffière's *Les Mythes d'Homère*, pp. 168–72. Michael Murrin calls attention to part of this passage in *Allegorical Epic*, p. 207, n. 17.

in the *Complaint of Nature*, who elaborately generates both the physical world and her own poetic figures while intensively demonstrating the need for each to be controlled, just as in proper grammar the 'adjective' is 'attracted' to the 'noun' (*DPN* X, 63–5).

Still, if Heraclitus' rather florid treatise only suggests the future, it nonetheless differs revealingly from the past. First, as these passages show, Heraclitus is not limited to Stoic interpretations, although he does include many of these in his work. He displays a broadly eclectic approach, even basing his allegory of the Athena/Achilles episode on the Platonic tripartite division of the soul. (Expectedly, he has a hard time fitting three elements into this two-character encounter.) As we shall see, this tendency to shift from *natura* to *humana natura* increasingly distinguishes not only late Stoic philosophy, but the interpretive tradition as a whole. The Ares/Diomedes critique nicely shows the transition from physical to human concerns in progress.

Second, at the same time that Heraclitus' philosophic approach is more flexible than that of the early Stoa, his literary approach is more concentrated. For all his obvious liberties with Homer's narrative (as in the 'Harmony' passage) and his selective stress on episodes concerning the gods, Heraclitus does not allegorize the gods randomly or even, to the degree of Chrysippus' extant exegesis, syncretically. Broadly speaking, his interpretation proceeds according to the narrative sequence of the *Iliad* and then continues according to the narrative sequence of the *Odyssey*. Nominally, if not practically, the text directs the interpretation.

Finally, and most significantly, Heraclitus strikes a self-consciously literary pose. Instead of being coolly detached from the text, like the early Stoa or his own more rigidly Stoic contemporary, Cornutus, he passionately defends Homer.[41] Even in the brief Ares/Diomedes selection quoted here, the enthusiastic tenor of 'clear,' 'very credible,' 'manifest proofs' might almost remind us of the supportive tone of twelfth-century claims about the *integumenta* of the *auctores*. In fact, Heraclitus

---

[41] See, e.g., pp. 1–2, 30, 83, 87–8, and the introduction to Buffière's edition, pp. xxxviii–xlii, which also notes Heraclitus' philosophic eclecticism. Contrast Cornutus, discussed on pp. xxxi–xxxii and in Tate, 'Cornutus and the Poets,' 41–5.

displays a certain imaginative flair of his own, as the 'Harmony'/
'lovely' passage suggests. Philosophy is here being composed in
a rhetorical key, if not in the rhetorical format it will achieve in
the *Cosmographia*. The philosophic, linguistic, and exegetical
reductionism of the Stoa is beginning to acquire a more expansive literary voice.

STOIC PSYCHOLOGY: *LOGOS* AND *PATHOS*

If we shift our perspective on Stoicism from the interpretation
of the gods to the delineation of the soul, we can see this compositional tendency developing from the other direction. Indeed, when the natural and human worlds reflect each other,
the study of cosmic principles inevitably implies the study of
psychic causes. To appreciate this process—and with it, the increasing interaction between the interpretive and compositional traditions—we might again consider texts from the early
and late periods of Stoicism.

The first of these documents is a valuable record of Chrysippus'
late third-century BC treatment of the soul, partially preserved
in a set of verbatim excerpts by the physician Galen.[42] The work
is important for our subject especially because Chrysippus,
unlike Plato, contends that the soul has no 'parts.' Instead, a
unitary soul, extending by pneumatic current from the
hēgemonikon, the seat of reason, permeates the body. When the
soul's pervasive 'tension' is equable, behavior is rational; when
it is imbalanced, by either abnormal expansion or contraction,
behavior is irrational. By contrast, Galen himself broadly
subscribes to the Platonic model of a tripartite soul, and he constantly plays it off the Stoic model he rejects. This is a testimony
not only to psychology, but to personification in the making.

Repeatedly, Galen is puzzled and perturbed that Chrysippus
should so often cite Greek poetry to support his view of a

---

[42] See *Claudii Galeni De Placitis Hippocratis et Platonis*, hereafter *DP*, ed. Iwanus
Mueller (Leipzig, 1874), cited by page number. In translating the Greek, I have con-
sulted the Latin translation in Mueller's edition and the Italian translation of brief
parts of this treatise, in *I frammenti morali di Crisippo*, tr. Rosario Anastasi, Vol. III of *I
frammenti degli stoici antichi* (Padua, 1962). The work is not available in English. For an
overview of some general principles in Stoic psychology, see, e.g., J. M. Rist, *Stoic
Philosophy*, esp. chs. 2, 11, 12, 14.

unitary soul (*DP*, p. 258 f.). Transcribing all these quotations
here, Galen complains, would fill a book (*DP*, p. 265). Besides,
argues Galen, verses such as the one Chrysippus cites from
Euripides' *Medea*—'But anger (*thymos*) is stronger than my de-
liberations'—clearly show, contrary to Chrysippus' position,
that the *thymos* is a distinct psychic agent, conflicting with
reason (*DP*, pp. 382–3). In terms deliberately recalling the
Republic, Galen elsewhere speaks of Medea's reason and *thymos*
'struggling' (*estasiaze*) against each other, of one part 'battling'
(*diamakhetai*) the other until it 'conquers' it (*nika*, *DP*,
pp. 272–4; cf. p. 306). Either Chrysippus really is at odds with
himself, as Galen slyly suggests as if to drive the point home
(*DP*, p. 382), or, in his constant appeal to poetry, Chrysippus is
exploiting a strategy that Galen, with his model of three actual
parts to the soul, can hardly appreciate.

When Galen lets Chrysippus speak for himself, the general outlines of that strategy become clear. Passion, says Chrysippus, is
the absence of proper psychic tension, or 'a-tensionality'
(*atonian*). When people are mentally disturbed we 'create the
expression' (*poioumetha ton logon*) that they are 'outside themselves' (*ou para heautois*), but this 'withdrawal' entails only a
'turning away' (*apostrophēn*) from reason. Indeed, it is possible
to hear just such expressions from the enraged, who say they
wish to 'indulge themselves in *thymos*' (*tō thymō kharizesthai
autous*), 'as the matter is fashioned at every turn'—or perhaps
we should translate, 'as the matter is depicted in every trope'
(*ek pantos ge tropon poiēteon*, *DP*, pp. 377–8, 383–4).

The tropes themselves, of course, long antedate Chrysippus,
as his own work demonstrates. Indeed, the tendency to treat
abstractions at least briefly almost as if they were discrete
figures occurs in nearly every period, and we can observe the
technique throughout antiquity, in historical, ethical, and
dramatic writing.[43] Chrysippus, however, is seeking to give

---

[43] See Charles Forster Smith, 'Personification in Thucydides,' *Classical Philology*,
13 (1918), 241–50; E. A. Barber, 'Alexandrian Literature,' in *The Hellenistic Age*, ed. J.
B. Bury, E. A. Barber, *et al.* (Cambridge, 1923), p. 66; and Lind, 'Roman Religion,'
cited in Ch. I, n. 2, above, 109. The abstractions of fifth-century BC Old Comedy to
which Lind points, however, along with similar figures in later drama, must be considered somewhat apart from the narrative tradition, with which I am mainly concerned
in this study. Drama automatically 'personifies' a concept if the concept is given a role
in the play. It thus differs considerably from narrative poetry, which can—and normally does—attribute effects to a concept without personifying it. For our purposes the

such rhetorical flourishes a philosophic rationale. For him, passions are not independent forces, but passivities, as their name (*pathē*) suggests, defects in the hegemony of reason. Unlike Plato, who makes the *thymos* a distinctive element in the soul, Chrysippus attributes human impropriety to a lapse in the dynamic continuum of the personality, and more importantly for our purposes, he is beginning to relate such improprieties to the oblique turns of language.

This strategy has impressive potential. With it, we could show how figurative language articulates our feeling that passion happens *to* us, while philosophic reflection demonstrates that passion is really something *we* undergo. We could retain the vividness of Homer's active agents or Plato's conflicting parts, while abandoning the awkwardness of these earlier psychologies. In short, we could make the allegory of self-division a counterpoint to the knowledge of personal identity.

Chrysippus himself, however, does not clearly articulate these allegorical possibilities here. It is 'not unfitting' (*ouk apo tropou*), he says, that passion is called a 'movement against' (*kinēsis para*) nature. Such movements are 'disobedient and averse' (*apeitheis kai apestrammenai*) to reason, although only in the sense of a 'turning away' (*apostrophēn*) from reason. Indeed, it is 'proper' (*oikeiōs*) that the enraged are said to be 'carried away' (*ekpheresthai*, *DP*, pp. 356–7, 386–7). Elsewhere Chrysippus even claims that the passions 'drive back' (*ekkrouei*) the rational processes, that they 'violently push forward' (*biaiōs proōthounta*) to actions contrary to reason (*SVF* III, 390). The crucial question is the sense in which we are to understand that such expressions are 'proper.' Chrysippus might, for example, have explained how the skewed perspective of emotional turmoil appropriately involves a shift in linguistic register, how the very figurative status of such language shows that it, like passion, needs to be transposed. We shall see in a moment that such explanations are quite possible in Stoicism, at least in a later period. But here we only dimly perceive just how the hands can be the hands of Plato, while the voice remains the voice of Chrysippus.

crucial issue is the transfer of a dramatic technique, *prosopopoeia*, to a narrative format; see App. II.

It is tempting to supply Chrysippus with the strategy implicit in his remarks. After all, he is not here writing a treatise on ambiguous language. Again, Galen (or Plutarch, in the 'violent' passage), for his own polemical reasons, may be extracting the most graphic expressions from Chrysippus' work without giving him a full opportunity to explain himself. Still, at least in the surviving fragments, Chrysippus never quite shows what it means to 'create the expression' or 'fashion the matter' as if *thymos* were a force in its own right.[44] Perhaps if the stylistic issue were clarified, Galen could not so sweepingly accuse Chrysippus of himself slipping into the tripartite model.

There may be deeper issues of causality contributing to these problems, as later developments will suggest. For now, the essential point is their literary effect. Whereas in Chrysippus' interpretation of the gods the philosophy tended to come at the expense of the poetry, now the poetry tends to come at the expense of the philosophy—a problem that was affecting the compositional tradition from the start. For all Chrysippus' appeals to poetry, the one procedure is only imperfectly complementing the other.

Such cooperation increasingly develops in later Stoic writing as a result of broad changes in philosophic and literary orientation. In the psychological tradition, for example, the first-century BC 'Platonizing' Stoic Posidonius argues for a distinct, irrational impulse in the soul. While this view challenges Chrysippus' oblique approach to passion, it also encourages a reassessment of psychic 'powers' important to the development of allegory. In the rhetorical tradition, influential Hellenistic treatises on style and the practical role of rhetorical persuasion in Roman education give special currency—sometimes excessive license—to the literary flourish. Indeed, it is in these treatises that the term *allegoria* first appears in its compositional sense.[45] We have already mentioned the rhetorical tendencies of first-century AD exegesis in Heraclitus. In his contem-

[44] For some other efforts by Chrysippus to apply linguistic transfer to the study of the soul, see, e.g., *DP*, pp. 276-8, 317-23, 377-8.

[45] On Posidonius, see I. G. Kidd, 'Posidonius on Emotions,' in *Problems in Stoicism*, ed. A. A. Long (London, 1971), pp. 200-15. On *allegoria* in early rhetorical treatises, see Reinhart Hahn, *Die Allegorie in der antiken Rhetorik*, Diss. Tübingen 1967 (Tübingen, 1967), and my Appendices.

porary, Seneca, we can observe the philosophic deployment of rhetoric by a man influential in both literary circles and late Stoic thought. In Seneca's writing on the soul, the allegorical procedure implicit in Chrysippus' work finally begins to acquire a recognizable, even dramatic, form.

Seneca's crucial contribution to the subject is his keen sensitivity to the relation between changes in behavior and shifts in language. A man's action is like his speech ('actio dicenti similis est'), he insists. As the equilibrium of the soul modulates, so does the tenor of language; the weaker the reason, the looser the talk. In effect, passion exposes itself by its rhetoric. When the soul is 'vitiated,' the 'ingenium' is 'inflated.' More particularly, 'an angry man talks in an angry way.'[46]

Here is a psychological basis for linguistic amplification, and Seneca's long treatise on anger shows its deployment in literary form.[47] The orator, Seneca points out, though not himself angry, may 'simulate' anger (II, xvii, 1), and in the *De Ira*, Chrysippus' passion expands into a picturesque, flamboyant figure. 'Raging with a scarcely human lust for weapons, blood, and punishment,' 'hurtling into the spearheads themselves,' 'like those infernal monsters fashioned by the poets,' the abstraction bursts into Seneca's treatise and wreaks considerable havoc for some thousands of lines (I, i, 1; II, xxxv, 5; cf. III, iv, 1–2). Its very amplification, however, betrays its bluster. Powerless over itself ('impotens sui'), a 'vacuous swelling,' like the 'rising winds,' recoiling upon itself ('in se revertitur'), gusty and empty ('ventosa et inanis'), the figure is only occupying a void left by a man's self-abdication (I, i, 2; I, xvii, 4; I, xix, 4; I, xx, 2). In effect, Seneca here makes the personification of passion a stylistic reverberation of the deviation from reason. Revealingly, when he applies this technique to a woman transported by

---

[46] See *Ad Lucilium Epistulae Morales*, ed. and tr. Richard M. Gummere, 3 vols. (London, 1918–25), on which my translations are based, *Ep.* 114, sections 1–3 and 20.

[47] Quotations from the *De Ira*, cited by book, section, and subsection, refer to the edition of John W. Basore in *Moral Essays*, I (London, 1928), on which my translations are based. For the ancient tradition of works on anger, see William S. Anderson, *Anger in Juvenal and Seneca*, University of California Publications in Classical Philology, Vol. 19, No. 3 (Berkeley, 1964), p. 174, n. 1. On Seneca's flair for the rhetorical flourishes of his day, see A. Bourgery, *Sénèque Prosateur* (Paris, 1922), pp. 114–20, and Eugène Albertini, *La Composition dans les ouvrages philosophiques de Sénèque*, Bibliothèque des écoles françaises d'Athènes et de Rome, Vol. 127 (Paris, 1923), pp. 223–6, 310–14.

passion in his own version of Euripides' play, Medea seems to beckon dementedly to a figure outside herself: 'wrath, where you lead, I follow' ('ira, qua ducis, sequor').[48]

While Seneca strikingly anticipates early medieval allegory, we may note three related elements of his work which still need development. First, although he vividly fleshes out an abstraction, his philosophic rationale is the Stoic view that the soul is corporeal (*Ep.* 106) and identical with its various states (*Ep.* 113), and that during the state of passion the mind transmutes itself into the vice (I, viii, 2). This radical notion of a psychic continuum not only deepens the tendency to pass from the personification to the individual (e.g., I, i, 1–7; III, iv, 1–3), a problem posed since Homer. It also seriously limits the possibility of sustained interior dialogue, since insofar as passion exists, reason does not. The closest Seneca comes here to an encounter between two abstractions is his brief contrast between reason's responsibility and anger's irresponsibility (I, xviii, 1–2)—not so much a conflict between personifications as a distinction between two ways a person can behave. As on the cosmic level the Stoic blending of agent and act leads Heraclitus to dissipate Ares into a series of material effects, so on the psychic level it leads Seneca less to delineate the personality than to diffuse it into its various conditions.

Second, the condition of passion has no genuine status in its own right; it is but the shadow of reason. Here the old notion of personification as a rhetorically thin trope, a limitation suggested since Prodicus, converges with the Stoic view that there is no independent 'impulse' responsible for passion. The principal action of Seneca's 'anger,' in fact, is self-destruction—a problem that will recur in Prudentius. It is significant that while Seneca is influenced by Posidonius, he rejects Posidonius' claim (similar to Galen's later complaint against Chrysippus) that reason's defection implies an interior agent of defection.[49] That pursuit of (infinitely receding) causes eventually produces the full-scale allegory of the soul.

Finally, whatever the degree of anger's personification in this treatise, it disappears (along with anger itself) when the

[48] See Seneca's *Medea*, l. 953, in *Seneca's Tragedies*, ed. and tr. Frank Justus Miller (Cambridge, Mass., 1917), I.

[49] See Pohlenz, *Die Stoa*, pp. 307–9, and Galen's *DP*, e.g., pp. 364–5.

soul is upright (I, ix, 3). This withdrawal into reason on the psychic plane parallels the conflagration into aether on the cosmic plane, and it accommodates only the apocalyptic (and terminal) mode of allegory. To develop a sustained psychic allegory like the *Romance of the Rose* or the *Divine Comedy*, it will be necessary to acquire a more Aristotelian sense of diverse powers integrated into a whole. That is, it will be necessary to articulate more than Stoicism the human sides of life, as well as the divine center. Indeed, this issue returns us to Homer's original problem: how it is possible to retain the *thymos* and yet listen to reasonable Athena. While Seneca creates a dazzling rhetoric of passion, perhaps Quintilian is right in more senses than one: 'He took too little trouble with philosophy.'[50]

EPIC MODULATIONS AND VIRGIL'S 'MARRIAGE'

Between the philosophic and rhetorical procedures we have seen interacting in this period there is an intermediate strategy, more eclectic in approach and more imaginative in inspiration. It is that philosophic poetry which nearly reduces the gods of mythology to an abstract level, on the one hand, while virtually raising the abstractions of the personality to a mythological level, on the other. Such poetry, more self-conscious than that of Homer and Hesiod, begins to appear early in the Greek tradition. It first develops systematically, however, in Virgil, near the end of the formative period we have been examining. By concentrating on the *Aeneid*, with brief glances earlier and later in the epic tradition, we can see the analytic and literary impulses emerging from Homeric epic begin once more to converge in an epic framework, now with a nearly allegorical force.

Perhaps the most dramatic case of this convergence is the brilliantly orchestrated 'marriage' scene of *Aeneid*, Book IV. The episode begins as the goddess Juno, seeking to divert Aeneas from his destiny and assuring Venus that she will see to the problem of Jupiter's will, reveals her plan to generate a storm when Dido and Aeneas join forces for a hunt. Virgil

[50] See *Inst. Orat.* X, i, 129, quoted by F. H. Sandbach, *The Stoics* (London, 1975), p. 159.

richly depicts the spirited hunters themselves and the
variegated terrain (IV, 129–59), and then suddenly shifts the
perspective upward, as 'the sky begins shaking with a great
tumult' (IV, 160–1). Everyone takes shelter:

> To the same cave come Dido and the Trojan chieftain. Primal Earth
> and Juno, patroness of marriage, give the signal; lightning fires flash,
> and the aetherial realm is witness to the mating, and from the highest
> hilltops scream the Nymphs. That day, the first of death and the first
> of woes, was the cause. For now Dido is affected neither by ap-
> pearances nor by reputation, nor does she think of furtive love. She
> calls it marriage, and with that name covers up her fault. At once
> Rumor runs through Libya's great cities, Rumor, swiftest of all
> evils. She thrives on speed, and by her going she gains strength. At
> first small through fear, soon she rises into the air; she walks the
> ground and hides her head in the clouds. . . .

>> speluncam Dido dux et Troianus eandem
>> deueniunt. prima et Tellus et pronuba Iuno
>> dant signum; fulsere ignes et conscius aether
>> conubiis summoque ulularunt uertice Nymphae.
>> ille dies primus leti primusque malorum
>> causa fuit; neque enim specie famaue mouetur
>> nec iam furtiuum Dido meditatur amorem:
>> coniugium uocat, hoc praetexit nomine culpam.
>>   Extemplo Libyae magnas it Fama per urbes,
>> Fama, malum qua non aliud uelocius ullum:
>> mobilitate uiget uirisque adquirit eundo,
>> parua metu primo, mox sese attollit in auras
>> ingrediturque solo et caput inter nubila condit. . . .
>>   (IV, 165–77)[51]

Rumor's tale, wildly agitating the entire region, provokes a
suitor of Dido to plead for Jupiter's intervention, which in turn
culminates in the confrontation between the lovers, Aeneas'
departure, and Dido's suicide. It is a decisive turning point in
the epic.

The spectacle, which begins with a hunt and ends with
a riot, is remarkable in the first place for its oscillating
movements of dilation and concentration. Between the frame
settings of countryside and city, the prospect first expands into

---

[51] Quotations from the *Aeneid* refer to *P. Vergili Maronis Opera*, ed. R. A. B. Mynors
(Oxford, 1969). My translations are based on *The Aeneid of Virgil*, tr. Allen
Mandelbaum (Berkeley, 1971).

the cosmic panorama of primal elements (ll. 166–70), then contracts into the close confinement of the cave (ll. 170–2), and finally expands once more as the tempestuous tale reverberates to the clouds (ll. 173–7).[52] This scenic pattern has its counterparts in social and tonal terms: from the demonic partnership of preternatural forces, to the private thoughts of Dido with regard to Aeneas ('meditatur,' l. 171), back to the spreading menace of Rumor; from the piercing stridency of the storm, to the silent recesses of the mind, back to the tumultuous uproar of the report. It is as if a burst of thunder shudders through every element of the story and echoes back to its celestial source. At the same time, the terrestrial center to which this impulse moves and from which it returns is the union of the two lovers. Virgil here fashions a comprehensive, imaginative continuum, organized by the reciprocal processes of expansion and contraction. It is almost as if the pulsating, dynamic world of Stoic physics were undergoing a poetic transformation.

In this continuum, the various levels of the epic begin to modulate into each other. Cosmic and personal processes nearly turn into degrees of a single, all-pervading 'tension' sustaining the epic. The underlying dynamism of this tension is the uneasy relation between volatile and cohesive forces. On the mythological plane, this relationship is expressed in the unstable union between Juno and Jupiter, here dramatized in her conspiracy to undermine his designs. This tendency to 'stir up a storm' is literally performed by the turbulent interaction of the physical elements. Whether or not Juno, associated (like Hera) with the windy element of air, openly announces her scheme to Jupiter, the chief of gods (like Zeus) in effect presides as does the 'aether' (l. 167), witnessing the event and flashing fire. The mythological and physical relationship, in turn, is acted out in the awkward 'marriage' of the two central human figures. Volatile Dido, devoted to Juno and increasingly agitated by Junonian 'furor' (e.g., IV, 69, 91, 101), darkly unites with 'pius Aeneas,' devoted to Jove and increasingly worthy of Jovian 'imperium' (e.g., I, 10, 229, 287). Finally, this convergence between Dido and Aeneas is internalized within each figure, as impulsive passion encounters responsible

[52] On Virgil's exploitation of visible space, see Theodore M. Andersson, *Early Epic Scenery* (Ithaca, N.Y., 1976), pp. 53–103.

reason. Self-consciously, Dido here seeks to 'cover up' her fault
(l. 172) and later plunges still deeper into guilt, while Aeneas,
whose inner life Virgil now veils in darkness, slowly emerges
into the light: 'Italiam non sponte sequor' (IV, 361).
Macrocosm does not merely parallel microcosm in this scene.
Each level of the continuum, from cosmic to psychic, blends
transparently and inseparably into the other.[53]

To appreciate Virgil's procedure, we might consider for a
moment the famous marriage at a cave site in the earlier epic of
Apollonius Rhodius, the *Argonautica*, composed in the third
century BC, near the beginning of the period we have been exploring. Apollonius of course has his own valid goals and attractive techniques, but it remains significant that unlike
Virgil, he tends to divorce the divine and human planes.

With respect to the gods, while Apollonius makes the pantheon
much more transparent than it is in Homer, he does not by that
token make it conceptual. The subtlest mythological episode in
the poem, Hera's conversation with Aphrodite (III, 36–112,
parallel to Juno's conspiracy with Venus), is depicted as a kind
of parlor scene, a brilliant but delicate little vignette in the
Hellenistic mode. Insofar as Hera has conceptual possibilities,
they are radically divided. She instigates Medea's passion, on
the one hand, but only to protect the heroic Jason, on the
other. Along with the other gods, she remains only distantly in
touch with most of the proceedings.

With respect to the people, Apollonius is distinguished for
his effort to bring amorous passion into the action of epic.
Medea's love, though, while subtly and poignantly portrayed,
never sustains the larger resonances associated with Dido's
demonic fury—or with the older Medea of Euripides and
Seneca. Insofar as the demonic element does enter Apollonius'
Medea, it does so only in her rather different role as the
sorceress who helps Jason to yoke the fire-breathing bulls and
finally to capture the golden fleece (III, 844 f.), or as the

---

[53] Here and throughout my discussion of the *Aeneid* I am particularly indebted to
Viktor Pöschl, *The Art of Vergil*, tr. Gerda Seligson (Ann Arbor, Mich., 1962),
hereafter Pöschl, and Brooks Otis, *Virgil: A Study in Civilized Poetry* (Oxford, 1963),
hereafter Otis, though my orientation is different in a number of respects. I have
drawn upon the notes in *The Aeneid of Virgil*, ed. R. D. Williams, 2 vols. (Basingstoke,
1972–3), and at times I have found useful Michael Murrin's discussion in *Allegorical
Epic*, pp. 3–25.

runaway who seeks to prevent the Colchians from capturing her (IV, 355–93)—a brief convergence of *amor* and *ira* that Virgil richly and elaborately exploits (*Aeneid* IV, 305 f., 365 f., 590 f.). As for Jason, his adventure has its own momentum, facilitated but not fully transfigured by either his love or the gods.[54] As a result, when the marriage at last takes place, Hera is largely a ceremonial marriage goddess, appearing structurally as a kind of afterthought (IV, 1152, 1185, 1199), and Jason and Medea, the poet explicitly tells us, marry at this time due to practical 'necessity' (*khreō*, IV, 1164) rather than urgent passion. Indeed, the whole treatment of the ceremony at the cave site deals less with cosmic and personal interaction than with the charming musings of fancy: graceful nymphs (IV, 1143–51; how different from Virgil's screeching ones!), splendid trappings (IV, 1180–95), current altars originally established by Medea (IV, 1217–19). Apollonius' narrative, like his Hellenistic aetiology, proceeds with a seemingly effortless ease. It is Virgil who turns such poetry toward the aetiology of allegory, the deep articulation of causes.

In fact, Virgil is constantly modulating the conceptual and poetic register of his poem. Thus, the storm of elemental fury (I, 81–123) that initiates the *Odyssey* half of the epic changes into the metaphorical 'storm' of martial fury (VII, 586–94) that dominates the *Iliad* half of the book. Between these two developments lies the stormy passion of Book IV, where the figurative 'wound' of love turns into an actual stabbing (IV, 1–2, 660–5). Dido, soon to go hunting, is imagined as a doomed 'deer,' helplessly fleeing through the forest (IV, 68–73); the 'deer' is later transformed into a slain stag, helping to provoke a war (VII, 481–502). In Virgil's epic, this kind of oscillation between figure and fact moves in both directions. It does not yet display the typological rationale it will later acquire in Prudentius and especially in Dante and Milton, where similes turn into facts which in turn are but figures of things to come. Already in the *Aeneid*, though, turns of language do not merely elaborate the story rhetorically; they interpret it philosophically, exposing and developing the meaning of events.[55]

[54] For the text, see *The Argonautica*, ed. and tr. R. C. Seaton (London, 1912). For the issues in my discussion, see Albin Lesky, *A History of Greek Literature*, tr. James Willis and Cornelis de Heer (London, 1966), pp. 728–37, and Otis, pp. 62–96.

[55] For attempts to find physical or psychological allegory in the *Aeneid*, see Richard

Virgil's technique has deeper implications for the development of allegory. By passing so smoothly between the outer
and inner worlds, he tends to blur the distinctions between
them. The clear, hard outlines of the Homeric world, which
limited the possibilities of allegory, are softening in focus.
Physical and psychological states overlap and reveal each
other: the darkened moon 'sinks' as troubled Dido 'falls' upon
the couch (IV, 80–3); conversely, the secret 'fire' of her passion
blazes into a funeral pyre (IV, 2, 661). In such a world, it is not
exactly possible to speak of a direct, 'objective' approach to
phenomena; the very definition of events has an oblique, subjective dimension.[56]

This subjective, human perspective is usually treated in
terms of poetic mood, the famous Virgilian *pathos*, but for us it
has two consequences of a more specific kind. First, the tendency
to see the world from the 'other side,' from the side of human
experience as well as divine destiny, from the side of passion as
well as action, implies an ethical orientation that will promote
the moral symmetries of allegory. In Virgil's work, *pathos*, passion, is neither an outside accessory to heroic action, as in
Apollonius' treatment of love, nor a sheer frustration of rational
activity, as in the Stoic treatment of 'anger.' Now it is a
necessary component in the creation of virtue, whether in the
form of the love affair through which Aeneas must pass or in
the form of the war fury that he must undergo. 'Pius' Aeneas is
not just an heroic or a rational figure; he is a compassionate,
sympathetic one—that is, he acts with passion, with *pathos*. In
this perspective, the old opposition between passion and
reason, *thymos* and *logos*, is no longer adequate. Both sides are
necessary to make the whole.[57] This dialectical symmetry
within a common framework of *pietas* is still diffused in the
Aeneid, implicitly rather than schematically presented. As we
shall see in a moment, Virgil's tendencies in this direction are
provisional, even uncertain. But when the general strategy of

Heinze, *Virgils Epische Technik* (Leipzig, 1903), pp. 284–92, 297–304, and Murrin,
Allegorical Epic, pp. 3–25; contrast Pöschl, pp. 21–2, 48–9, 72, 154, and Kenneth
Quinn, *Virgil's* Aeneid (London, 1968), pp. 300–7. For Virgil's modulation between
figure and fact, see Pöschl, pp. 65, 110, 140, 147.

[56] See esp. Otis, ch. 3, 'The Subjective Style.'

[57] See Pöschl, pp. 53–8, and Thomas M. Greene, *The Descent from Heaven* (New
Haven, 1963), pp. 89–99.

undergoing while acting is gradually transformed in a later milieu, it will help to consolidate abstract contraries within the common framework of divine love.

There is a second, more problematic consequence to this interaction between objective and subjective points of view. It puts extreme pressure on the conceptual categories of the world, thereby intensifying the need to discover underlying principles. We can see this pressure particularly during moments of crisis such as the 'marriage' scene, where actual events blend phantasmagorically into imagined ones. Lightning flashes seem to become wedding torches; the aetherial realm, an official witness to the ceremony; and wailing nymphs, the wedding chorus (IV, 166–8). Dido calls it all 'marriage,' but the term is only an integument covering her actual deficiency ('praetexit nomine culpam,' IV, 172). At this moment of moral and linguistic breakdown, just as the confusion is about to spread into the world at large, a personification takes over the foreground. Expansive 'Fama,' moving, gaining momentum, then lifting her head into the clouds (IV, 173–7), flies by shadow of night midway between heaven and earth (IV, 184), and perversely mixes truth and fantasy, as if to offer a new, abortive version of the *Aeneid* ('pariter facta atque infecta canebat: / uenisse Aenean Troiano sanguine cretum . . .,' IV, 190–1). Virgil's extraordinary transformation of Homer's expansive 'Strife' here shows how far the epic has come toward allegory. Unlike Homer's brief figure of social discord, the rhetorical flight of Virgil's 'Fama' is a comment on the stylistic and conceptual, as well as emotional, dilemmas of the poem. In a world turning inside out and outside in, it is necessary to find some conceptual category to encompass the action. In Chaucer's later, more playful *House of Fame*, Virgil's expansive figure finally turns into an amusing comment on the process of artistic amplification itself, based on a 'scientific' approach to the causal action of air waves: 'That whel wol cause another whel, / And that the thridde, and so forth, brother, / Every sercle causynge other.'[58] It is almost as if that professorial eagle were trying to steal Virgil's thunder.

[58] For the 'rhetorical progression' of 'Fama' in the *Aeneid* passage, see Piehler, *Visionary Landscape*, cited above in Ch. I, n. 6, pp. 25–6. For the quotation from the *House of Fame*, ll. 794–6, see *The Works of Geoffrey Chaucer*, ed. F. N. Robinson, 2nd edn. (Boston, 1957), to which all citations of Chaucer refer.

In the fluid continuum of Virgil's world, however, it is not always possible to specify scientifically the causes underlying events. At the crucial, transitional moment in the 'marriage' scene, when, in the terms of Chrysippus and Seneca, reason abdicates to passion, the precise agent of the transaction seems to slip away, and Virgil blames, as we might say today, the 'situation': 'That *day*, the first of death and the first of woes, was the *cause*' ('ille dies primus leti primusque malorum / causa fuit'). The parallel placement of 'ille dies' and 'causa fuit' emphasizes the problem. In the absence of a culprit, curse the day—or perhaps blame the nasty weather. But the bad weather is caused by Juno, and if we try to trace her motives, we pass rapidly through history into the inscrutable, mythological rivalries of Olympus (I, 12–28). How insidiously clever a work Virgil would have found Chaucer's *Merchant's Tale*, which 'resolves' the marital rivalry between two earthly figures only by shifting to a divine plane that repeats the rivalry in mythological form. In any case, if Virgil is pre-allegorical in his explanation of Dido's and Aeneas' 'marriage,' we tend to be post-allegorical. The lovers just let 'nature take its course,' as we might say—casually appealing to the very abstraction that the medieval allegory of *Natura* so painstakingly seeks to delineate.

The problem takes its most poignant form at the end of the epic, where Virgil in effect reverses the movement of the 'marriage' scene and seems about to subordinate passionate impulse to reason. This is the crucial moment of transition that seemed to elude definition in Homer and Plato, the moment when *thymos* is reconciled with rational reflection. Turnus, who has become almost a personification of anger (e.g. XII, 9, 45, 101, 680), finally surrenders and appeals to Aeneas. Although moved 'more and more' by the appeal, Aeneas suddenly sees on Turnus the belt of a slain comrade, and 'inflamed with fury and terrible in wrath' ('furiis accensus et ira / terribilis'), he slaughters Turnus as the epic ends (XII, 930–52). If *thymos* has become reasonable in this conclusion, it is distressing that Virgil emphasizes not the integration of Aeneas' impulses, but their disjunction. Servius' explanation that Aeneas shows 'pietas' both in initially considering Turnus' plea and in later avenging his slain comrade is tempting, but it, after all, only avoids a disturbing division of the 'I' by transferring the division to the abstraction. At any rate, in this crisis the old conceptual model is becoming insufficient.

It is possible, of course, to supply reasons for Aeneas' behavior, here and in the 'marriage' scene. 'Tout comprendre, c'est tout pardonner.' But the problem in the *Aeneid* is that we do *not* comprehend everything, that Virgil's world is a world in radical transition, always threatening to slip into incomprehensibility. It is said that Octavia, sister to the master of an empire, broke down upon hearing the poignant conclusion to Virgil's vision of Roman history, 'tu Marcellus eris' (VI, 883)—where the grammar itself seems to strain against the truth, as an indicative verb of the future is only a subjunctive condition contrary to fact. Octavia, it is true, was weeping for a son who would have inherited the empire, but her action illuminates the deepest strains in Virgil's work as a whole.

Virgil never completed his epic; perhaps the work does not lend itself to 'completion,' but only to perpetual reconstruction. The philosophic and poetic tendencies of the poem and its milieu intensify in the century following its composition. When Ovid transforms the Hellenistic metamorphosis tradition a few years after Virgil's death, he makes the radical modulation between disparate conceptual levels the organizing principle of an epic poem. In a sense, the *Metamorphoses* institutionalizes structural change, not only in the famous 'cuncta fluunt' of the 'Pythagorean's' philosophy (an influential passage for the *Cosmographia*), but in the ingenious inside-out formulations of the poetry. 'The greatest god is within me!' ('maximus intra me deus est!' VII, 55), cries Medea in love, and unlike the *Argonautica*'s Medea, she has not been mythologically wounded by the arrow of Eros—nor even, for that matter, embraced by the love god, as in the case of the *Aeneid*'s Dido. When Valerius Flaccus composes his own *Argonautica* in the late first century AD, he nearly turns Medea into the centering point for an extended, abstract encounter between 'amor' and 'pudor' themselves. When the more mannered Statius composes his *Thebaid* in the same period, the passion of *ira* seems to overtake a whole world, as if to schematize the deadly antinomies of Lucan's earlier *Civil War* and to fulfill the rhetorical warning of Seneca's treatise (*De Ira* III, ii, 2–6). Revealingly, the *Thebaid* ushers in the Fury of war at the summons of a man (not, as in the *Aeneid*, at the instigation of a goddess), and the frenzied war itself consists of paradigmatic, stylized struggles in which fury is constantly dissipating piety—a process that nearly reaches the breaking point in the encounter between the Fury and 'Pietas' herself near the end of the poem.[59]

Perhaps the single graphic sequence in which Statius describes the transition to war (III, 218–439) epitomizes the allegorical tendencies we have seen converging in the ancient world. Mars, sweeping toward Argos to incite it against Thebes, is intercepted by Venus, who seeks in vain to protect their child Harmony's offspring, the people of Thebes (III, 260–323). This fable of love seeking to prevent discord from disturbing the effects of harmony is a shift from mythology toward argumentation that almost reminds us of Heraclitus' exegesis. Meanwhile, that human figure of 'ira,' the bloodied Tydeus, is returning to Argos, where his frenzied call to arms is rhetorically exploited by the exiled claimant to the Theban throne. With 'variegated expression' Polynices obliquely utters ('obliquatque') his plea for war (III, 381–2), a rhetorical pose of which Seneca would approve—though he, like Statius, would condemn the anger that actually underlies it. Finally, mixing 'truth and falsehood' and inciting men to arms, 'Fama' spreads wildly through the countryside. Driven by the gods of war as storm winds are driven by the god of the sea (III, 425–39), she combines the tempestuous atmosphere of Virgil with the abstract temper of an age. In this sequence, the allegorization of a god is converging with the amplification of a passion by the dynamic motion of an abstract agent.

At the same time, this series of events, composed at the end of the first century AD, is not only a comment on Heraclitus, Seneca, and Virgil. It is also a striking sequel to that initial Homeric episode, composed nearly a millennium earlier, where Achilles obeys the god but does not let go of the anger. Statius, imitating that very episode near the beginning of his

---

[59] For the quotations from the *Metamorphoses*, see XV, 178 and VII, 55; cf. *Aeneid* IX, 184–5. For the abstract conflict in Valerius' poem, see his *Argonautica* VII, 153–466, and Hermann Fränkel, 'Das Argonautenepos des Apollonios,' *Museum Helveticum*, 14 (1957), 11. For the refs. to the *Thebaid*, see the edition of J. H. Mozley, 2 vols. (London, 1928), I, 46–143; VII, 217–18; XI, 457–96. For discussion of these issues in Lucan and Statius, see Lewis, pp. 49–56 (with caution on the psychic emphasis), and David Vessey, *Statius and the Thebaid* (Cambridge, 1973), pp. 55–133, 317–28.

own poem (II, 682–90), brings Athena to Tydeus just before his fateful return to Argos. But now the event does not just lead to disruption among the Argives and their opponents. More importantly, it finally begins to enact in narrative terms the allegorical potential of Homer's 'Strife,' a figure 'at first rearing up only a little, but then striding upon the earth with her head striking heaven.' Homer's work may be a recurring point of reference for the allegorical tradition. But the longer those who contribute to that tradition concentrate upon a source, the more they keep discovering a new center.

III *RITES OF PASSAGE: TRANSITIONS BETWEEN ANTIQUITY AND THE MIDDLE AGES*

Easy is the descent to Avernus . . . but to recall your steps, to rise again into the upper air—this is the task; this, the labor. (Virgil, *Aeneid* VI, 126-9.)

THE EARLY CHRISTIAN MILIEU: TEXT, BEING, TIME

The process of displacement by which allegory begins to emerge in the ancient world is not just a case of one fashion superseding another. It is the broad expression of a dynamic impulse inherent in the strategy of allegorical writing itself. As its early development suggests, there is a subversive element in the very technique of allegory, a tendency to disrupt philosophic and rhetorical norms that finally turns allegory even against itself. At the same time, however, this critical drive has its creative counterpart. In the very process of challenging the old frameworks allegory necessarily generates new ones. It is simultaneously committed to radical acts of destruction and reconstruction.

For such a technique, the more agitated the milieu, the more dramatic the possibilities. It is particularly appropriate, then, that the allegorical impulse intensifies during the complex passage from antiquity to the Middle Ages. In this restless period, the effort to dramatize the flux of shifting perspectives and changing conditions increasingly distinguishes the explicit designs of allegorical writing. Already in the earliest centuries AD, this tendency develops momentum in the rich mélange of interpretive movements that eventually produces the spectacular allegory of the third-century Christian exegete, Origen.

Perhaps the most immediately striking feature of allegorical interpretation during this early period, in fact, is its fluidity of poetic and intellectual approach. On the one hand, the range of texts subject to exegesis dramatically expands beyond the framework of Homer and Hesiod. Now it includes the mysteries of ancient oriental peoples, the mythology of the Egyptians, and the Scriptures of Jews and Christians. On the other hand, the strategies of interpretation themselves multiply and increasingly interact with one another. At times, in fact, the exegetes of this period appear to be commenting less upon poetic texts than upon other commentaries, as in the revision of the Apologist Justin's claims by the pagan philosopher Celsus, of Celsus' claims by the Alexandrian Christian Origen, of Origen's claims by the Neoplatonist Porphyry. Our civilization, it seems, is not the first to be preoccupied with hermeneutics and its discontents.[1]

In any case, the allegorists of the early centuries AD give self-conscious expression to their own interpretive interplay by their developing doctrine of a once single, now diversified revelation. According to this doctrine, the enigmatic poetry of various peoples over the ages expresses in oblique and sometimes confused forms an ancient, primordial wisdom, recoverable by the demystifying clarifications of philosophy. Perhaps the spirit of the age is best expressed in the celebrated phrase of that mysterious, hybrid, second-century figure Numenius, who draws upon Pythagorean, Platonic, and Jewish sources. 'What is Plato,' he asks, 'but a Moses speaking in Greek?'[2]

At the same time, this fluidity of approach is not exactly syncretic in effect. In the very act of borrowing from each other, such exegetes seek to qualify rival interpretations and to refine their own perspectives. A celebrated example of this process is the allegorical treatment of Homer's god Hermes, who gives Odysseus the magical herb 'moly' to protect him from the sorceress Circe. Perhaps the magical, esoteric element in this story particularly recommends it to the age; in any event, the overall treatment reads almost like a series of philosophic variations on the theme of Athena descending to Achilles.

---

[1] For detailed overviews, see Pépin, pp. 176–474 and Jean Daniélou, *Gospel Message and Hellenistic Culture*, tr. and ed. John Austin Baker (London, 1973), pp. 39–105, 197–300.

[2] For the 'wisdom of the ancients,' see Grant, pp. 1–30. Numenius' phrase is quoted by Clement of Alexandria, *Stromata* I, xxii, 150, 4.

Thus, at the beginning of the first century AD the Stoic Athenaeus argues that Hermes here gives Odysseus the 'logos' that makes him 'passionless,' an interpretation character-istically diversified in the same century by Heraclitus. At the turn of the first and second centuries, the Middle Platonist Plutarch offers an account evocative of the Homeric story but mixed with dualistic overtones and oriental mythology. About the second century, a Gnostic exegete associates Hermes with Moses, the Logos, and moly with the wood that sweetens the bitter waters of Marah—while heterodox artists portray Christ himself with the features of Hermes. This association, however, also develops in orthodox Christian circles, as the second- and third-century exegetes Justin and Hippolytus link Hermes, the messenger-Word, with the unique Logos made flesh. There is still some distance be-tween such interpretive strategies and Martianus' composi-tional allegory of Mercury (Hermes) as the 'Nous' of Jove who redeems mortal Philology, or Boethius' poetic exemplum of that 'numen' which rescues Odysseus from Circe. But the early exegesis of this god dramatizes the interplay of philosophic and poetic idiom that helps to bring a principle of reason down to earth.[3]

The gradual emergence of Christian exegesis during this period, though, depends upon deeper and broader changes of perspective. We might draw special attention to three such changes, associated with three overlapping movements— Jewish, Platonic, and Gnostic. The first change entails the shift to a text different in kind from texts allegorized in earlier inter-pretation. This is the central Jewish contribution to Christian exegesis. The second change entails the connection between levels of allegorical interpretation and orders of being. This is the principal Platonic element in Christian exegesis, although Gnostic writing also raises the problem in a revised form. The third change entails the relation between orders of being and the movement of time. While both Jewish and Platonic in-fluences operate here, it is the Gnostic challenge that par-ticularly dramatizes this issue for Christian exegesis during its early development.

---

[3] For these developments, see Hugo Rahner, *Greek Myths and Christian Mystery*, tr. Brian Battershaw (London, 1963), pp. 179–222 and Daniélou, *Gospel*, pp. 79–89.

The first of these changes, the shift in the text to be allegorized, produces a striking departure in exegetical strategy from that of earlier Greek interpretation. For Greek exegetes, the poetry of Homer and Hesiod is a diverting fiction. However inspired, it remains subject to the more rigorous discipline of philosophy, which transforms mere stories into facts. By contrast, when a different text, the Bible, is allegorized by Hellenized Jews, a reversal of priorities takes place. Because the Word of God, unlike the fictions of the Greek poets, is itself sacred and perfect, its interpretation can be only a form of inferior knowledge, not full knowledge. Accordingly, to apply philosophic interpretation to the Bible means not to place the text at the service of philosophy, but to place philosophy at the service of the text. This change offers at least the promise of a new logic and integrity to the 'literal' level, a need that was reaching a critical stage in the Greek tradition with the Stoics. If a first-century exegete like Heraclitus qualifies the Stoics' dissipation of the text with his enthusiastic gestures toward Homer, the Jews of the period make the endorsement of their text a matter of theological principle.[4]

While the Jewish philosophic approach to Scripture develops over time, its central representative is Philo, who flourishes in the early first century AD. Philo's own exegesis, it is true, often displays the extreme license of Greek allegorization, and at times he even denies the literal meaning of certain scriptural passages. The broad historical validity of the divine book, however, remains essential to his strategy, and his insistence upon its logical and inspirational priority helps to qualify even the most mystical allegorizations of the text. In the famous Philonic formula later repeated throughout the Middle Ages, philosophy becomes the 'handmaid' to Scripture.[5]

We can watch this reorientation of philosophy, the study of causes, toward the study of a sacred text in the very

---

[4] On the power and priority of God's Word in the Jewish tradition, see Thorlieff Boman, *Hebrew Thought Compared with Greek*, tr. Jules Moreau (London, 1960), pp. 58–69 and Wolfson, *Philo*, Vol. I, pp. 32–6, 138–40, 253–61.

[5] On Philonic allegorization, see esp. Wolfson, *Philo*, Vol. I, pp. 115–38; Erwin R. Goodenough, *An Introduction to Philo Judaeus*, 2nd edn. (Oxford, 1962), pp. 134–60; and the detailed study of V. Nikiprowetzky, *Le Commentaire de l'Ecriture chez Philon d'Alexandrie* (Leiden, 1977). On the 'handmaid' formula and its Christian afterlife, see Wolfson, *Philo*, Vol. I, pp. 143–54 and *Fathers*, pp. 97–101.

systematization of exegesis during the early Christian era. The most popular classification of philosophy during the first century is its division into physics, ethics, and logic, a classification endorsed in Platonic and Stoic writing of the period. In interpreting the Bible, the Alexandrian Philo states that his exegesis falls into two main categories, physical and ethical, a division reflecting the Greek philosophic interpretation of Homer, as we have seen. A century and a half later, the Christian Alexandrian, Clement, takes a fourfold classification of the Pentateuch as found in Philo and regroups it according to the tripartite division of Greek philosophy. It is significant that despite this philosophic parallel, Clement here calls the third part 'theological' and insists upon the transformation of Greek logic into the celestial logic of God. Similar transformations of the tripartite system recur in Origen and Jerome.[6] As in Philo's exegesis, this early Christian text-oriented philosophy does not exactly mean fidelity to the narrative in a modern sense. Indeed, for such exegetes the very efficacy of God's Word gives it a host of divergent meanings—a paradoxical counterpart to their official endorsement of the text that acts as a source of tension throughout the Christian tradition, as we shall see. In any event, the philosophic concentration on Scripture here deepens the broader tendencies of late antiquity as a whole to make the verbal arts central to philosophy itself, and it thus intensifies the interaction between the two allegorical traditions.

At the same time, such early systems of exegesis also reflect another tendency of late antique philosophy that we have seen developing in the late Stoic period: the shift from *natura* to *humana natura*. In his general division of the text into literal and allegorical senses, Philo compares the outer, literal meaning to the body, the inner, allegorical meaning to the soul. Clement supports the basic division by citing a scriptural verse (Prov. 22: 20) that in his text reads, 'Write the commandments doubly.' In the Septuagint, however, the text reads 'triply,'

---

[6] For these transformations of tripartite philosophy into exegesis, see Wolfson, *Fathers*, 24–72 and de Lubac, I, i, 193–4; 194, n. 6; 204–7; 205, n. 6. For discussion of an important crux ('in four parts' vs. 'in three parts') in the Clement passage, *Stromata* I, xxviii, 179, 3, see n. to l. 4 on p. 110 of Ludwig Früchtel's rev. 3rd edn. of vol. 2, *Stromata Buch I–VI*, in Otto Stählin's 4-vol. *Clemens Alexandrinus* (orig. pub. 1905–36; rev. edn. of vol. 2, Berlin, 1960).

and Origen invokes this passage to support his threefold division of Scripture into historical, moral, and spiritual senses. More revealingly, he associates this approach with the (Stoic) division of man into body, soul, and spirit, arguing that Scripture is aimed at the salvation of man. Like the tripartite classification of philosophy as a whole, this philosophic division of the personality is important not because it is easily applied to a book or because it is systematically followed in practice, but because the reference to it reveals an orientation, an effort to deploy the text to probe the depths of the spirit. This crucial tendency reaches its logical conclusion with Origen, who first conceives of the different kinds of interpretation as a simultaneous tripartite 'depth' within a given passage, rather than simply alternate strategies for various passages. The argument for exegetical depth is refined and elaborated by Jerome and Cassian (who also cite the Proverbs text) and later Christian exegetes. This is the principal foundation for the threefold and fourfold methods of exegesis which dominate the early Middle Ages.[7]

The issue of interpretive depth suggests the second change affecting early Christian exegesis, the connection between levels of interpretation and orders of being. Broadly speaking, this is preeminently a Platonic contribution to exegesis. In pre-Socratic and Stoic interpretation, there is little sense of genuine 'density' either in the poetic text or in the world the text reflects. The pre-Socratics simply transform the divine figures of Greek poetry into elements of the cosmos. More subtly, the Stoics treat them as extensions of a single, all-pervasive force. By contrast, for exegetes working within the Platonic tradition, the division between literal and allegorical meaning parallels the division between visible and invisible orders of being. The very 'texture' of poetry thus reflects the multilayered composition of the world at large.

In a sense, of course, this general perspective appears already in Plato—implicitly in fables such as the parable of the Cave (*Republic* VII) and explicitly in brief remarks about the

---

[7] For these associations between the division of the personality and the text, see Wolfson, *Fathers*, pp. 31, 47–9, 59, 65, 70 and de Lubac, I, i, 193–207. On Origen's central position in the development of multilayered exegesis, see de Lubac, I, i, 198–219.

link between levels of language and degrees of being (*Timaeus* 29B–29D). But it is Middle and Neoplatonic exegesis that decisively complicates and enriches the issue. Thus, in the famous interpretation of Homer's 'Cave of the Nymphs' (*Odyssey* XIII) that develops with the second-century Middle Platonists Numenius and Cronius and culminates in the extended third-century treatise of Porphyry, the issue is not exactly a one-to-one correspondence between the 'cave' of the material world and the expansive realm of the spirit. Rather, insists Porphyry, a cave can be the 'symbol' (*symbolon*) of either world—its darkness suggesting both the obscurity of the material cosmos and the mystery of the intelligible one—and even this particular cave of the lower world has a twofold portal, one (glossed as the constellation of Cancer) facilitating the descent to mortality, the other (glossed as the constellation of Capricorn) permitting the ascent to immortality. Similarly, inside the cave itself, the 'nymphs' symbolize both the powers of watery flux into which the 'dry' soul slips and at the same time the souls themselves. In such exegesis, a single poetic figure points in diverse directions. Conversely, the Neoplatonist Plotinus coordinates diverse poetic figures into a single hierarchy, by interpreting Hesiod's conflicting triad of Uranus, Cronus, and Zeus as a unified, orderly process of emanation from the One, to Nous, to Soul. The celebrated Platonic problem of the One and the Many here acquires an exegetical and poetic form.[8]

If these Neoplatonic strategies offer intriguing opportunities for Christian interpretation, they also present certain dilemmas. While the concept of the 'symbol,' for example, gradually enriches Christian exegesis, it is hardly a 'solution' to the

8 For Plato, cf. Meier, 'Zum Problem der allegorischen Interpretation,' cited above in Ch. I, n. 4, p. 269. For Porphyry, see *De Antro Nympharum*, ed. and tr. John M. Duffy, Philip F. Sheridan, *et al.*, Arethusa Monographs, Vol. I (Buffalo, 1969), chs. 5–13, 20–31; cf. the analysis of Buffière, pp. 419–59. For Plotinus, see Pépin, pp. 203–7. For the qualification of such a 'vertical' orientation by the 'horizontal' tendencies of Christian typology, see my discussion later in this section, with the refs. in n. 13, esp. Daniélou and Pépin. For the rather different argument that whatever the *interpretive* claims about 'levels' of meaning, allegorical *composition* itself actually 'works horizontally,' with meaning 'accreting serially' in polysemous language, see Quilligan, *Language of Allegory*, cited above in Ch. I, n. 4, pp. 27–33. The argument has its point, although compositional allegory in the Neoplatonic tradition explicitly incorporates conceptual 'depth' into its very design; see my analyses below.

allegorical problem, as has often been claimed since the time of the Romantics—who for that matter invoke the symbol some 1500 years after its sophisticated treatment by the Neoplatonists. The multivalence of the 'symbolic' cave of the nymphs, after all, only dramatizes the kind of deep ambivalence about the precise status of this world—now a mere shadow, now a reflection of the light—that preoccupies both the Christian tradition and any sophisticated philosophy, however 'esemplastic' its imagination. Alternatively, the attempt to order diverse elements of the world according to the progressive 'degrees' of a single force risks an emanationist or a subordinationist perspective dangerous not only to the Christian notion of the Trinity, but to any belief in a divine presence that is both outside and inside the world. Such problems appear during this period not only in Gnostic speculations about a shadowy world produced by an inferior Demiurge, but also, if more elusively, in orthodox Christian circles, as in Origen's ambivalence toward an earthly order that has been spiritually superseded and in his subordination of the Son himself to the Father.[9] In a broad sense, though, the dilemma of 'depth' affects the entire development of Christian exegesis, which seeks to give the sheer facts of existence a redeeming density and 'meaning.'

This effort to deepen the literal sense of the text and the material level of the world raises a third issue for Christian exegesis, the relation between interpretive depth and the development of time. The Christian response to this question—to show depth of meaning unfolding through the sequence of events—develops only gradually from the conflicting philosophic tendencies of this early milieu. Central to the Jewish tradition, for example, is the notion of progressive revelation, both textually, in the movement from the Written to the Oral Law, and factually, in the historical process of redemption. Indeed, quite apart from Philo, Rabbinic exegesis treats many scriptural passages as predictive allegories, referring either to events which have already occurred (e.g., the four rivers of

---

[9] For these general tendencies, see A. H. Armstrong and R. A. Markus, *Christian Faith and Greek Philosophy* (London, 1960), pp. 1–58. For their relation to the Gnostics and Origen, see, for example, J. A. Lyons, *The Cosmic Christ in Origen and Teilhard de Chardin* (Oxford, 1982), pp. 89–104, 118–19; and my discussion, below.

Eden signifying the four kingdoms of Babylonia, Media, Greece, and Rome) or to events yet to take place (e.g., the 'beloved' of the Song of Songs signifying the Messiah).[10] But to the early Christians, the Jewish refusal to expand such predictive strategies to the entire text and to apply the predictions to Jesus gives Judaism too limited an approach to textual and historical development.

By contrast, central to the Platonic tradition is a concentration on eternal stasis that tends to dissipate both the sequence of a text and the substantiality of events. Thus, in Plotinus' allegory of Hesiod's triad, a generative movement through time turns into a simultaneous and eternal process, and long before Plotinus, Platonic interpreters of the *Timaeus* insist that Plato here refers not to a temporal 'creation' but to the eternal dependence of the realm of Becoming upon the realm of Being.[11] If in the Jewish tradition meaning does not sufficiently unfold over time for Christian belief, in the Platonic tradition meaning seems too independent of time for Christian engagement.

Between these two approaches, in effect, lies a host of Gnostic and Christian perspectives. In its diverse forms, Gnosticism qualifies the Jewish view of Scripture, on the one hand, by endorsing various sequels to the text, or 'new' testaments. It qualifies the Platonic view of eternity, on the other hand, by claiming active, even agitated movement within the otherworld. But the effect of this Gnostic juxtaposition is more to undermine than to redeem the letter of the biblical text, while reserving decisive spiritual advance to a realm beyond the material world. Thus, Marcion rejects the Old Testament as the law of a Creator-God who is inferior to the supreme God. Saturninus, allegorizing away the central doctrine of even the New Testament, treats the Christ as a figure who only seems to be a man; the saving spirit cannot truly be incarnated in evil matter. Valentinus and his followers develop an elaborate mythology of spiritual 'Aeons,' one of whom, Wisdom ('Sophia'), falls, thereby generating (through various intermediaries) the world, the men of which are redeemable only insofar as they belong to 'spirit,' not merely to soul or

---

[10] See Wolfson, *Fathers*, pp. 24–9.
[11] See Pépin, pp. 503–5.

body.[12] A sense of disjunction dominates these and other Gnostic strategies, which compromise the possibilities of textual sequence and historical advance by the tendencies of abrogation and escape.

The principal Christian response to such challenges is the celebrated strategy of typological interpretation.[13] In this approach, the Old Testament anticipates a New Testament that fulfills it; the material world progresses toward a spiritual realm that consummates it. The crucial means of transition in both cases is the element of time itself. Over time, one level of the text or of the world deepens into another. Even more importantly, such deeper levels gradually become as literally plain and substantially present as the original ones, so that even the most divergent transfers from literal to allegorical, from material to spiritual, participate in a single continuity. This approach offers a certain control over that diverging tendency which always besets allegorical interpretation; it sets even contraries—types and antitypes—in correspondence with each other. Already in the second century, the anti-Gnostic exegete Irenaeus is systematizing the Pauline strategy: just as one man (Adam) doomed mankind through his disobedience, so another man (Christ) saved it through his obedience. Just as one woman (Eve) brought death into the world by listening to the serpent, so another woman (Mary) brought life into the world by listening to the angel.[14] Exegesis of this kind does not simply shift from letter to spirit—*Hēra* 'really' meaning *aēr*; now it makes the letter itself spiritual—*Eva* developing into *Ave*. The world is transformed, in the New Testament phrase, in the 'fulness of the time.'

While typology makes important contributions to the exegetical tradition, it does not, as is often claimed, resolve the

[12] For overviews, see François-M.-M. Sagnard, *La Gnose valentinienne et le témoignage de saint Irénée* (Paris, 1947); Grant, pp. 62–75; and R. McL. Wilson, *The Gnostic Problem* (London, 1958), pp. 64–148.

[13] For some controversies about the relation between Christian typology and other exegetical traditions, see Auerbach, 'Figura,' pp. 11–60; Henri de Lubac, ' "Typologie" et "allégorisme," ' *Recherches de science religieuse*, 34 (1947), 180–226; Daniélou, pp. 11–29, 61–5, 86, 110–12, 121, 136–7, 156–7, 169–70, 216, 219, 225–6, 234–5, 287–8; Grant, pp. 39–41, 46–51, 54–6, 76, 84, 96, 101–4, 137–9; Hanson, *Allegory and Event*, pp. 27–36, 48–53, 72–96, 117–20, 125–9, 243, n. 2, 248–54, 321–9, 345–56; Charity, *Events and their Afterlife*, pp. 25, 58, 67–80, 89–91, 172–8, 199, 247, 251, 258–9; Wolfson, *Fathers*, pp. 24–72; and Pépin's 1976 supplement, pp. 487–516.

[14] See Daniélou, pp. 11–21, 30–47.

subversive tendency implicit in allegorical interpretation from the start. Once the process of relegating one Scripture to the 'shadows' begins, it is difficult to stop the shadows from spreading. An early Christian exegete like Tertullian can insist that while the Old Testament is typological, the Incarnation story takes place neither figuratively ('non figurate') nor obliquely ('non oblique'), but we have already seen the Gnostics arguing just that, and the Montanist sect that Tertullian himself eventually joins originates in the claims of Montanus that his New Prophecy fulfills the New—now, nearly, Old—Testament. Both of these problems recur in revised form in Origen, who, while not denying the historical fact of the Incarnation, tends to diffuse it into a timeless figure for human 'gnosis,' and who, while not imagining a written sequel to the New Testament, allegorizes the Gospel itself as the prefiguration of that 'eternal gospel' (Apocalypse 14: 6) which will reenact the story on a celestial plane.[15] The persistence and elusiveness of the problem in Christian history is dramatized allegorically by Jean de Meun, who criticizes the latest (now millenarian) proclamation of an *Evangelium Aeternum*, while making False Seeming the spokesman for the critique. The central dilemma, indeed, is inherent in the very dynamics of Christian typology. It originates with the fact that the 'fulness of the time' did not, after all, constitute the end of time. Typology does not resolve the allegorical problem of constant displacement; it gives it a temporal dimension.

ORIGEN'S DESCENT; ANTONY'S ASCENT

Whatever the dilemmas posed by these three changes in exegetical strategy, they give a new richness to the interpretive tradition by the third century AD. With the coalescence of Jewish, Platonic, and Gnostic elements in early Christian exegesis, the different senses of a divine text come to imply different orders of the cosmos, which in turn imply different

[15] For various claims about these controversial tendencies in Origen, see Jerome, *Ep. ad Avitum* 12, quoted in G. W. Butterworth's tr. of Origen's *On First Principles* (1936; repr. New York, 1966), pp. 309–10, n. 7; Jean Daniélou, *Origen*, tr. Walter Mitchell (New York, 1955), pp. 120–7, 170–1, 262–5; Henri de Lubac, *Histoire et esprit* (Paris, 1950), pp. 195–232, 291–4; and Hanson, *Allegory and Event*, pp. 272–88.

stages in time, as an individual or a civilization converts from flesh to spirit. This is a more intricate, expansive design even than that of Virgil, with his simultaneous transitions between disorder and order on the divine, physical, and human planes. It is a more radical, mysterious vision than that of Homer, with his direct interplay between the impassioned man, Achilles, and the reasonable goddess, Athena. To suggest something of the change in perspective between that primal, Homeric event and early Christian allegory, we might consider for a moment the descent of a rational principle to earth as seen from the quite different viewpoint of Origen himself.

It is revealing that for Origen this kind of descent has a double valence. On the one hand, it is infinitely more reassuring than the descent of Athena to Achilles; it is the very pattern of the redemption by which the Logos condescends to man. Thus, in his vast critique of the Fourth Gospel, the first systematic Christian interpretation of a New Testament book, when Origen reads that Jesus and his retinue 'descended' to Capernaum and remained there 'not many days' (John 2: 12), he gives this brief episode a momentous meaning. The Logos, including those 'powers' (*dynameōn*) which accompany him, descends upon the 'field of consolation' (Greek Kapharnaoum; cf. Hebrew *Kfar Nachum*, combining *kfar*, 'village,' with *nachum*, related to *nachem*, 'console'), but this inferior region cannot receive much light, and accordingly the Savior does not stay long.[16] In this Christian allegorization, it is still possible to recognize the Jewish, Platonic, and Gnostic legacies. A word from the divine text ('descended') develops universal implications. A descent within this world becomes a descent between two worlds. Mysterious 'powers' accompany the Savior, whose limited time in the region, 'etymologically' defined, suggests the spiritual limits of its inhabitants. This is drama on a scale far beyond the descent of Athena, even in the ancient allegorical version of Homer, and it concerns only a single scriptural verse.

[16] See *Comm. in S. Joann.* X, viii, 37-X, xi, 60, in *Origenes Werke*, Vol. IV, ed. Erwin Preuschen (Leipzig, 1903). The *Commentary* is translated by Eugenio Corsini, *Commento al Vangelo di Giovanni* (Turin, 1968). For the etymological treatment of Capernaum, which appears also in Jerome, see Franz Wutz, *Onomastica sacra* (Leipzig, 1914), pp. 40, 643. On the meaning of Hebrew *kfar* and *Kfar Nachum*, see Samuel Krauss, *Kadmoniyyot ha-Talmud*, I, i (Berlin and Vienna, [1923?]), 22–37, esp. 32, to which Professor David Halivni has referred me.

By the same token, though, the expansion increases the allegorical dilemmas. The text itself, however divine, seems to recede with each daring insight. The distance between the two worlds exposes the uncertain status of this one. An historical interaction between Jesus and a particular people is diffused into the infinite recesses of time—a tendency confirmed in Origen's next remarks, which distinguish 'not many days' from 'all days' (Matt. 28: 20), meaning, Origen speculates, the 'aeon' itself. It is revealing that Marcion, followed by Heracleon (who produces the first sustained Gnostic interpretation of the Gospel), allegorizes the 'descent' of Jesus in dangerously similar terms. Origen criticizes Heracleon in this very passage for ignoring Christ's redemptive activity in Capernaum itself, but his own treatment here nearly leaves the text, the world, and time in limbo.[17]

In fact, that is just where Origen ends in his other, darker version of a rational principle descending to earth. If such a descent is the pattern of redemption, it is also the paradigm of deterioration. Thus, near the end of *On First Principles*, the first genuine attempt at a Christian *summa*, Origen concentrates on Ezekiel's prophecies about the rise and fall of Israel and neighboring peoples (Ezek. 19 f.). There is much in these prophecies, he insists, that should not be interpreted literally. Rather, just as there is a heavenly Judea, as well as an earthly one, so there may well be heavenly regions called Egypt, Babylonia, and the like, with their respective heavenly inhabitants. But no sooner does Origen thus transpose these prophecies to a higher key than the whole story tragically modulates downward:

From among these souls, according to the manner of life that they lead there, a certain captivity would seem to have taken place, by which they are said to have descended from Judea, from better and higher places, into Babylonia or into Egypt, or to have been dispersed among other nations.

And perhaps, Origen continues, just as people on earth who die are distributed, if judged worthy of Hades, according to the proportion of their sins,

[17] Here and below I am indebted to the seminal work of Daniélou, *Origen*, pp. 191–6; contrast de Lubac, *Histoire et esprit*, pp. 278–94. On Marcion, see Grant, p. 64. On Heracleon and Origen, see G. Quispel, 'Origen and the Valentinian Gnosis,' *Vigiliae Christianae*, 28 (1974), 29–42, and Lyons, *Cosmic Christ*, pp. 97–104.

so the souls there, if I may so speak, descend when they die into this Hades, and are judged worthy of different habitations, better or worse, in the whole region of earth.[18]

Here the three tendencies we have seen before acquire more radical form. So revealing is the Jewish text that its very geography is a map of heaven. The world is divided not merely Platonically into two, but Middle and Neoplatonically into degrees—as souls slip from one level of heaven to another (heavenly 'Babylonia'), from the heavenly realm as a whole to earth ('this Hades'), from the earthly realm to 'Hades' itself. (We shall see the Neoplatonist Macrobius exploiting a similar principle.) Finally, a prophecy of times to come becomes a Gnostic (and Platonic) vision of recurrent slippage from spirit into matter, a notion further radicalized a few lines later, when Origen strikingly adds that the process is reversible, and an 'Egyptian' sometimes slips back into 'Judea.' This is oscillation far more urgent than the eternal return of the Stoics: now human souls pass out of and into the divine drama, and they make their fates by choice.

The problems posed for orthodoxy by this kind of exegesis, of course, are notorious: the preexistence of souls, the evils of matter, the salvation of demons. Our central concern is their exegetical effect. As in the earlier passage about Capernaum, here the unique elements of text, being, and time are diffused into the most rarefied regions. Perhaps this is Ezekiel, but to paraphrase Numenius, it is Ezekiel speaking in Greek. While it is quite possible to find more conventional interpretations throughout Origen's work, perhaps these passages particularly display the sense in which he himself is a soul in transition. For him, wisdom's descent is from one perspective an Incarnation, but from another a Fall. As if to enact that problem, Origen himself sometimes seems divided about whether to bring his philosophy down to earth.

A complementary problem distinguishes the compositional tradition of this early Christian period: how to bring the soul up to heaven. The strategy of elevating the personality, of

[18] See *De Principiis* IV, iii, 9–10 in *Origenes Werke*, Vol. V, ed. Paul Koetschau (Leipzig, 1913). My translation is based on that of G. W. Butterworth, cited in n. 15. Because the extant Greek original is fragmentary, for part of this passage we must use Rufinus' Latin version.

course, is implicit even in the earliest Greek tendencies toward allegorization, as in Plato's analysis of the elements of the soul. But in the first centuries AD, the effort to distinguish a higher dimension within the human personality acquires a more explicit, systematic design. A correlation increasingly develops between the elements of the soul and the 'powers' of the spiritual world as a whole. From this perspective, the aspiration of the soul is by definition a cosmic process. Such an approach suggests possibilities of allegory greater than the apotheosis of the abstractions observed up to now. It places the drama of the soul simultaneously on two planes. It is often remarked that a 'turn inward' dominates the early centuries AD, and we have noticed this reorientation in the philosophic and interpretive tradition. But it should also be observed that this turn inward has its inverse compositional counterpart, as the articulation of the soul expands outward into the world at large. By the time of the *Cosmographia*, this process will become panoramic in scope.

The complex, late antique movement linking psychic causes with cosmic forces is still not fully understood; here we can only touch on a few of its facets. Already in Plato and Xenocrates, there are intriguing associations between the opposing forces of the soul and the various *daemones* of the world, who mediate between the realms of spirit and matter. By the Middle Platonic period, though, such associations become schematic. In the first century BC, Posidonius argues that every soul has two daemonic powers, one good and one evil. A century later, Philo, adapting the Platonic tradition to Jewish contexts, claims that daemons are the angels of God, who inhabit the intermediate realm of air and aid or punish man. The dualistic tendencies of such discussions intensify in Plutarch, who at times speaks both of two guardian daemons for the soul and of two governing powers (*dynameis*) in the world. With Apuleius in the second century, the 'guardian daemon' acquires a central, intimate role in the conduct of human life, a role also developed by late Stoic writers of the period. Meanwhile, the Gnostics and early Christians elaborate the cosmic side of these influences upon man, by identifying the good daemons with God's ministering angels, the evil daemons with a host of related villains: the fallen angels, the pagan gods, or the planetary powers. These diverse traditions converge in Origen, who divides both the soul and the world (and individual nations) between good and evil daemons—mediating powers (the evil ones associated with particular beasts and vices) who inhabit the air and help or hinder the soul's ascent to heaven.[19] Perhaps the most telling development of this period is the tendency among writers from various traditions—Jewish, Hermetic, and Christian—to conflate different senses of the term 'powers' itself (*dynameis*): psychic forces, angelic influences, and divine attributes. Such conflations tend to incorporate the middle realm of the *daemones* within the framework of man or God. The 'powers' are in a sense elements of each, but at some remove from both.[20]

To see the allegorical potential of this process, we can turn to the inner/outer struggle of an Egyptian Christian whose life spans the time from Origen's last years to the middle of the fourth century. The *Life of St. Antony*—the first genuine saint's life, composed by Athanasius shortly after Antony's death—explores a Christian's deepening withdrawal into the interior world, a movement enacted externally by Antony's relentless advance toward the 'Inner Mountain' of the Egyptian desert. This paradigmatic movement on the internal and external planes has its dynamic expression in a series of conflicts for Antony's soul, conflicts taking place, as it were, not only from the inside, but from the outside, as daemonic forces impinge upon the saint.

One day, for example, when Antony was about to pray,

he felt himself carried off in spirit, and—strange to say—as he stood he saw himself, as it were, outside himself and as though guided aloft by certain beings. Then he also saw loathsome and terrible beings standing in the air and bent on preventing him from passing through.

A dispute ensues between the two kinds of beings, and when the evil ones cannot give good reason to stop Antony's ascent,

---

[19] For these developments in their diverse contexts, see John Dillon, *The Middle Platonists* (Ithaca, N.Y., 1977), pp. 31–2, 46–7, 169–74, 202–4, 216–24, 317–20; Rist, *Stoic Philosophy*, pp. 212–17, 265–72; Claudio Moreschini, *Apuleio e il platonismo* (Florence, 1978), pp. 19–27, 90–2; and Daniélou, *Gospel*, pp. 427–41.

[20] See R. P. Festugière, *Les Doctrines de l'âme*, Vol. III of *La Révélation d'Hermès Trismégiste* (Paris, 1953), pp. 153–74, and Jean Pépin, *Théologie cosmique et théologie chrétienne* (Paris, 1964), pp. 374–89.

the way opened up to him free and unhindered; and presently he saw himself as it were coming to and halting with himself (*pros heauton estōta*); and so he was wholly (*holōs*) Antony again.

The vision past, Antony recalls Paul's admonitions about the 'prince of the power of the air' and the need to put on the 'armor of God.'[21]

If we compare this passage with earlier treatments of the divided soul, we can appreciate its extraordinary advances for our subject. First, even more than Homer's world, this is a world pervaded by daemonic agents. Such agents do not just intrude suddenly upon the soul; they are part of the very structure of the cosmos—'in the air,' as it were. Something of their pervasiveness can be seen in the account of a later Egyptian ascetic, Isidore, who recalls going to the marketplace to sell some goods, but 'when I saw anger approaching me, I left the things and fled.'[22] By the same token, the daemonic powers of this period are more graphic in form and more flexible in function than Homer's 'anger.' The devils in Antony's story not only intercept his ascent; they vividly assume the shapes of beasts, vermin, and even other people, in order to terrorize and tempt him with the most outlandish plots.

At the same time, this daemonic world has its psychic counterpart, as striking as any interior drama in Plato. In fact, the personal and cosmic levels of the soul's encounter are here coordinated more clearly than in Plato's work, which tends to oscillate between a psychological model in which reason is one part of a tripartite soul, and a metaphysical model in which reason is a *daemon* in its own right.[23] By contrast, the *Life of St. Antony* elaborately plays out the conflict between good and evil elements inside the soul by the conflict between good and evil daemons outside it. This is not to say that the psychology of this passage is more convincing than Plato's, but that it differs in purpose and design. Something of its ambitions can be seen in Antony's claim that the state of the individual determines the status of the daemons: 'in whatever state of mind they [the

[21] See ch. 65 of *Vita S. Antonii, PG* 26, 835–976, cited by chapter. My translations are based on that of Robert T. Meyer (Westminster, Md., 1950).

[22] The passage is quoted by Peter Brown, *The Making of Late Antiquity* (Cambridge, Mass., 1978), p. 88.

[23] See Guthrie, cited above in Ch. II, n. 22.

daemons] find us, so likewise do they represent their phantoms' (ch. 42). Such a perspective aggrandizes the soul while it personalizes the cosmos.

It also transforms certain problems raised by the Stoic treatment of the soul. Chrysippus had sought to make the passions not causes in their own right, but oblique conditions, defects in the power of reason, while Posidonius countered that such a defection itself requires an actual cause. In a sense the *Life of St. Antony* makes the passions both oblique and actual at once. During his ascent Antony encounters his daemonic adversaries in another dimension, posed, as it were, at an oblique angle to his own position, so that it is only after his vision that he again becomes 'wholly' himself. Yet these 'loathsome beings' are no less palpable or menacing on that account. Antony seeks to explain their ambiguous status by distinguishing between different kinds of power. While the daemons may affect power by their hideous transformations (ch. 23), their very threats, he insists, betray their actual powerlessness (ch. 28); all their stage effects are but the phantasmagoria of weaklings (ch. 29). This is more than Senecan contempt for blustery, windy passion, 'ventosa et inanis.' It is Christian disdain for the diabolical powers of air, vanquished by Christ's elevation on the Cross.[24] Because of that ascent, even overbearing forces seemingly above a man are actually subject to divine forces instilled within him. Here the conception of the suffering hero, the figure of Virgilian *pathos* who lives on the 'other side' of action, is not only transfigured by the majestic model of the divine Passion, but counterpointed by a Christian *apatheia* of active love. The daemons' flamboyant activities in air only dramatize the true power of the spirit on earth.

This sense of dramatic suspension, finally, is expressed formally by the portrayal of Antony's ascent as a vision. The telling shift in the register of the story here (and in similar daemonic scenes) is more than a stylistic or conceptual maneuver, as in Virgil's amplification of the figure of 'Fama.' It is a statement about the need to transpose not only a text, but a life, from one level to a higher one. Antony's spiritual *exstasis*,

---

[24] See Jean Daniélou, 'Les démons de l'air dans la "Vie d'Antoine,"' in *Studia Anselmiana*, 38, *Antonius Magnus Eremita, 356–1956*, ed. B. Steidle (Rome, 1956), pp. 136–47.

that is, his standing outside the self, has its literary counterpart in the text's transition toward a visionary mode—a mode that revealingly dominates much of his story as a whole. Whether or not we now treat Antony's encounters with beings of another order as hallucinations or insights, this basic rationale for vision literature is central to the development of allegory.

In the *Life of St. Antony*, then, a personal drama is daemonic in action yet psychic in orientation, resolved according to distinctions of causal power, and presented in visionary terms. Yet for all these developments, Antony's *psychomachia* does not quite display the allegorical form it will acquire nearly half a century later with Prudentius. In a sense, its limitations for compositional allegory are counterparts to the problems of interpretive allegory seen in Origen.

Thus, whereas Origen's divine text seemed to authorize the most sweeping speculations, here, conversely, in the compositional tradition, the concepts are still too limited to fashion a sustained text. The agents of Antony's story, darting in and out of the action, are genuinely daemonic powers, not allegorical agents. It is true that they impersonate various figures, but their masks are quickly stripped away, and they are exposed *in propria persona*. 'They do appear,' Antony assures his brethren, 'but disappear again the same moment, without harming any of the faithful' (ch. 24). Sustained compositional allegory requires a more expansive, more imaginative, design.

Again, as in Origen's exegesis the distinction between levels of being called into question the value of this world, so in Antony's story the distinction between spirit and flesh leaves human life in a kind of limbo. The uncertainty is perhaps most poignantly—or amusingly—displayed in the tendency of the *Life* to treat the people who keep knocking at Antony's door almost as daemons themselves, diverting the saint from his devotions (chs. 36, 48, 84). In terms of allegorical form, this is a problem of differentiating the level of real people from the level of daemonic figures, but it also has broader implications, in the conflicting attitudes of early monasticism toward human society and earthly life as a whole.

Finally, as Origen's interpretation tended to diffuse the redemptive movement of time into an eternal process, so the

Life of St. Antony tends to treat the distinctive history of an individual as a timeless paradigm. It is not only that each daemonic temptation is basically a replay of a single recurrent scheme, but that Antony himself scarcely undergoes a 'progress' at all. Though subject to temptation, his saint-like resolve prevails from the start; after nearly twenty years of ascetic rigor, even his body looks the same (ch. 14). While such a conception of the exemplary Christian life may have its own valid appeal, it is not conducive to sophisticated allegorical narrative, which requires the gradual emergence of conceptual issues and their organization into a developing plot. Nor does such a progress necessarily involve modern 'character development.' Augustine, born while Antony is still alive, undergoes a gradual progress from one state to another, and revealingly, his conversion scene gives new life to the allegory of temptation vs. sainthood, as obsessive attachments pluck at his garment of flesh, while serene Continence beckons him to cross the barrier (*Confessions* VIII). But by that time, the life of Antony has already passed into literary form, almost as if to present Augustine, who keeps recalling the story, with the dilemma that inspires his conversion—the problem of translating a mere paradigm into actual behavior, and thereby making the divine Book to which he finally turns a living document. This development, though, returns us to the interpretive tradition to which Augustine himself makes important contributions.

AUGUSTINE AND PRUDENTIUS: DIGRESSIONS AND PROGRESSIONS

The spiritual transition made by the Augustine of the *Confessions* as he opens his Bible to a Pauline exhortation on change exposes not only the centrality of conversion to the aims of Scripture. As early Christian exegesis suggests, conversion belongs in a sense to the very operation of Scripture, with its inspirational priority over other texts, its density of interpretive levels, and its interior progression from figure to fulfillment. Each of these approaches to the design of a text, expressing different tendencies of the age, develops its own complications in the late antique and early medieval period. In considering the first great handbook on Christian exegesis, Augustine's *On Christian*

Doctrine, written at the turn of the fourth and fifth centuries, we might concentrate on some of the complications involved in the last strategy, the argument that one part of the divine text fulfills another.

While this exegetical approach included the typological interpretation of Old and New Testament events, it also incorporated broader procedures from the start. The aim of developing correspondences between one part of Scripture and another, after all, was not only to elucidate the movement of history. It was also to insure the coherence and integrity of Christian doctrine. If God's scriptural work was a perfect whole, a doctrine worthy of that work had to consider how each divine detail fit into the Book at large. This was a formidable task, not only because Scripture included many apparently anomalous or obscure passages, but because the very efficacy of God's Word assured each passage of an explosive multiplicity of meanings, diverging in all directions from each other. In order to harness such divergences into correspondence with each other, an exegete needed more than the strategy of typological transfer. He had to draw upon every interpretive option available, whether or not it had a clear temporal dimension, allegorizing a phrase or even a word differently as the occasion demanded. In the end, this radical process promoted the kind of self-undermining effect that was working throughout the early allegorical tradition. The very effort to assure the full continuity of the sacred script tended to split Scripture into piecemeal interpretations, loosely arranged according to the most diffusive principles.

The difficulty of producing a convincing and consistent rationale for allegorical interpretation, of course, was not a distinctively Christian problem. Throughout the Greek tradition, exegetes relied upon rather general and arbitrary criteria for allegorization. Some claimed that if the literal meaning of a given passage was contrary to moral standards, it required interpretation; Heraclitus opened his treatise with this ancient defense. Others argued for allegory if the literal meaning was contrary to reason, another ancient position explicitly articulated by the first centuries AD.[25] When the allegorical

---

[25] See Jean Pépin, 'A propos de l'histoire de l'exégèse allégorique: l'absurdité, signe de l'allégorie,' in *Studia patristica*, Vol. I, ed. Kurt Aland and F. L. Cross (Berlin, 1957), pp. 395–413.

technique was applied to Scripture, however, such criteria in themselves seemed increasingly insufficient. Reason alone, for example, could hardly set itself up as arbiter of the true meaning of divinely revealed wisdom. The final criterion for determining the literal or figurative meaning of a passage was rather a broad rule of faith in basic religious truths. Any passage in Scripture that seemed to conflict with these truths was to be allegorized. As Augustine puts it in *On Christian Doctrine*:

Whatever appears in the divine Word that does not literally pertain to virtuous behavior or to the truth of faith you must take to be figurative. . . . But Scripture teaches nothing but charity, nor condemns anything except cupidity . . . [26]

Augustine realizes the consequences of this rule, and explains them openly in his treatise. We must not think that what a word signifies in one place it necessarily signifies somewhere else, he warns. In one passage (John 6: 51) the word 'bread' signifies the 'living bread' of God, but in another passage (Prov. 9: 17) it signifies the allurements of a foolish woman. The 'serpent' who seduced Eve cannot be the same serpent Christ had in mind when he urged his Apostles to be 'wise as serpents' (Matt. 10: 16; *DDC* III, 25). The rule of faith tells us otherwise. In order to apply this rule, it is clear that the actual reference of a text must keep slipping away from the apparent one, until the words of the text retain scarcely any consistency of their own.

Indeed, it is not only the apparent meaning that keeps receding into the distance, but the actual one, as well. The very basis for the figurative language of Scripture, Augustine emphasizes, is that the thing a text signifies should in turn signify another thing, until all signs eventually disappear in God. In this process of perpetual conversion, *res* themselves thus become *signa*, transitory vehicles moving toward a divine destination (*DDC* I, 4; I, 35; II, 10). As a result, the knowledge of things, as well as language, is essential to proper

---

[26] On the 'rules of faith' in Philo, Irenaeus, Tertullian, and Origen, see Wolfson, *Philo*, Vol. I, pp. 164–99, and *Fathers*, pp. 77–96; cf. Grant, pp. 35, 39, 51, 77, 92–3. For Augustine's formulation here, see *De doctrina christiana*, hereafter *DDC*, ed. William M. Green, *CSEL* 80 (1963), III, 10. Translations from the *De doctrina* are by D. W. Robertson, Jr., *On Christian Doctrine* (New York, 1958). Cf. *DDC* III, 15, and III, 28.

interpretation. We can understand Christ's injunction to be 'wise as serpents' only by knowing

> the well-known fact that a serpent exposes its whole body in order to protect its head from those attacking . . . That is, for the sake of our head, which is Christ, we should offer our bodies to persecutors lest the Christian faith be in a manner killed in us, and in an effort to save our bodies we deny God. (*DDC* II, 16)

In such exegesis, no sooner have we specified the parallel between the serpents and us than we recede yet further from both, by recognizing that our head—an item never mentioned in the scriptural text—is God himself. Like some serpent shedding its skin, we should shed our bodies in this life, and shed the body of the text in our interpretation, all for the sake of the spirit. Lest we fear that our similitude may stray even further from the text than does Augustine, the exegete reassures us in his next sentence, by making the comparison himself:

> It is also said that the serpent, having forced its way through narrow openings, sheds its skin and renews its vigor. How well this conforms to our imitation of the wisdom of the serpent when we shed the 'old man,' as the Apostle says, and put on the 'new'; and we shed it in narrow places, for the Lord directs us, 'Enter ye in at the narrow gate.' (*DDC* II, 16)

At this point, it is difficult to know any longer whether the original text, 'Be . . . wise as serpents,' corresponds to anything definite at all: the serpent's behavior, its head, our head, Christ, the serpent's skin, narrow openings, or the new texts, suddenly arising out of our previous interpretation. Augustine's whole point, of course, is that things should keep slithering away from the text, only to produce offspring which in turn slither away from them. In the process, the allegorical interpretation of Scripture expands beyond the text into the world at large, diverging radically from the initial correspondence between text and meaning. Such exegesis tends to replace the old encyclopedism of Homeric interpretation with an encyclopedism of its own. Scripture begins to turn into a series of splendidly written articles on the world, a book of God about that other book of God. In this respect, it is revealing that Augustine elsewhere applies the tripartite division of philosophy—once appropriated as a model for the threefold system of exegesis—to the working of the Trinity in nature itself.[27]

In a sense, Augustine's constant passage from words toward things toward a realm beyond both of them is the logical conclusion of an exegesis that links the progress of a text with the movement of the world at large. In the celebrated formula Augustine articulates in *On the Trinity* (XV, ix, 15), God writes allegory not only 'in uerbis,' but 'in facto'; he composes meaning not only by words, but by events. Such an approach encourages a rhetorical treatment of philosophic causes, a broad tendency of the age preeminently exemplified by Augustine himself, the rhetorician turned Christian philosopher.[28] Yet this interaction between the compositional and interpretive traditions has its problems. As even our brief look at Augustine's 'serpents' suggests, the intensive effort to shift between words and things, to turn each verbal item into a moral fact, requires the kind of *in bono/in malo* exegesis that weakens the consistency of the words and undermines the integrity of the things. From an allegorical perspective, such problems suggest the difficulty of clarifying just how and when a scriptural term passes from a literal status to a figurative one. This uncertainty about the text in turn reflects a deep sense of contingency about the status of the world. In any event, while early Christian exegetes might proclaim the value of the *historia*, the continuous texture of the letter that reveals the orderly dispensation of

[27] As Allen argues in *Ethical Poetic*, cited above in Ch. I, n. 1, p. 212, the exegesis of Augustine aims less to establish a 'fit' between text and interpretation than to develop an interpretation that makes 'true statements.' While this strategy has its potential, it produces deep tensions in the effort to implicate one frame of reference in the other; see my discussion and notes below in this section and in Chs. IV and VI. The textual questions raised by Augustine's exegesis might be relatively limited if the sole issue in scriptural interpretation were the inspired orientation of the mind. As important as such an orientation is to Augustine's program, it is inseparable for him in the end from the operation and design of the sacred text itself. The special status of that text, authored by God and played out in history, tends to pose the problems of correspondence and meaning discussed here and below. On the complications for Augustine of construing 'appropriate' scriptural meanings, see Rollinson, *Classical Theories of Allegory*, cited above in Ch. I, n. 1, pp. 42-64. On the two 'books' of God—Scripture and nature—see de Lubac, I, i. 119-28; Curtius, *European Literature*, pp. 319-26; and my discussion in Ch. IV, below. On tripartite philosophy and the Trinity in nature, see *De Civitate Dei* XI, 24-5; cf. *De Vera Religione* XVII, 32-3.

[28] See esp. H.-I. Marrou, *Saint Augustin et la fin de la culture antique*, 2nd edn. (Paris, 1949).

events, their actual exercises tended to produce piecemeal, if ingenious, allegorizations of isolated passages.[29]

It will be valuable to examine this tendency more closely in the Carolingian period, when it acquires a kind of cosmic scope. Already in Augustine's age, though, it is complicating the continuities of the divine text. Thus, Eucherius, in his fifth-century treatise on allegorical interpretation, *Formulas of Spiritual Understanding*, speaks in one breath of 'allegoria' as the historical prefiguration of events ('gestorum narratione futurorum umbram praetulisse'), as if to assure textual and temporal continuity—and in the next breath, speaks in piecemeal fashion of water, for example, as 'baptism, according to allegory; the angels, according to anagogy' ('aquae secundum allegoriam baptismus, secundum anagogen angeli'). The rest of his treatise, in fact, is a list of scriptural words taken in isolation from each other, each with the most divergent allegorical meanings.[30] By the sixth century and Gregory's *Moralia in Iob*, a model for allegorical interpretation in the early Middle Ages, the digressive, meandering approach to allegory is the ideal:

He that treats of sacred writ should follow the way of a river, for if a river, as it flows along its channel, meets with open valleys on its side, into these it immediately turns the course of its current, and when they are copiously supplied, presently it pours itself back into its bed. . . . Everyone that treats of the Divine Word . . . should, as it were, force the streams of discourse toward the adjacent valley, and when he has poured forth enough upon its level of instruction, fall back into the channel of discourse which he had prepared for himself.[31]

[29] On the *historia* and the problem of defining the literal sense, see A. Nemetz, 'Literalness and the *Sensus Litteralis*,' *Speculum*, 34 (1959), 76–89, qualified by de Lubac, I, ii, 425–87; on developments in the Carolingian and later medieval periods, see Spicq, pp. 20–1, 97–8, 267–88, and my discussion in Chs. IV and V.

[30] See the edition of Carolus Wotke, *Sancti Evcherii Lvgdvnensis*, CSEL 31 (1895), pp. 5, 7–62. On the volatile interpretation of selected passages about 'water' in earlier exegesis, see Daniélou, pp. 83, 88, 92–6, 171, 262, 270, with his comment on p. 93: 'it is the fault of certain exegetes to find Baptism whenever water is mentioned in the Old Testament.'

[31] See *Praef. in Iob* I, 6–7, quoted by Smalley, p. 33. On the ideal of meandering, cf. *DDC* III, 27–8, and de Lubac, I, i, 119–38; for some of its hazards, see Charity, *Events and their Afterlife*, p. 109, n. 1, on radical oscillation in Gregory, and M.-D. Chenu, 'Les deux âges de l'allégorisme scripturaire au moyen âge,' *Recherches de théologie ancienne et médiévale*, 18 (1951), 26, on the 'pulverization of the text' in later exegesis unrestrained by context.

The progression from one part of the text to another here demands the most diffusive movements in every direction. Allegorical interpretation depends from the start upon simultaneous tendencies of correspondence and divergence. In exegesis of this kind, the correspondence is strained to the limit.

Augustine began his treatise on scriptural exegesis in 396 AD, and after putting it aside, completed it some thirty years later. In the same period, the literary technique of personification finally emerged into full-scale form. The decisive event in this movement was Prudentius' *Psychomachia*, composed about the year 405 AD. Here the compositional tradition produced not only a complete allegorical story, but a kind of conceptual sequel to that philosophic poetry which we have seen developing from Homer to Virgil and his successors. At the same time, it fulfilled at last the compositional tendency to articulate a personal progress in cosmic terms.[32]

If we seek the direct origins of Prudentius' work, we can identify specific sources for his plot and particular antecedents for his personifications.[33] But in a deeper sense, all the compositional strategies examined up to now, however remote their original provenance, contribute to the *Psychomachia*, which in turn transforms them according to its own allegorical design. Thus, the dilemma of personal choice in Greek epic, which we examined in Homer, here acquires a fully schematic form, in which the forces of decision are inseparable from the instruments of human destiny. The rivalry of opposing principles in the moral fable, broadly sketched in Prodicus, takes on a new intensity, marked by a series of encounters between agents of virtue and vice. The interior analysis of the philosophic treatise, which we explored in Plato, not only develops a structure virtually independent of the individual 'man,' but also expands to incorporate the life of the Church as a whole. The

---

[32] For the text, see the edition by M. Lavarenne in *Prudence*, III (1948; 2nd printing, rev. and cor., Paris, 1963); on the poem's date, see p. 9. My translations are based in part on that of H. J. Thomson in *Prudentius*, I (Cambridge, Mass., 1949).

[33] See M. W. Bloomfield, 'A Source of Prudentius' *Psychomachia*,' *Speculum*, 28 (1943), 87–90; Macklin Smith, *Prudentius'* Psychomachia: *A Reexamination* (Princeton, 1976), hereafter Smith, pp. 22, n. 27, 126–41, 216–33; and Lavarenne, *Prudence*, pp. 13–24.

rhetorical figures of the psychological or moral essay, given early expression in Chrysippus and Seneca, turn into flamboyantly dramatic characters, theatrical in speech as well as action. The tempestuous and martial atmosphere of the Roman epic, elaborated in Virgil and Statius, provides the dynamics of an heroic plot, counterpointed by the humbler claims of the Christian spirit. The daemonic powers of the saint's life, which we considered in the life of Antony, finally take control of the narrative foreground, turning intermittent visions into an imaginative story. It is the convergence of such diverse compositional tendencies that consolidates the allegorical poem.

At the same time, compositional developments are inseparable from interpretive ones, and Prudentius' work reflects many of the strengths and weaknesses of Christian exegesis during this period. From one perspective, the allegorical interpretation of the Bible brought new depths into the literal level of the text. The spiritual events of the New Testament, which fulfilled the literal prefigurations of the Old, were part of a single, resonant, historical continuity. Nevertheless, the very efficacy of the text tended to break up historical continuity into isolated allegories, in which single words and phrases had a multitude of divergent meanings. The meanings signified by a text kept tumbling over themselves, as it were, in a breathless effort to disclose the depths of God's word. In the process, allegorical interpretation constantly suspended the movement of history into intervals of episodic exegesis.

In a similar way, Prudentius' compositional allegory is often at cross-purposes with itself. We may consider it first in its continuities, for though these are not its strongest points, the fact that the poem has them at all is in some ways its most remarkable feature, and one often strangely slighted. In both its general structure and its individual episodes, Prudentius broadly organizes his poem by the figural method of scriptural exegesis. In structure, he divides the poem into two parts. The first concentrates on historical events under the Old Dispensation: Abraham's victory over the evil kings, his nourishment by Melchisedech, the visit of three angels to his home, and the birth of Isaac (Genesis 14, 18, and 21). The second part, the core of the poem, treats these events as a 'figura' (*Praefatio*, l.

50) for spiritual life under the New Dispensation: the victory of the virtues over the vices, the arrival of the Lord in a newly-constructed temple, and the fruits of the Spirit. It is this second part, of course, that includes the famous battle among personified abstractions like 'Patience,' 'Anger,' 'Humility,' and 'Pride,' which was so influential in the Middle Ages. As we have indicated, Prudentius himself originates neither the personifications nor the figural interpretation of Abraham's victory. Nevertheless, he is the first to expand these personifications into a continuous narrative, just as he is the first to compose a sustained allegory reflecting the figural interpretation of the Bible. Elaborating his personified characters on a plane separate from their historical counterparts, he passes from one level to another without displacing either of them. Prudentius' strategy by no means completely reconciled the two allegorical traditions, as we shall see, but even in its limited way, it signalled the great changes which scriptural exegesis was working in literary allegory.

It is not only in its general structure, however, that the poem reflects the figural method. In individual episodes, Prudentius makes a clear distinction between the activity of historical figures under the Old Dispensation, and the activity of spiritual agents under the New Dispensation. Personification, as we have seen, emerges from the attempt to specify the causes of things. Whenever Prudentius describes an historical event before the New Dispensation, he attributes causal power to a human agent. This kind of recourse to the literal person had always limited antique personification in the end. Since the Incarnation, however, the flesh has been infused with spiritual power, and accordingly Prudentius attributes the main activity of the poem to the agents of the spirit—the *invisibilia* which make up the full-scale allegory.

Prudentius is careful to make this distinction even when the personified battle is at full pitch. Thus, Chastity ('Pudicitia') has just thrust her sword-point into the throat of the harlot, Lust ('Libido')—a rather lusty thing for modest Chastity to do—when, in the middle of her battle vaunt, she pauses to remember that early victory for chastity under the Old Dispensation. Judith, she recalls, 'checked the unclean passions' of

Holofernes by cutting off his head 'with no trembling hand.'
And yet,

> perhaps a woman still fighting under the shadow of the law had insuf-
> ficient force, though she prefigured ('figurat') our times, in which
> the real power ('Vera . . . uirtus') has flowed into earthly bodies to
> sever the great head by the hands of feeble agents. Well, since an im-
> maculate virgin has borne a child . . . all flesh is divine . . . That
> which we were, we are no longer, now that we are raised into a better
> condition.

> At fortasse parum fortis matrona sub umbra
> Legis adhuc pugnans, dum tempora nostra figurat,
> Vera quibus uirtus terrena in corpora fluxit,
> Grande per infirmos caput excisura ministros.
> Numquid et intactae post partum uirginis ullum
> ∙∙∙
> Inde omnis iam diua caro est
> ∙∙∙
> . . . nos quod fuimus, iam non sumus, aucti
> Nascendo in melius . . .　　　　　　　　　　　(ll. 66–84)

In the shift from the Old Dispensation to the New, the causal
agent changes from Judith to the 'vera virtus,' the real power.
The spiritual fulfillment of the New Dispensation allows the
personification to emerge from the literal person, and take over
the narrative foreground. Prudentius reinforces the distinction
with the play on the word *virtus*, as the personified Virtue
(*virtus*) of Chastity demonstrates that real power (*virtus*) has
passed into her spiritual realm. The figural method of exegesis is also the technical vehicle for the personified narrative.[34]

If Prudentius had sustained such insights, his poem would
have rated not only as the first full-scale personification
allegory, but as one of the best. Alas, the divine spirit did not
always flow into his trembling hands. If his strengths influenced

---

[34] For *virtus*, cf. Prudentius' *Apotheosis*, in Thomson's edition, cited above, ll. 1018
and 1047, which contrasts the old life, an imagined fable ('fabula'), with the new one,
invigorated by the power of Christ ('Christi virtute'). Barney's *Allegories of History,
Allegories of Love*, which reached me after I wrote my analysis of Chastity's speech, cites
part of the *Apotheosis* passage (p. 79) and makes some similar comments about Chastity's new power (pp. 68–70). Though Barney does not concentrate here on the
technical shift to personification, he aptly points out that for people, such spiritual vic-
tories remain incomplete.

both the general structure and the individual details of his poem, so did his weaknesses.

As for the poem's structure, it is now time to confess that Prudentius never truly made the second half of his poem fulfill the *figura* of the first part. In the first place, the battle of personifications is not itself an historical event, as it would be in true figural writing. It remains at one remove from history, presenting it on a fictional, personified plane. Lust, after all, cannot actually thrust ('Ingerit') a pinewood torch ('pinum') into the eyes ('Lumina') of chastity (ll. 43–5). Soberness cannot actually hurl ('Coniciens') a huge stone ('molarem') that loosens the teeth ('Dentibus resolutis') of indulgence (ll. 417–24). Lacking true personalities, these forces can act like people only in fiction. This limitation does not affect their power, of course. On the contrary, Chastity's emergence as a literary character dramatizes her 'vera virtus.' Nor does the lack of an actual personality restrict the scope of these forces. Indulgence, for example, may weaken not only an individual soul, but a whole society. The issue, though, is the way we express this power and scope. We may displace the abstractions from the foreground, and describe the chaste or lustful activity of literal men. Alternatively, we may displace the men from the foreground, and deploy the abstractions as imaginary people. Once personified, they can roam the world and refer to actual events, even though their deployment remains a fiction. For the second part of his poem, Prudentius chooses the allegorical alternative. As a result, part two of the *Psychomachia* does not so much fulfill the historical figure of part one, as add a literary figure onto it.[35]

[35] The view that Prudentius' abstractions are supra-personal ('überpersönliche') in status has been forcefully presented by H. R. Jauss; see 'Form,' pp. 186–9, 197; 'Transformation,' pp. 113–15, 132; 'Entstehung,' pp. 216–17. Jauss' important work qualifies Lewis' tendency to treat such abstractions as expressions of an individual soul. For their broader dimensions in the life of the Church as a whole, see Smith, pp. 4–6, 24–6, 111–13, 118, 142, 155–6, 162–3, and ch. 3, esp. pp. 169–71, 183–8; cf. Barney, *Allegories of History, Allegories of Love*, pp. 62–4, 73. The more radical claim that these abstractions are virtually mythological agents, like the 'deified abstracts' of Rome ('Form,' pp. 186–9, 195; 'Transformation,' pp. 113–15, 131), however, needs refinement. The test of an allegorical character, as we have seen from the start, is the predicate attributed to the abstraction, and the predicates Prudentius assigns to his figures are not literal. On the contrast between literal god and personification, see App. II. The crucial 'distinction between form and meaning' ('Differenz zwischen Gestalt und Bedeutung') that makes the poem allegorical is thus not that these abstractions

It is true that we may ask what this fiction represents, in its turn. Unfortunately, this question raises the second, more serious problem in Prudentius' figural scheme. Aside from the general correspondence of struggle and triumph, the events of part two do not clearly parallel the events of part one. This is not to say that part two makes no allusions to the Old Dispensation. On the contrary, it is riddled with them, as Chastity's reference to Judith suggests. The internal structure of the poem, though, its principle of organization, is scarcely typological. This is particularly true of the battle of personifications, which is a general description of the victory of virtue over vice, with only broad resemblances to the Abraham story, and which could apply to nearly any such victory. It is rather like Eucherius taking the general notion of 'water' in isolation and allegorizing it. The figural continuity of Prudentius' poem is only a thin veneer covering radical breakages between the two parts.[36]

In its details, too, the *Psychomachia* is full of discontinuities. Instead of developing a sustained, interlocking action, it presents a series of disjointed episodes, although the episodes do become longer and more intricate as the poem progresses. In this it is similar to the disjunctive tendencies we have analyzed in allegorical exegesis during the period. While the abstract events of Prudentius' poem cohere more closely than the fitful encounters of Antony, they never develop the kind of causal sequence vital to a convincing history, either personal or ecclesiastical.[37] Even within individual episodes of the poem, the

have a double reference to soul and Church ('Form,' pp. 185–6, 197; 'Transformation,' pp. 112, 132–3), but that their strict definitions are deflected by their predicates. When pride 'rides' a horse, such a duality emerges, regardless of whether the action as a whole refers to both a proud man and a haughty empire. Despite these reservations, Jauss' work provides a number of useful perspectives on the development of early personification.

36 For the broad use of typology here, see Jauss, 'Form,' pp. 188–9; 'Transformation,' pp. 114–15, qualifying Auerbach, 'Figura,' n. 36. The most extensive account of the poem's disordered allusions to the Old Dispensation is Smith, ch. 3, esp. p. 179; he admits 'inconsistencies of structure' (p. 178). The attempt to find verbal resemblances between parts one and two (pp. 206–22) only exposes the structural strain between the two sections.

37 See Lavarenne, *Prudence*, pp. 10–11, and Charles Muscatine, 'The Emergence of Psychological Allegory in Old French Romance,' *PMLA* 68 (1953), 1160–2, 1179–82, with caution against any strict 'moral'/'psychological' dichotomy. Smith argues for a movement from 'relative chaos' to 'relative symmetry' (pp. 114–26), but his further

action is basically an abrupt cancellation of one abstraction by another. Often, the two abstractions do not even directly touch, let alone interact fully with each other. Thus, in the battle between Anger and Patience, Anger unleashes a hail of weapons against Patience, to no avail. Beside herself with fury, 'mentis inops'—without a mind—Anger finally turns her anger inward, and slays herself. Perhaps it is not just Anger who here commits an act of desperation.

Behind Anger's suicide, though, lie genuine conceptual and artistic difficulties, and since we have been exploring the allegorical advance of this important figure since it first approached Achilles, we might consider briefly some of its current dilemmas. As a conceptual issue, the problem of anger lacking a mind, a fact that already restricted its allegorical potential in Plato's account of the *thymos*, here reaches a critical stage. Like the other agents of the *Psychomachia*, Prudentius' Anger is more than a Platonic element within the soul, more even than an individual succumbing to the passion, as in the case of Virgil's Dido, raging 'inops animi' (*Aeneid* IV, 300), or Statius' Polynices, likened to a man 'rationis inops' (*Thebaid* I, 373)—where even the phrases serve as types for Prudentius' later allegorical exploitation, 'mentis inops.' In scope Seneca's wide-ranging *ira* is closer to Prudentius' conception, but as a rhetorical amplification rather than a daemonic figure, its suicidal tendencies—'in se revertitur' (*De Ira* I, xix, 4)—are more conventional in effect. Prudentius' Anger, by contrast, exists in a different dimension, a dimension almost like that filled, as Antony briefly saw, with two kinds of 'beings.' Needing to make the inferior figure capitulate to the superior one, Prudentius turns Anger into a suicide. This self-defeating action momentarily displays the psychological and theological point,

---

claim that disorder in the plot reflects 'imperfection' in the soul (p. 125) is unconvincing. Even psychological disorder has its rationale, and it is not revealed by piecemeal alignments of vice against virtue, pasted together with the most primitive adhesives: 'Prima' (l. 21), 'Exim' (l. 40), 'Ecce' (l. 109), etc. The imperfection here belongs to the poet, not the soul. To enlist this 'rhetoric of confusion' (p. 155) in defense of the poem's unsystematic typology (p. 180) or its embarrassing excesses of Virgilian allusion ('purposeful irrelevance,' 'designed disorder,' etc., pp. 271–300), only betrays the poem's other weaknesses. Still, Prudentius can use Virgil to telling effect, as Smith himself often shows, and the *Reexamination* as a whole remains a valuable contribution to Prudentian scholarship.

but sustained allegory requires a more sophisticated conception of one allegorical force or abstract level yielding to another.

There is also an artistic issue at stake here, a counterpart to the dilemmas of interpretive allegory in Prudentius' day. In exegesis, the problem was to preserve historical continuity while fully allegorizing individual passages. In Prudentius' poem, this conflict takes the form of a pull between the needs of narrative continuity, on the one hand, and the requirements of allegorical integrity, on the other. Figures like 'Anger' and 'Patience' cannot fully interact because they are antithetical principles. To engage in a sustained battle, they would have to diverge at some length from their strict definitions, or find some third party to bridge the gap between them. It was all very well for Tertullian to *say* that in the Christian struggle, the gladiators were Shamelessness hurled down by Chastity, Pride defeated by Humility, etc.[38] It was quite another matter to produce a convincing narrative on that basis. Prudentius' problem was not only the celebrated dilemma of reconciling the epic battle with Christian subject matter. It was also the old restriction limiting sustained personification from the start. The moment a Prudentian abstraction diverged too much from its definition, it tended to undermine its very meaning, as in the case of Chastity's somewhat over-enthusiastic response to her opponent. Indeed, one of the illuminating failures of the *Psychomachia* is the constant anomaly between the behavior of a personification and its very meaning. Compositional allegory has not yet learned how to control sophisticated action, how to finesse the old narrow correspondence between the meaning of a character and the activity ascribed to it.

A single nuance exposes Prudentius' dilemma better than any extended analysis. It comes when Prudentius describes the fall of Pride into the ditch dug secretly by her own companion, Deceit. The ditch was meant for Pride's opponent, Humility, to trap her when she rushed into battle. 'At regina humilis'—but the lowly queen, although she knew nothing about the trap, stayed ('manebat') on the other side (l. 267). How Prudentius and his contemporaries must have delighted in those three words, 'At regina humilis.' In writing them, the

---

[38] This celebrated passage from *De Spectaculis* 29 is not necessarily Prudentius' direct source; see Smith, pp. 129–30.

poet was seeking to transform the elevated style and epic subject of Virgil into the low, humble action of the Christian, the
sermo humilis in all its force. 'At regina'—'but the queen':
Virgil had used the phrase three times in the fourth book of the
Aeneid, and each time the words signalled passionate, frenzied
activity. The first time the phrase appeared, in the opening line
of Book IV, it was not 'humilis,' but 'graui' that followed the
phrase—the severe sting of love that Dido felt for Aeneas. The
second time the phrase appeared (l. 296), it was 'At regina
dolos'—the deceit of Aeneas that sent the queen into raging action. The last time (l. 504), it was 'At regina pyra'—the blaze
that would soon become the queen's funeral pyre. *At Prudentius*—but Prudentius changed those lofty words to 'humilis,'
and followed them not by an action, but precisely by the lack of
action, 'manebat': Queen Humility stood still. The real continuities in this poem are the stoppages. In that one line,
Prudentius exposed not only the dilemma of reconciling the
epic style with the Christian one. He exposed also the
allegorical problem of reconciling progressive action with
digressive meanings. If the allegorical interpretation of
Prudentius' day fragmented the continuities of *history* by
diverging too much from the text, Prudentius' allegorical composition undermined the continuities of *narrative* by the inverse
procedure of restricting the legitimate capabilities of its
characters.

MACROBIUS' DREAM;
MARTIANUS' AWAKENING

The problem of bringing spiritual depth into the material
world, an issue complicating the interpretive treatment of progress and the compositional approach to plot at the turn of the
fourth and fifth centuries AD, is not an exclusively Christian
problem. As we noted at the outset, early Christianity itself
draws deeply upon the Platonic tradition for the very strategy
of giving 'density' to the text and the world. At the same time,
this Platonic association between levels of meaning and levels
of being—the second of the three major tendencies on which we
have been concentrating in this transitional period—not only
influences other traditions, but constitutes a tradition in its own

right. It reaches its most intricate form in Neoplatonic writing from the late third to the fifth centuries AD, a variegated movement that in turn leaves its own vital legacy to the later Middle Ages.

With respect to the Neoplatonic interpretive tradition, it would be possible to explore this appeal to allegorical density in several ways. Thus, the old tradition of allegorizing the gods increasingly takes a subordinationist or emanationist form, in which the hosts of Olympus constitute stages of descent between heaven and earth. We have already noted the Middle Platonic tendency to turn the gods into mediating daemons; indeed, in the second century Maximus of Tyre makes the Athena who descends to Achilles in *Iliad* I a daemonic intermediary. We have also called attention to the more rarefied formulation a century later by the Neoplatonist Plotinus, who orders the Hesiodic triad into a staged progression from the One, to Nous, to Soul. By the fifth century, this interpretive tendency reaches its logical conclusion, in Proclus' elaborate argument that the very defects of the Olympian gods—the original stimulus for their allegorization—actually express various daemonic degrees of degeneration within an infinite series extending from the supreme level of being to the lowest one. Homer's 'golden chain' here becomes a poetic figure with a full philosophic rationale.[39]

But it is not the allegorization of the gods that constitutes the central Neoplatonic contribution to exegesis, even if, as we shall later see, the philosophic strategy of cosmic hierarchy itself, with its three celebrated hypostases, plays a crucial role in the twelfth-century allegory of creation. Already by the late Stoic period, the center of allegorical interpretation had begun to shift from the analysis of the gods to the exploration of the personality. The Neoplatonists, for their part, tend to change this emphasis on the individual from a psychic perspective to a mystic one. Their interpretations concentrate on the mysterious passage of the soul from heaven to earth and back again.[40] In such exegesis, the descent of a rational principle to earth is not just a communication from a divine being to a human one, as in Athena's condescension to Achilles. It is a

39 See Buffière, pp. 521–58.
40 See Buffière, pp. 2–3, 393–5.

testimony to different levels of being within man himself, the split condition of a life poised, as Plato himself had indicated, between two divergent realms.

While Plato had depicted this division in his parable of the Cave, the Neoplatonists allegorize it on a panoramic scale. Thus, in his bold interpretation developing the Middle Platonic exegesis of Homer's 'Cave of the Nymphs,' Porphyry makes that *Odyssean* underworld a figure for the whole region below the Milky Way into which the sidereal soul falls. From such a perspective, the soul's fall into a body is like the individual's descent into hell—an infernal descent treated by different exegetes in physical and moral terms. About a century after Porphyry, when Servius encounters Virgil's reference to the 'ninefold Styx' (*Aeneid* VI, 439), he draws the appropriate conclusions: those infernal currents in the story represent the nine spheres of the cosmos, where the soul slips into its miseries. Such analyses give a new edge to the old claim that the body is really the prison of the soul.[41]

At the same time, though, these very allegorizations imply the prospect of the soul's escape. If the descending soul passes from one side of the galaxy through Cancer toward earth, the continuation of this movement allows it to pass out through Capricorn on the opposite side. If Aeneas learns about the infernal side of life in his underworld journey, this same journey teaches him about the blessed condition of Elysium. The tension here between allegorical descent and ascent dramatizes the internal strain between the two orders of human life. Even the Christian writers in the Origenist controversy of the late fourth and early fifth centuries, such as Epiphanius, Theophilus of Alexandria, Jerome, and Augustine, who revise the notion of the soul's imprisonment by arguing that the fall is not the soul's cosmic descent into a body but the composite fall of an embodied soul on earth, do not fully ease the strain.[42] Perhaps

[41] See Buffière, pp. 419–59, and the detailed discussions of Pierre Courcelle, *Late Latin Writers and their Greek Sources*, tr. Harry E. Wedeck (Cambridge, Mass., 1969), pp. 40–2; 'Interprétations néo-platonisantes du livre VI de l'*Enéide*,' in *Recherches sur la tradition platonicienne* (Geneva, 1955), pp. 95–136; and 'Tradition platonicienne et traditions chrétiennes du corps-prison,' *Revue des études latines*, 43 (1965), 406–43.

[42] See Courcelle, 'Tradition platonicienne,' 427–43; cf. C. J. de Vogel, 'The *Sōma-Sēma* Formula: Its Function in Plato and Plotinus Compared to Christian Writers,' in *Neoplatonism and Early Christian Thought*, ed. H. J. Blumenthal and R. A. Markus (London, 1981), pp. 79–95.

its most striking structural expression occurs in the *Cosmographia*, which allegorizes the process of descent by the downward passage of an abstract principle, Urania, to whom Nature correspondingly ascends, while literalizing that descent by the depiction of a host of actual souls, who dread their embodiment in the 'kingdom of Dis' ('imperium Ditis'). The manipulation of the allegory here suggests a tantalizing ambivalence about the fall.[43] Long after Dante transforms the sense in which the soul's descent is really an ascent, a Christian may still explore with interest—if not complete consent—the argument that 'oure present worldes lyves space / Nis but a maner deth, what wey we trace' (*Parliament of Fowls*, ll. 53–4).

The author of those lines had been reading Macrobius, whose *Commentary on the Dream of Scipio*, composed about the same generation in which Augustine wrote *On Christian Doctrine,* served the Middle Ages as a principal source book for the Neoplatonic treatment of the soul's descent.[44] But Macrobius' importance consists not just in his compilation of various doctrines, but in his intriguing association of them—as Chaucer himself unwittingly suggests by falling into sleep. It is in his discussion of dreams, after all, that this 'interpreter of dreams' ('somniorum interpres'), as Macrobius is called in a number of medieval manuscripts, first articulates the this-world/underworld strain that runs throughout his commentary.[45] Explicating Virgil's verse on 'insomnia' near the end of *Aeneid*, Book VI, he no sooner addresses himself to dreams of a lower order than he calls attention to the lower order itself:

'False are the *insomnia* sent by departed spirits to their sky.' He [Virgil] calls the region of the living the 'sky' because we who are above bear the same relation to the dead as the gods bear to us. (I, iii, 6)

This rather dark vision of the world and the world of dreams, however, is only one perspective. For like everything else in

---

[43] See *Cosm., Mic.* III, viii, and Édouard Jeauneau, 'Macrobe, source du platonisme chartrain,' *StM*, 3a ser., 1 (1960), 16–22.

[44] For the text, see *Ambrosii Theodosii Macrobii Commentarii in Somnium Scipionis*, ed. Iacobus Willis (Leipzig, 1963). My translations are based on that of William Harris Stahl (New York, 1952).

[45] For 'somniorum interpres,' see Stahl's introduction, p. 42. For a discussion of dreams and illusion in the near-contemporary commentary of Servius, see Murrin, *Allegorical Epic*, pp. 32–41.

Macrobius' Neoplatonic universe, dreams are divided into different orders, finally reducible to the two general orders of superior visions, which are worthy of interpretation, and inferior ones, which are not. Concluding his discussion of the subject by explicating the related Virgilian verses (*Aeneid* VI, 893–5) on the gates of horn (for true shades) and ivory (for false dreams), Macrobius notes, drawing partially upon Porphyry, that sleep itself may reveal, as well as conceal—like the substance of horn, thinned until it becomes transparent (*Com.* I, iii, 17–20). The very slippage into sleep here becomes potentially an awakening to the truth.

As before, Macrobius' distinction lies not in the basic argument itself, which had been developing earlier in this late antique period, but in the implication of the argument with related issues. Revealingly, his discussion of dream visions develops out of the comprehensive analysis of fiction that opens the *Commentary*—and serves as the starting point for twelfth-century treatments of narrative central to the development of allegory.[46] Here, in Macrobius' famous claims about the hierarchy of 'fabula' and 'narratio fabulosa' and the variegated covering ('vario . . . tegmine,' I, ii) of Nature itself, is a systematic treatment of the Platonic tendency to associate different levels of the text with different levels of the world. It is as if the claim that ends Macrobius' book, that 'nothing is more complete' (II, xvii, 17) than the fragment of Cicero's *Republic* which inspires his *Commentary*, were to apply to the *Commentary* itself, which seeks to consolidate the diverse orders of the Neoplatonic universe.

It is all the more distressing, then, that in his *Saturnalia* Macrobius notoriously contradicts the explicit criteria he himself advocates for the order of fiction, by philosophizing the very myth (Saturn's castration of Caelus) that the *Commentary* insists is inappropriate for philosophic interpretation—and philosophizing it, for that matter, in order to display cosmic harmony itself.[47] The fundamental issue here is not whether the *Saturnalia* precedes or follows the *Commentary*, although the allegorization may well not even have the 'excuse' of antedating the theory it contradicts. This same castration

[46] See Stock, pp. 11–62, and Dronke, *Fabula*, pp. 13–78.
[47] See *Saturnalia* I, viii, 6–8, and Wetherbee, pp. 119–20.

myth, after all, has impressive allegorical credentials throughout the Neoplatonic tradition; it is philosophized before Macrobius by Plotinus and after him by Proclus.[48] Rather, Macrobius' 'slip,' if we may use the term, dramatizes the dilemma of his whole *Commentary*, the effort to codify the conditions which make a fable truthful, and thereby to elevate the visionary part of Cicero's work into a philosophic whole.

Macrobius' problem, really, is the fundamental question of a fiction's 'integrity'—both in the sense of its propriety to its subject matter and in the sense of its own internal coherence. This problem preoccupies the critics of the Neoplatonic tradition, from Porphyry's student, Iamblichus, to the ingenious fifth-century exegete, Proclus, who consolidates the tendencies of his predecessors. Thus, Proclus daringly makes the 'impropriety' of myths, for which ancient exegetes had allegorically apologized, the very basis of their validity. Such apparently incongruous stories, he argues, are 'symbolic,' unlike more straightforward 'iconic' representations, which entail a one-to-one correspondence with their subject matter. For example, he continues, at the beginning of the *Timaeus* Plato prefigures his explication of the natural world by two representations of the human world—Socrates' recapitulation of ideal conditions in the *Republic*, and Critias' account of ancient conditions in the Atlantis myth. The very incongruity of 'symbolic' myths such as Critias' vivid tale provokes us to seek their higher meaning. They thus serve preeminently as mediators to the truth, like 'demons,' to which Proclus explicitly compares them in a later work, who make 'revelations to men through the medium of symbols, as happens when some of us during waking hours encounter demons or when, in sleep, we have profited from some inspiration from them.' Indeed, 'every myth is demonic on its surface,' but 'divine with respect to its secret doctrine.' Proclus' Neoplatonic treatment of the link between divinities and daemons is not just a theological claim about the hierarchy of the world, but an exegetical exposé of the order of myth, which recalls its divine source in the very act of diverging from it.[49]

[48] On the dates of the *Commentary* and the *Saturnalia*, see Stahl's translation, pp. 5–6. For Plotinus, see Pépin, p. 205; for Proclus, see Coulter, pp. 53–4.

[49] See Coulter, pp. 32–60, who translates these passages from Proclus' commentaries on the *Timaeus* and the *Republic*. On the tension between such 'intuitive' pro-

At the same time, this act of recall assures the internal coherence of a narrative's divergent elements. The more the ostensibly 'inferior' symbol is esoterically understood to depend upon its superior source, the more its partial condition is resolved into a comprehensible order. Like Iamblichus before him, Proclus even applies this principle to a brief portion of the *Timaeus'* introductory conversation, by arguing that Socrates' enumeration of the parties present and absent (*Timaeus* 17A)—a seemingly extraneous detail—suggests the ethical, physical, mathematical, and metaphysical levels of an integral doctrine. Such exegesis applies to the text that progressive process of diffusion and reversion which distinguishes the Neoplatonic world at large.[50]

However daring this strategy, it remains problematic, and its full exploitation awaits later writers in the Neoplatonic tradition, including the Pseudo-Dionysius, Eriugena, and especially Bernard Silvestris. First, the late antique Neoplatonists repeatedly mix the very terms, 'icon' and 'symbol,' which they seek to distinguish. Second, the internal rules for considering one representation straightforwardly 'iconic' and another mysteriously 'symbolic' (and superior) seem incompletely articulated.[51] Third, the bold effort to champion the impropriety of the 'symbol' deeply complicates the conditions of discourse. In one sense, the symbol is preferable to the icon, since its mysterious resonance suggests the loftiest secrets. In another sense, though, the symbol's elusiveness implies a role for the icon, which provides a framework for conceptual activity, even if this activity finally shows the need for a higher transport. Indeed, near the end of his hierarchy of narrative procedures (I, ii, 15), when Macrobius speaks of representing the supreme realm, he commends Plato's icon (*eikona*, *Republic* VI, 509A), the sun—an appeal to direct correspondence similarly endorsed

---

cedures and 'discursive' reasoning, see Trimpi, *Muses of One Mind*, cited above in Ch. II, n. 9, pp. 103–5, 128–9, 164–240, with my discussion of other Neoplatonic writing below and in Chs. IV and VI.

[50] See Coulter, pp. 59–60, 77–94, 128–30.

[51] See John Dillon, 'Image, Symbol and Analogy: Three Basic Concepts of Neoplatonic Allegorical Exegesis,' in *The Significance of Neoplatonism*, ed. R. Baine Harris (Norfolk, Va., 1976), pp. 247–62; cf. Coulter, p. 48, n. 16, and p. 56, n. 27.

by Porphyry and Proclus.[52] With their impressive efforts to distinguish different orders of fiction, the Neoplatonists refine the old Stoic principle that 'omne verbum ambiguum natura esse,' but the precise rationale of ambiguity here remains itself in doubt.

In the end, the antique Neoplatonists raise to a higher power the interpretive dilemma displayed from the start, the problem of turning fiction into philosophy. Their speculations on icons and symbols, dreams and visions, are really efforts to distinguish those parts of a text which diverge from the truth from those parts which correspond to it—that is, to establish criteria for allegorization. As Macrobius shows in his *Commentary* on a dream, it is quite possible to establish such criteria from the outside, as it were; a dream is legitimate if it turns out to be true, illegitimate if it does not (*Com.* I, iii, 3, 8–11). But the issue that troubles medieval (and modern) dreamers is how to know if a dream is authentic from the inside, while we are dreaming it. Every soul, after all, falls into the sleep of this world; the interpretive question is whether wisdom is revealed in the process.

This question has its compositional counterpart. Probably between 410 and 439 AD, shortly after Macrobius writes his commentary on a dream, Martianus Capella announces an awakening (*egersimon*) to a vision that popularizes the allegorical ascent to heaven.[53] The allegorical action itself, it should be stressed, constitutes only a limited portion of the *Marriage of Mercury and Philology*. Dominating the first two books, it dwindles into a general framework for the long didactic accounts of the Liberal Arts in the last seven books, which provide important source texts for the critical and curricular programs of the early medieval period. Yet the imaginative

[52] Courcelle, *Late Latin Writers*, p. 34, with n. 37, refers to these statements. On the Neoplatonic ambivalence toward conceptual frameworks of this kind, and the effort to specify the conditions of their use, see Coulter, pp. 95–126; Trimpi, esp. pp. 173, n. 10, 182–3, 200, 215, n. 50, 219–28; and my discussion below and in Chs. IV and VI.

[53] For the text, see *Martianus Capella*, ed. A. Dick, with addenda by Jean Préaux (Stuttgart, 1969). Citations refer to section numbers in this edition; e.g., *egersimon* (2). My translations are based on that of William Harris Stahl, Richard Johnson, and E. L. Burge, in *Martianus Capella and the Seven Liberal Arts*, 2 vols. (New York, 1971, 1977). On the date of the text, see Vol. I of this work, pp. 9–16.

framework develops a vivid life of its own during the Middle Ages, not only in the iconographic portrayal of the Liberal Arts themselves but in the mythographic treatment of the fable's introductory figures, and more immediately, Martianus himself poses problematic questions about the relation between his opening visionary movement and his later educational exposition. Nothing in the *Marriage of Mercury and Philology*, in fact, develops without twists and turns; the initial process of ascent itself actually consists of a series of transitions, in both directions, between one level of the universe and another.

Thus, at the start of the tale, Mercury, desiring a wife, traverses the 'mundi penita' (9) to seek the advice of Apollo. Apollo, recommending the learned maiden Philology, ascends with Mercury to the 'Tonantis palatium' (30) to petition for Jove's consent. Jove, consulting with Juno, receives from above, 'de quodam loco' (39), a visit from Athena, who urges him to convene a council of the gods and, if the assembly endorses the marriage, to immortalize the maiden. The assembly, hearing Jove's account of a maiden 'earthborn but starbound' (93), approves the accord, adding that all mortals of elevated stature should rise to the level of the immortals. With the marriage approved, Immortality itself ('Athanasia,' 134) appears to Philology, leading her through the initial rites of passage. At last, Philology ascends panoramically through the celestial spheres to the verge of the Empyrean itself (202), finally lighting down upon the divine dwelling of the Milky Way. There she receives her dowry—the seven maidens of the Liberal Arts, each of whom offers a protracted survey of her own principles before the drama is complete. Even this *Marriage*, it seems, has its ups and downs.

It also has its deeper point. However flamboyant this perpetual movement between one realm and another, it exposes the urgency of linking together different orders of the cosmos. As if to emphasize the point, Martianus makes concord itself the presiding principle of his work. He opens the *Marriage* by invoking the divine 'copula sacra' (1) that binds the dissonant elements of the world with a sacred embrace. He closes the tale as 'Harmonia,' the last of the Liberal Arts, celebrates in song the accord of the two lovers—one from heaven, the other from earth. Throughout the book he stresses, with Neopythagorean intensity, the role of harmonious number in the structure of his work and the world at large, and he frames the whole narrative by counterpointing the celestial scene of the gods with the terrestrial scene of the narrator and the listener, in which the composition takes form.[54] The *Marriage* thus not only draws upon the tradition of cosmic union—which pre-Socratic, Hermetic, and other writers had imagined as a *hieros gamos*, and Stoic philosophers had treated as a cosmic 'bond'—and not only exploits the tradition of psychic union, which Apuleius had developed in his story of Cupid and Psyche—a marriage that Martianus rather slyly claims to supersede (23), as if to stake out a claim for his own work.[55] It gives the tradition of union a more exotic, even ecstatic strain, dramatizing the initiation of human life into the life of the gods. It is revealing that Martianus' narrative of ascent serves as a principal model for the central allegorical ascent in the *Cosmographia*, as Nature aspires toward the heavens in order to consolidate man's creation on earth. If the *Marriage* does not offer so subtle or systematic a progress, it nevertheless also envisions the daring integration of a lower order with a higher one.

Such an intensive negotiation between diverse levels of the cosmos requires greater rhetorical flexibility than has appeared thus far in the allegorical tradition. In a fable that seeks to join the human and divine orders, each order must resonate with possibilities beyond the limits of its strict definition. On the one hand, the figures on both planes must be not only conceptually and emotionally implicated with each other, as in the 'marriage' scene of the *Aeneid*. On the other hand, they cannot be so fluid that they change pervasively into each other, as in Ovid's mythological metamorphoses. A figure like Mercury, for example, must be human enough to be personally diverted by his love affair, while cosmic enough to be astronomically delayed by retrograde motion (36). The challenge of a mythological allegory like the *Marriage of Mercury and Philology* is to retain the

---

[54] See the valuable but sometimes overenthusiastic study of Fanny LeMoine, *Martianus Capella: A Literary Re-evaluation* (Munich, 1972); the discussion of number occupies pp. 73–83, 196–208, 217–28.

[55] On these traditions, see Dronke, 'L'amor,' 389–408, and Michael Lapidge, 'A Stoic Metaphor in Late Latin Poetry: the Binding of the Cosmos,' cited in Ch. II, n. 34.

cogency of an allegorical argument while exploiting the versatility of the mythological flourish.

Later discussions of Martianus' work codify this conceptual and rhetorical challenge. Thus, near the beginning of a commentary on the *Aeneid* perhaps written by Bernard Silvestris himself, the commentator explains that allegorical works such as the *Marriage* depend upon 'equivocationes' and 'multivocationes': Mercury, for example, sometimes means 'eloquence,' sometimes the 'star.' A single name, he continues, can designate different natures, while a single nature can be designated by different names.[56] Although such later interpretations are more rigorous than the *Marriage* itself, it is clear that already in Martianus' time, the interpretive tradition of abstracting the personalities of the divine world is becoming inseparable from the compositional tradition of personifying the abstractions of the human world. More immediately, the original dilemma of compositional allegory—the problem of elaborating a concept into a fiction without undermining its integrity—is developing new urgency. A multileveled universe demands a multivalent language.

Now at times Martianus quite deftly executes this conceptual and linguistic maneuver. Perhaps the most dazzling episode of this kind—one that may influence both the *Cosmographia* (*Mic.* IX, iv–v) and the *Complaint of Nature* (IV, 18–63)—is the account of Mercury's and Apollo's celestial ascent. The very earth ('Tellus') and air ('aëria Temperies') are exhilarated by the breathtaking flight, and as Apollo passes beyond the aerial region,

suddenly his headband is transformed into rays of light, and the laurel, which he held in his right hand, bursts into a torch of cosmic splendor . . . At once he shone forth brightly as the Sun. The Cyllenian [Mercury], too, is changed into a glimmering star.

subito ei uitta crinalis immutatur in radios, laurusque, quam dextera retinebat, in lampadem mundani splendoris accenditur . . . Sol repente clarus emicuit. Cyllenius quoque in sidus uibrabile astrumque conuertitur. (29)

---

[56] See *The Commentary on the First Six Books of the* Aeneid *of Vergil Commonly Attributed to Bernardus Silvestris*, ed. Julian Ward Jones and Elizabeth Frances Jones (Lincoln, Nebr., 1977), pp. 9–10.

By breaking into a higher realm, the two figures burst into a new, astral dimension of themselves. Here the distance between the mythological and cosmological levels, which the Stoics had tried to conflate, is exploited to produce an expansive allegorical event.

But Martianus rarely equals this success. So intrigued is he by all the dimensions of his figures—Stoic, Neoplatonic, Neopythagorean, Hermetic, Orphic, Chaldean[57]—that he produces more an assortment of associations than a sustained abstract argument. Thus, it is not conceptually clear how the figure of Mercury himself relates to his passage across a terrestrial stream that corresponds to his own celestial sphere (14–16), or to his celestial sphere itself beyond which Philology must pass on her way to marry him (171–80), or to his bewildering array of identities—'sermo,' 'uerus Genius,' *nous*, Thoth, and the rest (91, 102). This is not to say that a cogent allegorical plot would require Mercury to be 'eloquence' alone—an interpretation that in any case scarcely does justice to Martianus' own rich conception, whatever its later popularity.[58] On the contrary, we have just seen that the *Marriage* is distinguished for the promise of conceptual flexibility it brings to personification allegory. But the multivalent *symbolon* has its risks, as well as its attractions. In order to exploit conceptual flexibility convincingly, it is necessary to organize it. Even the appearance to Philology of Eloquence herself ('Facundia') as a separate figure in the sphere of Mercury (171–3) would be discreet enough if Martianus did not hasten to add that Eloquence had already been reared in the house of Philology, who is presumably developing eloquence by her marriage to Mercury. Martianus is struggling here, really, with the difficult problem of degrees or levels of allegorical presence and absence, a particularly acute dilemma in a multileveled universe. Not until the *Cosmographia* will allegory begin to control this dilemma, by exploiting the distinction between potentiality and actuality—and even then, it will be necessary to refine the technique. As for Martianus, with his

[57] See, e.g., Courcelle, *Late Latin Writers*, pp. 211–19; LeMoine, *Martianus Capella*, pp. 65–70.

[58] On the interpretation of the work as an allegory of *eloquentia-sapientia*, see Gabriel Nuchelmans, 'Philologia et son mariage avec Mercure jusqu'à la fin du XIIᵉ siècle,' *Latomus*, 16 (1957), 84–107.

bizarre mélange of deities, concepts, and individuals, the allegorical ascent, however impressive its potential, keeps tending to turn into a flight of rhetorical fancy.

Martianus' technical problem of aligning *mythos* with *logos* reflects a deeper philosophic dilemma. Like the Neoplatonists, he seems profoundly ambivalent about the precise transition between one level of the text and the other—and between the world of appearances and the world of truth. It is revealing that Philology, about to attempt the transition, worries particularly about the prospect of forgoing myths and delights of poetic diversity ('mythos, poeticae etiam diuersitatis delicias,' 100). More drastically, her initiation by Immortality requires her to vomit the works she has assimilated:

Then that nausea and labored vomit turns into a stream of writings of every kind. (135)

The passage is not pretty; I have quoted it because it displays both the extreme demands of the initiation rite and the extreme pressures it places upon poetry. Philology is not a repulsive figure, like Spenser's 'Error,' disgorging repulsive books. She is an attractive, if still imperfect lady, and her books, it turns out, include the lore of those very 'Egyptians' who reveal Mercury's mystic name, Thoth. Martianus, of course, wishes to show that even her brilliance is dark when seen from a higher perspective, but something of his ambivalence surfaces later in the initiation scene, when Apotheosis blesses ('consecrabat') the very books Philology has just vomited (140)! In the rather 'fluid' status of those texts—if we may use the term—lies the ambiguity of Martianus' own work: whether the allegorical ascent means truly to elevate the fiction of earthly life or only to escape it.

In the end, this compositional question affects the very structure of the *Marriage*. As Martianus makes his transition between the marriage fable itself (Books I–II) and the doctrinal presentation of the Arts (Books III–IX), he self-consciously muses that 'mythos terminatur' (220), only to conclude that even in a doctrinal discourse, 'nothing can be composed' without 'figminis figura' (222). In his embarrassed acknowledgment here about the need to 'clothe' the truth (221–2), reminiscent of Macrobius' more solemn philosophic argument about covering Nature, and his rather disordered speculations later in the work about the value of imaginative language (e.g., 326, 512, 809, 997–1000), he is aspiring fitfully toward a theory of philosophic fiction that will not be systematically articulated until the *integumentum*-theorists of the twelfth century. As the long, labored exposition of the Arts shows, his own work remains divided between the charms of decoration and the demands of argumentation.

Martianus Capella thus brings the old allegorical problem of rhetorical decoration to a new turning point, by radically exposing both its luxuriant possibilities and its analytic limitations. He shares this divided tendency with the other mythological allegorists of the day. Claudian, who composes a marriage hymn that may influence the opening of Martianus' *Marriage*, enriches the allegorical tradition with his own exotic tableaux, imaginatively expansive but conceptually vulnerable. For all the suggestiveness of Claudian's celebrated portraits of "Natura" in the *Consulship of Stilicho* and the *Rape of Proserpina*, Nature's full conceptual and poetic deployment does not develop until its sustained analytic treatment in the twelfth century. Later mythological allegorists such as Sidonius Apollinaris, writing some decades after Martianus, and Ennodius, composing at the turn of the fifth and sixth centuries, conspicuously display both the promise of a visionary world and the need for intellectual rigor.[59] The ancient effort to unite rhetorical decoration with philosophic argumentation, eloquence with wisdom, had begun with the insight that 'speech' and 'reason' belong to a single word, *logos*.[60] But a convincing marriage between the two requires an orientation to *logos* in its third meaning of 'due proportion'—the equilibrium required to stabilize allegorical language.

FULGENTIUS AND BOETHIUS: INVERSIONS AND CONVERSIONS

The problem of giving logical coherence to imaginative language returns us not only to the interpretive tradition, but

---

[59] See Gordon Braden, 'Claudian and His Influence: The Realm of Venus,' *Arethusa*, 12 (1979), 203–31; Stock, pp. 73–7; Lewis, pp. 73–83.

[60] See Nuchelmans, 'Philologia,' 84.

to the first of the three broad movements upon which we have been concentrating in this period, the changing status of the allegorized text itself. As we have observed, one of the great changes in the antique interpretive tradition was the application of allegory by Jews and Christians to a biblical text different in kind from mythological poetry, which ancient allegorizers had tended to dissipate in the interests of philosophy. While even the earliest Christians enlisted Greek poetry at times to support their own doctrines, such allusions remained limited by the distinction between the mere eloquence of pagan fiction and the true wisdom of revealed Scripture. As Christianity consolidated its cultural and institutional position in the late ancient world, however, it gradually sought to expropriate, like the Israelites in Augustine's famous comparison (*On Christian Doctrine* II, 40), the 'gold of the Egyptians' for its own legitimate uses. This process never wholly resolved the distinction between human texts and divine Scripture, of course, but it produced increasingly sophisticated strategies to reduce the tension between them, by giving even mythical poetry an integrity of its own. The first great Christian allegorist in this movement is Fulgentius, who flourishes probably at the turn of the fifth and sixth centuries, and who writes (among other works) both an allegorical compendium of ancient mythology at large, the *Mythologies*, and an allegorical exposé of a central text, the *Aeneid*, the *Exposition of the Content of Virgil*.[61]

While the *Mythologies*, the earlier work, is less daring in conception than the *Content*, even it suggests an effort to reduce the disparity between poetic and philosophic language, and thus to ally the compositional and interpretive traditions as a whole. Exploiting a strategy developed by Macrobius and Martianus, Fulgentius calls his work at the start a 'fabula' (3. 17), a dreamy fiction ('somniali figmento,' 3. 18–19), as if to make the act of interpretation itself a visionary composition.[62] Its initial

---

[61] See Fulgentius' *Opera*, ed. R. Helm (Leipzig, 1898). The *Mitologiae* is cited by page and line number for the prologue, by book and myth number for the body of the text; the *Expositio Virgilianae Continentiae* is cited by page and line number. My translations are based on those of Leslie George Whitbread in *Fulgentius the Mythographer* (Columbus, Ohio, 1971). On the chronology of Fulgentius' works, see Whitbread, pp. 3–9.

[62] On the translation and tone of this passage, see LeMoine, pp. 35–6; cf. Courcelle, *Late Latin Writers*, pp. 220–3.

framework is an interchange between the narrator and the epic Muse, Calliope, who approaches him first in a shady spot, later in his own bedchamber. The narrator both encourages her early advances with poetic allusions and yet protests the false stories of the poets, and his whole orientation toward his plight—now humorous, now serious—oscillates rather uneasily throughout the prologue, as in Martianus' wry reflections about his art. Nonetheless, after the epic Muse herself commends to him Philosophy and Urania and promises him astral immortality (12. 3–15. 1), the prologue concludes with her as divine interpreter. There are intriguing ironies in making the same figure both the sponsor and the critic of myth, as the comic, self-undermining exchange on 'Satire' suggests (12. 9–13. 17; cf. 3. 10–16, 10. 11–19), and as Alan of Lille will show systematically in the twelfth century, but there are also promising possibilities—the promise of a link between mythological and logical discourse. As the interpretive Muse herself puts it (12. 7), this is labor suited to the versatile 'ingenium.'

Still, here such possibilities remain largely unfulfilled. It is not only that the Muse never reappears after the opening prologue—not even in the prologues to the second and third books of the three-part work—but that the *Mythologies* as a whole presents no really coherent poetic or philosophic design. Granted, Fulgentius' material is bewilderingly diverse. On the poetic level, he seeks to bind one story to the next by a kind of Ovidian linking technique, but this method becomes increasingly attenuated (e.g., I, 18; I, 21). On the philosophic level, he begins successive books with tales exhibiting a sort of macroto microcosmic progression—first the origin of the pagan gods and the system of the four elements (I, 1–5), then the division of human behavior into contemplative, active, and sensual lives (II, 1), finally the need for man to heed good counsel (III, 1)[63]—but this general design is too diffuse to be effective, and in any case it breaks down internally, as when three lessons about morality (Hercules, II, 2–4) rather abruptly yield to one about the seasonal cycle (Tiresias, II, 5). Allegorizing now 'physically' (Jove as fire, Juno as air, I, 3), now ethically (three-headed Cerberus as the threefold origin of envy, I, 6), now even historically, by the Euhemerist method destined for

[63] See Brinkmann, p. 186.

special favor in the Renaissance (Saturn as an Italian ruler, I, 2), Fulgentius aims less at conceptual order than impromptu invention.[64] But Martianus, no stranger to invention, would have been displeased to learn that his mystical Mercury is here reduced to the expedient status of trader ('negotiator') and thief ('furatrinumque'), and called Hermes from *ermeneuse*, translating, since translating is essential to traders (I, 18). Moderns specializing in *hermeneutics* may have their own divided thoughts about making a businessman the patron of their stock in trade.

In a sense, of course, Fulgentius' eclecticism is one of his valuable legacies to the mythographic tradition, helping to stimulate the interpretive imagination of allegorists from the Vatican Mythographers to the moralizers of Ovid. Further, his tendency to slip from the 'historical' treatment of certain figures to their 'moral' significance helps to give a kind of authenticity, even historical validity, to poetic fiction, almost as if it were not so distinct from the moral *historia* of his faith.[65] But his disjointed, sometimes arbitrary approach limits the logical cogency and historical consistency of his argument, and by extension the overall coherence of the myths. Perhaps nothing better exemplifies his atomistic treatment of mythological narrative than his extreme deployment of 'syllabic' etymology—deriving meaning not just from words but from syllabic fractions of them.[66] In the end, any claim here for the integrity of such fables is deeply qualified by the position taken at the beginning, when the narrator announces that he wishes to expose alterations from the truth ('Mutatas . . . uanitates,' 11. 12) and then opens the exegesis itself with a story about pagan idolatry (I, 1).

A bolder approach to the logic of poetry develops in Fulgentius' exegesis of the *Aeneid*. It is not only that the figure of the

---

[64] On Euhemerus, see Pépin, pp. 147–9; for some Euhemerist perspectives in the Renaissance, see Jean Seznec, *The Survival of the Pagan Gods*, tr. Barbara Sessions (New York, 1953).

[65] See Paule Demats, *Fabula: Trois études de mythographie antique et médiévale* (Geneva, 1973), pp. 55–60. For the radicalization of such tendencies in the late Middle Ages, see Judson Boyce Allen, *The Friar as Critic* (Nashville, Tenn., 1971), on the development of a 'spiritual sense of fiction,' and *Ethical Poetic*, pp. 219–29, on the movement toward exemplary figures through the 'assimilatio of parallel systems.'

[66] On this technique, see Klinck, *Die lateinische Etymologie des Mittelalters*, cited above in Ch. II, n. 36, pp. 16–17, n. 30; pp. 65–70.

creator who is his own critic (in the *Mythologies*, the Muse) now presides explicitly over the whole book, as the vatic Virgil (85. 11) explains sequentially the logic of his own poetic passages, almost as if he were fashioning an early *Vita Nuova*. Nor is it only that Virgil's self-interpretation is itself deepened by his ongoing dialectic with the narrator, the 'little man' ('homunculus,' 86. 7) who, while comically disparaged, contributes Christian insights at turning points in the work (e.g., 87. 6–87. 12). It is that the *Content*, for the first time in allegorical history, reads the whole epic as a single, continuous, allegorical plot, exposing 'the complete state of man' ('plenum hominis . . . statum,' 90. 1–2). Others before Fulgentius, like Macrobius in his *Commentary* and more broadly in the *Saturnalia*, had offered underlying meanings for selected parts of the *Aeneid*. Indeed, the *Aeneid* commentary of Macrobius' contemporary, Servius, includes over one hundred notes proposing sundry allegorical interpretations—physical, ethical, historical, cultic.[67] But Fulgentius seeks to turn the very poetic sequence of the *Aeneid* into the logical progression of human life.

The problem of logic applies even to the level of individual words. Explicating the opening verse of his poem (86. 21–90. 18), Virgil argues that the words 'arma' ('virtuosity of body') and 'uirum' ('wisdom of mind') seem to be arranged in reverse order, since according to the rules of logic ('dialecticam disciplinam') substance ('uirum') should precede accident ('arma'). The reversal of logical order here, Virgil continues, reflects the rules of praise ('laudis materia'), which exhibit the merit of a man ('arma') before the man himself ('uirum'). Nevertheless, this problematic tension between the rhetorical and logical orders—the old dilemma of interpretive allegory—is subject to some resolution. The same sequence of words displays the progressive deepening (or elevating) of human life:

first to possess, then to rule what you possess, and third to refine what you rule. Therefore, think of these three degrees as arranged in my one line, that is: 'arma,' 'virum,' and 'primus' . . .

---

[67] See Harrison Cadwallader Coffin, 'Allegorical Interpretation of Vergil with Special Reference to Fulgentius,' *The Classical Weekly*, 15 (1921), 33–5; J. W. Jones, Jr., 'Allegorical Interpretation in Servius,' *The Classical Journal*, 56 (1961), 217–26.

primum habere, deinde regere quod habeas, tertium uero ornare quod regis. Ergo tres gradus istos in uno uersu nostro considera positos, id est: 'arma,' 'uirum' et 'primus' . . . (89. 18–21)

In effect, Virgil here argues that the words are in their proper order after all, when the epic is read not as an inside-out movement (substance to accident), but as a movement from the outside in (or above)—the gradual consolidation of substance (89. 20–5): from 'natura,' to 'doctrina,' to 'felicitas' (90. 2–3). The horizontal movement of the poem's language enacts the vertical advance of man.

However contrived Fulgentius' approach here—and his constant verbal and philosophic reformulations threaten to disrupt even this fragile order[68]—it suggests at least potentially a vital shift in allegorical orientation. Even Heraclitus, whose exegesis nominally followed the sequence of Homer's poetry, proposed no continuous logical argument internal to the text. By contrast, Fulgentius aims not only to resolve a logical problem of individual words, but more extensively, a chronological problem of whole events, the celebrated question of temporal sequence raised by Virgil's opening in *medias res*. In terms of a continuous allegory of human progress from 'natura' to 'felicitas,' the shipwreck of Book I is not chronologically out of place with respect to the 'earlier' events at Troy and at sea in Books II and III. Rather, the shipwreck (the perilous process of birth, 91. 6–8) properly precedes, for example, the episode of the Cyclops (the wildness of youth, 93. 23–94. 11). Elements which were potentially allegorical in Virgil's original conception are now relentlessly interiorized as progressive stages of development: the storm of the 'marriage' scene becomes the young man's confusion of mind (94. 16–19); Turnus, the rage resisted by the power of wisdom (105. 13–15). (Vulcan, who played that disruptive role in the *Mythologies* ['the fire of rage,' II, 11], here develops into the redemptive figure of 'burning counsel' [105. 6], as if to enact that shift between the opposing values of Hephaestian fire which the Stoics had prepared for

---

[68] See, e.g., the problematic effort to apply the *uirtus/sapientia* scheme to the Homeric episode of Athena and Achilles (88. 17–89. 3); the shift of 'arma' (or 'uirtus') from 'accidens' to 'substantia' (87. 15, 89. 14, 89. 22); the tripartite terminology and treatment of 'substantia' (89. 22–5). Such involutions are not attributable simply to the limitations of the Virgilian character.

exploitation.)[69] Any systematic sense of personal advance in this allegory of *humana natura* is qualified by Fulgentius' episodic tendencies, but his broad approach unmistakably turns the psychomachic epic toward the allegory of maturation, a form later revised and exploited in the *Cosmographia*, the *Anticlaudianus*, and ultimately in the allegorical romance of the *Faerie Queene.*

Although the complex relation established here between the rhetorical and logical orders has antecedents in the ancient distinction between the *ordo artificialis* and the *ordo naturalis* of oratory, Fulgentius enriches and complicates the tradition.[70] While distinguishing the rules of praise from the rules of dialectic, he yet turns a rhetorical order into a logical one. While ignoring the chronology of Aeneas, he yet develops a chronology of man. By the time of the twelfth-century *Aeneid* commentary attributed to Bernard Silvestris, which expands the Fulgentian method, such paradoxes will be partially clarified by the argument that as poet, Virgil uses the *ordo artificialis;* as philosopher, the *ordo naturalis.*[71] In this formulation, Virgil's manipulation of his literary fiction (e.g., the apparent displacement of the shipwreck) is essential to the construction of his conceptual argument (birth as the initiating event). The very artifice of the poet *makes* the sequence philosophic. Even this formulation, however, implies a disparity between the sequence of fiction and the logic of life. It is revealing that the later twelfth-century *Éneas*, a romance version of the epic, tends to straighten out the line of Virgil's narrative to display the continuous history of its hero, and that Landino's much later interpretive allegory of the

[69] On the internalization of the epic, see the commentary *On the Thebaid* (Helm's edn., pp. 180–6) sometimes attributed to Fulgentius (but possibly a much later work) which turns Statius' panoramic story into an allegory of the soul's sequential development: 'Thebe id est humana anima' (186. 9–10).

[70] On the two *ordines*, see Edmond Faral, *Les Arts poétiques du xiie et du xiiie siècle* (Paris, 1923), pp. 55–60. For some complications, see Jerome Edward Singerman, 'Under Clouds of Poesy: Poetry and Truth in French and English Reworkings of the *Aeneid*, 1160–1513,' Diss. Harvard 1981, ch. 1, 'The Commentators' *Aeneid.'*

[71] See pp. 1–3 of the edition cited above in n. 56. Cf. Giorgio Padoan, 'Tradizione e fortuna del commento all'*Eneide* di Bernardo Silvestre,' *Italia medioevale e umanistica*, 3 (1960), 238–9; Brinkmann, pp. 292–317; and Allen, *Ethical Poetic*, pp. 89–91, 131–5, who explores this passage in terms of the distinction between the 'form of the treatise' (*forma tractatus*) and the 'form of the treatment' (*forma tractandi*) that develops in the later *accessus* tradition. For the relation between the argument of the commentary and the narrative procedures of the *Cosm.*, see Ch. VI, below.

Aeneid begins with Troy itself and explicates sequentially the stages of Aeneas' progress.[72] In any event, Fulgentius' own exegesis suggests the philosophic issue, the need to turn imaginative retrogressions into logical advances.

The central paradigm for this transformation is the *katabasis* of Book VI, a descent in the fiction that becomes an ascent toward the truth.[73] As before, Fulgentius' own treatment of this reversal is more suggestive than systematic, as he tells of 'darkness penetrated by higher knowledge' ('altiori scientia penetrata caligine,' 98. 6–7). Twelfth-century commentaries will distinguish more clearly the fortunate possibilities of such a fall, by making the soul's very slippage into a body the opportunity for its advance—the mind's engagement with the things of this world in order to turn its perspective to the world above.[74] In a sense, such clarifications of the different ways in which higher wisdom can descend to a lower world are themselves stages in an interpretive process developing since the descent of Athena to Achilles, and more immediately, in the exegetical ambivalences of Origen, Augustine, Macrobius, and others. But even in Fulgentius' rather disordered treatment of Aeneas' mysterious initiation, this central episode of conversion is beginning to consolidate the three broad issues of text, depth, and time which we have been exploring throughout this period. If the poetic text does not have the full integrity of Scripture, it nonetheless progresses impressively from accident to substance. By descending darkly into the depths, Aeneas passes into a higher order of enlightenment. By manipulating the movement of time, the poet transforms the temporal sequence into a spiritual design. Fulgentius ends the allegory by referring to Fortune's wheel, that is, 'the rotation of time'

---

[72] On this change in the *Éneas*, see Singerman, 'Under Clouds of Poesy,' pp. 29–108; in Landino's commentary, see the introduction to *Commentary on the First Six Books of Virgil's* Aeneid *by Bernardus Silvestris*, tr. Earl G. Schreiber and Thomas E. Maresca (Lincoln, Nebr., 1979), pp. xxix–xxxii. On Landino, cf. Murrin, *Allegorical Epic*, pp. 27–50.

[73] On the Neoplatonic and early Christian allegorization of this book, see Courcelle, 'Interprétations néo-platonisantes du livre VI de l'*Enéide*,' cited in n. 41, above.

[74] See Édouard Jeauneau, 'L'Usage de la notion d'*integumentum* à travers les gloses de Guillaume de Conches,' *AHDLMA* 24 (1957), 42, and Schreiber and Maresca, pp. xxvi–xxix.

('temporis uolubilitatem,' 107. 4). In the end, it is by moving around the circumference that he approaches the center.

About the time that Fulgentius was closing his interpretive allegory with the concept of Fortune's wheel, Boethius was turning that wheel into the starting point for his own compositional design. The early sixth-century *Consolation of Philosophy*, though, is not just a compositional counterpart to the interpretive effort to give poetry its own conceptual order. By seeking to transform the conceptual order into poetry, and then to deploy this poetry to address problems of depth and time, Boethius' work is in some measure a culmination of all three major tendencies we have been considering during this period, a work that completes the cycle of allegorical transition from late antiquity to the Middle Ages.[75]

With the *Consolation of Philosophy*, the late ancient and early medieval pattern of ascent and descent at last becomes the systematic principle of organization on every level of the text. In plot the work portrays the story of a conversion, the consolation for a fall that becomes an education by ascent, an *anamnesis* in which the human mind returns to its divine origin.[76] In argumentation it presents lapses of worldly condition as continuities in a divine plan, by turning the wheel of fortune (II, pr. i, 19) into the circle of fate (IV, pr. vi, 17) with Providence at the center. Its images—a bent sapling reverting toward the sky, a sun gone down only to rise again (III, m. ii, 27–38) —integrate the personal progress of man with the cosmic process as a whole, while the old metaphor of the body as prison of the soul acquires new urgency with the plight of the narrator, whose physical imprisonment puts the doctrine of spiritual liberation to the extreme test.[77] Even the language of the work dramatizes the point-counterpoint of the action, as in the clos-

---

[75] For the text, see *Anicii Manlii Severini Boethii Philosophiae Consolatio*, ed. L. Bieler in *CCSL* 94 (Turnhout, 1957). My translations are based on *Boethius: The Theological Tractates. The Consolation of Philosophy*, ed. H. F. Stewart, E. K. Rand, and S. J. Tester, rev. edn. (Cambridge, Mass., 1973).

[76] See Courcelle, *Tradition*, p. 114, n. 5 and p. 162; Luigi Alfonsi, 'Storia interiore e storia cosmica nella "Consolatio" boeziana,' *Convivium*, 23 (1955), 513–22.

[77] On the images in III, m. ii, see Helga Scheible, *Die Gedichte in der Consolatio Philosophiae des Boethius* (Heidelberg, 1972), p. 82; on the prison, see Anna Crabbe, 'Literary Design in the *De Consolatione Philosophiae*,' in *Boethius: His Life, Thought and Influence*, ed. Margaret Gibson (Oxford, 1981), pp. 237, 241–2.

ing line of the opening poem—'Qui cecidit, stabili non erat ille gradu'—where a slip down ('cecidit') can become a step up ('gradu') only if a man keeps his center of balance ('stabili')—or in the appeal to God to elevate the mind in the great hymn of Book III (m. ix, 22), itself a turning point in the composition and the center of interpretive attention in the later Middle Ages.[78] Despite considerable differences in philosophic orientation and artistic method between Boethius' advance and the imaginative journeys fashioned by Martianus Capella and Virgil, it is revealing that a twelfth-century commentary attributed to Bernard Silvestris treats this ascent as one stage in a continuous literary movement: 'Martianus, then, imitates Vergil, and Boethius Martianus.'[79]

In terms of allegorical activity, Boethius' work is in one sense far more restricted than the introductory account of Martianus, with its animated comings and goings. The brief dramatic maneuvers at the beginning of the *Consolation*, like the imposing entrance of Philosophy or the transformation of the 'Muses' from an allusion in the preliminary poem into an embodied troupe of downcast figures (I, m. i, 3; I, pr. i), broadly pass into the sustained dialogue that dominates most of the work. In a deeper sense, however, one of Boethius' most important contributions is his manipulation of the dialogue format to develop and clarify the tensions latent in such maneuvers, so that the opening dualities become a kind of initiation into the design at large—and a repeating pattern for works to come.[80] At the beginning of the work, for example, the internally divided, self-conscious narrator who was appearing piecemeal in Martianus and Fulgentius finally acquires the systematic form he will display in later medieval allegory. True, 'chained' as he is, he understandably loses here some of the comic ironies which he possessed in those earlier works and which he will regain with renewed force in Alan of Lille's later imitation. (The *Consolation*

---

[78] On III, m. ix as the work's turning point, see Joachim Gruber, *Kommentar zu Boethius De Consolatione Philosophiae* (Berlin, 1978), pp. 230–2. On the medieval interpretation of the poem, see Courcelle, 'Étude critique sur les Commentaires de Boèce (ixe-xve siècles),' *AHDLMA* 40 (1939), 5–140; *Tradition*, pp. 241–333; Brinkmann, pp. 318–47.

[79] See the quotation and discussion in Wetherbee, pp. 124–5.

[80] On the development of 'seminal images' such as Boethius' Muses into structural principles, see Piehler, *Visionary Landscape*, cited above in Ch. I, n. 6, pp. 21–68.

of Philosophy is not without humor, but to alter slightly
Johnson's judgment on *Paradise Lost*, no one ever wished it
graver.) Again, he is less a dreamer than a swooner, although
even a swoon has its visionary possibilities.[81] But the crucial
development in the treatment of this figure is that Boethius
clearly opens up a certain distance between the narrator's current condition and his 'true' self. 'He has for a little forgotten
himself' ('Sui paulisper oblitus est,' I, pr. ii, 6), comments
Philosophy at the start, as if to suggest the need for Platonic
reminiscence and personal reintegration. Because of this internal disparity, a genuine dialogue between two 'sides' of the
man can develop, a dialogue that escaped Homer's Achilles.[82]
The allegorical expression of this self-division is the narrator's
divided allegiance between two abstract figures, a schematic
format now beginning to develop in sustained, dramatic form:
'Fortuna,' on the one hand, the two-faced ('ambiguos
uultus'), fickle 'mistress' (II, pr. i, 11 and 18; cf. pr. ii, 6) to
whom he has disastrously given his loyalty,[83] and 'Philosophia,' on the other, the figure of integrity, who recalls
him to the love of wisdom. Finally, the 'I' of the narrative is
differentiated not only psychologically and conceptually, but
imaginatively, according to his abstract possibilities, slipping
into an elegiac mode (I, m. i) by his experience with misfortune, uplifted into dialogue by his encounter with reason.

Boethius' sensitivity to the allegorical nuances of the narrator gives a new sophistication to the abstract characters
themselves. What a philosophic and literary distance separates
that original descent of Athena from the descent of Philosophy!
The one had pulled Achilles around literally by the hair; the
other, philosophically deepened by the Neoplatonic exegesis of
this Homeric episode, turns the man about not physically, but
metaphysically, by a Platonic process of recollection.[84] The
one, for all her otherworldly radiance, was 'straightway'

[81] On the narrator's 'lethargum' (I, pr. ii, 5), see Dronke, 'Boethius, Alanus and
Dante,' *Romanische forschungen*, 78 (1966), 119–25, but cf. the plays on *somnium* and vision, e.g., III, pr. i, 5 and pr. iii, 1.

[82] On the *Consolation* as an 'autoconsolation,' see Alfonsi, 'Storia,' 515.

[83] On the association between Fortune and Love, see Howard O. Patch, *The
Goddess Fortuna in Mediaeval Literature* (1927; repr. London, 1967).

[84] See Volker Schmidt-Kohl, *Die Neuplatonische Seelenlehre in der Consolatio Philosophiae
des Boethius* (Meisenheim am Glan, 1965), pp. 1–3.

known by Achilles—'confessa deam,' as it were. The other, though explicitly emblematic in her garment marked with steps between Π (practical philosophy) and Θ (theoretical philosophy), remains conceptually obscure (II, pr. ii and m. iii) until she gives understanding to the narrator, as if she could act only by activating him. Above all, the one no sooner appeared than disappeared, a momentary visitant; the other stays to conduct an argument, explicating her mysteries as the dialogue advances. In effect, Boethius enhances the allegorical composition of his figure by the very process of interpretive elaboration. As in the case of earlier developments, the immediate issue here is not the degree to which the author deliberately revises a previous strategy, but rather the process by which allegory itself changes under the pressure of different conceptual and imaginative programs. However austere Boethius' conception, it displays a way of adjusting to the old problem of personification, giving dramatic flexibility to an abstraction without undermining its logical consistency. 'Philosophia' is neither so protean a revelation as to become a kind of shapeshifter, like 'Nous' in the Hermetic *Poimandres*, nor so restricted a concept as to remain an abstract counter, like 'Ratio' in Augustine's *Soliloquies*.[85] As a dynamic abstraction, she is closer to the 'Continentia' who beckons Augustine to cross the barrier in the *Confessions*, but her dialectical power enables her more than any philosophic or literary 'source' to shape the very movement of a whole book.[86]

Nothing more strikingly demonstrates her structural authority than her relationship to her abstract counterpart, Fortune. The remarkable fact about Boethius' Fortune is that she never utters a word *in propria persona*. Strategically removed from center stage (except, fittingly, in the early poetic interludes of the work), she speaks only through Philosophy herself, who 'personifies' her in the classical sense of *prosopopoeia*,

---

[85] For *Poimandres*, see chs. 1–12 of the edition in *Corpvs Hermeticvm*, ed. A. D. Nock and A.-J. Festugière, I (Paris, 1945); cf. Courcelle, *Tradition*, pp. 18–20, who cites the work to exemplify the 'revelation' genre upon which Boethius draws. For the *Soliloquia*, see Edmund T. Silk, 'Boethius's Consolatio Philosophiae as a Sequel to Augustine's Dialogues and Soliloquia,' *Harvard Theological Review*, 32 (1939), 19–39.

[86] On *Continentia*, see Crabbe, 'Literary Design,' pp. 254–5, 261; on other sources, see Courcelle, *Tradition*, pp. 35–7.

by composing a speech for the character.[87] The technical maneuver here has been noted before, but its full implications, I think, have yet to be explained.[88] Long before Boethius, of course, the Cynics and Stoics had shown how philosophic discourse could exploit rhetorical flourishes such as *prosopopoeia*.[89] But Boethius makes the personification of Philosophy itself fashion the *prosōpon* for another personification—the very personification, in fact, who is her abstract adversary. Such a 'bracketing' of one figure by another tends to subordinate Fortune logically, as well as rhetorically, to Philosophy. But this ingenious philosophic strategy is itself accomplished only by means of a rhetorical amplification. In short, Philosophy's daringly literary gesture here is the very guarantee of her conceptual control.

It is true that at this point the maneuver remains largely a rhetorical device. The narrator himself complains that the arguments in this *prosopopoeia* are 'covered with the honeyed sweetness of rhetoric and music' ('oblitaque rhetoricae ac musicae melle dulcedinis'), and Philosophy grants that the speech (like her initial poetic ventures) is only a provisional passage toward the truth (II, pr. iii, 1–4). She will fully assimilate her rival only by the end of the work, in her more abstract formulation about the circle of fate and its divine centering point. But Boethius' impressive allegorical achievement in this early passage is to 'layer' the characters of his text in order to differentiate the levels of his cosmos. If Fulgentius had made a poet speak philosophically in order to show that literature has its own logical force, Boethius makes Philosophy speak poetically in order to show that logic has its own literary expression.

The effort here to give philosophy a poetic dimension is part of a broader dialectic between *sapientia* and *eloquentia* that organizes the whole format of the *Consolation*. Already in the opening verses (I, m. i, 1–2), the narrator distinguishes be-

---

[87] See II, pr. ii and pr. iii, 1; on *prosopopoeia*, see App. II.

[88] F. Klingner, for example, in *De Boethii Consolatione Philosophiae* (Berlin, 1921), pp. 14–15, and Courcelle, *Tradition*, pp. 105–6, 115, note the use of *prosopopoeia*; Dronke, 'L'amor,' 404, and Wetherbee, p. 77, point out in more general terms that in the *Consolation* Philosophy 'superimposes' its vision on that of Fortune, on which see my discussion below.

[89] See Klingner, pp. 12–17; cf. Barber, cited above in Ch. II, n. 43.

tween the kind of poetry that renews the spirit, on the one hand, and the elegiac mode ('maestos modos') of his current, tearful condition ('flebilis'), on the other. In the following prose section, Philosophy allegorically dramatizes the distinction by substituting her own invigorating Muses for the enervating Muses of elegy. In the rest of the work, she in effect internalizes this dialectic by alternating between sections of intellectual argumentation and passages of lyric expression.[90] Here the *prosimetrum* format of Martianus Capella develops a systematic rationale, a kind of compositional and interpretive rhythm, as Philosophy seeks to implicate the conceptual order in the enigmatic language of human experience, and then to explicate that language in turn into higher conceptual levels. As in the case of her rivalry with Fortune, Philosophy aims not to exclude the world of imagination, but to assimilate and transform it.

Despite Boethius' impressive advances in this respect, the effort remains problematic. While Philosophy distinguishes her Muses from the Muses of passionate experience ('affectuum,' I, pr. i, 9),[91] she also concedes that her own poetry is an accommodation to such passions (e.g., I, pr. v, 11–12). As a result, a kind of poetic ground bass resonates insistently during her orchestration of the conceptual ascent. It is not only that the imaginative episodes repeatedly dramatize the sway of the emotions Philosophy seeks to order, but that the images themselves seem imperfectly translatable into philosophic terms. Thus, when Philosophy closes the central book with the 'fabula' (III, m. xii, 52) of Orpheus and Eurydice, it seems almost as if not only the singer in the tale, but the teller of it, is having difficulty turning a descent into an ascent. It is true that Orpheus converts even the ruler of the shades to his designs, but his singing is initially associated with those very 'flebilibus modis' (m. xii, 7) condemned at the start of the *Consolation*, and indeed he makes his way through hell with the poetry of passion (m. xii, 20–8).[92] At the same time, Eurydice (the very object of Orpheus' search) is problematically conflated with the infernal

---

[90] On the distinction between the opening elegy and the later poems, see Scheible, *Gedichte*, pp. 8–11; Gruber, *Kommentar*, p. 24; on the dialectic as a whole, see Wetherbee, pp. 77–82.

[91] On *affectus* vs. *ratio* in the *Consolation*, see, e.g., Scheible, *Gedichte*, pp. 8–9, 29; Gruber, *Kommentar*, pp. 87, 92.

[92] See Crabbe, 'Literary Design,' pp. 270–1, n. 93.

realm ('inferos,' m. xii, 58) from which Orpheus seeks to release her, in order that the episode may reflect the narrator's own opening mistake of looking backward rather than upward.[93] Such ambiguity about whether these characters exemplify good or evil is largely avoided by Fulgentius, whose interpretation prepares the way for allegorizing Orpheus as the *eloquentia* that needs the *sapientia* of Eurydice (*Mythologies* III, 10). But for centuries after Boethius and Fulgentius (and earlier tellers of the tale), mythographers such as Remigius of Auxerre, Arnulf of Orléans, Giovanni del Virgilio, and others are sorting out the difficulties caused by making a figure of poetry simultaneously a figure of reason, while leaving Eurydice, as it were, in limbo.[94] Revealingly, they themselves oscillate between condemning Orpheus as a falling sinner and championing him as an inspiring saint. Their fluctuations in a sense reflect Boethius' early compositional and interpretive dilemma, the problem of reconciling the spirit of poetry with the strictures of reason, and thereby drawing a lower order into a higher one.

In the *Consolation*, then, the problem of redeeming the imaginative world exposes the difficulty of salvaging the earthly one. This dilemma finally qualifies the literary and conceptual progression of the allegory as a whole. For the ascent of the narrator depends upon the possibility of making worldly diversions the very means of spiritual conversion, and this question seems to divide the author himself. At one point, the goods of this world are 'false' ('falsa bona,' III, m. i, 11), opposite to the truth; at another point, they are approximations to the truth, 'images of the true good' ('imagines ueri boni,' III, pr. ix, 30). The question is precisely how such falsehoods turn into figures of fact.

Now Boethius' basic strategy of transition is clear. As Philosophy announces at the start of the transitional book, she

[93] Cf. Edward Kennard Rand's protest in *Founders of the Middle Ages* (1928; repr. New York, 1957), p. 320, n. 65: 'But Orpheus was looking back at Eurydice, not at Hell.' On Boethius' orientation here, see Scheible, *Gedichte*, pp. 121–5.

[94] See John Block Friedman, *Orpheus in the Middle Ages* (Cambridge, Mass., 1970), pp. 86–145, esp. pp. 98–102, 109, 119–20, 122–3, 126–31. With respect to Remigius, the passage quoted here (pp. 98–9) to exhibit an interpretation by this ninth–tenth century writer actually comes from a twelfth-century Boethius commentary. Nonetheless, Remigius' actual commentary does raise the basic problem; see my discussion below in Ch. V, with n. 2.

will first show what happiness is *not* in order to direct attention to what it *is*, shifting from one side of the subject to its 'contrary' ('contrariam partem,' III, pr. i, 7). This shift from 'negative' to 'positive' argumentation, in fact, marks the structural turning point of the *Consolation*, as Philosophy repeatedly stresses (III, pr. ix, 1, 24, 31). The strategy itself is promising; the principle of turning from one side of a subject to its counterpart is central to the later development of allegory.[95] But for the strategy fully to succeed, it is necessary to elucidate a principle of transition between the two extremes, and here that principle never clearly develops. Instead, Boethius tends to oscillate between a world-renouncing and a world-redeeming perspective.[96] On the one hand, the things of this world are but slippages toward the void, 'proceeding from whole and absolute origins, lapsing into this last, exhausted condition' (III, pr. x, 5). On the other hand, such things are really passages toward the good; 'scarcely good when divided, they yet become good when they begin to be one' (III, pr. xi, 7). Between these two perspectives lies the elusive Platonic question of a defective world somehow 'participating' in a perfect one, and the more recent Neoplatonic problem of a cosmic procession 'reverting' to its source. But the problem has an allegorical dimension, as well, the question of transforming the dualities of imagination and the disparities of Fortune into the truth and integrity of Philosophy.

Nothing more strikingly displays the dilemma than the way in which the critique of the apparent 'goods' of this world passes in the following book into an exposé of moral evil, itself based on a 'slippage' from being ('esse . . . derelinquit,' IV, pr. ii, 36). The conclusion, that the power of doing evil 'derives not from strength, but from weakness' ('haec eorum potentia non a uiribus sed ab imbecillitate descendit,' IV, pr. ii, 37), is not itself surprising—already for Antony the apparent 'power' of evil daemons actually exposes their 'powerlessness,' and the basic strategy goes back to Plato's *Gorgias*—but the polemical resemblance between this 'negative realm' of evil and the 'counterpoint' world of Fortune tends to weaken the 'positive'

---

[95] See my article, 'From the *Cosmographia* to the *Divine Comedy*: An Allegorical Dilemma,' in *Allegory, Myth, and Symbol*, ed. Morton W. Bloomfield, Harvard English Studies, 9 (Cambridge, Mass., 1981), pp. 63–86.

[96] See the important discussion in Courcelle, *Tradition*, pp. 170–6, 221–31.

sense in which this world mirrors the otherworld. When the narrator protests that even worldly fortune must reflect a higher order in some way, and Philosophy responds with her famous 'Hydra-headed' argument (IV, pr. vi, 3) about the temporal progression as a circle turning about an eternal centering point and the disparity between the human and divine orders of perception, the resolution of the allegory seems to recede increasingly into the distance. By the end of the *Consolation*, Philosophy uncompromisingly links the imaginative dilemma with the philosophic one, by arguing that just as imagination is transcended by reason, so is reason transcended by divine intelligence, and it is only such intelligence—which reason, like imagination, fails to comprehend—that truly exposes the 'chains' of necessity as the constituents of freedom (V, pr. v and pr. vi).

The fact that the narrator does not respond after Philosophy's last discourse may suggest that he is transported to these rarefied altitudes,[97] but perhaps his silence is equally eloquent testimony to the difficulty of enacting—not only willing—the ascent. Later in the Middle Ages, when Thomas Usk adapts the *Consolation of Philosophy* into the *Testament of Love*, he seeks to resolve the problem by finally internalizing the otherworldly figure itself, as the allegorical 'Love' with whom the narrator has been discoursing suddenly leaps into his heart at the end of the work.[98] By Usk's period, of course, the very notion of conceptualization and mediation has undergone radical changes. But Boethius' relentlessly logical approach, which tends less toward principles of mediation than absolutes, qualifies not only the narrator's progress, but also the allegorical possibilities of the physical world and the literary text itself. When Philosophy seeks to show how Providence unfolds into fate, she seems singularly uninterested in speculating about the cosmological intermediaries (IV, pr. vi, 13) which will play such a large role in the later development of allegory; she is preoccupied with the logical issue. And for all her rhetorical maneuvers, she never directly acts out the story of ascent with other abstractions; instead, she conducts her

[97] Cf. C. S. Lewis, *The Discarded Image* (Cambridge, 1964), p. 90.

[98] See the edition of Walter W. Skeat in *Chaucerian and Other Pieces*, the *Supplement* to *The Complete Works of Geoffrey Chaucer* (Oxford, 1897), p. 137.

own peerless, intellectual argument. Only her rivalry with Fortune—a rivalry conducted, as it were, in *oratio obliqua*—suggests the possibility of an allegorical plot, and that plot scarcely develops before it ends. The *Consolation of Philosophy* presents an abstract drama; it is later allegory that produces a drama of abstractions.

Still, Boethius' last work remains an impressive effort to bring the pure order of logic into the variegated experience of life,[99] and it thus marks the most cogent (if austere) stage so far in the development of personification allegory, which from the start attempts to elaborate a concept into a story. In the process, the *Consolation* brings the late antique and early medieval tendencies we have been exploring not only to a logical conclusion, but to a literary one—maneuvering an abstraction rhetorically in order to dramatize the hierarchy of the world and thereby to center the movement of time. If Boethius' logical version of man's ascent to the stars still needs a more expansive cosmic and imaginative design before it can pass into full-fledged medieval allegory, it nonetheless at least suggests that prospect itself. Over the course of its argument, it translates a personal dilemma of misfortune into the universal question of mutability. As if to anticipate that upward movement of perspective, in the primal episode of descent that opens the book, Philosophy herself seems to stretch expansively between earth and heaven, now confining herself to the ordinary measure of man, now striking heaven itself with her head ('pulsare caelum summi uerticis cacumine,' I, pr. i, 2). Such an expansive vision has appeared before. Applied to Homer's 'Strife,' it signified the terrifying distention of social conflict. Adapted to Virgil's 'Fama,' it suggested the threatening breakdown of linguistic norms. Finally, transformed into Boethius' 'Philosophy,' it implies the cosmic dialectic of aspiring man. To that cosmic vision and its complications, the allegorical tradition—and our own study—now turn.

[99] See Alfonsi, 'Storia,' 514.

IV AGES OF RENEWAL:
THE EARLY MEDIEVAL
PERIOD

She is offspring to herself, her own sire, her own suc-
cessor. (Lactantius, *The Phoenix*, l. 167.)

GOD'S BOOKS AND
BEDE'S TROPES

If the transitional period between antiquity and the Middle
Ages passes on to later allegory the possibility of a broad,
allusive framework, it also underlines the dilemma of allegory's
own internal consistency. On the one hand, the rich interpretive
and compositional interplay from Macrobius and Martianus to
Fulgentius and Boethius produces a kind of critical/poetic index for transferring imaginative figures into cosmic or psychic
principles and, conversely, for exhibiting those principles in
imaginative form. Dramatized by the very content of such
writing, in which characters are themselves in states of transition from one dimension to another, this coordinating process
will intensify in the mythographic and visionary work of the
early Middle Ages, finally turning figures such as Vulcan and
Venus or Orpheus and Aeneas into complex reference points for
the problems of cosmic harmony or individual vision.[1] On the
other hand, as the allegorical writing of the formative period
itself suggests, the effort to reconcile philosophic systems with
imaginative designs produces interior tensions which expose
the need to clarify the very nature of the world underlying them
both. Insofar as allegory explicitly engages the dimensions and
nuances of that world, the allegorical study of causes turns with
increasing intensity into the study of the 'natures' of things.

The developing orientation toward *natura rerum*, of course,
involves a host of changes in conceptual and literary perspec-

---

[1] See Wetherbee, pp. 90-141; Demats, *Fabula*, cited above in Ch. III, n. 65;
Dronke, *Fabula*, pp. 13-78, 100-18; Brinkmann, pp. 169-206, 292-317; and my
remarks below in Chs. V and VI.

tive far beyond the allegorical tradition itself. In this and the following chapters, it is possible to touch on only a few of its allegorical aspects, with special attention to two important periods of regeneration in the Middle Ages: the 'Carolingian revival' of the late eighth and ninth centuries, and the celebrated 'renaissance' of the late eleventh and early twelfth centuries. As in other ages of renewal, the leading writers of these periods are oriented at once toward an old order and a new one, and the allegorical 'nature' they reveal reflects this problematic condition. To appreciate some of their efforts to integrate that 'nature'—and their own—it is necessary to turn both backward and forward with them, to consider certain sources of their energy, as well as the products of their own activity.

From its earliest forms, the allegorical tradition displayed at least potentially the dilemmas involved in developing an allegory of nature. Interpretive allegory originated with the effort to elucidate physical principles, although from the pre-Socratics to the Stoics, such exegesis tended to collapse *mythos* into *physis*, and thus to undermine the possibility of sustained allegorization. Compositional allegory, on the other hand, gradually delineated the principles of nature in order to display the soul's ascent, but as Martianus' work suggested, such personifications tended to slip out of analytic control into the vivid but volatile reaches of the imagination. Perhaps nothing more strikingly displays the difference between such early strategies and the later allegory of nature than the figure of Nature herself who fully develops by the central Middle Ages. The celebrated 'Natura' of the twelfth century is neither so nearly absolute a principle as the scientific *physis* of Stoic philosophy or the quasi-mystical cosmic goddess of Orphic writing, nor so sheerly imaginative a flourish as the brief abstraction at the beginning of Ovid's *Metamorphoses* or the picturesque presence in Claudian's poetry.[2] Rather, she emerges from these and other traditions to become a figure of both substantive depth and artistic range. In the *Cosmographia* and the *Complaint of Nature*, she finally

---

[2] On these and other early versions of 'Natura,' see Karl Kerényi, 'Die Göttin Natur,' *Eranos-Jahrbuch*, 14 (1946), 39–86; Curtius, *European Literature*, pp. 106–8; George D. Economou, *The Goddess Natura in Medieval Literature* (Cambridge, Mass., 1972), pp. 1–52.

becomes a full-fledged 'character,' mediating between different dimensions of the cosmos, the allegorical center for both the interpretation and the composition of the natural world.[3]

The developing early medieval concentration on *natura rerum*, in fact, gradually qualifies the basic distinction between allegorical interpretation and composition itself. Insofar as the 'nature' of the world, rather than a written text, becomes the object of philosophic investigation, while at the same time becoming the center of imaginative attention, the abstract categories of discourse potentially become at once both analytic and literary concepts.[4] 'Nature' itself—a category designed to explicate the world that can also be deployed to participate in a plot—is a case in point. This coalescence produces considerable tensions of its own: the precise degree to which such figures are rational or poetic in character; scientific or mystical in orientation; inherent in the world or imposed by man; illuminating, even transparent signs or dark, even diversionary symbols; akin to the truth or incongruous with it. Something of the pressures produced by this process can be seen from the fact that these apparent dualities themselves do not always parallel each other, but repeatedly appropriate terms from one 'side' of the opposition to another.[5] Indeed, by the twelfth century, no sooner is a broad reconciliation achieved than it is challenged; by the later Middle Ages, the challenge is so acute as to generate irresistible pressures on allegorical writing to shift toward a more 'naturalistic' mode of expression—the logical conclusion of allegory's tendency to be at odds with itself. Such intricate, later configurations, however, depend upon earlier, more general developments, the gradual conversion of the world itself into a realm of figurative reference.

Finally, these developments, which pose difficult questions about the 'meaning' of the natural world, deeply qualify the old critical distinction between a 'sacramental' or 'symbolic' procedure, on the one hand, and an 'allegorical' one, on the

[3] See the works of Gregory cited above in Ch. II, n. 34; Chenu, pp. 1-48; and my discussion below.

[4] Aspects of this process are suggested by Krewitt, pp. 468-9, and Brian Stock, *The Implications of Literacy: Written Language and Models of Interpretation in the Eleventh and Twelfth Centuries* (Princeton, 1983), hereafter *Literacy*, esp. pp. 241-325.

[5] See the important discussions of Chenu, pp. 99-145, and Wetherbee, pp. 11-73.

other[6]—a distinction that is at once too broad and too narrow. It is too broad in that the loose association between the 'sacramental' and 'symbolic' approaches tends to overlook the fact that these procedures may imply quite different values and operations for the figures of the natural world.[7] It is too narrow in that a strict separation between the 'sacramental' or 'symbolic' mode as a whole and the 'allegorical' mode in general seems to depend upon a problematic division between 'natural' and 'psychological' dramatization that overlooks the central principles shared by both strategies. It is true that the sacramental process of turning categories of the outer world (rather than categories of the inner one) into 'figures' of the truth complicates the question of signification, as we shall see, but as a technique of writing, it suggests less a shift from the broad strategy of allegory than a change in perspective. As Bernard Silvestris shows, it is no less possible to personify the powers of God than it is to personify the forces of the soul; the figurative movement remains, even while the center of causality changes. To suggest that those who make the natural world an image of the divine world are writing 'sacramentally,' 'symbolically,' or 'Platonically,' but not 'allegorically,' is not only to miss the broadening of allegory from psychic to cosmic forces since the late antique period, but to exclude from the allegorical tradition some of its most celebrated—indeed, some of its defining—representatives, including Bernard Silvestris and Alan of Lille themselves. Nor are these the only reasons for the limits of the distinction; both philosophic and linguistic principles are at stake.[8]

[6] Cf. Lewis, pp. 44-8, arguing that 'sacramentalism or symbolism,' first effectively appearing in Europe 'with the dialogues of Plato,' is 'almost the opposite of allegory.'

[7] For some distinctions between 'sacrament' and 'symbol,' see Chenu, pp. 124-41. Shifts in terminology—ancient, medieval, and modern—further complicate the issue; see, e.g., Jean Pépin, '*Mysteria* et *Symbola* dans le commentaire de Jean Scot sur l'évangile de Saint Jean,' in *The Mind of Eriugena*, ed. John J. O'Meara and Ludwig Bieler (Dublin, 1973), pp. 16-30.

[8] For some philosophic considerations, see, e.g., Jauss, 'Form,' pp. 179-91, 'Transformation,' pp. 108-18, 'Entstehung,' pp. 146-51, and A. D. Nuttall, *Two Concepts of Allegory* (New York, 1967); for some linguistic issues, see, e.g., Bertrand H. Bronson, 'Personification Reconsidered,' *English Literary History*, 14 (1947), 163-77, and Bloomfield, 'A Grammatical Approach to Personification Allegory,' cited above in Ch. I, n. 2. With respect to the sacrament of the Eucharist itself, factually 'composed' by God, there are revealing efforts in the early medieval period to make a kind of *interpretive* allegory coordinate with its composition; see Stock, *Literacy*, pp. 259-60.

In the broadest sense, the distinction between an 'allegorical' mode and a 'sacramental' or 'symbolic' one is intellectually
related to (although historically and operationally different
from) the aesthetic contrast between 'abstract' allegory and
'concrete' symbol popularized by the Romantics and still frequently repeated in various forms. Both claims, in effect, tend
to oppose 'conceptual' language to a more 'mystical' communication between the material and spiritual worlds, an opposition
that allegory itself, in fact, tends to mediate by its increasingly sophisticated strategy of implicating concepts in both
realms—to say nothing of other problems of definition and
theory in such claims.[9] The crucial distinction concerns not the
theoretical compatibility of Platonism with allegory but the
stimulating controversies over different versions of Platonism
which actually promote the allegory of nature itself.[10] In any
case, for all its debts to that *auctor* whose own work oscillates between philosophy and poetry, medieval civilization does not
quite consist of a series of footnotes to Plato. In at least certain
respects, it gradually writes a book of its own—at once a work
of exegesis and composition—founded upon sources originat-
ing with a higher authority.

Even the earliest traditions of systematic biblical interpretation
suggested the possibility of turning the exegesis of Scripture into
the allegory of nature. The belief that God authored not one
book, but two—the Bible and the world—implied that the
elucidation of the one complemented the understanding of the
other. Scripture itself, envisioning the heavens as a 'book' (Isa.
34: 4, Apocalypse 6: 14), had suggested the association between the two divine 'texts.' Philo, applying the philosophic
study of causes to the exegetical study of God's Word, had
argued that the 'Laws' of both nature and Scripture were central to the search for wisdom. Augustine, speaking of one book
'seen' and another 'heard,' gave the parallel an influential,

[9] See my remarks in Ch. III and App. I; my discussion of mature twelfth-century
allegory in Ch. VI; and, among many recent reassessments, the works by Honig,
Fletcher, Tuve, and Barney cited above in Ch. I, nn. 2, 4.

[10] See Chenu, pp. 49–145, though at times (e.g., pp. 35, 117, 131, 141–5) he too
slips into a 'symbol' / 'allegory' dichotomy (based in part on a limited association of
the literary procedure with a particular kind of exegesis) that his own analysis qualifies
and that more recent work supersedes.

discriminating formulation. Exegetes of the early Middle Ages increasingly transform the formula into a complex, continuous argument about the relative values of each revelation.[11] Indeed, already for Augustine the very dynamics of the divine text irresistibly drive exegesis toward the investigation of the world. A work of words that is also a revelation of events requires, as Augustine puts it, not only a knowledge of language, but a 'knowledge of things' (*DDC* II, 16). However constrained the late antique and early medieval analysis of the natural world, this basic impulse deeply transfigures early Christian exegesis, which keeps slipping away from the meaning of the text into the nature of the world at large.

There is a deeper tension, though, underlying this process, an exegetical counterpart to the broader dilemma of assessing the relative claims of a textual and an historical revelation. From the time that Paul applied the rhetorical term *allēgoria* to the typological relation between the two Covenants (Gal. 4: 24) and thus to two dispensations in history, the Bible problematically confronted Christian exegetes with different kinds of 'meaning.'[12] On the one hand, according to the traditional formula, the words of the text 'signify' facts; on the other, the facts themselves 'signify' other things in turn. Augustine, we have seen, articulated the contrast by distinguishing between 'allegoria in uerbis' and 'allegoria in facto.' Such neat formulas, unfortunately, begged the very question they sought to answer. It might be plausible enough to speak of words 'meaning' things, but it is less clear precisely how things themselves 'mean' other things. That is, the precise relation between language and being, between rhetorical and ontological 'signification,' remains unclear. The problem is especially acute when both kinds of signification are 'allegorical'—involving, that is, a shift in perspective from a provisional point of reference to a final one. It might be argued, of course, that such problems of signification are all part of God's mysterious

[11] For an overview, see Curtius, *European Literature*, ch. 16, 'The Book as Symbol,' esp. pp. 310–32; for Philo, see Nikiprowetzky, *Commentaire*, cited above in Ch. III, n. 5, pp. 6, 117–55; for Augustine, see Gregory, 'L'idea,' p. 27; for later exegetical attitudes toward the two 'books,' see de Lubac, I, i, 119–28, and my discussion below.

[12] See Hartmut Freytag, '*Quae sunt per allegoriam dicta*: Das theologische Verständnis der Allegorie in der frühchristlichen und mittelalterlichen Exegese von Galater 4, 21–31,' in *Verbum et Signum*, Vol. I, pp. 27–43; cf. Pépin, pp. 487–501.

design—they have provided innumerable opportunities for modern semiologists—but mystery is what interpretation seeks to clarify. In effect, Augustine and other early Christian exegetes were interpreting a text that 'turned' on two levels at once—the metaphorical level of words and the historical level of events. It seems almost a commentary on Augustine's own unresolved tensions between his early, secular, rhetorical training and his later, Christian, philosophic commitment that in all his works, he never clearly elucidates how these two different processes of simultaneous transfer—one linguistic, the other extra-linguistic—relate to each other. [13]

These complexities contribute to the increasing tendency in early medieval exegesis to treat metaphorical tropes as if they were metaphysical turns. By approaching the words of the divine text almost as if they were things in their own right, such exegetes tend to undermine the very distinction between allegory *in uerbis* and allegory *in facto* upon which they claim to base their exegesis. The tendency develops momentum in the first systematic effort since *On Christian Doctrine* to ally the rhetorical tradition with the exegetical one, Bede's *On Figures and Tropes*, composed at the beginning of the eighth century. [14] Determined to prove the Bible's literary (not only religious) superiority to other works (II, i), Bede argues here that the four meanings of Scripture—which had once been reserved for the actual facts of God's dispensation, *allegoria in facto*—can be signified not only by the things ('factis') to which Scripture refers, but by the words ('uerbis') themselves (II, ii, 12). [15] Citing both kinds of 'signification' for each of the four senses, he notes, for example, that 'tropological' perfection is signified by the 'allegoria facti' of Joseph's coat of many colors (Gen. 37: 3)—that is, explains Bede, the 'beauty of the many virtues' with which God has 'clothed' us—while the 'same' perfection is signified by the 'allegoria uerbi' of Christ's phrase about 'girded loins' and 'burning lamps' (Luke 12: 35).

[13] See Armand Strubel, ' "Allegoria in factis" et "allegoria in verbis," ' *Poétique*, 23 (1975), 342-7; cf. Krewitt, pp. 122-3.

[14] Citations refer to the edition of *De Schematibvs et Tropis* (with *De Arte Metrica*) by C. B. Kendall in *Bedae Venerabilis Opera, Pars I, Opera Didascalia*, CCSL 123A (Turnhout, 1975). The work is translated by Gussie Hecht Tanenhaus, 'Bede's *De Schematibus et Tropis*—A Translation,' *Quarterly Journal of Speech*, 48 (1962), 237-53.

[15] See Krewitt, pp. 164-7; Strubel, 'Allegoria,' 347-53.

The sentiment may be understandable, but it deeply complicates the old theory. In Bede's exegesis of Christ's phrase, the fundamental level of historical signification momentarily drops out; it is the words which signify—by metaphorical transfer—the tropological sense. This is not to say that the New Testament passage is not in fact using, as we should say, figurative language, but Bede simply juxtaposes such linguistic 'figuration' with the quite different historical figuration of events. As a result, the words begin to assume powers reserved by the theory for things.

Exegesis of this kind both promotes and limits the possibilities of allegorical writing. On the one hand, it gives rhetorical tropes like 'lamps' and 'loins' a rich, powerful resonance of their own, thereby enhancing the claims of imaginative language. On the other hand, it leaves the relation between rhetorical 'lamps' and actual ones so unclear as to call into question the precise status or identity of the actual items themselves. In such a world, figures of speech may be as 'significant' as facts, but by the same token, facts are thereby liable to be reduced to mere figures of speech.

Later in the Middle Ages, exegetes seek to discriminate more clearly between verbal and historical signification, by incorporating the figurative expressions of language *within* the literal sense of the *historia* itself, thus distinguishing such tropes from the turning of history that constitutes God's allegory *in facto*. This strategy, which gradually develops in the twelfth and thirteenth centuries, culminates in Aquinas' argument that the literal sense is not the trope itself (here, 'lamps' and 'loins'), but that which the trope signifies (here, the moral life)—a factual point of reference that participates in the continuum of such facts within God's allegory of events. Mere poetic fictions, Thomas scholastically concludes, end at the level of the historical sense—that is, the level of events where spiritual meaning actually begins.[16]

Such an analytic orientation to rhetoric, which develops unevenly within the scholastic tradition itself, severely constrains the spiritual resonance of imaginative language implied by Bede's treatise. Still, like every movement in the exegetical

---

[16] See the references to Spicq, Nemetz, and de Lubac in Ch. III, n. 29, above, and Strubel, 'Allegoria,' 353-7.

tradition, it no sooner undermines one kind of allegory than it generates another. By making imaginative tropes end where spiritual history begins, it in effect encourages compositional allegorists to develop strategies for giving their own poetry an *in facto*, scriptural dimension, a position that itself takes increasingly extreme (and finally desperately apocalyptic) forms—from Alan of Lille's claim to display the multiple senses of Scripture in his own imaginative work, the *Anticlaudianus* (*Prose Prologue*), which at its midpoint dramatically seeks to reverse the rhetoric of the 'poet' into the revelation of the 'prophet' (V, 268-9); to Dante's 'actual' movement through the other world, in which the imaginative displacement of one allegorical tableau by another becomes the substantive progression from potentiality to act; to Langland's constant disruption and regeneration of his plot by direct scriptural quotation, as if it were necessary for God himself to take over the tale.

Seen from this perspective, the extended controversies of recent years about whether or not such works deploy threefold or fourfold allegory seem at times not to engage the central issue. The crucial question is not how many or even which 'meanings' are theoretically discoverable in these texts; scriptural exegesis itself, even in the age of Bede, is practiced in this fashion only to a certain degree, with particular phrases and passages. The question is rather the more operational one of how the increasing need to write *in facto* urgently demands new strategies for a technique that arises from the very distinction between fiction and truth. In any case, such compositional efforts to move from turns on the level of language to turns on the level of being (a process partially anticipated even in Martianus and Boethius, but imaginatively flamboyant in the one, conceptually austere in the other) emerge later in the Middle Ages only as scholastic exegesis itself begins to organize rhetorical shifts into a continuous argument about historical change. Bede's treatise and the exegetical practice it reflects[17] suggest rather a relation so fluid between the transfers of language and nature that the integrity and continuity of each are constantly in danger.

By calling into question the very coherence of the natural world, such early medieval interpretations give exegetical ex-

---

[17] See Chenu, 'Deux âges,' cited above in Ch. III, n. 31, 25-7.

pression to broader tendencies of the age.[18] In the process, they transform the allegorical problem of the logic of language into the cosmological question of the propriety of things. Their allegorical limitations and possibilities appear most strikingly in the various early medieval encyclopedias, which seek to 'read' the book of nature as a whole. Already a century before Bede, Isidore of Seville had constructed his wide-ranging *Etymologies*, which applied the old exegetical technique of etymological explanation to the world at large, along with *On the Nature of Things*, which developed earlier allegorizations into a broad interpretation of natural phenomena.[19] It is not until a century after Bede, though, in the Carolingian age, that such allegorical techniques acquire their full, panoramic range— and with it, their most problematic designs.

RABAN MAUR'S SPRING; A CAROLINGIAN 'REVIVAL'

In the first part of the ninth century, one of the great figures of the Carolingian age, Raban Maur, expands the work of his predecessors into his own vast *On the Natures of Things*, a systematic interpretation of the world via scriptural authority.[20] Raban's work preeminently dramatizes the strain that exegetical strategies such as those of Augustine and Bede finally placed upon the interpretation of both Scripture and the natural world. In one sense, of course, nothing could seem easier for the theologian than to apply the rule of faith to both of God's books. Like Scripture, nature too teaches nothing but charity, nor condemns anything except cupidity. Accordingly we need fear nothing as we make our way through all this lore about rivers and landscapes, angels and flowers, beasts and men, for all of it will confirm the authority of God. On the other hand, we must

[18] See Gregory, 'L'idea,' pp. 27–34; Marc Bloch, *Feudal Society*, tr. L. A. Manyon (London, 1961), p. 83.

[19] See *Isidori Hispalensis Episcopi Etymologiarvm sive Originvm Libri XX*, ed. W. M. Lindsay, 2 vols. (Oxford, 1911), hereafter *Et.*, and *Isidore de Seville: Traité de la nature*, ed. and tr. Jacques Fontaine (Bordeaux, 1960), hereafter *Traité*.

[20] Citations refer to the edition in *PL* 111, which prints it under the title, *De Universo*. The work's earliest designation, however, was *De Rerum Naturis*; see Elisabeth Heyse, *Hrabanus Maurus' Enzyklopädie 'De rerum naturis': Untersuchungen zu den Quellen und zur Methode der Kompilation*, Münchener Beiträge zur Mediävistik und Renaissance-Forschung, 4 (Munich, 1969), hereafter *Enzyklopädie*, pp. 2–4.

be careful when we meet, say, a lion. Not because we are under attack—we are making our safari, after all, by turning the pages of Scripture, not by traipsing through the grasslands—but because, like Augustine's 'serpents,' the lion has opposite meanings. By his 'strength' ('per fortitudinem'), he typifies Christ, says Raban, quoting Apocalypse 5: 5: 'Behold the lion of the tribe of Juda.' By his 'strength and cruelty' ('ob fortitudinem et crudelitatem'), however, our guide adds, he signifies the Devil, as in Psalms 7: 3: 'Lest at any time he seize upon my soul like a lion.'[21] In such cases, the divergence displayed by Augustine's 'serpents,' interpreted *in bono* and *in malo*, has firmly established itself in the world as a whole. The problem, of course, is that Raban is isolating the general notion of 'lion' from various figurative expressions in Scripture, and then allegorizing lions themselves on this basis. It is only a short step from Bede's 'loins' which act like things to Raban's lions which act like tropes, and when a man takes it, the natural world, like the scriptural text, is always in danger of losing its coherence, of splitting apart even within a single word or object.

The dilemma affects Raban's analysis even when he turns to the most sustained, continuous motions of nature, the cycle of the seasons (*De Universo* X, 11; *PL* 111, 302–3). Beginning, as usual, with an etymological insight, Raban explains that the seasons are called 'curricula,' courses, because they flow ('currunt'). Then, he describes the cycle of natural growth throughout the year, starting with spring, which is called 'ver' because it is verdant ('quod viret'), and continuing through summer, autumn, and barren winter. In all of this, almost to the word, Raban has faithfully followed the account of the seasons in Isidore's *Etymologies* (*Et.* V, xxxv). At this point, however, Raban suddenly shifts into a higher register:

But mystically spring signifies the rejuvenation of baptism, or the renewal of life after the chill of infidelity and sluggish torpor; or the resurrection of the body after the slippage into death. Whence ('Unde') the Lord instructed in the Law that the ninth month should be observed, the beginning of spring, when the Lord led out the

---

[21] See *De Universo* VIII, 1; *PL* 111, 217D and 219A; cf. Augustine, *DDC* III, 25. For Raban's serpents (dual, but primarily diabolical), see VIII, 3; *PL* 111, 223–35. My translations from the Vulgate generally refer to the Douay-Rheims version, although in certain cases adjustments are made.

children of Israel from the land of Egypt across the Red Sea, and commanded that the Pasch should then be celebrated; in that time, also, the Savior after his Passion arose from death, and gave us the hope of resurrection. (*De Universo* X, 11; *PL* 111, 302D–303A)

Raban, of course, is not original in his interpretation of spring.[22] Even without the traditional Christian associations of the season, there is something of Raban's sense of rejuvenation in every spring. His interpretation is interesting for our subject rather because of its effect on the 'curricula,' the flowing course of nature, which he is claiming to describe. In attempting to give the underlying meaning of spring—that is, to interpret it allegorically—he ends by fragmenting the seasonal cycle of which it is a part. It is not that the other seasons lack such deeper meanings. On the contrary, each season has them: autumn, for example, is the 'time of universal judgment,' when each person harvests the fruits of his labors. It is rather that when we try to make these deeper levels correspond to the natural cycle, the pattern becomes rather confused.

Thus, it is all very well to argue that the spring of baptism leads eventually to the winter of death, which in turn gives rise to the eternal spring of resurrection. It is true that Raban's piecemeal presentation does not quite achieve even this clarification; but even if it did, what then becomes of the 'autumn of universal judgment,' which ought to be happening at the same time as the resurrection? Perhaps we could refine Raban's analysis still further, and argue that when the resurrection occurs, time stops. But then we would simply be conceding the point that our allegorical interpretation diverges radically from the seasonal pattern it was supposed to explain. The truth, of course, is that in Raban's *On the Natures of Things*, the deeper meanings of the 'courses of time,' the 'curricula,' correspond not really to time, but to the most timeless, abstract principles. In baptism, the return to fidelity, and resurrection, we have not the meaning of spring, but the meaning of revival in general, of which the natural season is only one more instance. Even sacred history is subject to these general principles, a fact

---

[22] For an overview of various allegories of the seasons, see Barbara Maurmann-Bronder, '*Tempora significant*: Zur Allegorese der vier Jahreszeiten,' hereafter 'Jahreszeiten,' in *Verbum et Signum*, Vol. I, pp. 69-101; on spring in particular, see pp. 75-9, 83-5, 91-3.

which perhaps accounts for that striking word 'Whence' ('Unde') to describe the placement of the Pasch and the Resurrection in springtime. It is as if these two events were linked less by a figural movement over time—the typological transition from an old redemption to a new one—than by a fixed relationship to the eternal principle of revival.

Raban's treatment of the seasons suggests the limitations of his work as a whole for a sustained allegory of nature. It is not that he does not see this world as an image of a higher (and a lower) realm. That broad strategy he shares with others who develop their own imaginative versions of the natural world, including the authors of those bestiaries, lapidaries, and herbals which increasingly proliferate in the centuries after his age[23] and which, when assimilated into more supple forms, make their own important contributions to later allegory, from the *Cosmographia* to *Pearl*. It is rather the way his imagery works. His encyclopedia reveals a world in which phenomena display their divine dimensions by splitting apart, in which historical sequence seems more a series of suspended moments than a continuous development, in which the very contingency that distinguishes an autonomous structure at times seems in doubt.

Still, for all these limitations, *On the Natures of Things* advances the possibilities of an allegory of the cosmos. However arbitrary its procedure, it marks an important stage in the effort to conceptualize the world, to give it a systematic rationale.[24] If Raban's account of the four seasons, for example, has its logical liabilities, it should be stressed that it nonetheless refines even less systematic earlier interpretations. These include not only the limited allegorical flourishes on one or two seasons in commentaries from the third to the eighth centuries by Origen, Augustine, Justus, Gregory, Bede, and others,[25] but also bolder attempts to explore the seasonal cycle itself. Already in

[23] See Brinkmann, pp. 93–121.

[24] See Friedrich Ohly, *Vom Geistigen Sinn des Wortes im Mittelalter* (orig. pub. 1958–9, repr. Darmstadt, 1966), pp. 15–17; on the fragmentation still affecting Raban's interpretive technique, see Heyse, *Enzyklopädie*, pp. 51–2.

[25] See Origen, *PG* 13, 183C–188B; Augustine, *PL* 36, 941 and *PL* 38, 216; Justus, *PL* 67, 971; Gregory, *PL* 75, 867A and *PL* 76, 499CD; Bede, *PL* 90, 517A. Some of these brief glosses (and others) are noted by Fontaine in *Traité* and Maurmann-Bronder in 'Jahreszeiten,' whose fine work has assisted my research on this issue, though neither of them really orders the problem chronologically or examines it from this perspective.

the fourth century, the Greek Father Gregory of Nyssa is evocatively elaborating the Song of Songs' vision of winter passing into spring, but his account concentrates on those two seasons and tends to be more connotative than strictly allegorical.[26] In the Latin tradition, the approach is more schematic, but by the same token, more disjunctive. Thus, earlier in the fourth century Lactantius briefly refers the seasons to the four points of the compass, associated in turn with the antithetical principles of life and death.[27] In the fifth century, Eucherius grants to each of three seasons—spring, summer, and winter—a short gloss and a scriptural allusion, but he omits autumn entirely from the account.[28] Two centuries later, in Isidore's *On the Nature of Things*, autumn still does not participate in the system, and the rest of the cycle remains unclear.[29] The spring of renewed faith seems in one sense to follow the winter of stormy tribulation, but in another sense to follow the summer of arid persecution. The confusion is reflected in the narrative order, where winter and summer enter first, to be succeeded by spring. Finally, in the early ninth-century *Key to Scripture* (*Clavis Scripturae*), Raban's probable source, all four seasons appear in order, each with its gloss and one or more scriptural prooftexts.[30] Still, the diagrammatic format inherited from Eucherius produces interpretations difficult to reconcile with the seasonal cycle.

There is still some time between Raban's more elaborate, slightly later ninth-century account, which reflects such earlier difficulties, and the twelfth-century interpretive continuum of Alan of Lille, who passes sequentially from winter to autumn in four allegorical stages which by their very logic transform time itself into a timeless presence: 'before the Law,' 'under the Law,' 'under Grace,' and 'under the aspect of eternity.'[31] But if Raban himself never quite develops this kind of dynamic conception, his rich consolidation of earlier fragments gives the

---

[26] See Maurmann-Bronder's discussion, 'Jahreszeiten,' pp. 76–9.

[27] See *Divinarum Institutionum Liber II, De Origine Erroris* 10; *PL* 6, 307B–308A.

[28] See *Formulae*, cited above in Ch. III, n. 30, II, pp. 11–12.

[29] See *Traité* VII, 6, pp. 203–5.

[30] See the edition of J. Pitra in *Analecta Sacra*, Vol. II ([Paris], 1884), IV, 60–6, pp. 20–1. For the date of this work, some time before 821 AD, and its influence upon Raban's treatise, see Heyse, *Enzyklopädie*, pp. 36–9 *et passim*, esp. p. 110.

[31] See Maurmann-Bronder's discussion, 'Jahreszeiten,' pp. 97–8; cf. p. 76.

seasonal cycle an allegorical dialectic more cogent than the designs it had in the past. At the same time, this logic displays its own poetic possibilities, still dominated, it is true, by the book that men should hear, but collated with the book that men can see.

If the interpretive dialectic of the Carolingian age sometimes evokes a kind of poetry, so, in the compositional tradition, does the poetry of the period exploit a kind of dialectic. Already in the *Consolation of Philosophy*, dialectic played a central role in compositional allegory, but there it essentially took the form of a conceptual exchange rather than a dramatic one. Further, insofar as the allegorical action itself was dramatic, it tended to be 'one-sided'—both in terms of form (an abstraction confronting a man) and in terms of orientation (the one philosophically assimilating the other). By contrast, the Carolingians give new vitality to a more symmetrical kind of literary argument, the 'poetic debate.' In this format, one personification disputes an issue with another personification, and even the resolution of the dispute tends to acknowledge the value of each contestant.

The format itself does not originate with the Carolingians. It has its sources deep in the rhetorical tradition of moral diatribes, law disputes, and pastoral contests between two shepherds, as well as in the folk tradition. Nevertheless, the Carolingians give the debate both a new conceptual edge and a new rhetorical fluency, and by the later Middle Ages it provides a literary forum for innumerable disputes between body and soul, wine and water, clerk and knight, rose and lily, and other figures.[32] In the end, it passes in and out of the allegorical mode, capable of schematizing a work like the *Consolation* into the 'Altercation between Fortune and Philosophy,' yet also able to inform a lyric as effusive as Dunbar's 'Thrissil and the Rois.'[33]

[32] On the nature of the 'poetic debate' and its antecedents, see H. Walther, *Das Streitgedicht in der lateinischen Literatur des Mittelalters* (Munich, 1920), pp. 3–54; F. J. E. Raby, *A History of Secular Latin Poetry in the Middle Ages*, 2nd edn. (Oxford, 1957), Vol. I, p. 208. On its later medieval development, see Walther, *passim*; Raby, Vol. II, pp. 282–308.

[33] For the 'Altercatio Fortune et Philosophie,' see Walther, *Streitgedicht*, pp. 232–4. For the 'Thrissil,' see *The Poems of William Dunbar*, ed. W. Mackay Mackenzie (London, 1932).

In the Carolingian debate itself there is a noticeable tension between the rhetorical and conceptual impulses, as there is in the exegesis of the period. Indeed, this tension pervades the age as a whole. If the Carolingian age impressively revives the interest in letters and logic, its achievements remain limited in both respects, and it is even more uneasy about the precise relation between the two realms. A man like Alcuin might be capable both of promoting keen logical investigations at the court of Charlemagne and of composing a gentle poetic lament about the absence of a friend, imagined pastorally as the departure of the cuckoo after the season of its song. Yet even he, who helped more than any man of the age to integrate the liberal arts with the discipline of truth, could argue that wisdom was to be found not in the lies of Virgil but in the Gospel.[34] In its own, more limited way, the early poetic debate is divided between a decorative, even chatty mode of discourse and a more substantial, cogent rationale. It is not until the twelfth century that the debate begins fully to exploit its potential, enhancing the rhetorical procedure with the subtle discriminations of the *disputatio*.[35]

Still, the Carolingian debate remains illuminating in its own right, not only because it provides the initial impetus for such later developments, but also because it is particularly distinguished for personifying forces in the world at large.[36] One of the earliest and most popular of these debates, in fact, was the 'Conflict of Spring and Winter' ('Conflictus Veris et Hiemis'), which received many variations throughout the Middle Ages. It may have been written by one of Alcuin's pupils; in any case, it belongs to the same period of revival in which Raban was composing his interpretive allegory of the seasons. Indeed, we could hardly choose a compositional allegory which more aptly portrays in style and subject that

[34] On these points, see John Marenbon, *From the Circle of Alcuin to the School of Auxerre* (Cambridge, 1981), pp. 30–66; Raby, *History*, Vol. I, pp. 185–6; Heinrich Fichtenau, *The Carolingian Empire*, tr. Peter Munz (1957; repr. Toronto, 1978), pp. 102–3. For an overview, see M. L. W. Laistner, *Thought and Letters in Western Europe: A.D. 500 to 900*, rev. edn. (1957; repr. Ithaca, N. Y., 1966), pp. 189–386.

[35] See Brinkmann, pp. 63–4; for its more exuberant side, which it continues to display, see, e.g., J. H. Hanford, 'The Medieval Debate between Wine and Water,' *PMLA* 28 (1913), 315–67.

[36] See Brinkmann, p. 63, n. 198.

tension between creative rejuvenation and conservative restraint which marks the Carolingian age as a whole.[37]

The poem has a simple plot. In spring, the older shepherd, Palemon, the younger one, Dafnis, and others in their party come down from the mountains to welcome the season in song with the cuckoo, herald of spring. Suddenly, two abstract characters appear on the scene: 'Spring,' attired with its flowery garland ('florigero succinctus stemmate'), and 'Winter,' hirsute with its frozen locks ('rigidis hirsuta capillis'). In alternating strophes of three lines apiece, the two seasons debate the question of whether or not the cuckoo should come. Winter claims that the cuckoo brings restlessness, work, and disruption, as opposed to the quiet hours by the hearth during the cold months. Spring counters that the cuckoo is welcome to all, since it brings natural growth and constructive activity, as opposed to the torpor of winter. At last, Winter thinks it has the decisive argument: the labors of spring are only preparations for the winter months, and thus subject to Winter's dominion. But Spring turns the tables: it is not Winter's dominion, but its impoverishment, that requires Spring's activity; winter could hardly nourish itself without the provisions of the previous season. At this point, Palemon, from his lofty seat ('sublimi e sede'), together with the other shepherds, silence Winter and urge the fields to burst forth in flower to welcome the cuckoo's arrival.

There is a certain surface prettiness about this poem, a kind of rhetorical finish that smooths the allegory out onto the literal level. First, the poem is self-consciously a literary product, constantly calling attention to its verbal polish. This appears in the self-reference of a song about singing, the artfully devised strophic structure, the incantatory repetition of phrases (cf. ll. 10 and 16; 14, 19, and 46), as well as the stock pastoral names of Dafnis and Palemon and the allusions to earlier texts by Virgil, Horace, and Calpurnius.[38]

---

[37] For the text of the 'Conflictus,' see *MGH, Poetae Latini Aevi Carolini*, ed. E. Duemmler, Vol. I (Berlin, 1881), pp. 270–2. On its authorship, see Max Manitius, *Geschichte der lateinischen Literatur des Mittelalters*, Vol. I (Munich, 1911), pp. 278–9, and Walther, *Streitgedicht*, p. 36, who also stresses the number of existing manuscripts and 'the international popularity of the piece.'

[38] See Duemmler's notes for the allusions to these three authors.

Second, although the poet substitutes for the standard singing contest between literal shepherds a debate between personifications, the personifications, too, glide smoothly along the surface of the poem. They display their identities less by exposing allegorical depth of character than by exchanging a series of vignettes about their effects in the world at large. The difficulty of giving a concept attributes without diffusing it onto the literal level affects personification from the start, but it is particularly acute in the poetic debate, which seeks to expose all the important effects of its personified contestants.

Finally, there is a third, related reason for the resistance of this poem—and to a degree, even later debate poems—to allegorical depths. The personifications are not quite something 'else,' the something else of allegory. They do not diverge enough from their proper definitions to interact on anything but the verbal level. Even on that level, Spring and Winter here do not speak with the deep resonances of primal forces—resonances such as Raban tried to develop in his interpretive allegory of the seasons. Occasionally, it is true, the personifications briefly suggest richer associations. Thus, gaily attired Spring and harsh, hirsute Winter may remind us momentarily of later courtly allegory's pleasant Fair Welcome and fierce, bristly-haired ('hericiez') Dangier, brandishing his club. So, too, one-word epithets like 'laetus' to describe Spring's joyous natural growth, as opposed to 'glacialis' to describe Winter's glacial sluggishness, may hint at deep contrasts—though the same word 'laetus' is used to describe Winter's feasts, as well (l. 25). We should not mistake the potential allegory, however, for the actual one. Spring and Winter remain virtually literal seasons, remote descendants of the old ritual struggle between gods of the natural cycle.[39] They are more conceptually disciplined than the mythological characters of Martianus, but not luxuriant enough to pass convincingly beyond the logical figures of Boethius. They thus raise on the cosmic level the old compositional problem of strict correspondence with conceptual principles, framing the seasons more than transfiguring them.

[39] In a rudimentary form, the pattern itself stretches back beyond Aesop, who has a dispute between Spring and Winter (Walther, *Streitgedicht*, p. 5), to the most ancient ritual dramas; see Theodore Gaster, *Thespis: Ritual, Myth, and Drama in the Ancient Near East*, rev. edn. (New York, 1961), pp. 12–13, 124–9, citing the figures in the Canaanite *Poem of Baal*.

It may be argued that the writer of this fragile little piece had no such intention from the start. The argument would be true, and itself indicative of the limitations of the allegorical debate at this stage. Yet if we look at the piece more closely, we can see the poet nearly breaking out of these limitations, trying to deepen the texture of his poem. The pastoral form, after all, already had a long history of at least implicit allegorization. Indeed, Quintilian had illustrated his remarks on compositional allegory by arguing that Virgil's shepherd 'Menalcas' was really Virgil himself (*Inst. Orat.* VIII, vi, 46–7). As for this particular pastoral, the words by which Palemon, Dafnis, and the other shepherds silence Winter—'Desine plura' (l. 45; 'say no more')—are the very words which Virgil used in his 'Fifth Eclogue' (l. 19) to begin the lament and deification of his own character Daphnis, perhaps an allegorical allusion to Julius Caesar.

In fact, if there is anyone who has divine 'depth' in this Carolingian debate, it is not the seasonal contestants, despite their cosmic affiliations with the old gods, but rather the shepherds themselves, judging the dispute as if they were exercising the jurisdiction of a higher court. The very names of the presiding shepherds come with impeccable credentials from the court of Charlemagne himself; 'Palaemon' was a bucolic title for the Emperor, and 'Dafnis' was the name by which Alcuin referred to the court friend in his own poem about the cuckoo of springtime.[40] On a higher level, the elder Palemon leads the judgment 'from his lofty seat' ('sublimi e sede'), almost as if he were Chaucer's figure of 'Nature,' 'vicaire of the almyghty Lord,' who sits 'upon an hil of floures' (*Parliament of Fowls*, ll. 302–3, 379). Opening the poem, he and the other shepherds remain strategically in the background while the agents of *prosopopoeia* conduct their debate in the foreground, only to enter again suddenly at the end, like *dei ex machina*, to determine the outcome. They have the last word, and it resonates with the kind of religious allusion that might appeal even to Raban Maur:

> All await you, sea and earth and sky;
> Hail, sweet splendor, cuckoo, throughout the generations, hail!

[40] See Brínkmann, p. 354. For the 'Fifth Eclogue' above, and Caesar, see the edn. and tr. of Virgil's works by H. Rushton Fairclough, rev. edn., I (1935), 34–41.

Omnia te expectant, pelagus tellusque polusque,
Salve, dulce decus, cuculus, per saecula salve! (ll. 54–5)

If we did not know that two centuries later, the famous 'Iam dulcis amica venito' of the *Cambridge Songs* would also integrate the Song of Songs with an earthly subject, we might smile even more than we do at the juxtaposition of 'sweet splendor' with 'cuckoo.'[41] And when the chorus of shepherds closes the poem with 'per saecula salve,' as if to hail their love forever, *et nunc et semper et in secula seculorum*, we may wonder whether a poem about springtime has turned into an allegory about the well-spring of life with which Raban Maur associates the season.

It has not, of course. We could turn this *jeu d'esprit* into an allegory of the spirit only by the most serious violations of its careful proportions. The allegorical dimension truly comes into play only when the personified action stops—when Winter falls into its own trap, like Prudentius' deceitful Pride, and Spring, like Queen Humility, stands still. That is, the narrative movement has not quite assimilated its allegorical potentialities—a problem on the level of plot that Raban faced on the level of history. Constricted at the center of the debate, the abstract characters remain imperfectly integrated with the expansive, almost impulsive celebration at the end.

Still, the fundamental strategy of this and other poetic debates suggests not only limitations, but opportunities in the allegorical tradition. First, if such exercises are rather stylized, even artificial in presentation, by the same token they help to shift abstract encounters into the realm of civilized discourse. Instead of the brute confrontations of Prudentius or the extravagant flights of Martianus, the poetic debate develops a subtler, more controlled interaction between its conceptual characters. It is true that this strategy, which was already developing in Boethius, loses some of the sheer energy of the earlier works, which after all were quite different in scope and intention. But it also anticipates the kind of verbal sophistication (though not the philosophic rationale) by which a later

---

[41] For the text of the 'Iam dulcis,' see *The Oxford Book of Medieval Latin Verse*, ed. F. J. E. Raby (Oxford, 1959), pp. 172–3. Both poems share notable reminiscences of the Song of Songs. On such reminiscences in the 'Iam dulcis,' see Peter Dronke, *Medieval Latin and the Rise of European Love-Lyric*, 2nd edn. (Oxford, 1968), Vol. I, pp. 271–3.

century, which itself revives the art of letters, will transfigure those bold early encounters into subtle imaginative designs.

Second, if the characters in the poetic debate tend to be leveled into a series of surface details, this is not only the sign of a diffusive, almost prosaic procedure. It also reflects the fact that the adversaries share a common frame of reference, that on some level they both contribute to a single continuity. Indeed, one of the salient features of the poetic debate is its effort to show contraries complementing, rather than simply opposing, each other, a feature that leads many debates to end either without a clear 'winner' or with some kind of reconciliation. This particular poem, in fact, though it has a winner, not only uses the same revealing word 'laetus' with reference to both contestants, but gives some of its most appealing lines to the loser, as when Winter describes the cozy indoors of the cold months: 'There is sweet peace, and the fire of the hearth is warm' ('Est requies dulcis, calidus est ignis in aede,' l. 26). In a larger sense, both Winter's final appeal and Spring's victorious reply depend upon the insight that both parts of the seasonal cycle imply each other, that each draws its power from the other. A more complex, cosmological approach to the strategy of interdependence, based on broader philosophic sources and principles, will develop by the twelfth century, but already in the poetic debate, there is a constant tendency to turn metaphoric figures into metonymic terms of a larger whole.[42]

Finally, this drive for resolution tends to turn the 'judge' at the end of the debate into not only an arbitrator, but a mediator. In the mature form of the debate, he (or it) keenly discriminates between the contesting forces in order finally to coordinate them, as when 'ratio' assesses the proper relationship between 'caro' and 'spiritus,' or elsewhere refines the dispute between 'cor' and 'oculus' by ascribing the 'causa' of sin to one, the 'occasio' for it to the other.[43] In the broader

[42] See Brinkmann, p. 63, on the opponents in the poetic debate as 'two correlated aspects of one superpositioned whole,' appearing 'rhetorically' as 'objectified metonymies.' On the exploitation of metonymy in allegory as a whole, see Holly Wallace Boucher, 'Metonymy in Typology and Allegory, with a Consideration of Dante's *Comedy*,' in *Allegory, Myth, and Symbol*, ed. Bloomfield, pp. 129–45, and more broadly, Fletcher, *Allegory*, cited above in Ch. I, n. 4, pp. 84–146; cf. my discussion of Eriugena below, with n. 67.

[43] On the first strategy, see Brinkmann, pp. 65–6; on the second, see Philip the Chancellor's 'Altercatio cordis et oculi,' ll. 49–56, in *Oxford Book*, p. 390.

allegorical exploitation of the debate pattern, this mediating principle becomes the literary, as well as philosophic, converging point of the whole drama, from Alan of Lille's 'Natura,' who no sooner cites the 'disputatio' between reason and sensuality than seeks (with ambiguous results) to deal with it by deploying both her own imaginative *ingenium* and the generative principle of Genius, to the more eschatological 'Everlasting Life' of the late medieval poem *Death and Life*, who changes from a mere phrase in the debate between Death and Life into an allegorical 'Lady' in her own right, a formal transition that becomes a spiritual one, as her articulation immediately anticipates the raising of the dead into the life to come.[44]

Such intricate rhetorical and conceptual maneuvers seem far removed from the capabilities of an early poetic debate like the 'Conflictus,' with its shepherds instinctively endorsing the spring season. But it is not so long after the 'Conflictus' that the celebrated *Eclogue of Theodulus* is composed, with its elaborate literary and philosophic debate between 'Pseustis' (Falsity) and 'Alithia' (Truth), the one invoking ancient mythology, the other responding with parallels from the Old Testament. In his rich late eleventh-century *accessus* to this poem, Bernard of Utrecht may be forcing the point to deepen each character by giving its *exempla* multiple senses of allegory while arguing that the sharp disjunction between these contrary figures of falsity and truth is really a sequential progression, from a dispensation 'before the Law' to one 'under the Law,' completed spiritually and historically by the figure of 'Fronesis' (the representative of the period 'under Grace'), who closes the debate as Pseustis asks for mercy.[45] But this interpretation,

[44] On Alan's 'Natura' presiding over ('ordinavit') the 'duellum' or 'disputatio' between reason and sensuality—a conflict that here passes beyond the logical format of the 'debate' into the broader traditions of opposing cosmological movements, ethical drives, and mythological transformations—see *DPN* VI, 51-68. On 'Natura's' problematic effort to resolve such oppositions, see, e.g., Richard Hamilton Green, 'Alan of Lille's *De planctu Naturae*,' *Speculum*, 31 (1956), 649-74; Wetherbee, pp. 188-211, with his article, 'The Function of Poetry in the *De planctu naturae* of Alain de Lille,' *Traditio*, 25 (1969), 87-125. On 'Euerlasting Liffe,' see ll. 394, 444 f. of '*Death and Liffe*: An Alliterative Poem,' ed. James Holly Hanford and John Marcellus Steadman, Jr., *Studies in Philology*, 15 (1918), 221-94.

[45] On Bernard's *accessus* to the *Ecloga Theoduli*, see Brinkmann, pp. 348-401, esp. pp. 369-73, 386-401.

which transforms the point-counterpoint of the debate into the gradual revelation of God, much as Alan of Lille transforms the seasonal cycle into a spiritual advance, at least suggests the impressive potential of the debate's abstract symmetry. Perhaps it also suggests a critical effort to inform such symmetries with a sense of process that is presented only in partial terms by the debate format itself. It requires a different, more radical kind of dialectical engagement with the world to display its movement according to a grand, panoramic design.

ERIUGENA'S THEOPHANY

That design acquires its most systematic expression during the early Middle Ages in a work that articulates the process of renewal not in terms of a mere seasonal cycle, but in terms of the act of creation as a whole. This work is the *Periphyseon* of John the Scot Eriugena, a spectacular, imposing vision of the cosmos, composed in the third quarter of the ninth century, only a few years after Raban's *On the Natures of Things*, but expressive (as if to reflect its subject) of a dimension outside its own time, belonging both to a Neoplatonic tradition of the past and to a Neoplatonic renaissance to come. It should be stressed that the *Periphyseon*, which consists of an intricate array of philosophic speculations, digressions, and resolutions, is itself 'allegorical' only in certain limited respects. Its principal importance to allegory lies in the broad metaphysical program that it implies by its own mode of operation, which tends to integrate in a particularly striking way the interpretive and compositional traditions at large. The book is at once an exegesis of creation (both the text of Genesis and the world of generation) and a kind of creation in its own right, turning the cosmic dialectic of 'procession' and 'reversion' into the basis for its own imaginative symmetry. Here it is possible only to touch on Eriugena's radical design, but even to appreciate something of his work's importance, it is necessary first to turn at least briefly to its Neoplatonic sources.

In a sense, the pattern of procession and reversion central to the *Periphyseon* is a strategy distinguishing the Neoplatonic tradition as a whole. The Stoics, it is true, had made the notion of an expanding and contracting universe central to their physics, but their doctrine of a physical 'continuum' tended to treat such changes as mere modulations of a single substance. By contrast, philosophers working within the Platonic tradition develop a more rarefied, metaphysical approach to cosmic differentiation. For them, there are different 'levels' to the cosmos, beginning with the radical distinction between a transcendent realm and the realm of phenomena, continuing with gradations within the world of phenomena itself. By the time of the third-century Neoplatonist Plotinus, this hierarchy turns into a full-fledged cycle of continuous emanation and return between the transcendent cause and its diffused effects, a process in which the degree of proximity to the 'One' coincides with the degree of fulfillment by the 'Other.' This bold conception, elaborated and diversified by Neoplatonists from the fourth to the sixth centuries, gives full cosmic expression to a central problem engaged by the Neoplatonic tradition from the start, the relation between levels of being and levels of meaning.[46]

By the same token, however, it produces extreme problems in each respect. In terms of being, it is not clear either how the transcendent 'One' can be responsible for the alien 'Other,' or conversely, how the 'Other' can be reconcilable with the 'One.' Though the approaches to this crucial issue by late antique Neoplatonists such as Iamblichus, Syrianus, Proclus, and Damascius vary in emphasis, their prevailing tendency is to treat the phenomenon of 'procession' and 'reversion' as a movement *by* the *effect* from its cause and back again. Such a strategy keeps the One transcendently undisturbed by the movement of the Other, while giving the Other a kind of self-fulfilling activity in its own right. On the other hand, it treats such activity as only a default from the aloof transcendence of the One, which remains remote from even the loftiest levels of emanation, the triad of 'Being,' 'Life,' and 'Intelligence.' In the end, the true fulfillment of the Other lies less in what it is than in what it is not.[47]

[46] For an overview of these and related developments, see A. H. Armstrong, 'Plotinus,' pp. 193–268, and A. C. Lloyd, 'The Later Neoplatonists,' pp. 269–325, in *The Cambridge History of Later Greek and Early Medieval Philosophy* (Cambridge, 1967).

[47] See the complex but vital discussion of Stephen Gersh, *From Iamblichus to Eriugena* (Leiden, 1978), pp. 27–45 on different kinds of 'potency,' 46–57 and 125–37 on 'self-determination,' 137, n. 61 on positive and negative 'hypotheses,' and 143–51

This philosophic tension between the positive and negative dimensions of being has its imaginative counterpart in the tension exhibited in Neoplatonic exegesis between positive and negative modes of meaning. Again, the Neoplatonic approach to this issue varies between exegetes, but this very diversity highlights the overall dilemma; the most systematic theorist, Proclus, displays something of the strain in his own right. On the one hand, as we recall, he endorses 'iconic' figures as direct analogies which affirm the truth (albeit in a limited fashion) by a kind of one-to-one, philosophic correspondence. On the other hand, he champions 'symbolic' figures precisely because their incongruous status undermines such a correspondence, thereby imaginatively displaying by default the utter transcendence of the truth. In effect, the divided Neoplatonic cosmos divides the Neoplatonic perspective itself between the potential for affirmation and the need for abnegation.

When such Neoplatonic strategies undergo adaptation by the great Christian Neoplatonists Pseudo-Dionysius, flourishing at the turn of the fifth and sixth centuries, and Maximus the Confessor, writing in the seventh century—both of whom enrich the Platonist approaches of earlier Christians such as the Cappadocian Fathers—the dilemmas are at once deepened and transformed. In terms of being, the fact that the Christian God creates without intermediaries tends to stress the dichotomy between him and the world, and thus to emphasize his sublime transcendence beyond mere creatures. At the same time, though, the absence of intermediaries brings him into direct rapport with his creatures, and thus tends to make him immanent in the world, energizing it from within.[48] This double vision of transcendence and immanence, imperfectly reconciled in both writers, simultaneously dramatizes the negative and positive perspectives toward both God and his creation.

Thus, Pseudo-Dionysius argues that while in one sense God is the cause of 'Being,' 'Life,' and 'Wisdom'—those originally 'emanating' effects ('Wisdom' here replacing 'Intelligence') which slipped from the Neoplatonic One—in another sense he *is* 'Being,' 'Life,' and 'Wisdom,' which are his attributes or

on the Neoplatonic triad. Gersh's study is the most thorough treatment of these developments, and I am indebted to it throughout this analysis.

[48] On this dual orientation, see Gersh, pp. 204–17.

'names.' From this perspective, God has not only a negative
dimension with respect to the world, but a strikingly positive
one; indeed, this direct divine assimilation of earlier cosmic
'levels' tends to make the order of God coincide (if not quite
merge) with the hierarchy of nature itself, which utterly
depends upon him.[49] If such an approach has its dangers—a
subordinationist God on the one hand, a pantheistic nature on
the other—it also has its defense, again by a revision of pagan
principles. Thus, the fact that the Christian God actually
becomes man helps Maximus to conceive of cosmic movement
at large not as the Neoplatonic slippage of an *effect* from an impassive cause, but as the momentous movement of the *cause*
itself, even a divine 'passion'—a 'blessed inversion' (*kalēn
antistrophēn*), he calls it, in which man is deified while God is
humanized.[50] In a broader sense, such perspectives help to
turn the whole deterministic cycle of nature into the creative
design of God, and thus to transform a Neoplatonic 'descent'
from perfection into a Christian ascent toward it.[51] If the world
loses autonomy in this scheme, it also acquires a certain divinity; it is at once radically humbled and elevated, suggesting
both what God is not and what he is.

The volatile double valence assigned by these Christian Neoplatonists to the realm of being has its counterpart in the realm
of meaning; as such philosophers argue, Scripture itself
displays both 'negative' and 'positive' modes of signification.
The crucial theorist of this duality is Pseudo-Dionysius, whose
division of scriptural language is similar to the Neoplatonic
distinction between 'symbols' and 'icons,' but whose belief in
the divine authority of his text intensifies the urgency with
which he defends the 'symbolic,' negative mode. It is preferable, he declares, for Scripture to represent the divine realm by
radically 'dissimilar figures' (*anomoiōn anaplaseōn*), rather than
apparently 'similar' ones (*homoiotētōn*). Such incongruous
figures prevent us more decisively from supposing that any

[49] The central document displaying these diverging and converging tendencies is *De
Divinis Nominibus*, hereafter *DN*, *PG* 3, 585–996. See René Roques, *L'Univers Dionysien*
(Paris, 1954), hereafter *L'Univers*, pp. 76–81, 111–15; Gersh, pp. 152–67.

[50] The quotation from Maximus' *Ambigua* appears in Gersh, p. 216; cf. pp. 166,
217–29, 253–60, and I. P. Sheldon-Williams, 'The Greek Christian Platonist Tradition
from the Capaddocians to Maximus and Eriugena,' in *Cambridge History*, pp. 492–505.

[51] See Gersh, pp. 181–90, 217–29, 240–3, 283–8.

representation can be truly appropriate to the transcendent realm, while at the same time, by their very impropriety, they provoke us more urgently to direct the intelligence upward (*noun anagousi*) beyond the world of figures as a whole.[52] They thus have an 'anagogic' force that lifts us (*anagetai*) from the variegated realm of Otherness to the simplicity of the One (see *DN* 705B, 913B). Such an intimate link between imaginative and actual transcendence gives the poetry of ascent both a powerful, scriptural authority and a new, compelling dynamism, beyond the more limited, earlier theories about 'incongruities' in a text pointing to the need for allegorization.[53] When Pseudo-Dionysius speaks of this purification as an upward 'catharsis' (*anakathairesthai, DN* 913A), it is plain that Martianus' rather baroque picture of heavenbound Philology cathartically vomiting earthly books has been left behind in a systematic drive—if only by constant default—to a higher linguistic and spiritual plane.

At the same time, this negative impulse seems imperfectly resolved with the positive movements implied by it. The very dynamics of ascent, after all, involve the passage from less to more 'congruent' levels of meaning and being—that is, from a 'symbolic' mode to a more conceptual one. Indeed, the same sentence in which Pseudo-Dionysius speaks of 'catharsis' includes the prospect of explanations more 'suitable' to the divine (*theoprepesi*)—clarifications which, as he indicates elsewhere, are accessible to us 'analogically' (cf. *analogikēs, DN* 825A), according to the 'proportion' of our knowledge. These possibilities of 'analogy,' involving modes of language and existence which at least approximate God, thus counterpoint the movement of 'anagogy' that tends to undermine such possibilities. The tension is most striking in Pseudo-Dionysius' twofold attitude toward the propriety of the divine 'names,' which we have already noted, and by extension, his deep am-

---

[52] See *De Coelesti Hierarchia*, ed. and tr. Günter Heil and Maurice de Gandillac, introd. by René Roques (Paris, 1958), II, 1141A; cf. 1137A–1137D.

[53] On this anagogic impulse in Pseudo-Dionysius, see Roques, *L'Univers*, pp. 200–44; Chenu, pp. 80–7; cf. Pépin's article on 'l'absurdité, signe de l'allégorie,' cited above, Ch. III, n. 25. On the importance of Pseudo-Dionysius' 'incongruous' figures to twelfth-century allegory, see Dronke, *Fabula*, pp. 43–7.

bivalence toward the value of philosophy.[54] In a sense, it is true, this interplay between affirmation and denial is precisely Pseudo-Dionysius' point, enacting on the level of discourse the double movement of a cosmos that is at once descending, asserting what it is, and at the same time ascending, conceding what it is not. But in a broader sense, the uneasy relationship here between positive and negative modes suggests a perspective in which rational categories of thought remain incompletely reconciled with the sacred mystery of the text, and finally, a world in which the natural process as a whole seems constantly liable to the rarefying impulses of the spirit. Long after Pseudo-Dionysius' own age, such conflicts will leave their legacy to the twelfth century, struggling to reconcile a 'symbolic' perspective with a conceptual theology, and in the end, seeking to turn a radically contingent universe into a world with its own integrity.[55]

These deep tensions developing in the Neoplatonic and Christian Neoplatonic tradition intensify in the striking activity of Eriugena, who not only translates central works by Pseudo-Dionysius and Maximus, but finally transfigures their strategies into the unique design of his *Periphyseon*.[56] As a critique of the relation between the One and the Other, the *Periphyseon* opens by incorporating 'all things which are and are not' into a single, comprehensive framework, 'Natura' itself (I, 441A). Yet Nature comprises the whole by virtue of its own self-division into four modes: Nature as the divine source of all, as

[54] See, e.g., *Epistola* IX, *PG* 3, 1108AB; cf. Krewitt, p. 472; Roques, *L'Univers*, pp. 59–64, 200–44; and Roques, *Structures théologiques de la gnose à Richard de Saint-Victor* (Paris, 1962), pp. 139–49, 164–79.

[55] See Chenu, pp. 23–6, 123–41. In the much broader terms of the imaginative tradition, the problem of formulating 'analogical' relationships both between a text and its points of reference and within the text itself increasingly preoccupies later allegorical writing; see my discussion below in this section and Ch. VI; cf. Allen, *Ethical Poetic*, pp. 179–287, on *assimilatio* or 'likening' in the later Middle Ages. The most intricate and important study of analogical patterns within a major allegorical work is James Nohrnberg's *The Analogy of* The Faerie Queene (Princeton, 1976).

[56] For Eriugena's collected works, see *PL* 122. My citations from Books I–III of the *Periphyseon* refer to the recent edition of I. P. Sheldon-Williams, 3 vols. (Dublin, 1968–81), the basis for my translations from this part of the work; citations from Books IV–V refer to the *PL* edition (entitled *De Divisione Naturae*). In all references I cite *Periph.* by both book number and *PL* page number. For an overview of Eriugena's activity, see Maïeul Cappuyns, *Jean Scot Érigène: sa vie, son œuvre, sa pensée* (Louvain, 1933), a valuable book that is gradually being superseded, however, by more recent studies, including those cited below.

the primordial causes, as the world of effects, and as the divine end of all (I, 441B–442A). Indeed, this very process of cosmic differentiation affirms a transcendent realm that is otherwise definable only by negation. Since the divine Nature is 'Nothing' ('nihilum') in its transcendent condition, it begins to 'appear' only by proceeding, in effect, 'from nothing into something' ('ex nihilo in aliquid,' III, 681A). In this progressive 'theophany' ('theophania,' III, 681A), the worldly effect at once inverts the otherworldly cause and fulfills it; the whole created cosmos is the 'manifestation of the hidden,' the 'affirmation of the negated' ('negati affirmatio,' III, 633A). More properly, it is the creative cause itself that undertakes what Maximus called this 'blessed inversion': 'descending' from his highest Nature, the Creator 'is created by his own self' ('a se ipso creatur') in the primordial causes; descending from that Nature in turn, he 'makes all things and is made all in all things, and returns into his own self, calling all things back into himself' (III, 683B). Here the dialectic of affirmation and negation, dramatized by the interplay of active and passive verbs, relentlessly turns the thearchy into the hierarchy of nature, so that the metaphysics of the *Periphyseon* becomes inseparable from its physics.[57]

However abstruse this extraordinary conception, it offers at least the possibility for an allegory of nature far more cogent than the improvisations of Eriugena's immediate predecessors, who are, so to speak, dissimilar in their very similitudes to him. Bede, adapting Augustine, had divided the creative process into a fourfold scheme suggestive in some respects of the fourfold 'Natura' of the *Periphyseon*.[58] Raban had seen the world as the visible manifestation of an invisible God. The author of the 'Conflictus' had treated the cycle of nature in dialectical terms. But working with more limited conceptual models, these writers could scarcely imagine the fearful symmetry that distinguishes the dynamic cosmos of the *Periphyseon*, a cosmos that is not merely a reflection, but a reflex action of God.

[57] See Jean Trouillard, 'Érigène et la théophanie créatrice,' hereafter Trouillard, pp. 98–9, 103–6, and Guy-H. Allard, 'La Structure littéraire de la composition du *De diuisione naturae*,' pp. 148–9, in *The Mind of Eriugena*, cited above in n. 7.

[58] For Bede, see Cappuyns, pp. 312–13; the Augustinian source, which Cappuyns does not specify, is *De Genesi ad Litteram* VI, x, 17; *PL* 34, 346. For the origins of Eriugena's own scheme, see n. 10 in Vol. I of Sheldon-Williams' edition, pp. 222–3.

At the same time, the *Periphyseon* marks not only a philosophic consolidation, but a formal one, enacting the dynamics of the cosmos by its own dialectical pattern. Self-consciously alternating between 'affirmative' and 'negative' (I, 458A) modes of discourse, the work displays by the very texture of its language that broader cosmic tension which pervades the realm of being. This strategy underlies Eriugena's repeated appeal to abstract terms prefixed by 'super-,' which no sooner posit a point of reference than transcend it. Terms such as 'superessentialis,' he writes, are expressly affirmative in 'form,' while sublimely negative in 'meaning' (I. 462C). In this sense, the whole conceptual scheme of the *Periphyseon* is a kind of dialectic of metaphors ('nomina . . . metaforica,' I, 458C; cf. 480B, 511C–513A, etc.), needing, like the cosmic process itself, to be 'translated' from an inferior level to a superior one ('metaforica . . . id est a creatura ad creatorem translata,' I, 458C). Here the tension between analogical and anagogic discourse in Pseudo-Dionysius acquires an integrated, systematic form.[59]

This 'metaphorical' design, of course, is too schematic to be a figurative story, as in the case of the *Cosmographia*; it remains a play of abstractions, not personifications. Nor is it clear to what degree the *Periphyseon* in its own right may directly influence either the *Cosmographia* itself or the generations between their composition.[60] On the one hand, Eriugena himself is a controversial writer whose work is unevenly known and assimilated during this period; on the other hand, even characteristically 'Eriugenist' positions overlap in part with perspectives developed by others in the late antique and early medieval Neoplatonic tradition. Beyond the question of specific influence, though, it remains useful to consider the *Periphyseon* as a particularly revealing expression of certain conceptual and

[59] On the interplay between positive and negative theology in Eriugena, see Cappuyns, pp. 274–331; cf. the strategy of Pseudo-Dionysius, discussed by Roques, *Structures théologiques*, cited above in n. 54, pp. 139–49.

[60] On the direct and indirect channels of Eriugena's later influence, see Paolo Lucentini, *Platonismo medievale: contributi per la storia dell'eriugenismo*, 2nd edn. (Florence, 1980), and the refs. below in Ch. V, n. 1, with my discussion. Lucentini, pp. 40–75, argues for the 'intensive circulation of Eriugenist doctrines' in the twelfth century, 'above all' through the *Periph*. Stock, Wetherbee in his tr. of the *Cosm.*, and Dronke in his edn. of the *Cosm.* specify possible relationships between the *Periph.* and the *Cosm.*; cf. my remarks in Ch. VI below.

imaginative possibilities later exploited in the twelfth century and the *Cosmographia* itself. With its elaborate account of 'theophany,' the 'manifestation of the hidden,' the *Periphyseon* suggests something of that dramatic 'projection' of divine figures in the *Cosmographia* who affirm a supreme realm otherwise accessible only by negation. Conversely, when two of those figures in the *Cosmographia*, Natura and Urania, approach this transcendent realm, Bernard Silvestris invokes terms like those of Eriugena; God himself is 'superessentialis,' a 'lux inaccessibilis' so brilliant that it produces a divine darkness ('caliginem').[61]

More broadly, the structural pattern by which Bernard Silvestris at once differentiates the divine whole into cosmic parts and resolves the parts back into the whole has a parallel in the (more austere) design of the *Periphyseon*, which is constantly dividing the 'uniuersitas' (II, 524D) into conceptual categories in order to reconstitute those elements on a higher plane. Every 'division,' writes Eriugena of the logic of the *Periphyseon*, is a kind of 'descent' ('descendens') from the general to the specific, while every 'reintegration' is a kind of 'return' ('reditus') from the specific to the general (II, 526B). In such a scheme, the cyclic movement of procession and return in the cosmos at large coincides with the dialectical format of the text itself.[62]

Finally, this daring effort to coordinate the differentiation of the cosmos with the dialectic of the mind implies a radical relation between macrocosm and microcosm that deepens the old formulas and engages problems central to the *Cosmographia*. For Eriugena, the whole formal pattern of cosmological and logical division or 'descent' is a counterpart to that dispersion of man into spatial and temporal diversity which constitutes the condition of his fall (II, 533B; IV, 807D). By the same token, however, the 'return' of the dialectical cycle implies man's transformation from the last, fragmented stage in the division of Nature into the divine goal of the entire process, from a ter-

---

[61] See *Cosm., Mic.* V, i, 9–10 and iii, 3–6, with Dronke's comments, pp. 29–30, 53.

[62] See the important n. 11 in Vol. II of Sheldon-Williams' edn., pp. 214–15, together with his chapter in *Cambridge History*, cited above in n. 50, pp. 524–6, and Marenbon, *From the Circle of Alcuin*, cited above in n. 34, pp. 75–7. Cf. *Periph.* II, 528C–529A; the internal 'recapitulationes' announced at II, 554C and III, 688A; and the preface to Eriugena's translation of Maximus' *Ambigua*, *PL* 122, 1195B–1196A.

minal part to the completed whole. In some respects, this approach to the correspondence between Nature and human nature is more extreme than that of Bernard Silvestris: Eriugena even oscillates over the degree to which the division of the One is an actual or a mental phenomenon.[63] It is revealing that such a radical consolidation of the cosmic cycle with human destiny is finally qualified by the *Cosmographia*, which ends by contrasting the cyclic process of nature with the mortal condition of the individual (*Mic.* XIV, 171–8).

Still, in its own way Eriugena's work too suggests the need to turn a Platonic recurrence into a Christian redemption. As the *Periphyseon* passes through the story of Genesis toward its conclusion, it brings a diffused Christological dimension into the tradition of the microcosm: in 'humana natura' is 'every creature constituted,' to 'revert' into it and be 'saved' by it (IV, 760A); in 'humana natura' does the whole world subsist ('totus mundus subsistit,' V, 911A).[64] In this sense, the *Periphyseon*, cast in the form of a dialogue between the sustaining master ('Nutritor') and the growing pupil ('Alumnus') and closing with the vision of darkness transformed into light (V, 1021B, 1022C), gives a scope to the drama of conversion beyond even the dialogue of Philosophy with Boethius.[65] It aims not only to align the divine and human orders, but to integrate them by generating the one and regenerating the other through the common framework of divine and human Nature.

For all its promise, this common framework is always in danger of slipping away in the *Periphyseon*. The inversions of Eriugena's world are so extreme that they no sooner suggest an allegory of Nature than they undermine it. Perhaps the most striking display of this volatile movement toward cosmic allegory, in fact, is the *Periphyseon's* treatment of 'creation' itself, its exegesis of the opening verses of Genesis (II, 545B f.).

[63] See, e.g., II, 525BC, 527D–528A, and Gersh, pp. 188–9, n. 273; 234, n. 135; 270–3; 279–82; 286–8; cf. Trouillard, pp. 99–101, 104.

[64] See Brian Stock, 'The Philosophical Anthropology of Johannes Scottus Eriugena,' *StM*, 3a ser., 8 (1967), 5–9, 15–20, 26–7, 46–53, and Trouillard, pp. 101, 107–11.

[65] For some parallels between the *Consolation* and *Periph.*, see Giulio d'Onofrio, 'Giovanni Scoto e Boezio: tracce degli "Opuscula sacra" e della "Consolatio" nell'opera eriugeniana,' *StM*, 3a ser., 21, fasc. 2 (1980), 742–5, 751.

Given the rarefied atmosphere of Eriugena's work, it may come as no surprise that he interprets the creation of 'heaven and earth' in the 'beginning' not as the making of heaven and earth themselves, but as the establishment of the 'primordial causes' in the *principium* of God (II, 545B–546B). Somewhat similar adaptations of the Platonic Ideas to the Genesis story, after all, had developed since Philo, and Eriugena himself cites such exegetical precedents. The really bold exegetical maneuver —only the author of the *Periphyseon* could dream of such a transport!—comes with the interpretation of 'waste and void' and 'darkness over the abyss' (II, 548A–551A). These passages seem to shift the perspective from God to the other side of the cosmos, but Eriugena argues that this apparent movement toward the circumference is actually a confirmation of the divine center. The 'waste and void earth,' he writes, refers here not to privation, but 'figuratively' ('figurate') to perfection—the sublime 'simplicity' of the primordial causes before their differentiation into effects, the mystical 'obscurity' ('obscuritatem') of the exemplary realm before its articulation into the forms of phenomena. In the very act of seeming to speak about the obscurity below, Scripture is directing our attention to the mystery above.

Now the basic strategy of exploiting figurative terms to coordinate mysteriously the extremes of the universe had already developed with the early Neoplatonists, as displayed in Porphyry's exegesis of 'caves,' which by their 'darkness' suggested both the murkiness of matter and the sublimity of the spirit. Eriugena, however, drawing upon more systematic speculations about 'inversion' from Iamblichus to Maximus, here turns the exegesis of the Bible into his own distinctive philosophic and imaginative synthesis. From a philosophic perspective, his interpretation suggestively plays upon the notion that what seems to be a terminal point in creation can yet be a goal; 'proceeding' in one sense from God, the 'earth' in another sense 'remains' with him. Indeed, it is precisely the attenuation of the primitive earth that suggests most radically the tenuity of the primordial causes; the intermediate levels of creation would not 'recall' each other so strikingly as the extremes. As a result, a story of the humblest effects ('waste and void') is transformed by allegory into a study of the highest causes—a reversion that dominates the whole allegorical operation, which keeps 'pulling back' the advance of the narrative ('And the earth . . .') to its starting point in God. The Book of Genesis itself 'proceeds' only to 'remain'; here indeed is a 'blessed inversion'!

Such a philosophic turnabout has its imaginative implications. Negotiating between the extremes of his world, Eriugena in effect passes from a 'symbolic' or incongruent mode of figuration to an 'iconic' or congruent one. In a provisional sense, it is the very divergence of a 'waste and void earth' from God that reveals its mysterious correspondence with him. In a stricter sense, though, it is most appropriate ('congruentissime') to apply the term 'abyss' to the divine causes, because of their unfathomable depth and infinite breadth.[66] By shifting his perspective from the apparent reference point (the effects) to the actual one (the causes), Eriugena thus aims to turn the most unlikely elements of the text into full conformity with the spirit. It seems particularly appropriate that the very act of creative partition from God—the making of 'heaven and earth'—should generate this movement of consolidation. Repeatedly in the *Periphyseon*, Eriugena makes a part of the universe a 'synecdoche,' as he puts it, for the whole—the 'soul' for the whole animal (IV, 744C–745A), the 'daystar' for the whole world (II, 560A–560C), the created world itself for the realm of primordial causes (V, 887–8)—as if each element of creation were a metaphor for the creation at large.[67] Such a drive toward completion had always been implicit in the notion of the *symbolon*, a term that originally denotes a 'part' needing to be joined to its counterpart.[68] But now the 'symbolic' transfer from part to whole is fully integrated with the cosmic

[66] On the related principle that negative terms are applied more appropriately than positive terms to the divine world—a development of Pseudo-Dionysius' doctrine—see, e.g., I, 461CD, 510B, 522B, and III, 684D–685A, with René Roques, *Libres sentiers vers l'érigénisme* (Rome, 1975), pp. 27–36, 90–5.

[67] On 'synecdoche' in Pseudo-Dionysius and Eriugena, see Roques, *L'Univers*, p. 213, n. 5, and Krewitt, pp. 472–3, 478. How much more dynamic is Eriugena's 'metonymic' strategy (I, 480B) than the metonymies we observed in the Carolingian debate! For Eriugena's somewhat different argument that the art of theology is a kind of 'poetry' fashioning 'imaginative fictions' to uplift the mind from imperfection to perfection, see *Expositiones super Ierarchiam Caelestem Sancti Dionysii*, II, in *PL* 122, 146BC.

[68] See Coulter, pp. 60–8.

movement from an inchoate world to the *principium* of its creation. The old question of Christian exegesis, the relation between linguistic and extra-linguistic transfer, between shifts of meaning and shifts of being, is finally beginning to receive a systematic response.

Nothing before the *Periphyseon*—nothing in heaven and earth —quite matches this dazzling exegesis of a dark creation. Still, with all its vertiginous shifts of perspective, Eriugena's work tends to blur the precise relationship between its two extreme points of reference, between the darkness below and the darkness above. It remains to define the exact means by which the obscure world of effects 'actually' signifies the mysterious world of causes, the precise principle by which the apparent meaning of the text turns into the authentic one. That is, it remains to clarify the philosophic and imaginative issue central to the allegory of Nature—the principle of transition between opposite ends of the universe.

It is thus revealing that between the exegesis of the first and second verses of Genesis, Eriugena inserts an exchange between 'Alumnus' and 'Nutritor' on the relation between the 'formlessness' of inchoate matter and the 'formlessness' of the primordial causes (II, 546B–548A). It seems hard to distinguish between the two, observes Alumnus; both seem to be the undifferentiated source from which the world emerges. Indeed, as we have seen, Nutritor himself uses terms traditionally associated with the 'nothing' below to express creation from the 'Nothing' above, as he tells of divine Nature passing 'ex nihilo in aliquid.'[69] Responding to his pupil's question, the

---

[69] For certain antecedents to this transfer (elaborately developed in III, 680C–688A) in Gregory of Nyssa, and some of its implications for later medieval philosophy, see Harry Austryn Wolfson, 'The Identification of *Ex Nihilo* with Emanation in Gregory of Nyssa,' and 'The Meaning of *Ex Nihilo* in the Church Fathers, Arabic and Hebrew Philosophy, and St. Thomas,' two articles conveniently available in his *Studies in the History of Philosophy and Religion*, ed. Isadore Twersky and George H. Williams, Vol. I (Cambridge, Mass., 1973), pp. 199-206, 207-21. On the more strictly logical question of whether the term 'nothing' has a positive status—a problem treated with increasing sophistication in the passage from the Carolingian period to the twelfth century and potentially (as Wolfson's studies suggest) and explicitly (as Anselm's work shows) related to the question of creation *ex nihilo*—see, e.g., Fredegisus, *Epistola de nihilo et tenebris*, ed. Ernest Duemmler, *MGH, Epistolae Karolini Aevi*, Vol. II (Berlin, 1895), pp. 552-5; Anselm, *Monologion* 6-9, 19 and *De Casu Diaboli* 11, in *Sancti Anselmi Opera Omnia*, ed. F. S. Schmitt, I (Seckau, 1938); and D. P. Henry, *The Logic of Saint Anselm* (Oxford, 1967), which undertakes a logical and linguistic analysis of the treat-

master slyly remarks that it is necessary to dispel such 'clouds of ambiguity' ('nebulasque ambiguitatis'), by distinguishing between privation of form, on the one hand, and transcendence of form, on the other. Yet in a sense, Nutritor's neat answer only dramatizes the fundamental question of how such disparate points of reference can seem so close to each other—the very unlikely likeness that is about to develop into the expansive exegesis of Gen. 1: 2 which we have just discussed, Nutritor's bold allegorical transfer from the 'abyss' to the heights.

Perhaps it is fitting that Eriugena, striving to resolve this question, should give his single most suggestive formulation here not to the confident Nutritor, but to the aspiring Alumnus, who makes a final effort to articulate the relationship before the exegesis of 'darkness' begins:

For the formlessness of things is nothing other than a certain motion departing from absolute non-being and seeking its rest in that which truly is . . .

Nil enim est aliud rerum informitas nisi motus quidam non esse omnino deserens et statum suum in eo quod uere est appetens . . . (II, 547B)

By turning his mind from matter's 'formlessness' to its 'motion,' Alumnus at last suggests in an inchoate—I had almost said creative—way both the principle of negotiation between contraries and the promise of the allegory to come. There is a certain pivot between the movements of procession and reversion, a point of transition between the extremes. It is that 'motus' which pervades all things, matter's sheer capacity to pass from nothing into something, its ability to be—and therefore to be divine—at all.[70] In effect, it is that which mediates between defection and perfection, almost that principle of 'potentiality'

ment of such privative terms (including 'nothing' on pp. 207-19). On the broader cosmological question of whether matter's emergence *ex nihilo* implies a rival to God—an issue that stimulates both heretical and more orthodox, though no less daring, strategies—see, e.g., the Wolfson articles; Ch. Thouzellier, 'Les cathares languedociens et le "Nichil" (Jean 1, 3),' *Annales Économies Sociétés Civilisations*, 24 (1969), 128-38; and my discussion in Ch. V below.

[70] For the development of this 'motus' principle in the *Periph.*, see, e.g., III, 729; IV, 790; for its importance to the *Cosmographia*, see *Cosm.* (tr.), pp. 37-8, 52-4 and *Cosm.*, p. 30.

which will one day help to reconcile the powerlessness of the material world with the power of the spiritual one in sophisticated twelfth-century allegory.

The *Periphyseon*, of course, is not composed in allegorical form. But even if it were, its orientation toward this *potentia* would still be too limited to produce the allegory of Bernard Silvestris and Alan of Lille. It will be necessary to separate more clearly the 'formlessness' of matter from matter itself before a character like Silva in the *Cosmographia*—graphically 'longing' ('Optat') for form, 'yearning' ('cupiens') for refinement (*Meg.* I, 18–22)—can emerge. Conversely, it will be necessary to implicate more extensively the perfection of the causes with the progress of the effects before a character like Noys—'troubled' ('Pertesum michi,' *Meg.* II, ii, 14) by the deprivation of matter—can develop. It will require an even bolder design to coordinate such extremes of powerlessness and power in a character like Nature in the *Complaint of Nature*—powerful in her own right, but powerless with respect to divine power ('meam potentiam impotentiam,' *DPN* VI, 137–8)—a figure who oscillates on that pivot between non-being and being which remains only an abstract point in Eriugena's treatment of creation. The *Periphyseon* is the brilliant culmination of one philosophic and imaginative tradition; a new renaissance is necessary before the world can 'yearn to be born again' (*Cosm.*, *Meg.* I, 35–6).

In the end, the Nature of the *Periphyseon* thus looks both backward to the allegory of the past and forward to the allegory of the future. It is finally divided not just according to the scheme of Eriugena, but according to those deep ambivalences about material, divine, and human 'Nature' which preoccupy earlier Christian Neoplatonists and which later philosophers in the tradition—even those who know little of Eriugena's work itself[71]—will seek in their own ways to resolve.

As it was for Boethius, Eriugena's material nature is in one sense the mere residue of a Neoplatonic descent from God, but in another sense the creative opportunity for a Christian ascent from the void.[72] The *Periphyseon* in effect dramatizes this ambiguity in its two-sided perspective toward a creation 'ex

---

[71] See n. 60, above, with my discussion below.

[72] See Tullio Gregory, *Giovanni Scoto Eriugena: Tre studi* (Florence, 1963), pp. 1–26.

nihilo,' the 'Nothing' above and the 'nothing' below (cf. III, 636D, 687AB). The issue at stake here, really, is the inherent value of matter, and it is revealing that for Eriugena, the declaration 'Let there be light' indicates at once a slippage from divine darkness and a passage toward divine clarification, at once a diminution and a revelation (III, 692A–693A).[73] The natural philosophers of the twelfth century will refine the broad question by reinterpreting the shadowy Platonic matter of the *Timaeus* in the light of Genesis, and finally making a disruptive matter into a constructive one.

As it was for Pseudo-Dionysius, Eriugena's divine Nature is in one sense inaccessibly transcendent, but in another sense pervasively immanent. The *Periphyseon* radicalizes this duality in its dazzling transition from the privative 'earth' below to the perfect 'earth' above, and it deepens the issue with each new exegetical turn, as when it oscillates over whether the 'Spirit of God' (Gen. 1: 2) is loftily 'borne above' ('superferebatur') the waters or intimately 'nourishing' ('fouebat') them (II, 552C–556A). Later exegetes, developing the association between the 'Spirit' of that verse and the Platonic World Soul, will fashion a crucial mediating principle between the transcendent Holy Spirit and the immanent, animating principle of life—a development that leads at last to the panoramic 'Natura' of the twelfth century.

Finally, as it was for the earlier Carolingians, Eriugena's human nature—which partakes of each of the other two—displays those arts of the mind which both raise man toward heaven and yet leave him short of it. The *Periphyseon* transforms this dilemma, insisting from the start that no concept can properly articulate the divine realm, yet proceeding to develop a conceptual design that not only explicates the divine Book of Scripture, but enacts that pattern of 'eternal' art which creates the Book of Nature at large.[74] This strategy underlies

[73] As if to expose the ambivalence, when Eriugena analyzes the 'anomalous' natures of Pseudo-Dionysius, he at once specifies more keenly than his predecessor the provocation of aberrant deformity and at the same time implies more strongly than Pseudo-Dionysius the potential for normative consistency; see Roques, *Libres sentiers*, cited above in n. 66, pp. 13–43.

[74] On Eriugena's daring association of the arts and the *intellectus* of man with the eternal *logos* of God—a principle central to his association between microcosm and macrocosm, as we have noted—see, e.g., I, 475C (on the inherence of the arts in 'mind'), I, 486CD (on the 'eternity' of both), III, 658BC (on their parallel 'descent'),

the dialectical pattern of Eriugena's whole work, which claims to reconstitute the order of the text and the cosmos more radically than anything earlier in the allegorical tradition, from Origen's *On First Principles* to Raban's *On the Natures of Things*. The early scholastic theologians of the age to come will produce their own abstract interpretive designs; that process will culminate (long after Christian Neoplatonism has been deeply qualified) in a *summa* that makes the originally Neoplatonic pattern of procession and return the formal principle of a comprehensive Christian exegesis.[75]

These expansive developments, though, await the future. However imposing it is in its own right, the *Periphyseon*, like its subject, is forever aspiring toward what it is not. Seeking to transform an explication into a composition, an act of exegesis into a form of genesis, it restlessly makes every point of possible stasis a volatile turning point, as if to systematize that self-undermining tendency to which allegory is liable from the start. In order to develop a sustained allegory of Nature, it will be necessary to make the potentiality of this world more than a pivot; it will be necessary to make it a center.

IV, 748D-749A (on the dialectical art as established in the very 'nature of things' by the 'author of all arts'), and IV, 778D-779A (on the parallel between the human mind and the divine *logos*), with the important discussion of Roques, *Libres sentiers*, pp. 45-98, 131, 190-1. Cf. Cappuyns, pp. 273-315, and Eriugena's internal 'recapitulations,' cited above in n. 62.

[75] See the analysis of the *Summa Theologiae* in M.-D. Chenu, *Toward Understanding Saint Thomas*, tr. Albert M. Landry and Dominic Hughes (Chicago, 1964), pp. 304-18.

V TWELFTH-CENTURY GENESIS

And this is the golden chain of Homer that he tells us God ordered to hang down from the sky to the earth. (Macrobius, *Commentary on the Dream of Scipio* I, xiv, 15.)

MOVEMENTS OF REGENERATION

Perhaps it is not surprising that the allegorical tradition produces no vision so panoramic as the *Periphyseon* until the *Cosmographia* itself. Aside from Eriugena's special access to the Greek tradition and the daring, controversial positions he assumed in this and other texts, few even among those acquainted with his work could maintain the diversity of perspective displayed by the *Periphyseon* as a whole. In the generations just after Eriugena, there are nonetheless partial reminiscences of the *Periphyseon* which suggest both the promise of developments to come and the limitations of the period in its own right. Perhaps the figure who best displays such tendencies is Remigius of Auxerre, flourishing at the turn of the ninth and tenth centuries. In his philosophic commentaries, he recalls, even develops, certain Eriugenist principles which both Eriugena himself and the allegorists of the twelfth century expand into bold designs: the preexistence of matter in the mind of God, for example (*Periph.* III, 636BC), a doctrine related to Eriugena's characteristic reversal from the depths to the heights and later exploited in a stunning reversal central to the *Cosmographia* (*Meg.* IV, viii, 1–5); or, conversely, the ultimate disparity between God himself and the mind of any creature, man or angel (*Periph.* I, 448B–448D), a doctrine related to the negative theology of 'theophanies' and later embodied in the problematic 'emblems of celestial theophany' ('theophanie celestis emblema') of the *Anticlaudianus* (*Prose Prologue*; cf. Book VI).[1] Remigius himself, however, never assimilates such

---

[1] For Remigius' adaptation of these doctrines, see Lucentini, cited above in Ch. IV, n. 60, pp. 29-30, n. 77, and pp. 31-2, n. 82, and esp. Giulio d'Onofrio, 'Giovanni Scoto e Remigio di Auxerre: a proposito di alcuni commenti altomedievali a Boezio, '

possibilities into a systematic formal structure of his own. It is as if such extremes of Creator and creation, which these more daring writers seek to consolidate, were keeping a certain distance from each other in his own more conservative interpretive activity.

Nor is this somewhat divided orientation only a philosophic problem. In his mythographic work, it is Remigius who openly displays by the different contexts of his commentaries that twofold approach toward Orpheus' 'descent' which was potentially complicating the story since Fulgentius associated it with the aspirations of art and Boethius with the failures of reason. In Remigius' commentary on Martianus' *Marriage*, Orpheus is a figure of human eloquence seeking its deeper foundations; in his commentary on the *Consolation*, Orpheus is a human soul slipping toward disastrous oblivion—a view vigorously developed by the sermonizing revisers of this commentary in the next century.[2] For all its explicitly acknowledged dilemmas, the first approach seems more suggestively to raise the prospect of linking the human imagination with divine wisdom, and revealingly, Remigius' interpretation does not come directly from Fulgentius, but appears almost verbatim in a set of *Annotations* attributed to Eriugena, who composed a Martianus commentary important to Remigius.[3] But then, even when Remigius is not writing in two different contexts he tends to

StM, 3a ser., 22, 2 (1981), 647-57, 688-90. For the passage of other Eriugenist themes from the late ninth to the early eleventh centuries, see the discussions of Lucentini and d'Onofrio; H. Silvestre, 'Le Commentaire inédit de Jean Scot Érigène au mètre IX du livre III du *De consolatione philosophiae* de Boèce,' *Revue d'histoire ecclésiastique*, 47 (1952), 44-122 (though the attribution to Eriugena himself is incorrect); Gregory, *Platonismo*, pp. 12-13; and the studies of Boethius commentaries cited below.

[2] On Martianus, see *Remigii Autissiodorensis Commentum in Martianum Capellam*, ed. Cora E. Lutz, 2 vols. (Leiden, 1962, 1965), Vol. II, p. 310; on Boethius (a commentary still only partially edited), see D. K. Bolton, 'The Study of the Consolation of Philosophy in Anglo-Saxon England,' *AHDLMA* 44 (1977), 45-6, 61-6 (with the problematic effort of the 'K' revision to combine both approaches). As noted above in Ch. III, n. 94, the analysis by Friedman, *Orpheus in the Middle Ages*, pp. 98-100, incorrectly ascribes to Remigius a commentary from the twelfth century; see Courcelle, 'Étude,' cited above in Ch III, n. 78, 24-6: *Tradition*, pp. 250-4.

[3] See *Annotationes in Marcianum*, ed. Cora E. Lutz (Cambridge, Mass., 1939), pp. 192-3. The precise extent to which the text of this edition represents Eriugena's own commentary, to which Remigius explicitly refers several times in his own work, is still uncertain; see Gangolf Schrimpf, 'Zur Frage der Authentizität unserer Texte von Johannes Scottus' "Annotationes in Martianum,"' in *The Mind of Eriugena*, cited above in Ch. IV, n. 7, pp. 125-39.

limit the impulse toward consolidation. In an important gloss on the Vulcan of the *Marriage*, the writer of the *Annotations* associates the figure not only with an enervating 'voluptatis calor,' but with that 'ingenium' which recalls man to his 'creator' and his own natural dignity ('naturalis dignitas')—an association between the physical and spiritual sides of 'ingenium' that we have seen developing episodically since the Stoic treatment of Hephaestus' 'craftsmanlike fire' and that will finally expand, with all its internal contradictions and ambiguous resolutions, into the Nature–Genius alliance of the *Complaint of Nature*. For his part, Remigius broadly allows the double association, but pointedly labels one side 'cupiditas' ('obscena,' he calls it twice), while not providing, on the other hand, an elaboration about 'natural dignity.'[4] In the end, perhaps Remigius' sense of a certain distance between this world and the other world is best suggested by the differing exegetical afterthoughts in these two commentaries concerning a particular 'woman' (*Marriage*, 131) who assists Philology's ascent to the stars. She is 'Philosophia,' observes the *Annotations* author, for 'no one enters heaven unless by philosophy,' 'semel splendoribus.' She is 'Philosophia,' comments Remigius, for 'no one can ascend to heaven unless by philosophy,' 'id est per amorem sapientiae.' Here not only Philology, but the new commentator, is shifting his perspective heavenward.[5]

Such nuances reflect a broader uneasiness about the possibility of ascribing genuine integrity both to the natural world itself and to the conceptual language devised by men to describe it. The most accurate gauge of that intellectual oscillation in the century after Remigius is the exegetical treatment of the principle that Plato had conceived to mediate between the world above and the world below, the World Soul—ancestress of 'Natura' herself. Placed by Boethius at the philosophic and literary center of his *Consolation* (III, m. ix), this principle preoccupies a host of commentaries on the poem from the late

[4] See *Annotationes*, p. 13; *Commentum*, Vol. I, p. 79. Wetherbee, pp. 117-21, explores some implications of the *Annotations* gloss, although he does not discuss Remigius' differences in tone here.

[5] See *Annotationes*, p. 64; *Commentum*, Vol. I, P. 171. On the holistic implications of the *Annotations* gloss, see Cappuyns, pp. 304-5; on Remigius' tendency to compile rather than synthesize, see Pierre Courcelle, 'La culture antique de Remi d'Auxerre,' *Latomus*, 7 (1948), 247-54.

ninth to the early eleventh centuries, critiques ranging from the suspicious to the sympathetic. In the tenth century, Bovo of Corvey warns that we must separate sharply the truth of the matter ('rei ueritatem') from the fictions of the philosophers ('philosophicis . . . figmentis'). Only then will we understand that the heavens revolve not by some vague World Soul ('ignotae . . . mundi animae'), but by 'the ineffable power of the omnipotent God.' Early in the eleventh century, Adalbold of Utrecht grants a certain immanent presence to this celestial principle, but at the same time he rebukes those men of physics ('physici') who impute the force of life to it rather than to the Creator. Such thinkers, Adalbold assures us, will perish by their own fictions ('ipsis suis figmentis perierunt'); they adhere not to the truth ('ueritatem'), but merely to what is similar to the truth ('ueri similia'). The World Soul is only 'minister' of life, not 'magister'; we must not attribute to it the 'power' that belongs strictly to God.[6] It is precisely the issues which Adalbold too briefly raises—the linguistic relation between verisimilitude and truth, and the cosmic relation between apparent and actual power—which determine the fate of the allegory of nature.

By the last half of the eleventh century, these dilemmas reach a critical turning point. On the one hand, men such as Peter Damian and Manegold of Lautenbach, seeking to defend the power of God, severely limit claims for the autonomous forces of nature or the conceptual designs of man. Damian, having been confronted during a conversation with Abbot Desiderius at Monte Cassino with the problem of whether an 'all-powerful' God has the power to restore a virgin after her fall, makes the challenge an opportunity to stress that the very course of nature is ultimately reducible to the Almighty: 'In-

---

[6] See the editions by R. B. C. Huygens, 'Mittelalterliche Kommentare zum *O qui perpetua*,' *Sacris erudiri*, 6 (1954), 394–5, 420; cf. Gregory, *Anima*, pp. 132–3 and *Platonismo*, pp. 1–15. For overviews of related questions raised by the commentaries of this period, including the association between the World Soul and the sun, located at the 'heart' of the cosmos, the relation between the threefold nature of the World Soul and of the human soul, or alternatively, between the World Soul's motion and the contrary movements of reason and sensuality, and the figurative treatment of the human soul's astral 'chariot,' see Courcelle, 'Étude,' 52–76; *Tradition,* pp.275–99; Brinkmann, pp. 188–9; Jacqueline Beaumont, 'The Latin Tradition of the *De Consolatione Philosophiae*,' in *Boethius*, ed. Gibson, cited above in Ch. III, n. 77, pp. 278–305; cf. my discussion later in this chapter.

deed, the nature of things has its own nature—that is, the will of God.' At the same time, while recognizing the use of logical investigation and drawing upon its techniques, he nonetheless urges caution toward the 'ars dialectica' and the 'entanglements of words' ('consequentia uerborum') which in such cases appear to limit divine power.[7] It is true that Damian acknowledges an allegory of nature, but for him, as for Raban Maur, it is still ordered largely by the evocations of Scripture—or the formulations of a bestiary.[8]

On the other hand, already in Damian's period different forces, however restricted initially in scope and influence, are promising to strengthen the claims of both the world and the arts. At the same time (the 1060s) and in the same monastery (Monte Cassino) at which Peter Damian had been posed that provocative question about God, Constantine the African was beginning to translate into Latin those Arabic medical works which would help men to analyze not only man's body, but the world's, as a sentient creature with its own sources of vitality, including that (originally Stoic) fiery 'pneuma' which would help the twelfth century to transform the world's radiant Soul into the 'craftsmanlike fire' of Nature.[9] At nearly the same time and in the same place, Alberic of Monte Cassino was stimulating that *ars dictaminis* which, while limited in its contributions to *ars poetria* (to say nothing of *ars dialectica*), would

[7] For overviews of *natura* seen from the perspective of Damian and Manegold, see Gregory, 'L'idea,' pp. 36–8; *Platonismo*, pp. 17–30. For Damian's responses here to the problem on power originally formulated by Jerome, see *Lettre sur la toute-puissance divine*, ed. and tr. André Cantin (Paris, 1972), p. 450 (*PL* 145, 612C), p. 416 (*PL* 145, 604B); on 'natura' as 'uoluntas Dei,' Damian is adapting Augustine, *De Civitate Dei* XXI, 8. While defending divine power, Damian oscillates in his approach toward what is 'possible' for God; see Cantin's assessment in his edition, pp. 129–31, 140, 178–80. For Damian's divided approach toward dialectic, see J. Gonsette, *Pierre Damien et la culture profane* (Louvain, 1956), pp. 43–61; Cantin's remarks in his edition, pp. 35–7, 40, 184–7, 221, 231, 308–10; and Cantin's *Les Sciences séculières et la foi: Les deux voies de la science au jugement de S. Pierre Damien (1007–1072)* (Spoleto, 1975), pp. 417, n. 123, 433, 437–50, with the observation on p. 439: 'few men probably had a spirit more removed from all forms of abstractions.'

[8] For Damian's moralizations of the elephant, the bull, etc., see J. A. Endres, *Petrus Damiani und die Weltliche Wissenschaft, Beiträge*, 8/3 (Münster, 1910), p. 32, n. 3.

[9] On these points see Paul Oskar Kristeller, 'The School of Salerno: Its Development and Its Contribution to the History of Learning,' orig. pub. 1945, repr. in his *Studies in Renaissance Thought and Letters* (Rome, 1956), esp. pp. 508–19; Stock, pp. 26, 30, 146, 152, 212–13; Gregory, *Anima*, pp. 152, 165, 171, n. 3; *Platonismo*, pp. 135–6, n. 1.

teach men to organize the 'entanglements of words' into cogent rhetorical patterns and rhythms, and would finally count Bernard Silvestris among its twelfth-century masters.[10] If only Damian had known that his pious polemic *On the Omnipotence of God* was conceived, so to speak, in the very cloister where that 'cursed monk,' 'daun Constantyn,' produced his rather more earthly treatise *On Coitus*, on which the *Cosmographia* itself may have drawn at its close (*Mic.* XIV, 153–78) to dramatize those seminal principles which keep regenerating both mankind and nature even while they perpetually flow away.[11] But such 'blessed inversions,' alas, have a way of turning into less fortunate falls; later in the Middle Ages, January in the *Merchant's Tale* (ll. 1805–30) seems virtually to have made *On Coitus* his bedtime reading; his heaven slips a bit lower than that of the *Cosmographia*.

The regenerative movement of the early twelfth century, though, depends upon more than the vitality of selected individuals and institutions.[12] It involves a broad, dynamic drive to discover the underlying causes of things, an aim exemplified by its own internal activity of seeking simultaneously to recover old resources and to develop new ones. If this striking process never wholly resolves the conflicts of earlier generations, it nonetheless transforms those dilemmas into a new, panoramic dimension.

From the perspective of theology, Anselm explores those *rationes* and Abelard, more radically, those *quaestiones* which begin to turn the exegesis of Scripture into a science, while Hugh of St. Victor, though himself developing the ordered sequences of the sacred *historia*, finally stresses the sacramental

---

[10] See Janet Martin, 'Classicism and Style in Latin Literature,' in *Renaissance and Renewal in the Twelfth Century*, ed. Robert L. Benson and Giles Constable (Cambridge, Mass., 1982), hereafter *Renewal*, pp. 537–68; Wetherbee, pp. 14, 104, 145.

[11] For Bernard's possible use of the *Liber Maior de Coitu* here, see Dronke, 'L'amor,' 415, n. 92, and Stock, p. 219, n. 103, though Wetherbee's translation, p. 164, nn. 110–11, also notes pertinent passages from Constantine's *De Communibus Locis*.

[12] Among many overviews of the twelfth-century renaissance since the stimulating work of Charles Homer Haskins, *The Renaissance of the Twelfth Century* (Cambridge, Mass., 1927), see esp. M.-D. Chenu, *La Théologie au douzième siècle* (Paris, 1957), partially translated in Chenu (1968); M. de Gandillac and É. Jeauneau (eds.), *Entretiens sur la renaissance du 12ᵉ siècle* (The Hague, 1968); and *Renewal*, cited above in n. 10. For personal discussions with me on the twelfth century, I am particularly grateful to Prof. Winthrop Wetherbee, Prof. Brian Stock, Fr. Nikolaus M. Häring, and Mlle Marie-Thérèse d'Alverny.

mysteries of a divine revelation. [13] Such tensions between scientific and sapiential tendencies acquire their own expression in cosmology, as William of Conches, adapting the *imago mundi* of Plato, integrates the cosmic process into a conceptual system of complementary, elemental forces, while Honorius, drawing upon the *universitas* of Eriugena, spreads that system into the hierarchical progression of a transcendent principle. [14] These dynamic approaches to the cosmos, in turn, develop new complexity with the growing interest in astrology; thus, Adelard of Bath translates a set of Arabic astronomical tables vital to the astrolabe, and Hermann of Carinthia translates the systematic astrological work of Abu Ma'shar, developments which stimulate a vision of interlocking motions from the celestial spheres to earth—a vision that seems simultaneously to bind man to a deterministic order and yet to grant him the power to explore the contingencies of his destiny. [15]

At the same time, the question of the powers of man provokes diverse speculations in psychology, from technical inquiries about the faculties of the soul to mystical transports on the return of man's *imago Dei* to its source. [16] Such explorations of human potentiality complement the imaginative range of a revitalized poetry, from the wistful reverie on nature and human nature in 'Levis exsurgit zephirus' to the typological regeneration of Adam of St. Victor's vigorously advancing 'Easter Sequence.' [17] This flourishing of literary artistry, in turn, has its broader dimension in the developing arts and sciences curriculum of the cathedral schools, while the dazzling

---

[13] See M. Grabmann, *Die Geschichte der Scholastischen Methode*, 2 vols. (1909 and 1911; repr. Graz, 1957), esp. Vol. I, pp. 28-37, Vol. II, pp. 13-24, 157-68; J. de Ghellinck, *Le Mouvement théologique du XIIe siècle*, 2nd edn. (1948; repr. Brussels, 1969), pp. 83-7, 125, 174-5, 197-202, 224-33; G. R. Evans, *Old Arts and New Theology: The Beginnings of Theology as an Academic Discipline* (Oxford, 1980); Chenu, pp. 103, 112-14, 165-73, 289-90.

[14] See Gregory, *Anima*; Lucentini, cited above in Ch. IV, n. 60, pp. 56-75; M.-Th. d'Alverny, 'Le Cosmos symbolique du XIIe siècle,' *AHDLMA* 28 (1953), 31-81.

[15] See Olaf Pederson, 'Astronomy,' in *Science in the Middle Ages*, ed. David C. Lindberg (Chicago, 1978), hereafter *Science*, pp. 308-13; Richard Lemay, *Abu Ma'shar and Latin Aristotelianism in the Twelfth Century* (Beirut, 1962), hereafter *Abu Ma'shar*; Gregory, 'L'idea,' pp. 48-61.

[16] See Pierre Michaud-Quantin, 'La Classification des puissances de l'âme au xiie siècle,' *Revue du moyen âge latin*, 5 (1949), 15-34; Robert Javelet, *Image et ressemblance au douzième siècle de St. Anselme à Alain de Lille*, 2 vols. (Paris, 1967); Colin Morris, *The Discovery of the Individual: 1050-1200* (1972; repr. New York, 1973).

[17] See *Oxford Book*, pp. 173-4, 234-7.

cathedrals of St. Denis and Chartres themselves finally testify both to a new technological ingenuity that transforms man's physical environment and to an aesthetics of form and light that redirects human perspective upward to the metaphysical art of God—the starting point for the whole process.[18]

In the end, though, these extraordinary transformations of old potentialities into new powers—to say nothing of decisive shifts in geographical boundaries, commercial activity, and social ambience—remain largely descriptions, not full explanations, of the renaissance of the twelfth century. Like every rebirth, the twelfth-century revival emerges from a complex, simultaneous movement backward and forward in orientation, in which the interest in a source is inseparable from the pursuit of an end, while the vision of the end is inseparable from the inspiration of the source. Significantly, this 'renaissance' is at once more ancient and more modern than any earlier revival in the Middle Ages; the very dynamics of its regeneration preeminently expose that endlessly receding movement in both directions which simultaneously stymies and provokes every search for causes.

One vivid expression of those dynamics is allegory, the philosophic and literary articulation of the search for causes. By directing the study of causes to the very powers of the cosmos, the allegory of nature seems to enact on a grand scale this simultaneous movement toward an underlying source and away from it, the reductive and expansive process of regeneration. On the one hand, in a movement we have seen dramatized even in cosmic allegory before the twelfth century, an allegory of nature requires a principle of cohesion, the 'conservation' of all powers in a single, divine source—however elusive that source may ultimately be. On the other hand (though this demand we have seen thus far much less successfully fulfilled), the flexibility of the allegory depends upon a principle of expansion, the 'delegation' of power by that source to figures who act in their own sphere—however reducible those figures may finally be. The allegory of nature, that is, requires the world to

---

[18] See R. W. Southern, *The Making of the Middle Ages* (1953; repr. New Haven, 1975), pp. 170–218; Brian Stock, 'Science, Technology, and Economic Progress in the Early Middle Ages,' in *Science*, pp. 25–32, 45; Otto von Simson, *The Gothic Cathedral* (New York, 1956).

be simultaneously one with God and other than him. Whether this dilemma is expressed in terms of reconciling immanence with transcendence, a 'positive' with a 'negative' theology, a center with a circumference, it is the cosmic consummation of the reductive and expansive tendencies informing allegorical interpretation and composition from the start.

For all their promise, the cosmic schemes examined up to now remain only partial expressions of these allegorical possibilities—Raban Maur's encyclopedic nature, for example, neatly indexed by scriptural authority to its divine author —even Eriugena's Nature, rather abstrusely undertaking a reflex action by which its very procession returns upon itself. It is only when the twelfth century scrutinizes the elemental nature of power and causality itself that it finally transforms the allegorical study of causes to a new, decisive level of sophistication. Seeking to direct the material world to its spiritual source while keeping the spiritual world distinct from the matter it informs, the natural philosophers of the early twelfth century impressively, if imperfectly, try to articulate the fundamental constituents of both worlds. Their activity remains abstract, not fully allegorical, in procedure, and it produces internal contradictions and external controversies. But by interpreting the powers of the cosmos conceptually, they simultaneously compose the prototypes of those graphic figures who will people the first magisterial allegories of the Middle Ages: Matter ('Hyle' or 'Silva'), the divine Mind ('Noys'), 'Natura,' and others. They thus help not only to consolidate the extremes of the cosmos in the middle ground of the natural world, but to join the interpretive and compositional traditions at large in an allegory at once intensive in concentration and comprehensive in scope.

MATTER: THE CONSERVATION OF POWER

It seems appropriate to begin a discussion of this process with the power which seems to occupy the other side of the universe from God—Matter itself, a force apparently so alien, 'obdurate,' 'hostile,' 'abounding in darkness,' that at the start of the *Cosmographia* it seems able to 'frighten its Creator' ('Auctorem terrere,' *Meg.* I, 18–31). As in the past, our aim is not to provide an exhaustive source study of Matter in the *Cosmographia*, much less in the early twelfth century as a whole,[19] but to explore certain strategies critical to the allegorical exploitation of the principle. Here we might concentrate on three such strategies, which may be loosely labeled the 'scientific,' the 'mystical,' and the 'creationist.' It should be stressed that these general approaches often overlap with each other, even in the earliest sources; they are not rigid categories defining a particular document or passage, but broad tendencies to facilitate analysis. In any event, as the natural philosophers of the early twelfth century seek to reconcile matter with God, to 'conserve' all power within a single divine source, they also tend gradually to transform and consolidate these diverse strategies, finally producing not only a distinctive interpretation of the material world, but an incipient composition in its own right, a 'matter' fit for poetry.

From the beginning, the 'scientific' sources for the Matter of the twelfth century tended to make it a principle limiting divine power, rather than enhancing it. As the earliest systematic account of the subject, Plato's *Timaeus*, puts the problem, the Demiurge who fashioned this world used for his model the perfect world of eternal Being, but the copy of this model was only an imperfect world of perpetual Becoming (27D–29D).[20] The Demiurge, it is true, had desired that 'so far as possible' (*kata dynamin,* 30A) all things should be good, but a recalcitrant 'Necessity' (*anankē,* 47E) restricted his power. Under such conditions, the principle of Reason (*nous*) needed to 'control' Necessity by 'persuading' (*peithein*) it to conduct to the best end 'the most part' of the things coming into existence; indeed, only through 'Necessity yielding to intelligent persuasion' (*anankēs hēttōmenēs hypo peithous emphronos,* 48A) did the cosmos arise.

[19] See Theodore Silverstein, 'The Fabulous Cosmogony of Bernardus Silvestris,' *MP* 46 (1948), 98–104; Gregory, *Anima,* pp. 189–212; *Platonismo,* pp. 104–22; Stock, pp. 97–118 *et passim; Cosm.* (tr.), pp. 36–8 and esp. the notes to *Meg.* I, II, IV; and the works cited below.

[20] Quotations and translations refer to the text in *Timaeus, Critias, Cleitophon, Menexenus, Epistles,* ed. and tr. R. B. Bury (Cambridge, Mass., 1929). For the *Timaeus'* decisive influence in the Middle Ages, see, e.g., Taylor, *Commentary,* cited above in Ch. II, n. 21, pp. 1–2; R. Klibansky, *The Continuity of the Platonic Tradition during the Middle Ages* (London, 1939), pp. 27–8, 30, 33–4.

Nonetheless, as Plato acknowledges, Necessity is the 'Errant Cause' (*tēs planōmenēs . . . aitias*, 48A), a kind of sheer truancy alienated by its very nature from authority.[21] It is thus difficult to see just how the stubbornness inherent in material things can be convincingly 'persuaded' at all. As Aristotle would later argue, 'necessity is held to be something that cannot be persuaded—and rightly, for it is contrary to the movement which accords with purpose and with reasoning.'[22]

Plato's cosmological problem here is somewhat similar to the psychological problem complicating his earlier work, when he tried to bridge the gap between the rational and irrational sides of the soul. How could the rational side 'persuade' the irrational one, if by definition the irrational has no 'mind' of its own? Plato had sought to resolve that dilemma by developing in the *Republic* a mediating principle distinct from either extreme, the *thymos*, but this principle seemed to succeed only by compromising its distinctive status, and acting as if it were 'rational' in its own right. Just such an argument, in fact, would later be applied directly to the realm of matter: if God persuaded it, it must have its own soul, since only animated beings can be persuaded.[23] Plainly, a Necessity that was open to persuasion required some interior susceptibility to Reason.

As if to address himself to this concern, Plato no sooner introduces 'Necessity' than he confesses the need (48E–49A) to revise his original account of a two-sided transaction between the perfect model of Being and the imperfect copy of Becoming. There must be something, he argues, *in which* the copy arises. This ground for material things Plato calls the 'Receptacle,' since it receives the model that will become a copy. It underlies

---

[21] See Cornford, *Plato's Cosmology*, cited above in Ch. II, n. 21, pp. 162–77, 206–10.

[22] See *Metaphysics* V, v, 1015a31-3, tr. W. D. Ross in *Basic Works*, cited above in Ch. II, n. 24. Glenn R. Murrow, 'Necessity and Persuasion in Plato's *Timaeus*,' *Philosophical Review*, 59 (1950), 147–63, tries to explain this 'persuasion' as the prudent selection of necessary contingencies into a purposeful design. Nevertheless, he underestimates the core of intractability here. The problem is not merely to order matter, but to penetrate it, as it were, with intelligibility. Cf. Cornford, *Plato's Cosmology*, pp. 176–7, 209, 361–4.

[23] Calcidius notes the argument, which may come from Numenius, but does not accept it; see *Timaeus a Calcidio Translatus Commentarioque Instructus*, ed. J. H. Waszink, rev. edn. (Leiden, 1975), in *Plato Latinus*, IV, in the Corpus Platonicum Medii Aevi series, hereafter Calcidius, to which all quotations from this work refer, ch. 300, p. 302.5-11, and J. C. M. van Winden, *Calcidius on Matter: His Doctrine and Sources* (Leiden, 1959), hereafter Winden, pp. 122–3.

everything, but has no character of its own. Later Plato calls it 'Place' (*khōra*, 52B), since it is the 'room' in which all things must exist. By being perfectly plastic, it can receive every form. In this sense materiality cooperates with Reason and 'yields' to it.

Even while the Receptacle enables Reason to pursue its plans, however, it spoils them in part. Because it is the medium in which the perfect model must degenerate into an imperfect copy, it thwarts Reason's perfection. It is thus both the necessary condition for Being to come to exist at all, and at the same time the necessary resistance to Being. Plato's God, as it were, cannot do without it; even in helping him, it thus displays his limitations.[24]

There is a deeper sense, however, in which Necessity must always remain outside Reason's camp. Not only is there no reason *in* Necessity by definition, but also there is no reason *for* it. Necessity has no *aitia*—cause or reason—precisely because nothing caused it in the first place. As Plato says of his Receptacle, it is *aei* (52B), always-existing. Such an independent reality could never be wholly reduced to Reason, which was not responsible for it.[25] If we may paraphrase Plato's abstract scheme, it was *necessary* that Reason's power should be limited. As we shall see, only when divine power is completely conserved will matter's 'rivalry' with God become oblique enough to make it fully suited for allegory.

Though this possibility remains limited in the 'scientific' tradition itself, even with the 'mythological' tendencies of Plato's model, it advances somewhat in the work that transmits the *Timaeus* to the Middle Ages, Calcidius' fourth-century AD *Commentary*. In this treatise, matter becomes a graphic figure of diverse dimensions, some of them scientifically quite irreconcilable with each other; Calcidius identifies it not only with

---

[24] See Harold F. Cherniss, *Aristotle's Criticism of Plato and the Academy*, I (Baltimore, 1944), hereafter Cherniss, pp. 172-3, and Leonard J. Eslick, 'The Material Substrate in Plato,' hereafter Eslick, in *The Concept of Matter*, ed. Ernan McMullin (Notre Dame, Ind., 1963), hereafter *Concept*, pp. 70, 74. While Plato himself did not explicitly identify his Receptacle with 'matter,' by the Middle Ages, Receptacle, matter, and Necessity were all identified; see below.

[25] See R. P. Festugière, *Le Dieu cosmique*, Vol. II of *La Révélation d'Hermès Trismégiste* (Paris, 1949), p. 148; Cornford, *Plato's Cosmology*, pp. 35-7, 164-5, 193, 209-10; Eslick, p. 71.

Plato's 'Necessity,' but also with Hesiod's 'Chaos,' the confused mass in Genesis, Aristotle's 'hyle,' and 'silva.'[26] It is a many-faceted 'Hyle' or 'Silva,' of course, that will take a leading role in the *Cosmographia*, but in Calcidius the figure is still far from an oblique principle expressing divine power, much less an allegorical character. In fact, although Calcidius knows that according to the Jews (ch. 276) matter was made by God, and although he himself is a Christian, he considers matter an independent reality.[27]

The consequences of this view are grave, and despite the diverse attitudes exhibited by Calcidius, he cannot entirely avoid them. If God is responsible for good, and matter is something for which he is not responsible, then matter must not be good. 'According to Plato,' notes Calcidius with approval (schematizing and moralizing a brief flourish in *Timaeus* 50D on the Source of things as a 'father,' the Receptacle as a 'mother,' and the result of their interaction as the 'offspring'), the world received its good things from God, as a 'father,' but evil 'clung' to it through 'the defect of matter, its mother' (ch. 298, p. 300. 4–5). In such a divided universe, good and evil are not only eternal opposites; they have opposite causes: 'Deum . . . initium et causam bonorum, siluam malorum' (ch. 296, p. 298. 13–14).[28]

Like Plato, Calcidius tries to ameliorate this opposition; he discusses at length, for example, Reason's 'persuasion' of Necessity (chs. 269–70). We have already seen the pitfalls of this notion in Plato. As usual in hopeless situations, the more Calcidius tries to step out of the trap, the deeper he slips into the mud. Necessity, he insists, willingly offered itself ('se facilem praebente') for adornment. Reason, after all, dominated it not as a tyrant, but as a wise ruler, who improves

---

[26] See Calcidius, ch. 268, p. 273. 15; ch. 123, p. 167. 6; ch. 276, p. 280. 1–5. On the conflations (some antedating Calcidius) and inconsistencies in this treatment of matter, see J. R. O'Donnell, 'The Meaning of "Silva" in the Commentary on the *Timaeus* of Plato by Chalcidius,' *Mediaeval Studies,* 7(1945), 19; Winden, pp. 31, 245, *et passim.*

[27] On matter's eternity, see ch. 295, p. 297. 15–16; ch. 312, p. 311. 10–11; ch. 319, p. 315. 22–3; ch. 330, p. 325. 3; on Calcidius' rejection of creation *ex nihilo,* see ch. 31, pp. 80. 20–81. 1. Cf. Winden, pp. 8, 53, 108, 220, 239; R. M. Jones, 'Calcidius and Neoplatonism,' *Classical Philology,* 13 (1918), 208; and below.

[28] My translation of the first passage is based on Winden, p. 114, who associates 'Oriental dualism' (p. 117) with the incriminating remarks following it.

his subject ('melius efficit quod regit'). By 'salutary persuasion' ('salubri persuasione') Reason urged the harshness of
Necessity ('rigorem necessitatis') to the best ends. As a result,
Necessity itself became 'provident' in its obedience ('prouida
parentia'). With this, of course, Calcidius gives away the
game. He is trying to define out of existence the very Necessity
to which he grants independence. Necessity in his account
becomes 'provident' ('prouida'), which was presumably the attribute of Providence, its opposite number. The very principle
of adversity must not, as he says a few lines earlier, be 'adverse'
('aduersum').[29] The fact is that by definition Necessity has no
'reason,' and it therefore seems rather difficult to reason with
it. Calcidius himself began the discussion by conceding that
Reason and Necessity were 'separate elements and principles'
('diuersis elementis initiisque,' ch. 269, p. 274. 7-8). Insofar as
Calcidius attributes reason to Necessity, he denies the very
premise with which he started.

In the end, the rivalry between matter and God seems to in-
here in the very structure of Calcidius' universe. Approving of
Pythagoras' view that matter is intrinsically evil, Calcidius
observes that for Pythagoras, the existence of Providence
necessarily ('necessario,' ch. 296, p. 299. 7-10) involves evil
alongside it. Here Calcidius seems to be referring to a broad
tradition in which one opposite necessarily implies its counterpart;
it is as if his world had fallen from the start into 'that doom which
Adam fell into of knowing good and evill, that is to say of knowing
good *by* evill.' Unlike Milton, though, Calcidius sees this two-
sidedness from all eternity and in the very nature of things, not
merely in our fallen knowledge about them.[30] Now the basic principle that one side of the universe implies the other will become
central to the *Cosmographia*, but as we have seen in the partial an-
ticipations of Bernard's strategy by the Neoplatonists Boethius

---

[29] See ch. 270, p. 274. 21-2; later (ch. 298, p. 300. 16), nonetheless, 'aduersatur
prouidentiae.'

[30] For Milton's comment (my italics), see *Areopagitica*, ed. Ernest Sirluck, in *The
Complete Prose Works of John Milton*, ed. Douglas Bush, John S. Diekhoff, *et al.*, Vol. II
(New Haven, 1959), p. 514. For Calcidius' approach, see Winden, p. 113, and my article, 'From the *Cosmographia* to the *Divine Comedy*,' cited above in Ch. III, n. 95, pp.
66-8, which distinguishes the 'absolute' correlation of opposites (which Calcidius suggests) from two different but related traditions (including the 'epistemological' claim
that Milton invokes), all three of which contribute to medieval allegory.

and Eriugena, its success depends upon the degree to which this world does not simply invert the other world, but converts toward it. The medieval allegory of nature begins to develop fully only when the adversary of God convincingly becomes an aspirant toward him.

Despite its limitations, Calcidius' commentary itself provides a philosophic basis for that aspiration by partially incorporating a third 'scientific' approach to matter, the approach of Aristotle. For Aristotle, it is true, matter is still independent of God, but it is not a principle opposite to him, nor does it act against his designs. Plato, of course, had argued that his Receptacle had no activity of its own, but it always tended to slip from neutrality into adversity, like some *thymos* gone wrong.[31] By contrast, Aristotle explicitly inserts between the opposing principles of the world a 'third thing,' a means by which one contrary can develop into the other. In terms of the famous Aristotelian example, while the unmusical *per se* can never change into the musical, an unmusical *man* can become musical.[32] This keen conception of a material subject, distinct from both privation and form, yet susceptible to either, tends to free matter from any necessary connection with evil itself. Instead of being contrary to form, matter becomes the potentiality for form, definable not only by what it is, but by what it can be. As Calcidius puts it, paraphrasing Aristotle, unformed bronze is 'potentially' ('possibilitate') a statue, even though it is as yet unformed ('informe'). Split between its limitations and its possibilities, the material subject has a divided identity; the bronze both 'is and is not a statue' ('Est ergo statua et non est'); the shift in its identity embodies the dynamics of change.[33]

[31] See above, with n. 24, and Eslick, pp. 60, 64–6. At the heart of the problem is the mismatch in Plato between Being and existence; see Étienne Gilson, *Being and Some Philosophers*, 2nd edn. (Toronto, 1952), pp. 1–73. For the attempt to make the Receptacle 'neutral,' see *Tim.* 50BC, 51A, and Calcidius, chs. 309–22.

[32] See *Physics* I, vi, 189a26 and vii. It remains questionable whether Aristotle is fair in charging that Plato wholly divides the world into irreconcilable opposites which cannot interact; see, e.g., *Phaedo* 102D–103C, *Sophist* 257B–259B, and Cherniss, pp. 92–101. George S. Claghorn, *Aristotle's Criticism of Plato's 'Timaeus'* (The Hague, 1954), pp. 5–19, in his attempt to reconcile Aristotle's 'matter' with Plato's 'Receptacle,' tends to treat Aristotle's criticisms more as friendly suggestions than as the serious charges they are.

[33] For Aristotle's broader exposition (not explicitly included in Calcidius) of matter as potentiality, see, e.g., *Metaphysics* V, vii, 1017b1–9, xii, and *Metaphysics* IX, and cf.

The movement of material aspiration implied by this approach is articulated by Calcidius in only a fragmentary and confused fashion, but his one sustained quotation-paraphrase (ch. 286) from the *Physics* (I, ix, 192a3–33) provides the early twelfth century with perhaps its most vital source of Aristotle's doctrine on matter. Matter, begins the quotation, differs from privation. Privation, the opposite of form, resists ('renititur') formative activity, whereas matter desires ('appetit') form, 'just as the female desires the male, and deformity, beauty' ('ut femineus sexus uirilem et deformitas pulchritudinem'). And this deformity belongs to matter not 'ex natura,' but 'ex accidenti.' However laconic in its own right and complicated by Calcidius' glosses, this crucial passage promotes the possibilities of 'matter' in three critical ways. First, it distinguishes more than one principle on the other side of form—not just formlessness, but a principle of transition between the extremes, the sheer capacity for form. Second, it conceives this capacity in terms of a drive for fulfillment, thus changing the old maternal 'Receptacle' from a 'receiving' principle into a 'desiring' one. Third, it makes the 'deformity' of matter a condition that belongs to it not properly, but only obliquely, thus enhancing its aptitude for the beauty it seeks. The 'matter' of this passage is still not allegorical; a split identity is not a split personality, and as for 'desire,' Calcidius points out that it is not that of living things (ch. 287, p. 292. 4–6). But in the passage from Plato, to Calcidius, to Calcidius' Aristotle, a scientific foundation is emerging for the complex opening scene of the *Cosmographia*, where Silva, though obdurate ('rigens'), desires ('Optat') form, and, as a mother containing the original natures of things diffused within her womb ('parens . . . genetiva tenet, gremio diffusa'), yearns ('cupit') to be born again ('Rursus . . . nasci').

For all these 'scientific' contributions to the reborn world of the *Cosmographia*, the matter of the twelfth century has at times a

Joseph Owens, 'Matter and Predication in Aristotle,' pp. 110–13, and Ernan McMullin, 'Four Senses of "Potency," ' pp. 295–6, in *Concept*. Even when Calcidius is not directly expounding Aristotle, however, Aristotelian notions infiltrate his approach; see, e.g., his tendency to oscillate between a Platonic principle that is 'impassive,' and thus immutable, and an Aristotelian matter that is 'passive,' and thus movable, discussed by Winden, pp. 31–2, 120, 124–5, 142, 147, 149, 152–3, 159–60, 166, 169, 171–3, 189–90, 203, 233, 235, 241–5.

more exotic, even mystical dimension. The most important (though not the only) source of this exotic approach is the Hermetic *Asclepius,* probably composed in the early centuries AD and translated into Latin perhaps about the time of Calcidius.[34] Itself drawing upon a mélange of philosophic sources, with a considerable Stoic component, the *Asclepius* transmutes these elements in an aura of mystery, in which the revelation of divine Love ('diuinus Cupido') from above is an initiation of enraptured man from below (ch. 1). Framed, as it were, by a diffused Stoic-Platonic perspective—from its opening declaration that 'all things are one, and the One, All' ('omnia unum esse et unum omnia,' ch. 2, p. 297. 23-4) and its fiery cosmology of an 'ignis' fashioning the world (ch. 2, p. 298. 5-12), to its closing argument about a comprehensive Destiny, *heimarmenē,* necessitating ('necessitas') the concatenation of events (chs. 39-40)—it contributes, along with more rigorously philosophic sources, to vital twelfth-century speculations about matter's oneness with God, the formative activity of the *ignis artifex,* and the orderly pattern of temporal succession, even helping to inspire the abstract figure of 'Imarmene' in the *Cosmographia* (*Meg.* IV, xiv).[35] For all its pantheistic tendencies, it displays at times a dualistic strain, declaring that in the beginning 'there was God and *hylē,*' and that '*hylē,*' with its 'spiritus,' is 'ungenerated' (ch. 14). Yet even this duality it seeks to resolve by energizing matter with an autonomous power of generation ('in se nascendi procreandique uim,' ch.

---

[34] Quotations refer to the edition in Vol.II of *Corpus Hermeticum* (Paris, 1945), cited above in Ch. III, n. 85, hereafter *Asc.* For its diverse sources, the problematic question of its composition and unity, and its influence in the twelfth century, see Walter Scott, ed. and tr., *Hermetica,* Vol. I (Oxford, 1924), pp. 51-81; *Asc.,* pp. 267-8, 284-95. For other sources of Hermetic lore in the twelfth century, see, e.g., the introduction to *Liber Hermetis Mercurii Triplicis de vi rerum principiis,* ed. Theodore Silverstein, *AHDLMA* 22 (1955), 217-302 (a work probably later than the *Cosmographia*), and Stock, p. 207, n. 86. For a different kind of 'mystical' orientation to matter influencing the twelfth century, see my discussion of Eriugena above and below.

[35] On the One, see *Asc.,* n. 15, with Todd, 'Monism,' cited above in Ch. II, n. 30; on fire, see *Asc.,* n. 18, with Hahm, *Origins,* cited above in Ch. II, n. 29; on *heimarmenē* and 'necessitas,' see *Asc.,* nn. 331-6, with Sambursky, *Physics,* cited above in Ch. II, n. 30, pp. 52-7. On the qualification of these principles for the twelfth century by Platonic sources (esp. Boethius) and astrological writings (esp. Firmicus Maternus and Abu Ma'shar), see, e.g., Gregory, *Anima,* pp. 59-97; Stock, pp. 83-4, 146-50, 204-7; Lemay, *Abu Ma'shar,* pp. 60-1, 76, 88, 113-32, 181-2, 257, 268-71; R. B. Woolsey, 'Bernard Silvester and the Hermetic Asclepius,' *Traditio,* 6 (1948), 341-2; *Cosm.* (tr.), pp. 31, 152-3, nn. 115-18, pp. 154-6, nn. 137, 141-50; and my discussion below.

14, p. 313. 21–2), as if it were no sooner separating God from matter than finding him inside it. Matter here is less an object of scientific analysis than an opportunity for mystical ascent.

In this charged, cosmic continuum, the extremes of the universe tend to blend into each other. God, once divided from matter as the 'father' from the 'mother,' is now 'utterly filled with the fecundity of both sexes' ('utraque sexus fecunditate plenissimus,' ch. 20, p. 321. 9–10). At the same time, matter incorporates the same opposites within itself, as the two sexes of 'all things, animate and inanimate,' mingling in the God-given 'mystery of eternal reproduction,' pour out into each other their issue ('utraque in utramque fundat nature progeniem'), so that the female acquires a masculine vigor ('uirtutem . . . marum'), and the male is relaxed in feminine languor ('femineo torpore,' ch. 21).[36] In such an erotic 'mysterium,' matter becomes not only an aspirant toward God, but an animating principle in a pulsating universe, a world both 'vivified' and 'vivifying' ('uiuificatur . . . uiuificatque,' ch. 30, p. 338. 3-4). Before the material world of the *Asclepius* can pass fully into medieval allegory, it will be necessary to turn this teeming birth process into a more metaphorical conception, and to distinguish more clearly the generative movement of matter from the creative power of God. But here already is an embryonic expression of the fecund Matter of the *Cosmographia*, 'fertile and prolific' ('pregnabilis et fecunda'), preexisting in the 'spirit' of eternal vitality ('preiacebat in spiritu vivacitatis eterne,' *Meg.* II, vi, 6–7; IV, viii, 5).

While the *Asclepius* helps to turn matter into a principle cooperating with God, neither its 'mystical' orientation nor the 'scientific' arguments we have explored make the material world an agent of God, a figure seeming to exhibit power in its own right but actually displaying the power of God. This is the distinctive legacy to later allegory of the 'creationist' perspective on matter. Developing ambiguously already in Hellenistic Jewish writing at the turn of the first centuries BC and AD, the notion that God creates the world *ex nihilo* acquires increasingly systematic expression in Christian theologians from the second

---

[36] See *Poimandres* 9, in *Corpvs Hermeticvm*, I; *Asc.*, nn. 173, 180; Dronke, 'L'amor,' 397, 407-8; Stock, pp. 102–5.

to the fourth centuries.[37] In making matter originate with God's creative activity, such early writers may not yet fully exploit the metaphysical principle that a God who said 'I am who am' (Exod. 3: 14) encompasses existence itself,[38] but they at least express the need to safeguard the comprehensive power of the sole Creator.

Thus, in the second century Theophilus of Antioch distinguishes a full-fledged creator from a mere artisan working with preexisting materials. In the third century, Tertullian argues that such a preexisting matter would imply that God was 'in want' of it. In the fourth century, Athanasius observes that a God of this kind would be powerless to create without matter.[39] By contrast, all power is conserved in a God who creates *ex nihilo*. By the same token, 'matter' in such a creation is transformed; no longer a mere aspirant, much less an adversary, now it is virtually an aspect of God.

While this early Christian perspective seems at last to make the material world the very expression of the divine one, it nonetheless presents a final obstacle to matter's allegorization. Even if a creationist God has no evil principle countering him from all eternity, the God of Scripture seems himself to have created on the other side of the universe a chaos almost as ungodly as any such counterpart. Revealingly, already in Augustine's work there is a tentative effort to give the 'formless' mass in Genesis a kind of form, as if to make it more akin to God, and this problematic strategy, developed in the twelfth century, has its effect upon the *Cosmographia*, with its primordial 'elements' already appearing in the midst of confusion.[40] The chaos of Genesis, however, raises broader questions about how a primeval darkness can fit from the start into

---

[37] See 2 Mach. 7: 28; Wolfson, *Philo*, Vol. I, pp. 300–10 (an analysis not wholly convincing, but exemplifying the ambiguity of the issue at this stage); and two important articles by Wolfson reprinted in *Studies*, a collection cited above in Ch. IV, n. 69, 'Plato's Pre-existent Matter in Patristic Philosophy,' pp. 170–81, and 'Patristic Arguments Against the Eternity of the World,' pp. 182–98.

[38] See Étienne Gilson, *The Spirit of Mediaeval Philosophy*, tr. A. H. C. Downes (New York, 1936), pp. 68–71, with notes, and *History of Christian Philosophy in the Middle Ages* (London, 1955), pp. 19–20, relating the principle to early treatments of creation in the *Pastor of Hermas*, the *Cohortatio ad Graecos*, and Theophilus of Antioch.

[39] See Wolfson, 'Plato's Pre-existent Matter,' p. 179.

[40] See *Meg.* I, 23–7; cf. I, 43–7 and II, vi, 1–3. On the general strategy, see Silverstein, 99–100; cf. Augustine, *Confessions* XII, 6; XIII, 33.

a divine design. It is true that theologians from Ambrose to Bede to Hugh of St. Victor might claim that such a darkness allowed God to illuminate man by showing (in Hugh's words) how great a distance separated bare being ('esse') from adorned being ('pulchrum esse').[41] But such defenses come perilously close to the old position that in some sense God 'needs' an opposite after all in order to display his power. It would be ironic if the creationist perspective undermined Plato's 'Necessity' only to allow it, in a different form, to be born again.

If each of these early approaches to matter—'scientific,' 'mystical,' and 'creationist'—makes certain direct contributions to twelfth-century allegory, none of them quite displays the *Cosmographia*'s unique perspective. That perspective finally begins to develop only as the natural philosophers of the early twelfth century, probing the very structure of the physical world, increasingly play these sources off each other, thereby altering the abstract characterization of matter itself. Whether these extraordinary men constitute a 'school' is questionable; their institutional affiliations are fluid, and their attitudes toward the precise value and operation of the natural world, even toward matter itself, differ in important respects.[42] Nor do they themselves produce allegorical poetry. Rather, in interpreting both the foundations of the material world and the ancient language of their sources, they develop an angle of vision and a pattern of analogies which begin to shift the concept of matter into an oblique realm one day to be exploited by the *Cosmographia*. Here we might concentrate on two of the most innovative and influential of these philosophers, William of Conches and Thierry of Chartres, with brief glances at some of their contemporaries, to suggest how their efforts to integrate

[41] For the positions of these three figures, see Gregory, *Platonismo*, pp. 105-6, n. 2. Cf. M.-D. Chenu, 'Nature ou histoire? Une controverse exégétique sur la création au XIIᵉ siècle,' *AHDLMA* 20 (1953), 25-30.

[42] The degree to which it is appropriate to speak of a 'School of Chartres' has been the subject of considerable controversy since R. W. Southern's challenge in *Medieval Humanism and Other Studies* (Oxford, 1970), pp. 61-85. More recently, see Southern, *Platonism, Scholastic Method, and the School of Chartres* (Reading, 1979), and 'The Schools of Paris and the School of Chartres,' with bibliography in n. 1, in *Renewal*, pp. 113-37. On the diverse approaches of such philosophers to matter, see Heinrich Flatten, 'Die "materia primordialis" in der Schule von Chartres,' *Archiv für Geschichte der Philosophie*, 40 (1931), 58-65.

these three broad approaches to matter tend to make each perspective qualify the others and be qualified by them in turn—beginning with the last approach, the creationist.

A particularly revealing case of this transformation is William of Conches' *Glosses* on the *Timaeus*.[43] Here the systematic effort to reconcile a creationist approach with a scientific account enriches both traditions and produces a 'matter' at some remove from either of them. Opening his discussion of Plato's natural philosophy by citing the four (originally Aristotelian) causes—efficient, formal, final, and material— William at once qualifies this scheme by indicating that only the first three are truly 'causes,' the Being, Wisdom, and Goodness of the Trinity. The material cause, after all, is really an 'effectus' (98–9).[44] By a series of interpretive transfers, William subtly revises Plato's argumentation in the very act of seeming to endorse it. The *auctor* argues that nothing comes to be without a cause; 'ergo nec mundus,' stresses the commentator (103, 106, 108). Plato says that the source of this world is an artisan; 'opifex, id est Creator,' glosses William (112, 126).[45] In this process, the preexisting matter and the imperfect divinity of the *Timaeus* turn into philosophic expressions of a single creative act with two complementary dimensions. What once resisted God now becomes his ally; matter, observes William, is the Creator's 'creatura,' testifying to his comprehensive 'potentia' (260).

As a result of this affinity between matter and God, William is spared some of the embarrassment Plato and Calcidius displayed when it came time to describe the cooperation between Necessity and Reason. Plato had claimed that Necessity

[43] See *Glosae super Platonem*, ed. Édouard Jeauneau (Paris, 1965), hereafter *Glosae*, cited by page number. For its period of composition and 'redactions,' see pp. 12–16, 45–8. For William's reputation and the distinction of his *Glosses* amid other twelfth-century glosses to Plato, see pp. 10–11, 29–30, and Gregory, *Platonismo*, pp. 55–8.

[44] On the transmission of the four Aristotelian causes via Boethius, see J. M. Parent, *La Doctrine de la création dans l'école de Chartres*, Publications de l'Institut d'Études Médiévales d'Ottawa, Vol. 8 (Ottawa, 1938), hereafter *La Doctrine*, p. 43. On the importance of Boethius to William's *Glosses*, see *Glosae*, pp. 27–8. For other identifications of the first three causes with the Trinity, see *Commentaries on Boethius by Thierry of Chartres and his School*, ed. Nikolaus M. Häring (Toronto, 1971), hereafter cited as *Thierry* (with the caution on authorship noted in the discussion of Thierry and his circle below), pp. 555. 18–556. 34, and John of Salisbury, *Policraticus* VII, 5.

[45] For various strategies by which William turns the artisan into a Creator *ex nihilo*, see 104, 108, 116, 287, 289. Cf. *Thierry*, p. 77. 76–8.

yielded to 'intelligent persuasion,' while Calcidius grandly held forth on the effectiveness of a wise ruler. If Necessity was persuaded by such posturing, it is doubtful that anyone else was. William, by contrast, starting from the view that God and matter are not alien principles, but related ones—however distant from each other—develops no such rivalry. When he reaches Calcidius' words, 'with Reason dominating' ('dominante tamen intellectu,' 261), he indicates that even the most unrefined matter already has being, albeit a 'rudimentary being' ('rude esse'). Form, on the other hand, gives that matter 'the being that it is' ('esse id quod est'), just as a statue is called a statue of Achilles not from the fact that 'it is of bronze, but from the fact that a certain form is impressed upon it.'[46] There is now an irresistible force, but no longer, as in Plato and Calcidius, an immovable object.[47] William therefore conveniently omits Calcidius' next words, 'salubri persuasione' (*Tim.* 48A); matter no longer needs to be implored, like some truant, to obey authority. It belongs from the start to an author refining his own design.

If William's creationist approach modifies his scientific analysis, the process of revision also works in reverse. Thus, when he reads in Calcidius' translation that God 'marshalled the elements from a disorderly turbulence into order' ('ex inordinata iactatione redegit in ordinem,' *Tim.* 30A), he does not say: 'iactatio, id est caos.' Instead, he boldly denies a primordial chaos either in the *Timaeus* or in Genesis (118–19).[48] He knows the old theological argument, articulated in his own period by Hugh of St. Victor, perfectly well: God created chaos 'in order to show how great a confusion there would be in things unless the divine power and wisdom ordered them.' To whom, though, William asks, would God show the difference between this initial confusion and its later order? To an angel? An angel already knows the natures of things 'by its own

---

46 The direct source of this analogy is Boethius, *De Trinitate* 2; cf. *Thierry*, p. 271. 87–8. For the non-pantheistic sense in which God is *forma essendi*, see Gregory, *Anima*, pp. 80–97.

47 See the almost Aristotelian formulation that matter 'transit in ("passes into") aliud, ut es in statuam' (258); cf. *Thierry*, p. 167. 52–4, and Winden, p. 32.

48 The analysis here closely parallels his discussion in *Philosophia Mundi* I, 21; *PL* 172, 53–4. For the controversy between William and Hugh of St. Victor on this issue, see *Didascalicon*, tr. Taylor, cited above in Ch. II, n. 34, pp. 227–8, n. 3.

nature and by divine grace.' To man, then? No man yet existed, and if God had made such confusion to show it to man, he would not have ordered it before man's creation. The old argument, then, is 'inconveniens.'

Even more explicitly, William prefaces this critique by appealing to the physical principles at stake here (118). It is quite impossible, he observes, for the four elements to 'rise and fall simultaneously,' as the believers in chaos claim. After all, there is no 'place' outside the elements ('extra elementa nullus locus est'). Accordingly, fire, the highest of the four elements, could not 'rise' with the others; by definition, 'there was nowhere for it to rise.' Similarly, earth, the lowest element, could not 'fall' with the others; there was nowhere for it to go, either. It is almost as if Plato's *khōra*, 'Place,' which once limited the divine design, now guaranteed it. God, concludes William, must have created the elements from the start in their present order, even if they were not 'disposed' ('disposita') as they are now. That is, they had their 'substantial' qualities, but not their 'accidental' qualities of refinement.[49] The tumultuous disorder, though, that had for so long seemed the necessary concomitant to divine order, had at last disappeared even from that primeval darkness. 'What would be the place of disorder, with God disposing all things' ('quis enim locus esset inordinationi, Deo cuncta disponente')?[50]

William's argument was not widely accepted, but even many who took other positions shared its spirit.[51] Alan of Lille himself later argues against the notion of an 'inordinatam materiam.' 'If it was made by God, how could it be disorderly'?[52] Indeed, for all the differences in orientation between William and Alan, the earlier philosopher is already suggesting that matter's problematic condition can be seen from not only a direct, but an oblique point of view. 'From a disorderly turbulence,' William reads in his source, hastening

---

[49] See 118-19, 122-3, 258-9, 288-9, and William's commentary on Boethius, ed. Parent in *La Doctrine*, cited above in n. 44, p. 129.

[50] Cf. 'Des commentaires inédits de Guillaume de Conches et de Nicholas Triveth sur la Consolation de la philosophie de Boèce,' ed. Charles Jourdain, *Notices et extraits des manuscrits de la Bibliothèque Impériale*, 20 (1862), 61.

[51] See Chenu, 'Nature ou histoire?,' cited above in n. 41.

[52] See *Summa 'Quoniam homines,'* ed. P. Glorieux, *AHDLMA* 20 (1953), 128; Gregory, *Anima*, pp. 200-1, n. 3, quotes the passage.

to explain, 'not that which *was* but that which *could* be' ('non
que fuit sed que esse potuit,' 123). It is as when, he says in
elaborating this very critique of 'chaos' in his own *Philosophia
Mundi*, by the warning of a friend, we escape that which *would*
have happened had the friend not been there. In such a case,
we say that he 'freed' us from this evil, not because the evil was
there in the first place, but because the evil *would* have happened
to us had he not been there (*PL* 172, 54A). Chaos is thus not
something that actually happened, but something that would
have happened had not God instilled his orderly presence in
matter from the beginning. It is a way of expressing what is
always threatening in possibility, but permanently stymied in
actuality. In saying that God freed the world from such a
villain, we are really saying indirectly that he supported his ally.
In the end, his evil opponent displays by its limited status as a
figure the good that matter possesses in fact. No longer spoiling
the divine design, 'chaos' here becomes a foil for God's own
comprehensive power.

If William of Conches alters the language of 'chaos' to distance
matter from its lower capabilities, it remains to shift the concept of matter more clearly toward its higher possibilities. The
most radical tendency to elevate matter in the sources for
twelfth-century speculation develops within the second of the
broad approaches we have explored, the 'mystical' doctrine of
the *Asclepius*, proclaiming that 'all things are one, and the One,
All.' Such exotic doctrine, however, has its pantheistic implications, and it is revealing to see the more rigorous analyses
associated with the twelfth-century philosopher Thierry of
Chartres—to whom Bernard Silvestris dedicates the
Cosmographia itself—seeking to integrate this approach with
both the theological and scientific traditions. It is not always
possible to know how closely the works which have been linked
to Thierry preserve his teachings in their original form.[53] While
there is evidence for Thierry's inspiration in their argument
and method, at least some of these writings, or passages within
them, may belong to students adapting his work. Until ques-

[53] See the overview of Häring in *Thierry*, pp. 19–52, and the questions raised by
Southern, *Platonism, Scholastic Method, and the School of Chartres,* cited above in n. 42,
pp. 25–40.

tions of authorship are further clarified, it seems best to refer these texts—including three important commentaries on Boethius' theological writing, classified as the *Commentum*, the *Lectiones*, and the *Glosa*[54]—not strictly to Thierry himself, but to the circle of Thierry and those immediately influenced by him. The works themselves, in any case, articulate certain linguistic and philosophic distinctions vital to the broader characterization of matter as a figure pointing beyond itself.

The most striking example of such a strategy in the group of writings from Thierry's circle appears within a discussion that concentrates not on the material side of the universe but on the divine one. Analyzing Boethius' *On the Trinity*, the author of the *Commentum* is about to explain the relation between the Aristotelian categories and God when he breaks into a discussion of his own on 'predication' (p. 95. 1) in order to free certain statements of any heretical implications.[55] He argues, for example, that it is legitimate to say not only that 'God is all things' ('deus est omnia'), but that certain other subjects, like 'matter,' are 'all things' ('materia iterum omnia,' p. 97. 77–80). Now the Church had long debated the precise sense in which God is 'all things' (a claim suggested by Scripture itself in a number of celebrated passages), and the twelfth century does not end the speculation.[56] Our more immediate concern is how the commentator seeks to reconcile such a position with the claim that 'matter is all things'—and more broadly, what it might mean to say, as 'in *Trimegistro* Mercurius asserit' (the *Asclepius* passage quoted in the *Commentum* and in our own discussion above), that 'omnia unum esse' (p. 97. 88–90).

'Predication,' explains the commentator, is variable (p. 98. 8–16). For example, we can say that 'an egg is a living creature' ('ouum esse animal'), even though strictly speaking such is not the case. It is called a living creature according to its

---

[54] These are the titles given to the first, third, and fifth texts in Häring's edn. The first text, perhaps the most celebrated of the commentaries, is also known as the *Librum hunc*.

[55] On this discussion, see Stephen Gersh, 'Platonism—Neoplatonism—Aristotelianism: A Twelfth-Century Metaphysical System and Its Sources,' in *Renewal*, pp. 512–34, hereafter 'Platonism,' to which I am deeply indebted throughout my analysis.

[56] See, e.g., 1 Cor. 15: 28, Rom. 11: 36, and John 1: 3–4; Augustine, *De Natura Boni* 26–7; Gregory, *Anima*, pp. 80–97; Maurice de Wulf, 'Le Panthéisme Chartrain,' in *Beiträge*, Supplementband III, 1 (1935), pp. 282–8; and Étienne Gilson, *La Philosophie au moyen âge* (Paris, 1944), p. 383.

'potentiality' ('natura possibilitatis'). For 'from an egg it is possible for a living creature to be made' ('ex ouo animal fieri
possibile est'). Indeed, such potentiality applies to creation at
large. It is stated, the commentator continues, that God
'created all things at once' (Eccli. 18: 1). But it is not exactly
the things themselves which were so created. Rather, all things
were created at once in the sense that at a single stroke the sum
total of the matter ('materiam') for all things was created.

In this compact analysis, the three broad approaches to matter which we have examined converge: a mystical notion of
oneness between matter and God is qualified by a scientific
doctrine of potentiality to elucidate a creationist approach to
the world. In the process, 'matter' acquires a striking capacity
for signification, even while its actual power is carefully circumscribed. 'All things' can be attributed to it in discourse
because all things are generated from it in fact. Its linguistic
predicates correspond to its physical potentialities; an 'egg' is
said to be (indirectly) a 'living creature' because it turns (eventually) into one. If this writer from Thierry's circle (like Aristotle
himself) never fully clarifies how the linguistic turn relates to
the physical one, he at least correlates these shifts in linguistic
and physical perspective more clearly than anyone since
Eriugena.[57] Indeed, with his Aristotelian sense of potentiality,
he suggests perhaps more strongly than Eriugena how matter—not just the divine 'Nature' as a whole—can be seen as a
universe ('uniuersitatem,' p. 98. 14) in its own right.
Moreover, in applying the principle of potentiality to the
'simultaneous' creation of the world, he almost suggests a
strategy for resolving a problem that had tended to elude

---

[57] The problem of this relationship in Aristotle is notorious; revealingly, Dominicus
Gundisalvus' later twelfth-century *De Processione Mundi*, which in some respects
displays a stronger Aristotelian influence than the *Commentum*, seeks to distinguish *hyle*
as subject to *form* ('subiecta formae') from a subject in *logic* ('in logica subiectum'); see
the edition by Georg Bülow, *Beiträge*, 24/3 (Münster, 1925), p. 31. 6–11. On the
general question of Eriugena's relation to the *Commentum*, see Gregory, *Anima*, pp.
84–92; Lucentini, cited above in Ch. IV, n. 60, pp. 51–2; Gersh, 'Platonism,' p. 519,
n. 40, p. 523, n. 52. Gersh notes Augustinian, Hermetic, and Boethian influences on
the different categories of the passage as a whole; see also his revealing remarks, pp.
528–9, on the commentator's approach: 'among Chartrian writers' truth is 'ap-
proachable from a number of perspectives,' each of which, as already in earlier
Neoplatonic writing, 'reflects a different aspect of a dynamic truth. The doctrine . . .
finds a special expression in the twelfth-century use of "integuments" (*integumenta*).'

Eriugena, the development of creation over time. That problematic issue, though, is explored at greater length in a separate treatise, *On the Works of the Six Days* (the work perhaps most convincingly assigned to Thierry in his own right, although even here the received text may be an adaptation of his teaching), which itself quotes the *Asclepius* on a divine 'spirit' immanent in the world while carefully omitting the immediately preceding (heterodox) passages we have cited earlier on matter's autonomous generative powers.[58] In effect, such works are suggesting a way to reconcile matter's generative capacity with both Christian orthodoxy and Greek science. The matter they depict possesses not only the capacity for new birth, like an egg becoming a living creature, but the potential for a whole world.

The most remarkable aspect of this potentiality, though, is that it testifies finally to the conservation of all power in God. Matter itself, observes the commentator, is the sheer capacity to receive ('aptitudo recipiendi') diverse states of being. In the writer's rather Aristotelian terms, it has no 'actus' of its own; God alone is pure act. By contrast, prime matter is pure possibility—'absoluta possibilitas,' in the phrase of the *Lectiones*.[59] While it is thus on the other side of God, it serves as a kind of coordinate of his comprehensive power, enfolding in itself ('conplicatio') the universe of things—only all things in possibility, not in act. This universe of potentialities ('rerum uniuersitas'), in turn, unfolds ('explicatio') insofar as it is

---

[58] On the possibility that the received text is a recasting of Thierry's treatise by his student, Clarembald of Arras, see Southern, *Platonism, Scholastic Method, and the School of Chartres*, pp. 31–4, who argues, however, that 'we may accept Clarembald's assurance that the main part comes from Thierry.' For this particular passage, see *De sex dierum operibus*, hereafter *Six Days*, ch. 26, p. 566. 32–43 in Häring's edn., which cites first *Asc.* 14, p. 313. 4–6 on 'there was God and *hylē*,' continues immediately thereafter with *Asc.* 16, pp. 315. 17–316. 4 on God governing the world through 'spirit,' and thus omits the particularly dangerous intervening passages on 'ungenerated' matter possessing the autonomous 'power of generation,' *Asc.* 14, pp. 313. 7–314. 4; 15, p. 314. 16–22.

[59] On 'aptitudo,' see *Thierry*, p. 75. 18–19, p. 74. 6–7, with Clarembald of Arras, *Life and Works of Clarembald of Arras,* ed. Nikolaus M. Häring (Toronto, 1965), hereafter *Clarembald*, p. 94; on God as 'actus,' *Thierry*, p. 75. 21–3; on matter as 'possibilitas,' *Thierry*, p. 74. 2–3; on 'absoluta possibilitas,' *Thierry*, p. 157. 11–13. Häring, 'The Creation and Creator of the World according to Thierry of Chartres and Clarenbaldus of Arras,' *AHDLMA* 22 (1955), hereafter 'Creation,' 171, n. 4, observes that while the term 'possibilitas' had been used by Calcidius to designate matter, 'the term *possibilitas absoluta* seems to have been coined in the school of Chartres.'

activated by God.[60] While such matter thus lacks the force it had in Calcidius, by the same token it loses its former evil; in the most elemental sense, its 'power' is now an expression of the power of God.

This is a far more profound conception than the vague notion that the material world 'reflects' the divine world. In some respects, it is a more symmetrical view even than that of Eriugena, with his divine 'Nature' acting reflexively upon itself. Beyond 'reflection' and 'reflexivity,' these commentaries suggest the prospect of seeing matter almost in a reciprocal relation to God—and thus of seeing God's own activity from the point of view of matter's possibilities.[61] This orientation is central to the dynamics of the *Cosmographia*, where Hyle or Silva dramatically emerges from below at the very moment that divine power converges with it from above.

It is true that the 'matter' of Thierry of Chartres and his circle is not an allegorical figure, nor even as integrated a conception as that of Bernard Silvestris. When, in *On the Works of the Six Days*, the author examines prime matter from a more strictly physical point of view, he pictures it in far more disorderly terms than pure 'possibility'; 'confusio,' he calls it.[62] That is, Thierry's circle never quite clarifies just how its metaphysics relates to its physics—a problem dramatized within the treatise itself, which shifts *in medias res* (ch. 30) from the physical exposition of creation to the metaphysical mathematics of God. Perhaps the most striking feature of the *Cosmographia* is that it demonstrates (more vividly even than the *Periphyseon*) how the effort to resolve this issue is inseparable from the workings of the human imagination. Bernard's work opens with a scene of

---

[60] See *Thierry*, pp. 157. 3-158. 15; *Clarembald*, pp. 125, 235.

[61] The increasing tendency in this period to enhance the role of matter with respect to form complements this perspective; see, e.g., Gersh, 'Platonism,' pp. 522-3; Hermann of Carinthia, *De Essentiis*, ed. P. Manuel Alonso, Miscelánea Comillas, Vol. 5 (Comillas, Santander, 1946), pp. 37-8, with Lemay, *Abu Ma'shar*, pp. 220-38; Dominicus Gundisalvus, *De Processione Mundi*, cited above in n. 57, pp. 21-6. In strict theological terms, of course, the infinite cannot itself enter into an exactly 'reciprocal' relation with the finite.

[62] See *Six Days*, ch. 24, p. 565. 12; cf. chs. 2, 23, 28; contrast *Thierry*, p. 157. 11-13: 'Absoluta autem possibilitas . . . uocatur a phisicis primordialis materia siue caos.' The degree of common authorship in all these texts remains uncertain; see n. 53, above. Flatten, 'Die "materia primordialis," ' cited above in n. 42, stresses the contrast in the approaches to matter associated with Thierry, although he perhaps insufficiently considers the differences in context.

cosmic disarray as graphic as any spectacle of chaos, but it places that scene on a level of images linguistically and ontologically distinct from—yet parallel to—the level of God, for whom the turbulent movement from disorder to order is only the effortless passage from potentiality into act. If Thierry and the more strictly philosophic members of his circle do not themselves achieve such a synthesis, they nonetheless show more suggestively than anyone before them the possibility of elevating the material world even in its inchoate state. As one of Thierry's students, Clarembald of Arras, fashions the matter in the tractate he attaches to *On the Works of the Six Days:*

And just as the egg is the living creature in possibility ('ovum animal est possibiliter'), and in the egg are all the parts of the bird enfolded ('per complicationem') in possibility, so also in a single seed of grain are many seeds, and the stem, and the chaff, and so in matter are all things in possibility. But it itself is not anything in act.[63]

This coolly Aristotelian formulation is enough to make a Romantic hold forth on the 'meanest flower that blows.' The wise restraint, however, appears in the last sentence. Matter, whatever it is in possibility, is nothing without God.

This approach, finally, transfigures the initial Platonic question with which we began this discussion, the relative claims of matter and God. Plato had measured their rivalry in terms of a certain 'Necessity' in the universe, and nothing more strikingly displays the transformation of the Platonic 'science' of matter than the radical revision of this notion by Thierry and others as they consolidate various scientific, creationist, and mystical strategies. In a world wholly activated by divine power, the old threat of necessity finally recoils upon itself. 'Necessity' no longer designates the limitation of God's design by matter; now it is matter that 'needs' God's design. In the words of the *Lectiones*:

Simplicity itself does not need ('non requirit') matter for its being. But matter needs ('requirit') Simplicity for *its* being. (p. 162. 85–6)

Far from compromising divine power, the 'need' in the universe now confirms the power of God.

[63] See *Clarembald*, p. 235; on the egg, cf. Dominicus Gundisalvus, *De Processione Mundi*, p. 32; on the seed, cf. Hermann of Carinthia, *De Essentiis*, p. 37.

Indeed, it is precisely the fact that twelfth-century matter (unlike Plato's substratum) owes its very existence to God which radicalizes this need. As the *Commentum* puts it:

It is well said that Oneness ('unitas') creates matter ('materiam creare'). For from Oneness descends otherness ('alteritas'), and from Immutability, mutability. For otherness always *needs* ('exigit') Oneness. For the other is called 'other' by reference to the One. (p. 81. 86–8)

Clarembald, commenting on the opening verses of Genesis, consolidates the point. Primordial matter, he argues, is nothing but possibility, which in turn is mutability, and

mutability descends from Immutability by *necessity* ('ex necessitate'). But Immutability is the eternity of God. Therefore, it is *necessary* ('necesse est') for mutability to descend from eternity, and thus, primordial matter descends from God. (p. 237)

Such a primeval 'descent' from God has a parallel in the *Periphyseon*, although Eriugena perhaps tends to give too much of the 'need' for descent to divine Nature as a whole, rather than to matter in its own right. In any case, matter has here changed from the necessary resistance to God to the needy petitioner for him.

At the same time, a compelling Necessity does not exactly disappear from such a universe. Rather, shifting in meaning, it is now displaced to the other side—to God, who necessitates all things. This change in perspective is facilitated by the *Asclepius*, with its deft instinct for a cosmic continuum, a divinely ordained concatenation of events to which it gives the very name 'necessitas,' as well as by other more strictly scientific or philosophic texts, including astrological discussions on the causal nexus of the heavens, and Boethius' *Consolation*, with its keen analysis of the interlocking pattern of 'fate' resolved in the providence of God.[64] So when the writer of the *Glosa* lists the various names for matter, in the way Calcidius does, or his own contemporary, Gilbert of Poitiers, he omits (unlike them)

---

[64] For the *Asclepius*, see *Asc.* 39–40, esp. p. 350. 1–6 on 'necessitas omnium . . . catenatis nexibus uincta,' associated with the supreme God ('deus summus') or ('aut') with the chain of procession from God, and cf. my discussion of *Asc.* above and in n. 65 below; for astrological texts, see n. 35 above; for the *Consolation*, see esp. IV, pr. vi and V, pr. vi.

one of its traditional names: 'necessitas.' Some call primordial matter 'chaos,' he says; some call it 'hyle'; some, 'silva.' He does not say, however, that people had been calling it 'Necessity' for 1500 years. For him, that word applies rather to God, the 'absolute necessity' ('necessitas absoluta'), compared to which matter is merely 'possible.'[65] Defining that necessity as the 'vinculum in esse,' he cites in support the celebrated proof-text for creationist theology, 'I am who am.'[66] But the very language of Thierry's circle exposes the diverse provenance of the concepts linked in its new configuration: 'Act without possibility,' in the words of the *Commentum*, is 'necessity,' and 'this is called by everyone God.' As Clarembald explains, 'Absolute Necessity' is

divine providence, in which all things are enfolded ('complicantur'). And it is called 'absolute' because it owes to nothing what it is. For it is that divinity to which all other things owe what they are.

God has finally replaced his old adversary. Matter, it is true, enfolds all things in possibility. But that capacity is only the converse of the activity of God, enfolding ('conplicatio') all things in act, according to the *Lectiones*, and finally unfolding ('explicatio') that necessity to order the world.[67]

In the end, there are thus two sides to 'Necessity,' as there are to the twelfth-century universe as a whole. One of the great achievements of the period is that it tends to consolidate such divisions, not by denying the duality, but by transfiguring one side into a counter for the other. Playing their ancient scientific, mystical, and creationist sources off each other, the natural philosophers of the period seek not only to resolve the old opposition between matter and God, but more importantly, to enhance simultaneously the integrity of each. By conserving

[65] For the *Glosa*'s list, see *Thierry*, p. 272. 15-17; for Calcidius, see ch. 268, p. 273. 15; for Gilbert, see *The Commentaries on Boethius by Gilbert of Poitiers*, ed. Nikolaus M. Häring (Toronto, 1966), p. 80. 62-8 (*PL* 64, 1265); for the ancient association of matter with 'Necessity,' see Winden, p. 31. For the contrasting use of 'necessitas' in the writings associated with Thierry, see Häring's 'Glossary,' s.v., in *Thierry*. For 'necessitas absoluta' see p. 272. 97; cf., for example, p. 156. 85, p. 157. 3-7. Häring, 'Creation,' 171, n. 6, notes that this use of the term *necessitas* 'goes back to *Trismegistus*,' but that 'the specification *absoluta* was introduced by the school of Chartres.'

[66] See *Thierry*, pp. 271. 91-272. 98, and my discussion above.

[67] For these points, see *Thierry*, p. 75. 17-23; *Clarembald*, p. 124; *Thierry*, p. 157. 8-10, p. 156. 55-63, and *Clarembald*, pp. 124-5, 235-6.

God's power in fact, they allow an incipient figure to emerge on the other side—a foil to dramatize God's plan, a subject to reciprocate his activity, a material petitioner for spiritual fulfillment. They thus acknowledge the force of matter in this world while turning it into the potential for a better world. In their treatment of Matter, they not only transform an ancient source of generation; they produce a new resource for the regeneration of allegory itself.

CREATION: THE DELEGATION OF POWER

If there is a decisive sign of the movement toward complex allegory, it is the tendency to implicate the philosophic analysis of causes with the imaginative development of them. The twelfth-century investigation of the material world suggests such a prospect. In their systematic effort to integrate all power in a single source, the natural philosophers of the period turn matter itself into an agent of divine activity—a figure that by its very potentiality only dramatizes the power of God. Nonetheless, this consolidating movement has its philosophic and imaginative limitations; it tends finally to reduce the mere figures of this world to the fact of God himself. When we say that the presence of the divine constitutes the being of all creatures, cautions the author of *On the Works of the Six Days*, it is not the divine that exists 'in' the matter, but rather the matter that 'has existence from the presence of the divine' ('ipsa materia ex presentia diuinitatis habeat existere').[68] All such effects are ultimately reducible to their source; the conservation of divine power may be a necessary condition for the allegory of creation, but it is not a sufficient one.

Such an allegory demands not only a reductive impulse, but an expansive one. These complementary demands, developing in allegorical writing from the start, increase in philosophic and imaginative urgency when the allegorical framework is the cosmos itself. If in one sense the world is one with God, after all, in another sense the two are quite distinct. In a universe of this kind, power needs not only to be conserved in God, but diffused, delegated, as it were, to a realm outside him. Such a division would mean that even while God retains all power in fact, others can act obliquely on his behalf, thereby safely distinguishing him from his work. At the same time, the philosophic distinction between actual and apparent levels of power implies an imaginative distinction between actual and apparent levels of meaning—the development of a level of discourse parallel to the truth but at some remove from it. Such a distinct philosophic and imaginative dimension, critical to any multileveled universe, had begun to develop with new cogency when matter, in order to ascend to God, turned into a figure of his power. That development would be complete only when God in turn descended to matter through a series of figures of his own.

In broad terms, of course, such a mediated descent had marked the Platonic tradition from the start. Plato himself had declared that 'it is not possible that two things alone should be conjoined without a third,' and to link the perfect world of Being with the imperfect world of Becoming he had inserted the intermediary of Soul *(psykhē)*, a principle partaking of both realms.[69] In early Neoplatonism, this World Soul becomes the third in a descending hierarchy of principles linking God to his work: the supreme God, the One or the Good *(to hen* or *to agathon)*; the providential design of creation *(nous)*; and the World Soul *(psykhē)*, animating the world as a whole. While late antique Neoplatonism develops still more intricate systems of procession and return, as we have seen, it is this threefold scheme of emanation, adapted and popularized by Calcidius and Macrobius, that passes most widely into the currency of the later Middle Ages.[70]

In Bernard Silvestris' allegory of the creation, the figures of 'Noys' and the 'World Soul' will play important roles. In their original Neoplatonic condition, however, they could scarcely solve the Christian problem of a God who creates matter without implicating himself in it. On the one hand, the Neoplatonic supreme God remains aloof from all that is below him, and so does not directly 'create' in the first place. This is

[69] See *Timaeus* 31BC, 34B–35B; Cornford, *Plato's Cosmology*, p. 63.

[70] See Macrobius' *Commentary*, cited above in Ch. III, n. 44, I, xiv, 15; Calcidius, chs. 176–7.

hardly the God of Genesis, who was directly responsible for the world. Already in the early centuries AD, Christians are insisting that God, as sole creator, admits no intermediate cause between himself and his work, and when in the early Middle Ages Pseudo-Dionysius and Eriugena seek to adapt Neoplatonic strategies of gradation to a Christian perspective, they tend to transform an emanation of beings into a system of direct, formative activities, while bringing the thearchy into a more intimate relation with the hierarchy of nature itself.[71]

On the other hand, insofar as such a Neoplatonic deity does set the world in motion—deity in its third stage, via Nous and the World Soul—then it is a deity that compromises itself by its work. This tendency is particularly striking in Macrobius' influential account of how the divine World Soul imparts the faculties of reason, sensation, and growth to the earthly realm. The World Soul has the pure faculty of reason, of course, from its divine superior, Nous (*mens*). Something, however, has to explain the existence of less rational faculties on earth, and so the World Soul, 'out of its own nature, takes on' ('ex sua natura accipit') the faculties of sensation and growth.[72] In effect, the last stage of divinity has made contact with the material world only at the cost of lowering itself. Even the more sophisticated divine Nature of Eriugena is liable to such internal difficulties—or at least to being interpreted as a cause slipping too deeply into its own effects—as it 'is created' in things,

[71] For various challenges to hypostatic intermediaries from Philo to the early Church Fathers, see Wolfson, *Philo*, Vol. I, pp. 226–52, 269–71, 282–9; *Fathers*, pp. 257–86; Gilson, *Spirit*, cited above in n. 38, p. 110; but cf. Origen, with my refs. above in Ch. III, n. 9. Intermediaries of a different kind, the 'daemons,' are gradually reinterpreted and assimilated (with some difficulty) into Christian contexts; see my discussion above in Ch. III, with the refs. in nn. 19 and 20. For the transformations of Pseudo-Dionysius and Eriugena, see my discussion above in Ch. IV; Roques, *L'Univers*, cited above in Ch. IV, n. 49, ch. 3; Gersh, *From Iamblichus to Eriugena*, cited above in Ch. IV, n. 47, pp. 160, n. 158, 204–17, 283; Chenu, pp. 52–4. For the twelfth-century effort to redefine the notion of emanation, see Chenu, pp. 53–5; Gregory, *Anima*, pp. 92–3, n. 2, 96–7; and my discussion below.

[72] See *Commentary* I, xiv, 7; cf. the compromising description here in which incorporeal Soul 'degenerat' (cf. 'degenerans,' I, xiv, 9) into a corporeal framework. Plotinus, *Enneads* V, ii, 1, writes that the soul 'in some sense' (*tropon tina*) reaches the order of plants (growth). Gersh, 'Platonism,' p. 520, n. 43, discussing the prior passage from Mind to Soul, observes that by making Soul a result of Mind turning *away* from the One, Macrobius 'introduces an ethically negative element quite absent' from the Plotinian original, and 'in that way possibly limits the usefulness of the whole scheme for Christian Platonists such as the 12th-c. Chartrians.'

and Eriugena's elaborate efforts to distinguish different modes of a single Nature testify to the excruciating difficulty of keeping God immanent and transcendent at the same time.[73]

In an 'ascending' form, we have already seen similar problems of negotiating between the rational and the irrational both in psychic and cosmic terms. Plato had tried to attribute reasonable behavior to *thymos* in order to coax the irrational side of the soul into reason's camp. Calcidius had tried to ascribe a 'provident obedience' to incorrigible Necessity, though this was presumably the attribute of Providence, its opposite number. In such accounts, the irrational seemed able to accommodate the rational only by undermining its own definition. Now, from the other direction, as divine reason itself attempted to accommodate its counterpart, there were even higher stakes in the possibility of self-contradiction. To retain both his creativity and his integrity, God needed to make a world while remaining unworldly, to extend his power while reserving it wholly to himself. The problem with earlier views of the creation was their directness, the literal attachment of God to his work. What was needed was an account that recognized God's responsibility for his work while keeping him at one remove from it. What was needed, that is, was an oblique account of his action, an allegory of the creation.

This was the allegory that the twelfth century finally developed. The split reference of allegorical language uniquely suited the needs of a God who had somehow to be distanced from what was his own. Of course, since God was indivisible, there could be no question of separating him into 'parts,' and distancing one from the other. An orthodox distinction, however, provided the twelfth century with its opening. This was the division of God into three distinct persons. While these three persons were a single Trinity, it was proper to distinguish among them in the terms of the Nicene Creed. The Father was the begetter; the Son was the begotten; and the Holy Spirit proceeded from them both.[74] At times in the history of the Church,

---

[73] See my discussion above in Ch. IV and the refs. in Ch. IV, nn. 63 and 72, with Gersh, *From Iamblichus to Eriugena*, pp. 157, n. 147, 209, n. 29.

[74] For the early Church's struggle to define the distinctions among the persons of the Trinity, see Wolfson, *Fathers*, pp. 287–363; Jaroslav Pelikan, *The Emergence of the Catholic Tradition (100–600)*, Vol. I of *The Christian Tradition: A History of the Development of Doctrine* (Chicago, 1971), pp. 200–25, 269–70.

the distinction of the three persons was reinforced by assigning to each a particular characteristic. In one such formulation, the Father's special attribute was power (*potentia*); the Son's was wisdom (*sapientia*); and the Holy Spirit's was goodness (*bonitas*), or love, or will. To many, this formulation was a dangerous one, though some argued that it had been supported by Augustine. It threatened, after all, to divide God into various functions, and so to make one person unequal to another. Over the course of the twelfth century, the issue acquired systematic form, and the controversy reached a turning point. Although Abelard, who maintained the distinction, was condemned at the Council of Soissons (1121), by the end of the century the differentiation was more carefully articulated and widely accepted in the Church.[75]

This internal distinction among God's attributes was the first step in separating, as it were, one part of him from himself. Once again, there could be no question of dividing God in fact. But there was now, at least, a way to conceptualize one aspect of him without immediately posing the interlocking set of relationships of begetting, begotten, and proceeding. This conceptual framework provided a way to speak about God not only in terms of his internal relations, but in terms of the particular functions of each concept. In short, it opened the way to see God not only in relation to himself, but in relation to his work—and thereby, to see him from a point of view outside himself.

This possibility was preeminently exposed by William of Conches, who assigned to each of these three personal attributes a specific role in the creation of the world. The Father is God's power ('potentia'), which creates all things. The

[75] For supporters and opponents of the three attributes, see J. G. Sikes, *Peter Abailard* (Cambridge, 1932), pp. 156-7, 161-3; Chenu, p. 276; and Jean Châtillon, 'Unitas, Aequalitas, Concordia vel Connexio,' in *St. Thomas Aquinas, 1274-1974: Commemorative Studies* (Toronto, 1974), Vol. I, pp. 337-79, esp. pp. 359-60, n. 98, on Augustine's position and Abelard's role. For different strategies in support of the distinction—endorsed, among others, by William of Conches, Thierry of Chartres (in the transmitted version of *Six Days*), and John of Salisbury—see my refs. above in n. 44, with Parent, *La Doctrine*, pp. 70-1: A.-M Éthier, *Le 'De Trinitate' de Richard de Saint-Victor*, Publications de l'Institut d'Études Médiévales d'Ottawa, Vol. 9 (Ottawa, 1939), pp. 102-19; Jaroslav Pelikan, *The Growth of Medieval Theology (600-1300)*, Vol. III of *The Christian Tradition* (Chicago, 1978), pp. 265, 278. Dante later exploits the distinction; see *Convivio* II, v, 8; *Inferno* iii, 5-6.

Father begets the Son—'that is, divine power begot wisdom ("sapientia")'—by foreseeing how to create all things. Finally, the Holy Spirit proceeding from Father and Son is 'nothing other than' ('nihil aliud quam') God's will ('voluntas'), which stretches out toward the creation to govern it; this is the goodness ('bonitas') of God in his creative effect ('effectu').[76] In his analysis, William thus tended to define God's three attributes not on the basis of God's own nature, but in relation to what God created. That is, he began to shift the divine attributes away from God, and toward the world. It was as if, by turning into concepts, the persons of God had broken off from him, and descended slightly earthward.

Such dire consequences from such subtle changes might not occur to moderns, but they were not lost upon one of William of Conches' contemporaries, William of St. Thierry. The abbot of St. Thierry, in a letter to Bernard of Clairvaux, condemned the 'man of physics' ('homo physicus') for such a creatural approach to God. This heretic, wrote the abbot, argues that God, who is that which he is 'in and from himself' ('in semetipso et ex semetipso'), is rather all that he is in relation to his creatures ('ad creaturam'). He applies the names of Father, Son, and Holy Spirit to God not because of their true, internal relationship of begetting, begotten, and proceeding, but rather 'by a certain metaphorical transfer' ('nomina . . . aequivocali quadam affinitate translata'), since he supposes the true distinction to lie in the creational concepts of power, wisdom, and goodness. Thus, the Father is not what he is in relation to the Son, but in relation to the creation ('non ad Filium, sed ad creaturam'); not in his own internal nature, but in his creational disposition ('non natura, sed affectu').[77] In effect, William of St. Thierry sensed that the conceptualization of God had placed a wedge between his persons and his inmost nature, so that even the three persons applied only 'by a certain metaphorical transfer' to him.

The conceptualization of the three persons into power, wisdom, and goodness, however, did not in itself provoke the

[76] See *Philosophia Mundi*, hereafter *Ph. Mundi*, I, 6–10; *PL* 172, 45. Augustine, *De Civ. Dei* XI, 24, does not put the case so strongly.

[77] See *De Erroribus Guillelmi de Conchis*; *PL* 180, 335B, 338C. Cf. *Ph. Mundi* I, 5 (in the text—defective in *PL*—printed by Dronke, *Fabula*, p. 51, n. 4) on 'transferred' ('transferentes') names.

kind of split in language needed for allegory. Others before William of Conches had applied such terms to persons of the Trinity without remarkable results. The decisive factor was William's emphasis on the *causal* function of these attributes, which tended to define God from outside himself, as it were, from the point of view of his creation.[78] In particular, the third of these attributes, goodness ('bonitas'), had this effect. Goodness, on the authority of a host of different sources—the Bible (Gen. 1), the *Asclepius* (ch. 26), the *Timaeus* (29E–30B, 37CD)—was the attribute of the world. It is true that the reason for the world's goodness is the goodness of God, but this explanation has a double edge. Because God is good, and that which is good begrudges existence to nothing which can exist, God could hardly *refrain* from creating a good world.[79] In a sense, that is, the goodness that the world *could* possess *necessitated* God to create it. Obviously, it would be heresy to attribute determinism of any kind to God. Those who followed the premise of God's goodness to its conclusion, however, came very close to saying that God is not only the subject *of* goodness, but subject *to* it. To such a degree is God in all that he does mindful of the good, said Abelard,

> that he is said to be induced to make individual things rather by the value of the good there is in *them* than by the choice of his own will . . . This is in accord with what Jerome says, 'For God does not do this because *he* wills to do so, but he wills to do so because *it* is good.'[80]

Goodness, that is, is a two-sided word. It is a force that issues from God, but it is also a force that seems to compel him to act, from the outside. Through its two-sidedness, goodness—one of

---

[78] On the three attributes as three Aristotelian causes, see my discussion earlier in this chapter, with n. 44. Cf. Gregory, *Anima*, p. 107: 'the Trinity is thus explained essentially in its function of creative activity and not as an aspect of the interior life of God.'

[79] The classic study of this implication is Arthur O. Lovejoy, *The Great Chain of Being* (Cambridge, Mass., 1936); see pp. 49–50 on 'omne bonum est diffusivum sui,' with *Timaeus* 29E.

[80] See *Introductio ad theologiam*; *PL* 178, 1093–1101; quoted by Lovejoy (my italics), p. 71. Cf. Augustine on the cause of creation as the fact that 'every *creature* of God is good ("omnis creatura Dei bona est"). And what is more appropriate than that a good God should make good things . . . ?' *Ep.* V, 15; *PL* 33, 727; quoted by R.-H. Cousineau, 'Creation and Freedom: An Augustinian Problem,' *Recherches augustiniennes*, 2 (1962), 256, an article to which I am indebted in my discussion of divine goodness. Cf. also *De Civ. Dei* XI, 24; *PL* 41, 338.

the three persons of God—could seem subtly to separate itself from him, and begin to assume a force of its own.

It was the unique causal function of goodness that especially promoted this shift. For William and his contemporaries, God's goodness was the 'final cause' of the creation, the end toward which the created world itself moved.[81] In its role as final cause, 'goodness' was particularly liable to detach itself from God, as it were, and establish a separate vantage point from which to see him. Ever since Aristotle, the notion of a final cause implied a certain passivity on the part of God, a Mover who moved by *being* loved. The fact that there is an end which is passively loved implies that there is something else which is actively loving it. Love, that is, is as two-sided a concept as goodness. It may mean the love that *God* shows for all things, or, alternatively, the love that all *things* show for God.[82] It is the *Divine Comedy* that preeminently displays this reciprocal motion in allegory, demonstrating that from one perspective creatural activity has its own force, while from another perspective it simply reveals obliquely the force of the Creator. 'L'amor che move il sole e l'altre stelle' is at once the love from *God* that moves the universe and the love that motivates the *universe* to God.[83] There had been prefigurations of this principle before Dante and before the twelfth century. But in easing God's goodness or love away from him, so that something outside him could echo his summons, the early twelfth century first developed the systematic basis for the exploitation of that duality in allegory.

It was through such conceptual and causal perspectives on goodness or love, then, that an internal attribute of God might seem to become an external force, acting in its own right. The fact that this point of view developed out of the third person of the Trinity externalized God, as it were, at his most internal point, for as we have observed, the third person was also identified with God's will ('voluntas'), the internal source of his action.[84] Do not seek, Augustine had warned, a cause for creation

---

[81] See, e.g., *Glosae*, pp. 98, 116; *Six Days*, ch. 3.

[82] See Dronke, 'L'amor.' For the identification of the third person of the Trinity with love, see, e.g., William's *Glosses* on Boethius, ed. Jourdain, cited in n. 50 above, 75-6; *Thierry*, p. 80. 69-70.   [83] See Dronke, 'L'amor,' 389-90.

[84] See, e.g., Augustine, *Confessions* XIII, 11; William of Conches, *Ph. Mundi* I, 9; *PL* 172, 45.

outside God's will. To 'explain' the creation beyond God's will would subject his will to something else that caused it to be the way it is—'quod nefas credere'—a truly criminal thought. God's will is antecedent to everything else.[85] Nevertheless, because God's internal source of action was identified with his expansive tendency for goodness, goodness threatened to become a rival explanation for the creation, as if something outside God's will were responsible for the world.

In an incipient form, this rivalry appears already in Augustine. Augustine scarcely completes the thought that 'the cause of all that he made is his will ("voluntas"),' than he adds, 'God made by his goodness ("bonitate"), of nothing that he made was he in need.'[86] Similarly, it is goodness that seems to explain the creation when Augustine declares that 'by no need of any advantage to him, but only by goodness ("nulla suae cuiusquam utilitatis indigentia, sed sola bonitate")' did he make that which is made.[87] Such a conceptual recourse to divine goodness is not in itself remarkable, of course, and long after Augustine, others—including William of Conches—make similar statements.[88] But in probing the causal force of goodness, William tends to bring this latent rivalry into the open. In fact, just when William is stressing God's independence from external causes, an internal 'cause' seems almost to make God its own object:

God made this world not impelled by any external cause, that is, by any indigence such as we are impelled by to do anything, but impelled by goodness alone.

Deus fecit mundum istum non impulsus aliqua extrinseca causa id est indigentia quemadmodum nos impellimur ad agendum aliquid sed impulsus mera bonitate.[89]

Suddenly, the subject that opens the sentence—God—is subject *to* the abstraction that has momentarily taken over the foreground: 'impelled ("impulsus") by goodness alone.'

---

[85] See *De Gen. contra Manichaeos* I, ii, 4; *PL* 34, 175, with the other refs. in Cousineau, cited above in n. 80, 245.

[86] See *Ennar. in Ps. 134*, 10; *PL* 37, 1745; quoted by Cousineau, 256.

[87] See *De Civ. Dei* XI, 24; *PL* 41, 338.

[88] See, e.g., Peter Damian, *PL* 145, 605C; William's *Glosses* on Boethius, ed. Parent, *La Doctrine*, p. 128.

[89] See *Glosses* on Boethius, ed. Parent, *La Doctrine*, p. 61, n. 2.

Once again, there is no question here of an actual separation between God and goodness. The issue is rather the tendency to place goodness in relief, to give it a dimension in its own right. Indeed, an abstraction performing the divine will (*voluntas*) can almost develop a will of its own:

. . . God made the world because he is supremely good. But the supreme generosity wishes to be diffused and to share with others what it has.

. . . Deum ideo fecisse mundum quia summe bonus est. Summa autem largitas vult largiri et participare aliis quod habet.[90]

As if to enact his own overflow, God here seems to pass into the very principle of generosity.

Language of this kind is still abstract, not allegorical. Yet it displays a shift in perspective deeply susceptible to allegorical exploitation. Revealingly, when Abelard comes to describe the creation, the third person of the Trinity itself briefly yields the narrative foreground to divine goodness, which animates the embryonic world like a bird brooding over an egg:

Just as the bird brooding on the egg and devoting herself to it with exceeding ardor warms it with her heat, as it is said, forms the chicken, and brings it to life; so divine goodness ('bonitas'), which is understood ('intelligitur') as the Holy Spirit and properly ('proprie') called the love of God . . . is said to be set over ('praeesse') that yet fluid and unstable mass as over waters, that presently it might produce living creatures from it . . . [91]

---

[90] This passage is from the so-called 'second redaction' of William's *Glosses* on Boethius, ed. Parent, *La Doctrine*, p. 127, n. to l. 22. Whether it is his own or that of one of his followers, the revealing turn of language remains the central point. Augustine had approached such language in *Ennar. in Ps. 134*, 10; *PL* 37, 1745, without quite displaying its specificity. On the convergence of *bonitas* and *voluntas* in the gloss to the Boethian passage, cf. *Saecvli noni avctoris in Boetii consolationem philosophiae commentarivs*, ed. Edmund Taite Silk (Rome, 1935), pp. 176–7, a twelfth-century work (despite the title) probably composed after William's *Glosses*; see Courcelle, *Tradition*, p. 251.

[91] See *Expositio in Hexaemeron*, *PL* 178, 736AB, quoted in Dronke, *Fabula*, p. 159; my translation is based upon Dronke's, pp. 95–6. Cf. his acute comments: 'On the one hand he has a series of abstract concepts . . . on the other, a series of physical realities . . . How can the conceptual and the physical entities be related? What can it mean to speak of an abstract principle—goodness or love—acting upon a physical mass, warming, shaping, quickening it? . . . [T]he abstracts are not enough . . . they call out for an extension into images . . . '

For a crucial moment, the abstract agent of goodness ('bonitas') acts in its own right, mediating between divine love in all its propriety ('proprie') and the material realm in its teeming confusion. The effort to bring God to the world without compromising his perfection, though, has a momentum of its own. The vivid image of the bird and the striking disparity between the abstraction and its assigned activity—as 'goodness' is 'set over' the turbulent mass—reveals that gulf between the spirit of God and the matter he inspires which only allegory can bridge. It is possible that Abelard draws his analysis of the cosmic egg itself from William of Conches' own discussion of this figure in a quite different context. The image as a whole, in any case, develops from a complex interaction of mystical, theological, and literary traditions.[92] Such a rich mélange differs considerably from the more rigorous scientific analogy of matter as an 'egg' potentially emerging into a 'living creature.' But it seems almost a commentary on a broader convergence in this milieu that the figure of a matter waiting to be born here converges with the figure of a God fostering its birth.

However revealing these developments, they alone would not have produced the full-fledged allegory to come. At the same time such philosophers were developing divine goodness as a conceptual figure mediating between God and the world, though, they were remaking that ancient candidate for this mediating role, the World Soul. The World Soul, after all, shared many of the features applied by Christians to God's goodness or love—a vital spirit nourishing and sustaining the world. This vital spirit, however, together with related conceptions, had acquired the most diverse philosophic and literary guises: in the *Timaeus*, a cosmic soul animating the world's body; in the *Aeneid*, a kind of internal Stoic life-force; in the *Asclepius*, a mystical current suffusing the world; in the *Consolation*, the moving power motivating all things.[93] We have seen the early medieval commentaries on the *Consolation* struggling to adapt such a principle to Christian faith. The decisive con-

---

[92] For the relation between William and Abelard here, see Dronke, *Fabula*, p. 95; for the general image of the cosmic egg, see pp. 79–99.

[93] For such diverse early developments, see Gregory, *Anima*, pp. 123–32, with *Asc.*, ch. 6.

vergence came when William of Conches and his contemporaries joined the abstract notion of divine 'goodness,' or
'love,' or 'will,' with a systematic reinterpretation of that vital
principle. 'According to some,' wrote William of Conches, 'the
World Soul' ('anima mundi') is

the Holy Spirit ('Spiritus sanctus'); for by divine goodness and will
('bonitate et voluntate'), which is the Holy Spirit, as we have said, all
things which are in the world live. (*Ph. Mundi* I, 15; PL 172, 46)

It was not the first time that Christians had suggested the
association, but William, Abelard, and others in the early
twelfth century gave it a critical new edge.[94] By consolidating
a divine abstraction with a cosmic agent, they produced a
composite figure pointing in two directions. In its Christian affiliation with divine goodness, this principle could remain
otherworldly in its dimensions. In its pagan character as the
World Soul, it could be deeply implicated in the world. We can
watch William of Conches exploiting this very duality. When
he encounters Calcidius' statement that the World Soul is a
'tertium genus,' a third kind of being, he argues that the
phrase may be taken in either of two ways. On the one hand, it
may mean that the World Soul is that third being which proceeds from both the 'essence' and 'wisdom' of God—in short,
the third person of the Trinity. On the other hand, adds
William, it may also mean that the World Soul has a threefold
nature, by being responsible for the earthly powers of reason,
sensation, and growth. The powers of sensation and growth
were precisely what compromised Macrobius' World Soul,
which was responsible for earthly faculties not fully compatible
with the divine. In effect, William's dual approach to this new
figure allowed it to be both divine and worldly at once, thus

---

[94] For associations between the Holy Spirit and the World Soul (along with reservations) in the early Church, see Courcelle, 'Interprétations,' cited above in Ch. III, n.
41, 107–10; Gregory, *Anima*, pp. 125–8, 142, n. 1. For different strategies of association in the twelfth century by William, Abelard, Thierry of Chartres (in the transmitted
version of *Six Days*), Arnold of Bonneval, and the authors of the *Tables of Marseilles*,
Bibl. Nat. lat. 8624 (Paris), Bibl. Naz. Conv. Soppr. I. l. 28 (Florence), and Univ.
Libr. Mm. i. 18 (Cambridge)—some tending toward strict identification, some,
toward metaphorical affiliation—see the full discussions in Gregory, *Anima*, pp.
133–58; *Platonismo*, pp. 122–34; Dronke, *Fabula*, pp. 103–4, 110–12, 178–9, 182.

enforcing that delicate division between God and himself in the creation of the world.[95]

William's very diction displays this subtle distinction. Thus, in his *Glosses* on Boethius, after describing the World Soul's responsibility for the earthbound faculties of reason, sensation, and growth, he gestures to the earth with his verb, as

God stretches out ('extendit') the World Soul, that is, his love, since by love alone he creates all things and governs them.[96]

On the other hand, in his *Glosses* on Macrobius, when he comes to the word 'degenerare' ('descend'), which Macrobius applies to the World Soul, he hastens to explain:

But it is said to descend ('degenerare'), not because the Holy Spirit in itself ('in se') descends, but because it descends in its creational disposition ('affectu').[97]

So, too, when Abelard—who is sometimes more radical than William in his efforts to reconcile Christian doctrine with pagan discourse[98]—interprets Macrobius' argument that the World Soul has a beginning, he insists that there Macrobius is speaking of its earthly effects ('effecta'); in its eternal state, of course, it is the Holy Spirit:

Spirit, indeed, is the name of its nature ('naturae'); Soul is the name of its function ('officii').[99]

The very nuances of language expose different orders of being. As Abelard argues, writings about the World Soul, sensitively

[95] See *Glosae*, pp. 149–50, with Jeauneau, 'L'Usage,' cited above in Ch. III, n. 74, 67–9, 78–80. Dronke, 'L'amor,' 410–11, writes of William's strategy that 'it is unmistakably God himself who in physical things assumes the attributes of *vegetatio, sensualitas, ratio.*' In view of the duality we have been describing, this statement should perhaps be refined.

[96] See the edition of Jourdain, cited above in n. 50, 76.

[97] See the quotation by Jeauneau in *Glosae*, p. 145, n. c. Jeauneau thinks 'affectu' may be a textual error for 'effectu.' On this possibility, cf. William's 'effectu,' n. 76 above, and the *Sententie Parisienses*, cited by Gregory, *Anima*, p. 147, n. 3; but cf. William of St. Thierry's 'affectu,' n. 77 above. Whether the explanation for the word lies in a textual error or a contemporary looseness of terminology, William of Conches' careful distinction about the World Soul's 'descent' remains the same.

[98] See Jean Jolivet, *Arts du langage et théologie chez Abélard* (Paris, 1969), p. 253; Wetherbee, pp. 38–44; Dronke, *Fabula*, pp. 55–67.

[99] See *Introductio ad theologiam* II, 17; *PL* 178, 1082; quoted by Gregory, *Anima*, p. 147, who points out (p. 145) that whereas William gives the World Soul a 'cosmological' function, Abelard gives it the 'charismatic' function of dispensing grace.

interpreted, refer by a most beautiful figural covering ('pulcherrima involucri figura') to the Holy Spirit.[100]

Such nice distinctions were part of that careful movement in which God eased his way toward earth. The third person of the Trinity turned into the abstract agent of goodness or love. Goodness or love, in turn, affiliated with the World Soul, through the exegesis of that concept in a range of philosophic and literary texts. Finally, the World Soul itself was splitting in two, its head turned toward heaven, its feet planted firmly on earth. In short, it was in allegory that the twelfth century achieved what eluded its Neoplatonic sources: the progressive descent of God from himself without compromising his divinity.

At the same time, this is allegory somewhat different from anything we have seen in an earlier period. Written by philosophers, it belongs not quite to either the compositional or the interpretive mode alone, but to a kind of intermediate strategy drawing upon both procedures. On the one hand, such writers are conceptualizing a dimension of God as 'goodness' or 'love.' On the other hand, they are reinterpreting the figure of the World Soul to conform with that concept. They thus tend to consolidate a strategy of abstraction with an act of exegesis. This kind of convergence between compositional and interpretive technique, it is true, had been broadly developing throughout the allegorical tradition. Nevertheless, early allegorists tended either to conflate the abstraction with the figure, as in the Stoic exegesis of a Heraclitus, equating 'war' with Mars, or conversely, to diffuse the figure in a host of conceptual directions, as in the exotic vision of Martianus, diversifying Mercury as 'eloquence,' 'Genius,' *nous*, and the rest. By contrast, these twelfth-century writers subtly play the two sides of their composite principle off each other, thereby negotiating not only between its constituent elements, nor only between its Christian and pagan sources, but between the worlds of spirit and matter themselves. In the process, they begin to develop an intermediate level of discourse between strict truth and mere fiction, a level of *integumenta* that accommodates the different dimensions of a multileveled universe.[101] Indeed, in the effort

---

[100] See *Introductio ad theologiam* I, 19; *PL* 178, 1021-2.

[101] On the diverse twelfth-century approaches contributing to the development of *integumenta*, see M.-D. Chenu, '*Involucrum*: le mythe selon les théologiens médiévaux,' *AHDLMA* 30 (1955), 75-9; Jeauneau, 'L'Usage,' cited above in Ch. III, n. 74,

to consolidate their universe, they help to consolidate the compositional and interpretive traditions at large, promoting the possibilities of an allegory that simultaneously displays both conceptual control and imaginative versatility.

Some in the twelfth century, however, were not much impressed by gestures toward allegory in these matters. If the Holy Spirit is the soul of the world, objected the author of the *Disputation against Abelard*, then it is inextricably bound up with the world, just as the human soul is bound up with the body. And if that is the case, then the world is made holy, and must be worshipped ('colendus') and adored ('adorandus') by us.[102] The debate reached the breaking point at the Council of Sens in 1140, which condemned the proposition that the Holy Spirit was the World Soul. The general strain, though, had been building for some time. Abelard, retracting his previous views, confessed that some 'have adhered too much to allegory' ('allegorie nimis adherentes') in trying to match the (Neo-) Platonic triad with the Holy Trinity.[103] For his part, William of Conches grew increasingly reticent about associating the World Soul with the Holy Spirit. Whereas in his early *Glosses* on Boethius he had confidently declared that the Holy Spirit was the World Soul, by the time of his *Philosophia Mundi*, he says that 'the World Soul, *according to some*, is the Holy Spirit.' In his *Glosses* on the *Timaeus*, he observes that some call the World Soul the Holy Spirit, 'which we now neither deny nor affirm.' Finally, in his last great work, the *Dragmaticon*, he does not mention the World Soul at all.[104] Plainly, the increasing con-

35–100; Stock, pp. 49–62; Wetherbee, pp. 28–73; Dronke, *Fabula*, pp. 13–78; Brinkmann, pp. 169–214.

[102] See *Disputatio adv. Abaelardum*, *PL* 180, 266B. Contrast William's appeal for a metaphorical understanding of 'Soul' in *Ph. Mundi* I, 15; *PL* 172, 46–7.

[103] See Abelard's *Dialectica*, ed. L. M. de Rijk, 2nd edn. (Assen, 1970), pp. 558–9. The date of the passage seems to be later than 1135; see de Rijk's introduction, pp. xxi–xxiii. Cf. Gregory, *Anima*, pp. 148–51.

[104] For these positions, see the edition of Jourdain, 75; *Ph. Mundi* I, 15 (*PL* 172, 46); *Glosae*, p. 145; Gregory, *Anima*, pp. 148–9; cf. Silverstein, 'Fabulous Cosmogony,' 114–15, and Dronke, 'L'amor,' 410–13. The chronological relation between the *Glosses* on the *Timaeus* quotation and the *Ph. Mundi* passage (cited here from texts which may be revised versions of these works) is uncertain; see Southern, *Platonism, Scholastic Method, and the School of Chartres*, cited above in n. 42, pp. 16–17, n. 17, pp. 22–4, who notes some additional texts in arguing for a similar shift in William's orientation.

troversy that led to the condemnation of 1140 was taking its toll. But it scarcely mattered. In the movement William and his contemporaries began, traditional theology was being overtaken by events.

It was the condemnation itself, in fact, that promoted this movement. As so often in attempts at censorship, the censors hastened the very process they were so zealous to stop. The concern that God was being undermined by that figurative composite, the World Soul, led to the formation of a new composite far more imposing and enduring: the abstraction of 'Nature.' It was precisely the exclusion of the World Soul from the divine plane that led to a new emphasis on its connection with the earthly plane. Eventually, this vital *anima*, confined to the natural realm, was replaced by the figure of an animating 'Nature.'[105]

We can watch the shift take place in mid-paragraph in William of Conches. The World Soul, he had said, 'according to some,' is the Holy Spirit. Then he continued: 'Others say that the World Soul is a natural power ("naturalem vigorem") implanted in things,' which is responsible for the earthly faculties of growth, sensation, and reason.[106] Not long after William wrote these words, Hermann of Carinthia applies a different interpretation of the Soul's tripartite nature to 'natura' itself, that 'germinating force of the world' ('mundi germen'), which 'Plato calls' the World Soul.[107] A few years later, John of Salisbury explains that according to some, 'natura' is 'a certain life-giving force, implanted in all things' ('vis quaedam genitiva, rebus omnibus insita').[108] Shortly thereafter, in the *Complaint of Nature*, Alan of Lille dispenses with the World Soul, attributing its powers instead to the full-

---

[105] See Gregory, *Platonismo*, pp. 135, 144. For full documentation of this process, here presented only in the briefest overview, see Gregory's seminal work in *Anima*, pp. 123–246, *Platonismo*, pp. 122–50, and 'L'idea,' pp. 42–51, to which I am deeply indebted. While Gregory deals mainly with the philosophic issue at stake, I have hoped to suggest some of the relations between the philosophic and linguistic issues, along with certain consequences of their interaction.

[106] See *Ph. Mundi* I, 15; *PL* 172, 46, with the textual readings printed by Dronke, *Fabula*, p. 175.

[107] See *De Essentiis*, cited above in n. 61, p. 63. Gregory, *Platonismo*, pp. 140–3, cites the passage, along with the identification of 'anima mundi' and 'natura' in the later *De septem septenis* and the descending triad of 'causa, racio, natura' in *De vi rerum principiis*.

[108] See *Metalogicon* I, 8; *PL* 199, 835.

grown figure of 'Natura.' Now it is 'Natura' that is the generative principle of things ('genitrixque rerum'), the binding force of the world ('Vinculum mundi').[109] She is the culmination of that compositional and interpretive process which eased God down to earth in stages, finally transforming a divine allegory of 'love' into the allegory of nature itself.

This transfiguration uniquely suited the paradoxical needs of a God whose power had to be at once delegated and conserved. It was only by 'yielding' his power, in effect, that God could be saved from undermining it, from implicating himself too directly in the world. It was only by obliquely 'surrendering' part of himself that he could achieve that 'generosity' ('largitas'), that self-surrender, which distinguished him. In facilitating such a movement, the natural philosophers of the period were not only explicating the spiritual origins of their world, but helping to stimulate a mediating world of discourse, an allegorical testimony to divine power.

God's abstract agent on earth, 'Nature,' displayed an autonomy scarcely exhibited by her conceptual predecessors. Among the most important sources of her 'life-giving force' were those originally Stoic, then Neoplatonic (and more rarefied) *rationes seminales*, which held in embryonic form all subsequent natural growth. In his influential account of Genesis, Augustine had adapted those seminal principles to explain the generative process of nature, but for him, such seeds were material principles programmed by their divine Creator, not autonomous forces of efficient causality inside nature itself.[110] In the mid-twelfth century, some attempted to reconcile the two theories, as when Clarembald of Arras defined 'ratio seminalis' as 'the hidden force implanted in the elements' ('vis occulta inserta elementis').[111] But in the end, the *rationes seminales* were too matter-bound, too literal in their attachment to earth to act as expansive figures of divine power. It was Nature in whom God breathed the breath of life, and

---

[109] See *DPN* VII, 1–2; cf. Gregory, *Anima*, p. 153.

[110] See my discussion in Ch. II; Gregory, *Anima*, pp. 179–81; Gilson, *Spirit*, cited above in n. 38, pp. 135–6, and his *Introduction à l'étude de Saint Augustin*, 3rd edn. (Paris, 1949), p. 269, n. 5. For the broader sources of 'Natura,' see the refs. in Ch. IV, n. 2, above; for its relation to the *ignis artifex*, see my discussion below.

[111] See *Clarembald*, pp. 233, 238. Cf. *Six Days*, chs. 16–17, and É. Jeauneau, 'Simples notes sur la cosmogonie de Thierry de Chartres,' *Sophia*, 23 (1955), 178.

who thereupon emerged almost as a living thing, sharing his spirit through allegory.

As a result, when William of Conches interprets the biblical account of man's creation, a new abstraction appears in the story, the unmistakable ancestress of Bernard Silvestris' and Alan of Lille's 'Natura.' Adam, says William, was created from the earth ('ex limo'), and so was Eve, he adds, even though Scripture plainly says that she was created from Adam's side ('ex latere Adae'). This text, William explains, must not be taken literally ('Non enim ad litteram credendus est'). The truth is that all men and women are born, then as now, through 'natura.' Some will say, he points out, that such a view detracts from divine power.

To whom we respond, on the contrary, this is to *confer* power to God ('ei conferre'), since we attribute to him both that he gave such a nature to things ('rebus naturam'), and also that he created the human body through the operation of nature ('per naturam operantem').[112]

Far from compromising God's power, his earthly delegate is seeing to it that his orders are carried out. As William says elsewhere, we do not 'detract' from God when we call the creation of men, which continues to this day, the work of 'nature':

All things which are in the world, except evil, God made, but some things he made through the operation of nature, which is the instrument of divine work ('operante natura rerum que est instrumentum divine operationis') . . . [113]

Thus, when God allows other agents to operate, he is magnifying not only them, but himself. By distancing himself from direct contact with his work, he can fill the world with testimonials to his creative power. Into that distance between God and his effects would soon rush the whole host of 'secondary causes' which the twelfth and thirteenth centuries developed to express God's manifold action—as they themselves expanded their own intellectual range with a new influx of scientific and astrological texts. The process advanced by William and his contemporaries culminated a century later,

---

[112] See *Ph. Mundi* I, 23; *PL* 172, 56; cf. *Glosae*, p. 122.
[113] See *Glosses* on Boethius, ed. Parent, *La Doctrine*, p. 128.

when Aquinas confidently declared: 'To detract from the perfection of *creatures* is to detract from the perfection of *divine power.*'[114] God's ability to establish new agents of power was a testimony to his plenitude, not a diminution of it.

In the end, this expansive movement produced the opportunity not only for an interlocking series of philosophic causes, but for an intermediate range of oblique figures, set at varying angles to the truth. It would require a more literary perspective to explicate such possibilities fully in allegorical terms. But already in this incipient 'Natura,' the natural philosophers of the early twelfth century were intensifying the development of conditions critical to allegory: the tendency to consolidate the philosophic study of causes with the imaginative expression of them.

To some, nonetheless, such an approach to nature and language threatened to abandon God altogether. The ever-vigilant William of St. Thierry was shocked by William of Conches' account of the creation. The man is an outright Manichaean ('manifestus Manichaeus'), the abbot of St. Thierry declared, and a materialist at the same time—the abbot occasionally sacrificed consistency in the interests of truth—who follows the opinion of those stupid philosophers ('stultorum quorumdam philosophorum') who believe that there is nothing but the material world. This deluded 'man of physics' tells us that the human body is made not by God, but by *nature* ('dicit corpus ejus non a Deo factum, sed a natura'). In his novel approach to the creation of Eve, which he interprets according to the 'sense of physics' ('physico sensu interpretans'), how foolishly, how proudly, he slights the historical sense of divine authority ('quam stulte, quam superbe irridet historiam divinae auctoritatis').[115] Although William never retracted his general views on the instrumental power of nature, he did confess, in the face of such attacks, that he had previously taken the story of Eve's creation from Adam's rib 'translative'—metaphorically. This interpretation, he added, must be condemned ('damnandum'). To replace it, William exhumes the safe old exegesis of the Church Fathers, the piecemeal allegory of tradition. God really did make Eve from

---

[114] See *Summa Contra Gentiles*, III, 69; quoted by Gregory, *Anima*, p. 237, n. 1.
[115] See *De Erroribus Guillelmi de Conchis*, PL 180, 339–40.

Adam's rib, William now says, and in so doing he both signified ('significaret') that woman should be subject to man, and prefigured ('praefiguraret') that the Church issues from the side of God.[116] Reading this retraction is almost like watching the old exegesis make a last stand against the new continuities of physical interpretation. Not that the old exegesis ever disappeared, of course, but that forces it could no longer contain were beginning to displace its old authority.

The process of displacement, however, has its own problematic momentum. In a cycle seen throughout this investigation, the very study of causes which provided William with his bold conceptual categories increasingly produced new categories which displaced the old concepts in turn. Nature no sooner emerged as a full philosophic concept than it was refined by new scientific perspectives and transformed from the inside, while the abstraction as a whole passed into wide literary currency. Perhaps the most striking early twelfth-century anticipation of the scientific side of this process is the famous exposition of creation 'secundum phisicam et ad litteram' attributed to Thierry of Chartres, *On the Works of the Six Days*.[117] It is often remarked that the treatise's importance lies in removing God from the formation of the world once the initial instantaneous act of creating matter has been performed. And it is true that once God creates the four elements, he withdraws from the scene, as the element of fire sets in motion a series of processes which result in the formation of the firmament, the appearance of dry land, and the development of life.[118] There is another feature of the author's analysis, however, which is perhaps more revealing of both his own method and the changes to come. He began his treatise by dividing creation according to the four causes. God, on the one hand, was the efficient, formal, and final cause; matter, on the other, was the material cause (ch. 2). Later in the treatise, however, once God has created matter and withdrawn from it, the material world acts out *within itself* the very relationships which God originally

---

[116] See *Dialogus de substantiis physicis (Dragmaticon)*, ed. G. Gratarolus (1567; repr. Frankfurt/Main, 1967), pp. 7, 77.

[117] For the phrase itself, see *Six Days*, ch. 1, p. 555. 2.

[118] See Jeauneau, 'Simples notes,' cited above in n. 111, 172-83.

acted out with the material world as a whole—and in similar terminology:

For fire only acts ('agit'). But earth only undergoes ('patitur'). And the two elements which are in the middle both act and undergo. . . . So, therefore, fire is like a craftsman ('quasi artifex') and efficient cause ('efficiens causa'); but earth is its subject, like a material cause ('materialis causa'). And the two elements which are in the middle are like the instrument ('instrumentum') or coordinating factor by which the action of the highest is administered to the lowest. (ch. 17, p. 562. 4–12)

The original distinction between God and the world has here given way to a distinction within the world itself. In such a world, a comprehensive framework like 'natura' requires constant, interior articulation. Here, one of nature's own internal components, fire, takes over the causal foreground both from God and from the 'instrumental' nature that we have already seen beginning to displace God's direct activity. It is fire, not the Lord, that is now in a sense the 'artifex et efficiens causa' of events. More pointedly, it is not exactly 'natura' as a whole, in the famous definition, that constitutes the 'ignis artifex,' but a fiery principle with a kind of elemental, creative dimension in its own right.[119] In the face of such a text, the opposition of some of Thierry's contemporaries to the new physical doctrines is understandable. It was not only their world that was being dismantled; in a sense it is ours, too, as our own *physici* no sooner specify the agent of a natural process than probe inside it, find its constituent parts, and pinpoint a new agent—only to have it displaced in turn.

[119] On the movement from God to fire as 'quasi artifex' in *Six Days*, cf. Peter Dronke, 'New Approaches to the School of Chartres,' *Anuario de estudios medievales*, 6 (1969), 133–6; on the nuances of this movement and its relation to other orientations, see below. For the (originally Stoic) definition of 'natura' as 'ignis artifex' and its variegated passage to the twelfth century, see my discussion and notes below, and Hugh of St. Victor, *Didascalicon*, tr. Taylor, I, 10, with the refs. in Taylor's n. 71, pp. 193–4. It is important to distinguish the different (although often overlapping) approaches to an 'ignis artifex' in texts available by the mid-twelfth century; see, e.g., the cosmic agent in *Asc.*, ch. 2; the solar source in Macrobius, Remigius, and others, cited by Taylor; the activating power (with certain astrological implications) in Abu Ma'shar, cited by Lemay, *Abu Ma'shar*, pp. 60–1, 88, 100–1, 105, 110–13, 181–2,190, 193; the physiological force in Constantine the African, noted by Gregory in the refs. cited above in my n. 9.

Broadly speaking, of course, all these 'efficient causes'—God, Nature, fire—are reconcilable with each other; they reveal a single divine cause unfolding on different but parallel planes. But this very question of reconciliation brings the whole issue full circle, to the sources of the treatise's conception and their allegorical afterlife. While Thierry and others draw upon a variety of texts for the notion of an *ignis artifex*, the ultimate source of such a conception, of course, is the Stoic cosmology discussed near the beginning of this study. For the Stoics, God or Nature—their oscillation in this definition is revealing—is 'a craftsmanlike fire going on its way to genesis.'[120] It is true that the Stoics, as we have noted, articulate a complex physics elaborating this principle, but their whole impulse is to conflate the divine cause with the material effect, and so to minimize the kinds of distinctions to be made between them. The author of the *Six Days*, like others in the *avant garde* of twelfth-century science, is no less possessed of a consolidating impulse, but he insists more clearly than the Stoics upon its differentiating counterpart, the careful 'explication' of the divine from one level to another. His God is at once more conservative and more expansive than the God of the Stoics; he retains for himself a unique creativity while granting to his creatures a distinctive autonomy in their own right.

When, in the *Cosmographia*, such simultaneous impulses toward convergence and divergence are adapted and enriched by a range of mystical, astrological, and theological perspectives, they acquire striking imaginative form.[121] The scientific account of an interplay between fire and earth turns into a sensitive dramatization of the interplay between this interior cycle itself and the cosmic cycle at large. In the brilliant vision that closes *Megacosmos* (Sec. IV), the elemental forces (i) of fire and earth begin to interact in the figurative terms of lover and beloved (ii), but as Providence brings the creation from above

---

[120] See my discussion in Ch. II; the definition itself was available in Cicero, *De Natura Deorum* II, xxii, 57, with a variant in Victorinus; see Taylor, cited in the previous note.

[121] For the different traditions of the interaction of the elements, see the refs. to *Asc.* and Abu Ma'shar in n. 119, above; Endres, *Petrus Damiani und die Weltliche Wissenschaft*, cited above in n. 8, p. 31, n. 2; d'Alverny, 'Le Cosmos symbolique du XIIᵉ siècle,' cited above in n. 14, 76 and 78, n. 4; Dronke, 'L'amor'; and the refs. in *Cosm.* (tr.), pp. 152-4, nn. 115-18 and 128-32.

to below 'in a continuous revolution full circle' ('repetitis am-
fractibus rerum originem retorquebat,' iii) according to the
procession of 'time,' the perspective shifts to the totality
('Rerum . . . universitas,' iv), where the maker himself is
strictly the 'eternal cause,' while informed matter as a whole is
his perpetual subject—a totality that at once passes back
through the cycle, initially into the rarefied 'image' of the
divine ('imago,' v) and such abstract attributes as 'sapientia,'
'voluntas,' and 'bonitas' (v–vi), then into the diverse
characters of the text ('Yle,' 'Natura,' 'Noys,' vii–ix), and
finally, with the cyclical movement of 'time' (x–xiii), back to
the other side of the universe ('universa,' xiv) in a visionary
retrospective. Here the very shift in linguistic register enacts
the contractive/expansive movement of the cosmos as a whole.

In his scientific account of creation, of course, the author of
the *Six Days* does not aspire to such a synthesis. Even with his
more austere format, however, he displays a distinct effort to
negotiate between different linguistic and cosmic orders in a
temporal context. Beginning with a section on the divine and
material 'causes' of creation ('de causis,' chs. 2–3), he shifts
into a physical analysis of the six days themselves, the 'order of
times' ('de ordine temporum,' chs. 4–17), then incorporates
those physical categories into an 'exposition of the letter' of
Genesis ('ad expositionem littere,' chs. 17–29), an exposition
that finally, with 'Let there be light,' provokes an ascent to the
abstract 'theology' ('theologia,' chs. 29–47) of the One.[122] Not
since Eriugena's *Periphyseon* had an exposition of Genesis
sought to develop such a multileveled, panoramic movement.[123]

---

[122] The extant treatise ends at ch. 47, and it is possible that Thierry himself did not
complete it; see Häring, 'Creation,' 144–5. The crucial point is the author's movement here between diverse levels of analysis.

[123] With respect to this analytic drive, see the almost parallel phrasing at the start of
Six Days (ch. 1, p. 555. 1–6) and *Periph.* III, 693BC (where Eriugena begins to
elucidate the systematic passage 'causarum in effectus,' as he puts it): the *Six Days*
author declares his intention to concentrate on the 'sensum littere hystorialem'
(Nutritor: 'secundum historiam') and to leave aside the 'allegoricam et moralem lec-
tionem' (Nutritor: 'allegoricis intellectibus moralium interpretationum'), which, the
Six Days author notes, 'a sanctis doctoribus aperte execute sunt' (Alumnus: 'Satis enim
a sanctis patribus de talium est actum'). The parallel, which I think has not been cited
before, is perhaps too general in strategy to be pressed, and the twelfth-century writer,
with his keener sense of 'physics,' proceeds to develop a very different approach
toward the six days; see below. Nonetheless, the similar declarations reveal certain

The *Six Days* treatise itself, with all its structural deficiencies and its eagerness for a new learning that will not be fully assimilated for another century, hardly matches Eriugena's work in intention, orientation, or impact. Nonetheless, it suggests how the twelfth century is beginning to clarify issues of text, being, and time which we have seen problematic not only for Eriugena—with his abstruse modes of 'Nature'—but for scriptural exegesis as a whole since its rich formative period in the early centuries AD. The 'letter' of the text here becomes central to the exposition, even while the very meaning of 'literal' is changing, acquiring new conceptual depth. The orders of being include a 'physical' level increasingly distinguished from a strictly 'theological' one both in cosmic and linguistic terms. The development of time, while still severely limited in conception, turns into the dynamic framework for the organization of the elements. It is as if the expansive movement of divine creation at large were demanding a new diversification of human discourse itself.

In response to that demand, Thierry and his contemporaries carefully maneuver between the original formulations of their texts and the abstract categories of their analysis. They thus carry into the realm of 'physics' the conceptual tendencies of early scholastic theology as a whole—the effort to articulate formal structures of exegesis which do not undermine a text, but reconstitute it on an abstract plane.[124] In their concern for sustained, continuous designs, perhaps they share a certain spirit even with those who most impressively display alternative attitudes toward the works of God—the Victorines. It should be stressed that deep differences separate the kinds of continuities developed by men of such different orientations.[125] The 'naturalistic' interest in cosmic order in the exegesis of a Thierry of Chartres is not the same as the 'naturalistic' concern for historical sequence in the exegesis of a Hugh of St. Victor.[126]

common tendencies toward the conceptual reconstruction of the *littera*. For Eriugena's general influence upon writing associated with Thierry, see the refs. to Gregory, Lucentini, and Gersh in n. 57 above.

[124] See the refs. in n. 13 above, with B. Geyer, *Die Patristische und Scholastische Philosophie* (Berlin, 1928), pp. 152-7; A. Forest, F. Van Steenberghen, and M. de Gandillac, *Le Mouvement doctrinal du IXe au XIVe siècle* (Paris, 1951), pp. 147-52.

[125] See, e.g., Chenu, pp. 9-10, 17-18, 22-5, 33-5, 103-6, 112-14, 137, 199, 290; Wetherbee, pp. 49-66.

[*for n. 126 see next page*]

The one tends to stress the analogical possibilities of this world; the other, the anagogic progression toward a higher world. Common to both, however, is an effort to enrich the very notion of textual 'signification,' to show that depth of meaning depends not just on a fourfold exegetical method, with its piecemeal tendencies, but on the construction of sequential wholes and coherent causalities.[127]

Traditional exegesis continues to be practiced throughout the Middle Ages, and some perhaps have underestimated its currency in the twelfth century and later. Even the author of the *Six Days* never rejects 'the allegorical and moral reading, which the saintly teachers have plainly elucidated' (*Six Days*, ch. 1). But when, at the start of his treatise, he announces that he will leave such readings aside to concentrate on creation 'according to physics and the letter' (ch. 1), he displays a drive toward conceptual reformulation that is destined to transform traditional modes of interpretation, expanding the 'letter' in a way scarcely dreamed of by the old practitioners of the fourfold method. In fact, for all its fourfold meanings, it was that inherited method which often proved to be the most restricted, the most text-bound in procedure. When William of St. Thierry accused William of Conches of 'slighting the historical sense of divine authority,' it was with the intention of harnessing his exegesis to the old literal story of Adam's rib and its authorized spiritual meanings. Exegesis of that kind too often became constrictive, impeding a broader transfiguration of the text ('translative,' admitted William of Conches). In the end, a full account of the amplitude of creation required not the mere affiliation but the deep integration of spirit with the body of the letter.

Such was the process that God himself enacted in his gradual 'descent' to earth, passing into a series of figures to which he delegated his own power. The passage provided for him by the early twelfth century did not develop in neat chronological stages, of course—from the third person of the Trinity to abstract goodness or love, from love to the World Soul, from ·

126 On the dimension of the *historia* in Hugh and Adam of St. Victor, see Spicq, pp. 80-4, 94-101; Smalley, pp. 83-106, 112-85; Chenu, pp. 165-73.

127 See esp. Chenu 'Deux âges,' cited above in Ch. III, n. 31, 19-28; *La Théologie*, cited above in Ch. V, n. 12, pp. 200-6.

the World Soul to Nature. Parts of this process took place roughly at the same time, in certain authors tentatively, in others, decisively, with some variations even within the works of a single author. Further, as we have noted, there were important distinctions in emphasis and approach even among those who agreed upon a general strategy. Broadly speaking, however, these diverse developments reinforced each other, so that together they provided a composite framework for such a descent. To facilitate that movement, along with the corresponding ascent of matter, the natural philosophers of the period developed figures which pointed in two directions. In the process of developing them, they helped to consolidate the two sides of their own activity, at once performing acts of interpretation and composition. In effect, these writers were really celebrating two creations. God, it is true, had brought heaven down to earth. They, on the other hand, were bringing both into poetry.

VI *THE ALLEGORY OF CREATION: THE* COSMOGRAPHIA

Since you cannot reach to what he is, reach to what he is
not. (Augustine, *In Joann.* XXIII, 9.)

If the twelfth century marks a decisive stage in that broad convergence of interpretive and compositional activity which we
have been exploring in allegory since antiquity, the *Cosmographia*
is not the only sign of the transformation. Even in examining earlier developments, we have noted certain changes in
twelfth-century philosophic and imaginative procedures, sometimes related only indirectly to allegory, which prepare the way
for such a convergence. From the *quaestio* and the *summa* to the
accessus and the gloss on ancient authors, the exegesis of this
period increasingly develops abstract designs with a new sensitivity to literary nuance.[1] At the same time, the literary tradition itself, from the mythological vision and the love lyric to
the poetic debate and the sequence, gradually consolidates its
allusive movement with a new conceptual cogency.[2] By the
later twelfth century, even forms belonging rather strictly to
either the philosophic or the rhetorical tradition may be intriguingly implicated in the other. Thus, the exegetical *distinctio*
turns scattered allegorizations into a kind of intricate matrix for
rhetorical exploitation, while conversely, the typological lyric
organizes the very texture of its language by the categories of
scriptural exegesis.[3] It is as if philosophy and rhetoric as a

---

[1] See, e.g., the remarks corresponding to Ch. III, nn. 59, 70–1, 74, 79, 94; Ch. IV,
nn. 1, 16, 45, 55, 75; Ch. V, nn. 13, 14, 43, 44, and the last section of the chapter;
with the refs. in the notes.

[2] See, e.g., the remarks corresponding to Ch. II, n. 35; Ch. IV, nn. 1, 35, 41–4;
Ch. V, nn. 10, 17; with the refs. in the notes.

[3] On the *distinctio*, see Smalley, pp. 246–63, esp. p. 248; Stephen Barney, 'Visible
Allegory: The *Distinctiones Abel* of Peter the Chanter,' in *Allegory, Myth, and Symbol,* ed.
Bloomfield, cited above in Ch. I, n. 4, esp. pp. 91, 96–7, 102–7; Allen, *The Friar as
Critic,* cited above in Ch. III, n. 65, pp. 32–4, 102–8; and *Ethical Poetic,* cited above in
Ch. I, n. 1, pp. 100–6, 142–66, on the broader relation between the *distinctio* and the
'normative array' of full-fledged literary forms in the later Middle Ages. On the

whole were each developing by exploring the strategies of the other.[4]

Beyond such general tendencies, however, the twelfth century produces more direct interactions between the philosophic and rhetorical traditions of allegory itself. Such are those variegated, composite forms, systematically developing from the early twelfth century, in which one tradition passes almost imperceptibly into the other: the suggestive sketch of Honorius *On the Exile and Homeland of the Soul* (*De Animae Exsilio et Patria*), for example, which explicates the Babylonian exile in the guise of an abstract journey; the mystical treatises of Bernard of Clairvaux or Richard of St. Victor, which trace the soul's ascent by passing into elaborate metaphor or even the conceptual deployment of scriptural 'persons'; the exotic visions of Hildegard of Bingen, which ceaselessly transfigure didactic principles into a fabulous mode.[5] The most strictly allegorical of these diverse, composite forms, and yet at the same time, perhaps the most conceptually and artistically versatile work among them, is the *Cosmographia* of Bernard Silvestris, composed almost at the midpoint of the twelfth century. Here interpretive and compositional allegory at last converge with full force, and in the process, decisively transform the allegorical tradition as a whole.[6]

typological lyric, see Krewitt, pp. 450–2, and esp. the striking poetry of Walter of Châtillon; e.g., poems 1, 3, 5, 9, in *Die Lieder Walters von Chatillon*, ed. Karl Strecker (1925; repr. Berlin, 1964), and the more sustained compositions in *Moralisch-Satirische Gedichte Walters von Chatillon*, ed. Karl Strecker (Heidelberg, 1929), poems 1, 14, 17.

[4] See Richard McKeon, 'Poetry and Philosophy in the Twelfth Century: The Renaissance of Rhetoric,' *MP* 43 (1946), 217–34.

[5] See Heinz Meyer, '*Mos Romanorum:* Zum typologischen Grund der Triumph-metapher im "Speculum Ecclesiae" des Honorius Augustodunensis,' in *Verbum et Signum*, Vol. I, esp. pp. 47–8; Chenu, pp. 113–14; Stock, *Literacy*, cited above in Ch. IV, n. 4, pp. 408, 413, 435–8, 452; Barbara Nolan, *The Gothic Visionary Perspective* (Princeton, 1977), pp. 20–5, 30–8; Grover A. Zinn, Jr., 'Personification Allegory and Visions of Light in Richard of St Victor's Teaching on Contemplation,' *University of Toronto Quarterly*, 46 (1977), 190–214; Dronke, *Fabula*, pp. 96–9, and his *Poetic Individuality in the Middle Ages* (Oxford, 1970), pp. 150–79.

[6] The edn. and introd. of Dronke, the tr. and introd. of Wetherbee, and the study of Stock, cited in the introductory list of abbreviations, offer stimulating approaches to the poem, and I am deeply indebted to these works. In citing the text at places where the printed line numbering is incorrect (e.g., line indicator '10' at line number of a section), for convenience of reference I treat the last line indicator (e.g., '10') as the starting point for identifying the lines after it; thus, e.g., the third line after '10' is cited as '13,' though this line may in fact be the twelfth line of the section. For the date of *Cosm.*, probably between 1143 and 1148, see Stock, p. 11, n. 1.

The subject of the poem is the original transformation itself, the fashioning of rudimentary matter into an orderly world. The work is divided into two books. In Book I, *Megacosmos*, 'the greater universe,' Nature complains to Noys (the divine Mind) about the confused condition of Hyle (prime matter), and pleads that the universe be more beautifully wrought. Noys willingly agrees to the appeal, and organizes the amorphous state of matter into the four elements. From Noys emanates the World Soul (here called 'Endelichia'), which animates and sustains the world. The universe unfolds in a magnificent panorama: the angelic host; constellations and planets; mountains, rivers, and trees; animals, fish, and birds; all in their orderly arrangements.

At the opening of Book II, *Microcosmos*, 'the smaller universe,' Noys glories in the refinement of the greater universe, and promises to create man as the completion of her work. To achieve this task, she bids Nature seek out Urania, the principle of celestial knowledge, and Physis, the principle of earthly understanding. Nature ascends through the heavenly spheres and finds Urania at last in the highest level of the firmament. Together, Nature and Urania descend toward earth. Alighting in the paradisal garden of Gramision (many mss, 'Granusion'), they discover Physis, accompanied by her daughters, Theory and Practice. Suddenly, Noys appears, and assigns her charges the task of creating the microcosm, man. Urania is to give man his soul; Physis is to put together his body; and Nature is to unite the two. As aids in their work, Noys gives to each of the three a separate model of Noys' own divine understanding, each model progressively more restricted in scope. Urania receives the 'Mirror of Providence.' Nature receives the 'Table of Fate.' Physis, at last, must be content with the 'Book of Memory.' After some difficulty, man takes shape, and with the fashioning of the smaller universe, the universe as a whole is complete.

Beyond its intriguing details, the most immediately striking feature of the *Cosmographia* is its overall design. Bernard Silvestris' poem is at once an interpretive and a compositional performance. On the one hand, the author is explicating the story of creation. On the other hand, he is conducting that explication by creating an allegorical story in its own right. That is, he *acts out* his *exegesis* by the *composition* of *allegorical agents*. This is a crucial turning point in the development of allegory. If the earlier works we have explored increasingly associate allegorical interpretation and composition, the *Cosmographia* decisively integrates them. Indeed, as we shall see, the poem constantly turns its very subject, the primal act of creation, into a comment on its own creative processes, as if to make itself an act of genesis. Here at last the two traditions of allegory radically merge with each other, setting in motion an allegorical world with its own autonomy, evolving as it passes into the later Middle Ages.

As in every merger, each of the component parts in the process undergoes a change. We might briefly consider first Bernard's manipulation of interpretive allegory. It is true that the *Cosmographia* follows the general process of the Genesis story, and so in a sense remains within the long hexaemeral tradition of Christian exegesis.[7] Bernard deeply enriches this tradition with other interpretive strategies, however, adapting the very categories of his analysis—Noys, the World Soul, Nature, Hyle—from the systematic reinterpretation of such pagan principles in the twelfth century. Indeed, a figure like Bernard's Noys is the product of the whole complex interaction of sacred and secular exegesis that we have explored since antiquity. Affiliated here with 'Minerva,' 'divine Providence' ('divina Providentia'), and the 'mind of the most high' ('mens altissimi'), she has her remote origins in the ancient interpretive interplay between Homer's Pallas Athena (Minerva) and abstract 'wisdom'—a principle transformed by Greek philosophy into the divine *logos*, formulated by Hellenistic Judaism and early Christianity as God's own plan of creation, implicated by Stoic and astrological treatises in the direct administration of the cosmos, fashioned by Martianus' invocation to 'Pallas' as the principle of 'fate' and the 'sacred Nous,' and interpreted in Remigius' commentary on Martianus' Pallas as that 'wisdom' which issues from 'the mind of

---

[7] See Étienne Gilson, 'La Cosmogonie de Bernardus Silvestris,' *AHDLMA* 3 (1928), 5–24, esp. 8; contrast Curtius, *European Literature,* p. 112, and see Silverstein's reply, 'Fabulous Cosmogony,' cited above in Ch. V, n. 19, esp. 94–5; cf. my qualifications below. Isidore of Seville, incidentally, used the word *cosmographia* to describe the Pentateuch itself; see Stock, p.21.

the supreme God'—developments all contributing in some measure to Bernard's multifaceted figure.[8] At the same time, by exploiting such sacred and secular texts, the *Cosmographia* develops a continuous exegesis of that other 'text' central to the interpretive tradition, the book of nature. Perhaps the range of Bernard's orientation is best exemplified by Nature herself, a figure addressed by Noys in the almost sacramental register that acquires new resonance from Raban Maur to Hugh of St. Victor—'uteri mei beata fecunditas'—yet engaged in the contemporary 'physics' of a William of Conches—'Natura . . . elementans.'[9] If such diverse interpretive strains produce certain tensions in the work, by the same token they constitute a uniquely bold interpretive composite, a rich, abstract counterpart to the story of creation.

In order to produce that composite, the *Cosmographia* exploits the tradition of allegorical composition. The activities attributed by the Bible to a quite literal God Bernard distributes among various abstract powers who seem to act on their own. As a result, the single, all-powerful agency of a divine source is divided into a series of partial, independent transactions. Instead of saying, with the Bible, that God brought chaos into order, Bernard says that chaos itself, Hyle or Silva, petitioned Noys, the divine Mind, for form. Instead of saying, with the Bible, that God created man from the dust of the earth, Bernard says that the agent of the physical world itself, Physis, fashioned man's body, while the agent of celestial knowledge, Urania, was responsible for his soul. Such versatile characters are neither so metaphysically abstruse as the 'emanations' of the late antique Neoplatonists or the 'inversions' of Eriugena, nor

[8] For the refs. to Noys in *Cosm.*, see *Meg.* I, 6 and 66; II, vii, 1-2; II, xiii, 2. For her remote ancestry (along with other direct and indirect contributions to her development), see my discussion of Athena in Ch. II; the refs. to Armstrong and Markus in Ch. III, n. 9 and to Wolfson in Ch. V, n. 71; Silverstein, 107-12; Stock, pp. 87-97. The various affiliations of Noys in *Cosm.* suggest different levels on which the divine design operates, and while I use, e.g., 'divine Mind' as a shorthand for these diverse levels, Noys herself is not to be confused with the second person of the Trinity; see Silverstein, 102-7; *Cosm.* (tr.), p. 39. (The n. to *Meg.* III, 17-18 on pp. 164-5 of *Cosm.* needs a more careful sense of the modulations of this figure.) On the transformation of the hexaemeral tradition by pagan sources in the *Cosm.*, see Stock, pp. 227, 264, and 278-9, nn. 116-17, although he perhaps underestimates Bernard's effort to incorporate such categories within a Christian, even scriptural, framework.

[9] For these refs. to Nature and their implications, see *Meg.* II, i, 3-4 and IV, vii, 1, with *Cosm.* (tr.), pp. 54-6 and p. 153, n. 128; cf. my broader discussion below.

so decoratively exotic as the gods of Martianus and the figures of Claudian—although they owe much to such earlier models. They constitute a set of uniquely articulated, carefully composed allegorical agents, acting out on their own terms the story of creation.

As a work that simultaneously criticizes and composes a story, the *Cosmographia* thus marks the culmination of a long allegorical process. That process had intensified as the interpretive tradition increasingly developed an abstract mode of discourse which the compositional tradition increasingly deployed in its own right. These complementary procedures finally coalesce in the *Cosmographia*, which makes the activity of interpretation abstract, while making the activity of abstractions interpretive. It is as if the two halves of Plato's broken egg, each looking for its counterpart, were rejoining each other. A critical need is converging with a compositional method.

In constructing his allegory of creation, Bernard Silvestris dramatizes the fact that the study of causes underlies both allegorical traditions. As an interpretive act, the *Cosmographia*, like all its philosophic ancestors since the earliest exegesis of Homer, attempts to reach the underlying principles of the world. As a compositional act, the *Cosmographia*, like all its predecessors in the rhetorical tradition, attempts to expose those principles by elaborating them in a narrative. Causation, in fact, is the very subject of the poem, the activity of the First Cause in the making of the world. At the same time, this comprehensive source of creation acts in accordance with the two fundamental principles we have seen developing in the twelfth-century orientation to divine power. First, even when it seems that something else is acting, God's power is totally conserved. Second, and conversely, even when God conserves his power, he can delegate it, and this will cause something else to seem to act. This twofold perspective on power has its rhetorical expression, as we have observed, in the split reference of figurative language, seeming to point in one direction, actually pointing in another. In composing a world filled with such figures of divine power, Bernard Silvestris turns the philosophic duality into a starting point for allegory.

In fact, the *Cosmographia* develops these principles into an expansive narrative. In terms of the conservation of power,

Bernard carefully specifies that even figures central to the poem are really at some remove from the truth. Noys herself is but 'the *image* of unfailing life' ('Vite viventis ymago,' *Meg*. I, 4), or, as Bernard later puts it, as if to check himself,

the image, or perhaps I should call it a face inscribed with the image of the Father.

imago nescio dicam an vultus, patris imagine consignatus.[10]

As for Endelichia, Nature, Urania, and Physis, they are products of Noys, herself an image.[11] Indeed, the very employment of these principles in the creation of the world directly implicates them in an imagistic realm. The cosmos they are laboring to construct, after all, is but 'the image of a better world' ('mundi melioris ymago,' *Mic*. X, 9), the better world of God himself. Every divine 'theophany' here is only a figure of God's own propriety. Divine power is fully conserved.

Yet even while God conserves his power, he can delegate it, and this will make it seem that something else is acting. It is this delegation of divine power—more philosophically rigorous than the 'reflections' of earlier cosmic allegory yet more imaginatively luxuriant than the 'theophanies' of the *Periphyseon* —that generates the elaborate activity of Bernard's narrative, activity that in strict truth belongs to God. The most dramatic of these delegations of a power wholly conserved comes in the first scene of the *Cosmographia*, and revealingly, it is the best piece of allegory in the poem. It describes the primal moment when Silva, the mere 'appearance of Being' ('Usie vultus'), pleads for refinement:

Silva, obdurate, a formless chaos, a hostile coalescence, the motley appearance of Being, a mass discordant with itself, longs in her turbulence for a tempering power; in her crudity for form; in her rankness for cultivation. Yearning to emerge from her ancient

10 See *Meg*. IV, v, 2; cf. *Cosm*. (tr.), p. 153, n. 124. On the more strictly philosophic twelfth-century notion of 'imagines' as forms both ontologically and linguistically at some remove from their 'proper' ('proprie') origins, see, e.g., *Thierry*, p. 88. 12–17; p. 176. 54–6; cf. Gregory, *Anima*, pp. 78, 89–97; M.-Th. d'Alverny, *Alain de Lille: Textes inédits* (Paris, 1965), pp. 167–9; Gersh, 'Platonism,' cited above in Ch. V, n. 55, pp. 518–23.

11 See *Meg*. II, xiii, 16–18; *Meg*. II, i, 3–5; *Mic*. IV, 15–16; *Mic*. X, 1; cf. *Mic*. VII, v, 5–8.

tumult, she requires the shaping influence of number and the bonds of harmony.

> Silva rigens, informe chaos, concretio pugnax,
> Discolor Usie vultus, sibi dissona massa,
> Turbida temperiem, formam rudis, hispida cultum
> Optat, et a veteri cupiens exire tumultu,
> Artifices numeros et musica vincla requirit.
>
> (*Meg.* I, 18–22)

In this famous passage, it is almost as if allegory, like prime matter itself, were emerging into sophisticated form. By exploiting the split reference of language, Bernard expresses the divided condition of an incipient world, a world that in the very act of exposing its own powerlessness—its utter dependence upon God—seems to exert a certain power of its own. In the attributes longing ('Optat'), yearning ('cupiens'), and requiring ('requirit'), Bernard plays on the double-edged concept of 'want,' referring on the one hand to the passive need of the recipient, on the other hand to the active desire of the petitioner. Such predicates confirm the philosophic point that matter is actually defective, while hinting just enough about aspiration to make matter imaginatively effective. Severely constricted in fact, matter begins to expand in the fiction. What she actually requires she seems to request; what she actually lacks she seems to seek. In a sense, her literal liabilities are her allegorical competences, impelling her toward her divine counterpart.

It is true that this twofold dimension of matter has philosophic precedents, as we have seen, in the diverse approaches of philosophers such as Aristotle, the late antique Neoplatonists, Eriugena, and Thierry of Chartres. And as for the twofold dimension of words like 'want,' such *double entendres* are available in any age. 'It is a truth universally acknowledged,' wrote Jane Austen at the beginning of *Pride and Prejudice*, 'that a single man in possession of a good fortune must be in *want* of a wife.' Bernard's achievement is to integrate systematically the duality of the world with the duality of discourse, to implicate turns of being with turns of language. In fact, the very capacity of his allegorical world to exist seems almost to coincide with its ability to speak—as if the parallel between matter's ontological and linguistic attributes applied not only to predication *of* it, as in the argument of the *Commentum* of Thierry's circle, but to predication *by* it:

As if within a cradle, the infant universe squalls, and pleads to be clothed with a new form.

> Has inter veluti cunas infantia Mundi
> Vagit et ad speciem vestiri cultius orat. (*Meg.* I, 39–40)

Here the inchoate movement toward refinement is inseparable from the inarticulate drive toward articulation; the *infans*—that which cannot speak—is seeking to speak. From its earliest treatment in the ancient rhetorical tradition (App. II), *prosopopoeia* was 'impersonation,' the attribution of speech to that which cannot speak. It seems almost a comment on Bernard's deepening of that tradition that he puts the whole 'speech' of inarticulate matter into *oratio obliqua*, expressed within the opening appeal of a higher principle, Nature. It is true that the broad strategy of 'internal' personification, in which one figure inside the text fashions the *prosōpon* for another, had already developed in Boethius' *Consolation*, where Philosophy maneuvers rhetorically around her counterpart, 'two-faced' ('ambiguos uultus') Fortune. But perhaps it is a sign of the deep shift in philosophic and linguistic perspective here that now the speaker conducting the maneuver (Nature) acts not at the figure's expense, but on its behalf, and that the figure itself (two-sided matter) exhibits not just a deficiency, but a potentiality in its own right.

It is precisely personification, in fact, in its fundamental meaning of 'characterization,' of 'adopting guises,' that helps Bernard to engage the chronic philosophic problem of defining prime matter, as well as the chronic literary problem of sustaining a convincing allegory. Philosophically, we have seen that since the time of Plato, the 'scientific' tradition had been preoccupied with the issue of matter's adversity. It seemed difficult to make an intractable 'Necessity' susceptible to 'Reason.' The source of this dilemma, Aristotle argued, was that matter could not be contrary to form and at the same time desirous of it. It must rather be a third thing between formlessness and form, capable of the one, but receptive of the other. While this Aristotelian doctrine of potentiality was transmitted by Calcidius in fragmentary form to the twelfth century, Calcidius was hardly a model of clarity on such issues, and the matter of his commentary at once exhibits Platonic and Aristotelian features. Confronted with such obscurities, the twelfth century only slowly assimilates the notion of matter as a 'third thing' between evil and good; even Thierry of Chartres and his circle scarcely reconcile the notion of 'potentiality' with the 'physics' of *On the Works of the Six Days*. [12] While Bernard Silvestris himself displays his own ambiguities on this question, [13] perhaps his crucial contribution is to give the philosophic principle of potentiality an imaginative dimension, by making matter a *character,* the fictional subject *of* formlessness, but by the same token, subject *to* form. That is, by turning matter into a personification, he tends to make it the bearer of the deficiency, rather than the deficiency itself, and thus, conversely, susceptible to fulfillment. It is finally as an allegorical figure that matter develops an oblique relation to the two extremes.

Even in his most apparently 'Manichaean' statements about matter's association with evil, Bernard never quite equates Hyle or Silva with evil itself. He speaks, rather, of 'the evil *of* Silva' ('malum Silve,' *Meg.* II, ii, 7), or 'the ancient evil *of* Silva' ('antiqua Silve malicia,' *Mic.* VII, x, 5), or even, at its most incriminating, 'the ineradicable evil *of* Silva' ('inextricabile Silve . . . malum,' *Mic.* XII, 19–20). All the while, however, Silva herself is in the genitive case, possessor *of* evil, just as she is susceptible *to* good, but identical with neither. As with so many of the momentous changes displayed in earlier works, they take shape through almost imperceptible shifts in language and perspective. Calcidius had put *evil* in the genitive case, making Silva itself the origin of the evil: 'God is the principle and cause of good; Silva, of evil' ('Deum . . . initium et causam bonorum, siluam malorum'). [14] The matter of the *Cosmographia*, by contrast, even when its malicious inclination is strongest, remains a third thing, poised in 'a certain two-sided condition, suspended between good and evil' ('ancipiti quadam est conditione, inter bonum malumque disposita,' *Meg.* II, ii, 1–2). However 'disheveled in appearance'

[12] On these points, see Ch. V, above.
[13] See esp. the treatment of matter's refinement in *Meg.* II, vii–viii, which plays on both 'asperitas' and 'aptitudo,' 'in ea' and 'ex ea'; cf. Winden, cited above in Ch. V, n. 23, pp. 31–2, and see my discussion below.
[14] See ch. 296, p. 298. 13–14, quoted above in Ch. V, with Ch. V, n. 28.

('vultibus incompositis'), she is a character subject to 'reform' ('reformabitur,' *Meg.* II, ii, 13).

Indeed, her status as a character helps to distinguish her not only from sheer adversity, but from the problematic autonomy sometimes ascribed to her in the 'mystical' atmosphere of the *Asclepius.* Initially 'wrapped' ('obvoluta') in obscurity, Bernard's Hyle 'puts on other appearances' ('vultus vestivit alios') only as she is 'given definition' from above by 'visible images of the ideal' ('ydearum signaculis circumscripta'). It is then that matter displays at last her full generative capacity, 'opening forth the womb of her fecundity to give birth' ('ad parturiendum sinus fecunditatis exsolvit,' *Meg.* II, viii, 5–10). Her generative autonomy is a function, as it were, of her imaginative development. Shifting from the old 'vultibus incompositis' to the new 'vultus alios,' like some character in a divine *prosopopoeia,* displaying new *prosōpa* or guises, she gradually develops a rich personality, finally bursting into life.

In seeking to engage a philosophic problem of matter, Bernard thus tends to accommodate a literary problem of personification—if it is possible any longer to separate the two in an allegory that fuses the exegetical and rhetorical traditions. The recurring problem of personification was the relation between a concept's definition and its legitimate activity. The concept tended either to confine itself rather closely to its definition, as with abstract 'anger' from Homer to Seneca, or, conversely, to move rather awkwardly in diverse directions, as with the personified gladiators of Prudentius or the exotic gods of Martianus. In either case, it seemed difficult to construct a figure that was at once philosophically cogent and imaginatively versatile. By contrast, Bernard shows how a figure can become cogent precisely by becoming versatile, how by moving away from its strict definition, it can meet itself, as it were, on the other side. If, strictly speaking, matter is the passive need for form, then the other side of this need is the active desire for form, its eager search for it. If, strictly speaking, matter is the motley appearance of Being ('discolor Usie vultus'), then the other side of that appearance is its orderly manifestation of Being, its 'vultus alios.' Poised in 'a two-sided condition,' matter can adopt opposite roles, yet remain true to itself, like some sophisticated fictional character. In effect, Bernard Silvestris opens up an interior distance within the figure of matter, so that in moving from one side of herself to the other, the character can grow, change, develop. If Aristotle had suggested that in a sense matter had a divided identity, Bernard finally gives it a divided personality, a literary counterpart to the dynamics of potentiality. In the process, personification breaks out of its ancient constraints, just as prime matter itself bursts forth into a new world. The *Cosmographia* shows that what matter is not, it yet can be—indeed, that these are two sides of the same dynamic process. The poem thus begins to expose the full potential of a literary technique based upon the very distinction between what something is and what it is not—the technique of allegory.

Pointing in two directions, the old material Necessity at last meets its divine counterpart. As if to draw upon the opposing uses of that term in twelfth-century natural philosophy, Bernard deploys 'necessitas' in the center of his work at one point to depict the disturbing 'necessity' displayed by the world itself (*Meg.* IV, ix, 8), at another point to portray the consolidating 'necessity' that coordinates the world (*Meg.* IV, xii, 1; cf. xiv, 6–8). In fact, the *Cosmographia*'s very first use of the word is a sly reversal of Necessity's traditional spoiler role. Nature has been complaining about Silva's uncultivated condition, and Noys patiently explains:

The nativity of creatures is celebrated first in the divine mind; the effect that ensues is secondary. . . . Unbending and invincible *necessity* ('Rigida et inevincibili necessitate') and very intricate bonds had been imposed, so that the cultivation and adornment which you desire for the world might take place no sooner. (*Meg.* II, i, 12–19)

The very nativity of the created world depends upon the design of the creating mind. By the same token, matter's constriction at this stage—its ancient 'necessity'—now becomes part of Providence's necessary plan. Transforming the twelfth-century figure of matter, the *Cosmographia* thus transmutes not only the 'scientific' and 'mystical' traditions, but the 'creationist' tradition itself, into material for a new creation story. No longer constraining God, matter now belongs to him; no longer undermining Reason, she now pleads for it.

Divine Reason, for her part, responds in kind. Just as Bernard shows an uncanny sensitivity to the two sides of Matter, so he displays the consequences of this two-sidedness for Matter's counterpart, Noys. He sees that by distinguishing Matter from its actual constriction and attributing to it a fictional yearning toward Reason, Reason, conversely, must in some sense be receptive to Matter, even though in truth she is perfectly transcendent. The other side of a Matter that speaks is a Mind that listens.

This insight leads to three related changes in the traditional approach to divine Reason, all of which occur in Noys' attitude toward Silva's plea. First, it transforms the ancient account of Reason's perfection. In Plato and Calcidius, we recall, Reason in its isolation is serene and self-sufficient; it is only when it has to stoop to Necessity that its difficulties appear. In the *Cosmographia*, however, a remarkable change takes place. In her complaint, Nature points out to Noys that her splendor seems compromised, not because she *is* dealing with Necessity, but precisely because, as yet, she is *not*:

By your leave, bountiful Noys, let me speak: supremely beautiful though you are, your rule over Silva, your dominion, is exercised in a barren and ugly court; you yourself seem old and sad ('vetus et gravis ipsa videris,' *Meg.* I, 55–7).

Later, Noys admits that she is 'indeed troubled' ('Pertesum michi,' *Meg.* II, ii, 15) by the deprivation in the universe. Indeed, it is only when she *has* stooped to reform Silva that Noys exults in glory (*Mic.* I–II). Far from being too lofty to soil her hands with materiality, Noys' very perfection depends on her assistance to matter. If Bernard's orientation here owes something to the Neoplatonic (and especially Eriugenist) principle that a transcendent God can 'appear' only by becoming immanent in the world, it nonetheless suggests in some respects a more radical, yet intimately sensitive critique of Reason.

Second, this change in approach toward Reason involves a divergence from the very definition of the 'divine Mind.' Whether in Plato, Calcidius, the *Asclepius* author, or the Church Fathers, God's Providence might well be 'provident' or 'wise,' but it is certainly not 'sad' and 'troubled.' Instead of the secure divine Reason of such philosophic traditions, Bernard's Noys is unmistakably a *character* who can be affected. There is no question, of course, of claiming that God himself, or God's actual 'mind,' is sad; Noys and all the other characters in this drama, after all, are at some remove from the truth. It is rather that through her 'concern,' this divine figure is exhibiting, from the other side, the implications of matter's struggle. Something of this double orientation toward divine 'compassion' is already developing systematically in the early scholastic tradition at large; as Anselm puts it, God both 'is and is not compassionate' ('es et non es misericors'). He is 'compassionate' with respect to 'our sense' ('nostrum sensum'), but not with respect to his own condition ('secundum tuum'):

For when you look upon us, wretched as we are, *we* feel the effect of your compassion, but *you* do not feel emotion.[15]

Yet such scholastic discussions seek essentially to dissipate the linguistic problem, whereas Bernard exploits it. There is an irreducibly poetic and spiritual dimension to his Noys, exhibiting *pathos* with reason. Beyond the broad religious model of his faith and the traditional philosophic metaphors of divine descent, it is almost as if the mood of that ancient epic which implicated *pathos*, passionate experience, in the very movement of reason had passed into his poem.[16] Now, though, the 'subjective' style of an *Aeneid* acquires symmetrical expression in the 'lacrimae rerum' of a Mind deeply engaged in designing the universe itself. In a sense that Virgil could hardly have imagined, 'mortal matters touch the Mind.'

Finally, and most strikingly, in diverging from her strict definition, Noys tends to draw closer to her opposite number,

[15] See *Proslogion* 7, in *Opera*, cited above in Ch. IV, n. 69, p. 106; tr. based on *A Scholastic Miscellany*, ed. and tr. Eugene R. Fairweather (1956; repr. New York, 1970). On God's 'impassibility,' see the refs. in Fairweather, p. 77, n. 34.

[16] On the importance of the *Aeneid* and the notion of undergoing to the *Cosm.*, see Wetherbee, *Cosm.* (tr.), pp. 18–19, 22–6, 35–6, 48–9, although he largely approaches the motif of 'experience' from the other side, where it is prominent. My point here is that the symmetry of action and passion in the poem as a whole is incorporated to some degree *within* each figure, even the lofty figure of Noys; see below. Cf. my analysis of symmetries in the *Aeneid* in Ch. II, above, and my discussion later in this chapter of the *Aeneid* commentary often attributed to Bernard Silvestris. For some later literary treatments of the configuration of action and passion, see Georgia Ronan Crampton, *The Condition of Creatures: Suffering and Action in Chaucer and Spenser* (New Haven, 1974).

Silva. Throughout the 'scientific,' 'mystical,' and 'creationist' traditions, there was a tendency to define Reason by reference to its counterpart. In the *Cosmographia*, that opposition is *internalized* within each figure, so that just as Matter displays both her own deficiency and divine vitality, so does Noys display both her own vigor and earthly melancholy. As a result, an extraordinary convergence between the most divergent principles begins to develop. Silva, a 'mass discordant with itself,' continually troubled in her own nature, is somehow bursting with vitality, yearning for the formative power of Noys. Noys, on the other hand, who is by definition perfectly vital and filled with form, is troubled and concerned. By seeing each opposite from the point of view of its counterpart, by showing that Matter's defective 'necessity' can be seen as its need *for* Reason, while Reason's effective 'necessity' can be seen as its need *for* Matter, Bernard Silvestris dramatizes in literature what philosophy had long been yearning to show. Seen from both sides, God's condescension to matter *is* matter's ascension to God. In the process, he develops narrative *motion*, even between the most apparently irreconcilable principles, so that a personification can stray outside its own boundaries, and yet find itself in its counterpart. He thereby eases, at the extreme borders of existence itself, those paralytic constraints which had tended either to constrict personification allegory to a naive simplicity, or to embarrass it with illegitimate breakages of literary and philosophic decorum.

Decorum, in fact, is above all the watchword of Bernard's drama. So careful is he to show that the two sides of each character are really aspects of one truth, that in every major encounter between two characters, there is an eerie sense that the action has already been anticipated, as if one figure were not so much acting upon the other as confirming the other's nature. Thus, in this very first exchange, when Nature appeals to Noys on Hyle's behalf, Noys informs her petitioner (*Meg.* II, i) that divine Reason acts in accordance with divine will ('divine voluntatis'), without which any effort to bring order to the cosmos is 'in vain.' Since, however, Noys continues, Nature appears 'at the proper time' ('tempestive'), and according to 'causes which concur in the impulse to order' ('causisque ad ordinem concurrentibus')—since all this occurs, 'tuis desideriis deservitur.' Typically, we may translate Bernard's phrase (literally, 'it is served according to your desires') in two opposite ways. It may mean that since Nature appeals with the concurrence of Noys and divine will, *Nature*'s desires are served. Alternatively, it may mean that since Nature appeals with such concurrence, *God*—or even Silva—is served by your desires. The point is that it scarcely matters which way we take the phrase. Bernard's whole effort is to show that Nature's appeal has already been granted, that in fact her appeal is only the other side of God's own purpose.[17]

Indeed, Nature herself knew from the start that by the nature of things, her wish was granted the moment she expressed it. At the beginning of her address, before Noys has replied, Nature points out:

Surely God . . . wills the melioration of all things . . . Thus you [Noys] cannot be envious, but will bestow upon the unwieldy mass a full and perfect grace, *if I recall rightly the hidden ways of your deliberation* ('Consilii si rite tui secreta recordor,' *Meg.* I, 11–17).

That is, in the pattern repeatedly observed, Nature's long, eloquent appeal and Noys' majestic, considered response are but two fictional sides of a single truth, with God's actual will to create poised instantaneously in the center. Because of this unifying truth, the figure entreating and the figure entreated share the same secret, each knowing the other's mind.

The pattern recurs throughout the story. The next major allegorical exchange between characters is hardly an exchange at all. At the beginning of Book II, *Microcosmos*, Noys recounts the fulfillment of her promise to Nature, while Nature simply listens. Finally, Noys instructs Nature to find Urania, in order to enlist Urania's help in the creation of man. Nature searches through the heavens, and at last finds Urania, gazing at the stars. Nature is about to inform her of their mission, but

Urania knew at a glance both who had come and her reason for coming. Cutting short the business of salutation, she preempted by divine

---

17 Wetherbee, *Cosm.* (tr.), p. 69, interprets the phrase to mean Nature's desires are served; Stock, p. 90, interprets it to mean God is served. Cf. William of Conches, *Glosae*, p. 122: 'in order that anything may be with *nature* operating, it is necessary for divine *will* to precede' ('ut aliquid sit natura operante, necesse est divinam voluntatem precedere'); cf. *Ph. Mundi* I, 22; *PL* 172, 56AB. What Bernard has done is to separate

insight ('ingenio diviniore prevenit') Nature's attempt to speak. 'You bring, Nature, the decrees of the supreme God, and what the divine Mind has even now willed to come about. . . .' (*Mic*. III, xiii, 3–5; IV, 1–2)

If Urania's knowledge of the stars here grants her the power of prediction,[18] Bernard incorporates that astrological dimension of his period in a broader concatenation of events. Since Urania is part of the same cosmic whole as Nature, Nature's expansive movement toward her in the fiction is but the sign of a truth that simultaneously binds the two figures together even before the one reaches the other. As Urania puts it, she and Nature are both 'sisters' born of Noys. While directed to their respective realms, they remain of one 'kind' ('Nempe tuum genus unde meum,' *Mic*. IV, 16–18). Accordingly, just as Nature's appeal was but the other side of Noys' consent, so is Nature's potential question but the other side of Urania's actual answer.

As Nature and Urania descend toward earth to complete their mission, occasionally pausing in wonder at the sights, Nature suggests that they turn aside at the paradisal garden of Gramision, where she thinks Physis might be found:

Spontaneously, the beautiful place took on a greater luster, for it had sensed in advance that Nature, mother of generation, was at hand ('matrem generationis Naturam presenserat adventare'). The earth, through that fecundity it had received from the genius of Nature, suddenly teemed with life . . . (*Mic*. IX, iv, 1–4)

It is not merely that Gramision rises to the occasion. It is rather that the natural garden is but the other side of Nature itself, completed when the two sides come together. The activity *of* Gramision is its activation *by* Nature.[19] This striking scene, as

the two parts of this confluence from each other, and then bring them together through a narrative progress.

[18] See Stock, pp. 164–5, who contrasts her in this respect with Martianus' Urania. On the other hand, Martianus does show other figures knowing each other's minds; see *Marriage* 20, 24, 25. Bernard gives such alliances a more cogent philosophic rationale, a more pervasive role in the action, and a more sensitive relation to the imaginative coalescence of the plot; see below.

[19] The tr. of this passage is based on both *Cosm*. (tr.) and Stock, p. 190. On 'Gramision' vs. 'Granusion,' see *Cosm*., n. to *Mic*. IX, ii, 1 and 4, pp. 171–2. The correct reading of the phrase 'Nature igitur Genio,' here translated as 'the genius of Nature,' may be 'Nature igitur gremio,' 'the womb of Nature'; see *Cosm*., n. to *Mic*. IX, iv, 3,

we 'sensed in advance,' owes much to Martianus' account of
the world's exhilaration when Mercury, Apollo, and the Muses
fly to heaven.[20] The difference is not only that Bernard changes
a unilateral movement of ascent into a multilateral pattern of
descent and ascent. It is also that he transforms the very relation between the mythological and cosmological dimensions
of allegory that had limited Martianus even at his most successful moments, as in that splendid episode from the *Marriage*.
For Martianus, the earth bursts into flower because Mercury
(along with his myriad other roles) is the god of spring; the air
shines clearly because Apollo is the god of the sun; and so forth.
For Bernard, the generation of nature takes place because the
Nature of generation is at hand. His poem displays a kind of
doubling up, a reciprocal movement that integrates *mythos* and
cosmos even as it allies the separate figures of the narrative.

At last, Nature and Urania find Physis in the garden of
Gramision. Again, though, it is almost a question of just who is
finding whom. For before anyone even speaks, Bernard tells us
that in a sense Physis was *already* following Nature:

By those principles established by supreme divinity through genera,
species, and individuals, she [Physis] followed nature, and whatever
is included under that name, by an unwavering path ('naturam, et
quicquid eo / nomine continetur, indeflexo vestigio sequebatur,' *Mic.*
IX, vi, 6–8).

Physis, like Gramision, is an aspect of that natural world en-
compassed by Nature (and 'whatever is included under that
name')—indeed, conversely, the very name *physis* means
'nature'[21]—so that Physis' investigation of 'nature' is an expression of Nature's search for herself. After all, Physis too,
like everyone else in this poem, is already in on the secret
before being told it:

Physis was dreaming about the making of man, divining it as if in an
image, from the potentiality of nature . . .

p. 172. Either reading preserves the symmetry of the transaction with 'Nature, mother
of generation'; the reading 'Genio' almost anticipates, as it were, the Genius/Nature
alliance of the *Complaint*.

[20] See *Marriage* 27, with Stock, pp. 189–90, and my discussion above in Ch. III.

[21] The two figures are distinguished by their functions, with Physis providing a particularly practical, empirical approach to nature; see Stock, pp. 193–7, 221; *Cosm.*
(tr.), pp. 42–3.

when Urania, Nature, and finally Noys appear, and turn that image into the truth.[22] The narrative progress fulfills in 'act' what was physically a 'potentiality.' Like Nature's journey to Urania, her journey to Physis is ostensibly an effort to find someone 'else' to help, but that someone 'else' turns out to be very nearly her own self. If allegory says one thing and means something else, here that divergence is at last beginning to produce a generative motion carefully controlled by the very affiliation of the figures.

At last, Noys gives her charges three models for the creation of man (*Mic.* XI), but each model only complements its counterparts in the act of diverging from them. Urania's Mirror of Providence, Nature's Table of Fate, and Physis' Book of Memory all present the panorama of creation, in progressively shifting perspectives. While the Mirror of Providence, the 'mens eterna,' encompasses the extremes of the universe, including the form of Silva itself, in the 'exemplaria,' this radical consolidation is somewhat attenuated in the Book of Fate, which exhibits only 'vestigia' of the divine and concentrates on 'naturalia' passing through time, and the whole is still further attenuated in the Book of Memory, the 'intellectus,' which includes the 'same accounts of all the preceding natures, but not with the same clarity' ('eadem—sed non eodem iuditio—naturarum omnium qui precesserant argumenta'). Long before Bernard, it is true, Boethius (and others) had suggested how a single cosmic order could be distinguished according to shifts in orientation: when contemplated by the divine mind that disposes all things, that order is called 'providentia'; when referred to the things so disposed, it is called 'fatum' (*Consolation* IV, pr. vi). Bernard, however, not only elaborates this kind of distinction into a threefold progression that includes the disposition of man, but almost makes the array of models a kind of dramatic staging of the Neoplatonic passage between orders of being, each attenuating the previous one while 'recalling' it. It is as if the three *ecphrases* were themselves exhibiting in the narrative sequence the movement from macrocosm to microcosm that concludes the poem.

---

[22] See *Mic.* IX, viii, 1–2: 'Plasmaturam quoque hominis—de nature possibilitate coniciens—quadam velud sub ymagine sompniabat.' The coordination of figures is further reinforced if, as Wetherbee translates, 'nature' is capitalized.

At the same time, even that procession implies a return to its source. If the last model in the sequence, the human 'intellect,' displays lesser clarity than the models preceding it, it nonetheless recalls in 'memory' the 'same accounts.'[23] In this sense, Bernard is at once more guarded and more demonstrative in his approach to the creations of the mind than Eriugena, who oscillates over the degree to which the division of Nature is an actual or a mental phenomenon (Ch. IV, n. 63). While in the *Cosmographia* the human imagination does not actually create the modes of the cosmos—it is repeatedly stressed that man himself appears but faintly at the end of each of the three models—the mind at least potentially re-creates those modes in its own sphere, not only in the 'Book of Memory' as a whole, but in a particular book that retells the story of creation, a work that passes from the 'eternal mind' to the human 'intellect' by fashioning a series of images which suggest by their very progression the operation of the original model. In this carefully qualified sense, Bernard's book, with all its limitations in kind, begins to converge with its object, the book of creation, and its creator begins to converge . . . But that strategy fully develops only when such a convergence is radicalized in the *Divine Comedy*, where the author himself gradually progresses toward his divine source, so that his own creation of images turns into an authorial reenactment of the book of God.

This presiding pattern of convergence between diverging elements in the *Cosmographia* has never before been systematically exposed, but it is perhaps the most important feature of the poem.[24] Besides its broad implications, it serves certain specific philosophic and literary purposes. Philosophically, the technique of making the flurry of activity in the fiction only a deepening, an intensification, of potentialities latent in the characters offers a strategy for resolving a dilemma about time that had preoccupied the exegesis of creation since

---

[23] For a valuable discussion of Dante's later transformation of a personal 'Book of Memory' in the *Vita Nuova*, see Barbara Nolan, *The Gothic Visionary Perspective*, cited above in n. 5, pp. 84-123.

[24] The pattern is outlined in my article, 'From the *Cosmographia* to the *Divine Comedy*,' cited above in Ch. III, n. 95. The works of Stock, Wetherbee, and Dronke include a number of suggestive observations, though their orientation is rather different.

Augustine. On the one hand, Genesis 1 seemed to indicate, and Exodus 20: 11 to confirm, that God made the world in 'six days'; on the other hand, Ecclesiasticus 18: 1 declared that he 'created all things at once ("simul").' Traditionally, the apparent discrepancy had been explained by the argument that God created all things simultaneously, implanting in his original work those 'seminal principles' which, in unfolding, accounted for all later developments. As we have seen, however, the notion of 'rationes seminales' was itself gradually undergoing qualification in the twelfth century. In the *Commentum* associated with Thierry of Chartres, the 'simultaneity' verse was explained in terms of the 'potentiality' ('possibilitas') of matter, while in *On the Works of the Six Days* itself, it was explicitly argued that the other verse referred to 'the distinction of forms, which should then be treated according to physics' ('distinctione formarum de qua deinceps secundum phisicam tractandum est').[25] Others broadly expressed this physical principle through the figure of 'Nature' itself. In a sense, Bernard seeks to consolidate such strategies, by turning 'Nature' into a figure who is gradually 'informed'—both in the sense of learning about herself from Noys and Urania, and in the sense of being filled out, finding her own component parts as she progresses through the narrative. She and the other characters of Bernard's text mature by finding their counterparts, by complementing each other, by fulfilling in act what their 'other sides' achieve only in potentiality—only, as in the case of Physis, 'in an image.' As a result, the elaborate movement of the plot is but the 'six days' expression, as it were, of the 'simultaneous' truth of God's action.

This ingenious strategy, nonetheless, has its complications. It tends to interlock the contingencies of history with the instrumentalities of the cosmos, and thus finally to enclose sacred history itself within a natural cycle of reciprocal transactions.[26] Such implications are particularly prominent in the astrological speculations of Bernard's poem, which seem at times to program the very history of man in the motion of the stars.[27]

[25] See *Six Days*, ch. 4; cf. Silverstein, 99–100, and Chenu, 'Nature ou histoire?,' cited above in Ch. V, n. 41.

[26] On this problem and strategies of resolving it, see Stock, pp. 140–1, 161–2, 234–7; *Cosm.* (tr.), pp. 16–19, 26, 47–55; Chenu, pp. 86, 95, 117; and below.

[27] On the astrological dimension in Bernard's poem and his age, see the refs. in Ch. V, nn. 15, 35, 119.

For the firmament is inscribed with stars, and figures-forth all that can come to pass through the decree of fate.

> Scribit enim celum stellis, totumque figurat
> Quod de fatali lege venire potest.   (*Meg.* III, 33–4)

It is as if history were revealed not so much by the 'figural' procedure of Christian typology as by the 'figural' ('figurat') procedure of astral motion. In such a world, the line between the 'signification' of events and the 'generation' of events is very thin: the entire historical sequence, Bernard continues, pre-exists ('Preiacet') in the stars, unfolding ('Explicet') from them in time (*Meg.* III, 37–8). It is true that this perspective suggests a way to resolve certain problems preoccupying Christian typological and allegorical writing since its ancient formative period (though it will not be fully developed until over a century after Bernard, in the works of Aquinas and Dante). By implicating the notion of historical prefiguration with the notion of physical activation, it tends to integrate 'meaning' with 'being' in the very dynamics of natural objects and to organize the rather disparate relationships of Christian typology within the coordinate framework of cosmic interaction. But by the same token, it raises the larger question of what that interaction as a whole 'means' and what constitutes its own source of 'being.' Thus, it no sooner demonstrates the 'order of times,' in the phrase of *On the Works of the Six Days*, than it implies the need to pass out of time toward a transcendent principle. There is a glimpse of this vision even in the astral catalogue itself, which observes Christ's own birth prefigured in the stars.[28] The vision is fully realized in narrative terms, however, only when Bernard so radicalizes the convergence of his cosmic figures that he not only deepens each of them, but transfigures the whole of which they are parts.

That intensive vision, though, which we shall later explore, depends not only upon such philosophic issues, but on certain literary implications of the *Cosmographia*'s narrative pattern. From the age of the first great epic incorporating time into its very design, the *Aeneid*, the effort to reconcile the artistic design of a poem with the actual sequence of history had been deeply problematic. In the first full-scale allegorization of the *Aeneid*, Fulgentius sought in effect to resolve the problem by ignoring the

---

[28] See *Meg.* III, 53–4; cf. *Cosm.* (tr.), pp. 47–8.

chronology of an individual, Aeneas, and concentrating on the chronology of man himself, thereby turning the 'displaced' shipwreck of the opening, for example, into the proper starting point for an art of life: hazardous childbirth. With the twelfth-century commentary on the *Aeneid* often ascribed to Bernard Silvestris, this strategy acquires systematic formulation: the very artifice of beginning *in medias res*, the *ordo artificialis* of the poetry, gives Virgil's story its authentic philosophic order, the *ordo naturalis* of human history. However impressive this formulation, it still implies a disjunction between the sequence of the plot on its own terms and the philosophic order attributed to it. With respect to the story, after all, the shipwreck 'really' takes place after events later recounted; with respect to the allegorization, the shipwreck must remain just where it is. In order to solve such problems in a text that deliberately counterpoints the designs of artistry and the movement of history, it would be necessary to rewrite the *Aeneid*—a task the Middle Ages in fact begins to undertake in the twelfth century.[29]

Bernard Silvestris does not rewrite the *Aeneid* itself, but in merging the poetic and philosophic traditions of allegory while composing his own epic, he transforms both the *ordo artificialis* and the *ordo naturalis*, and in the process integrates the two orders more boldly than any allegorist before him. For Bernard, as we have seen, the *ordo artificialis* is not only a narrative sequence, but a conceptual development. At the same time, the *ordo naturalis* is not only a conceptual development, but an historical sequence.[30] As a result, when Bernard deploys his characters to fashion the world, the very sequence of the allegorical plot orders the historical process, while the historical process orders the sequence of the allegorical plot. Chronology —both narrative and historical—no longer proceeds in opposition to meaning, but in congruence with it. As we shall

[29] See my discussion in Ch. III, with nn. 70-2.

[30] On this conception of the *ordo naturalis*, see my discussion above in this chapter and in Ch. V, with Stock, pp. 9, 243, 250-1, 271, on the twelfth-century scientific tendency to apply 'strict, logical rationalism to the problem of natural causality,' thereby allying '*ratio*' with the '*ordo naturalis*.' As Bernard integrates this philosophic order with his artistic one, he approaches that 'special case' described by Allen, *Ethical Poetic*, pp. 91-4, in which the 'forma tractandi and forma tractatus are the same'; cf. Ch. III, n. 71, above. Such a consolidation has still broader dimensions in the convergence of interpretive and compositional procedure in the *Cosm.*; see my discussion above and below in this chapter.

see, even this magisterial strategy is transcended in the
Cosmographia's intense vision of the end of time. But nothing
more strikingly displays Bernard's coordination of the kinds of
problems posed by the *Aeneid* and its commentaries than the
opening scene of his own epic. According to that twelfth-century
Aeneid commentary, the chaotic turbulence of *Aeneid* I is an
allegory of the elements at the birth of a child, whose body, like
a stormy sea, is a 'whirlpool of ebbing and flowing humors'
('intracium et exeuntium gurges humorum').[31] Now, at the
opening of the *Cosmographia*, that whirlpool has turned, as it
were, into an elemental, cosmic mass 'ebbing and flowing'
('fluit refluitque'), and the child has turned into a 'squalling,
infant universe' ('infantia Mundi vagit'), pleading to be clothed
with new form. In addition to all the other shifts in perspective
here, now the allegorical character—unlike Aeneas—is *itself* in
its natural infancy; the *ordo artificialis* of the allegory meshes
with the *ordo naturalis* of history. And as for that 'displaced' speech
in *Aeneid* II, which the commentator treats as the beginning
of speech itself from 'infantia'—explained by him etymologically
as 'not to speak'—that process of progressive articulation for
the 'infantia Mundi' constitutes the very dynamics of the
Cosmographia from the start.[32]

In the broadest sense, finally, such philosophic and literary
strategies of order and development depend upon Bernard's
transformation of the two allegorical traditions as a whole.
From its beginnings, allegory had been compromised by two
opposite problems. Interpretive allegory, on the one hand,
tended to diverge from the apparent meaning of a text, fragmenting the text if necessary, in order to reach underlying
principles. Compositional allegory, on the other hand, tended
to require a close correspondence with such principles, so that
its personifications were either severely restricted in their

---

[31] See the Jones edn. cited in Ch. III, n. 56, pp. 4–14; for the quotation, p. 5. 13–
14, tr. Schreiber and Maresca, cited in Ch. III, n. 72.

[32] For the *Aeneid* commentary, see p. 14. 17–25; cf. my discussion above on 'infantia'
and *prosopopoeia*. To my knowledge, these passages and the ones cited above have
never before been explicitly related to each other. Whether or not Bernard knows the
commentary itself (he is the likely author), its discussion in some respects exposes certain *allegorical* issues at stake in the *Cosm.*'s opening scene which are not exhibited by
the specific sources normally cited (though they are themselves deeply influential, and
are explored above in Ch. V).

legitimate activity or problematically implicated in flights of fancy. The increasing interaction between the two allegorical traditions gradually refined these problems, if it did not wholly resolve them. That interaction reaches a decisive stage in Bernard's *Cosmographia*, which interprets the story of creation while creating allegorical agents to act out the story. There is a deeper, more complex sense, however, in which the two traditions mesh in his poem.

On the one hand, as we have observed, the characters of his poem present the 'other side' of each other. That is, each character *interprets* its counterpart, either by exposing the implications of its counterpart's action, as in Noys' sadness, the other side of Silva's yearning; or by reading its mind, as in Urania's foreknowledge of Nature's proposal; or by fulfilling in act what was otherwise a potentiality, as in Nature's fulfillment of Physis' dream. In this inclination of one figure toward another, the characters move, grow, diverge from their own definitions. Thus, by definition Noys cannot be 'sad'; she can be so only as a fictional character, in her relationship with Silva. Silva, in turn, cannot actually 'desire' anything, marginally existent as she is; she can do so only as the other side of her need, her lack of Noys' formative power. Urania, the principle of celestial knowledge, can hardly 'descend' to earth without diverging from her own definition; as she herself puts it, she will be 'drawn away' ('abstrahor,' *Mic.* IV, 20) from her proper place. Nature, for her part, begins the story as the grand cosmic ally of Noys, but as the narrative progresses, she becomes a character who is constantly learning new things, growing, changing.[33] And Physis is roused from her slumber only with the arrival of Urania and Nature, and in fact fulfills her own duties only with the help of these other characters (*Mic.* XII, 49–54; XIII, iii, 7–9). In short, each character fulfills itself only by moving toward its counterpart, by diverging from its own definition. And in the process of so diverging, each character illuminates the others, interprets their full implications. Such divergence we have seen to be characteristic of all interpretive acts. Its striking effect in Bernard's poem is to

[33] See Silverstein, 106–7; Stock, pp. 66, 77, 174.

act as a counterpoint to the chronic problem of compositional allegory, the constriction of personifications to a limited sphere of legitimate action. By diverging from themselves, and interpreting each other, the characters grow, and thereby develop an interlocking network of narrative events.

Even this, however, is only half the expression of a world moving toward equilibrium. For the same interplay of forces that tends to modify the old constraints of compositional allegory by the process of interpretive *divergence* also tends, conversely, to regulate the old licenses of interpretive allegory by the pull of compositional *correspondence.* That is, as the diverse characters in the poem imply each other, expose the 'other side' of each other, they confirm that by moving *away* from themselves they are moving *toward* a single, all-embracing truth. By diverging in their fictional roles, they are corresponding to their true natures as expressions of God's instantaneous act of creation. Though such transactions are partial and their impulses variegated, together they tend to fuse the interpretive and compositional traditions not only in the broad design of the work, but in the very heart of its procedure. On the one hand, the correspondences of compositional allegory begin to *expand* as the characters diverge from *themselves.* On the other hand, the divergences of interpretive allegory begin to *coalesce* as the characters correspond with each *other,* and in so doing, converge upon an underlying truth. It is a dizzying transformation of the allegorical problem, but one that is suitable to Bernard's very subject: the bursting of inactivity into vitality, and the taming of wildness into order. While such a process has far-reaching imaginative implications, here it is inseparable from the fundamental pressures of Bernard's philosophic concerns. It gives a new dimension to that expanding, contracting universe which we have explored since the time of the Stoics and the early Neoplatonists, while integrating the two broad principles of causal power which we have seen developing in the twelfth century. God might delegate his power to a thousand oblique agents, all going about their own duties, diverging from their common origin. Yet by the same token, in the very act of divergence, they would merely confirm their interlocking correspondence with each other, and finally reveal the conservation of all power in God.

Before we examine the central, decisive expression of that insight, however, it would be well to assess the limits of Bernard's procedure. They are the signs of an allegory that is only beginning to emerge into maturity, and that, while founded upon cogent principles, has not yet fully mastered them.

First, the complementary technique by which one character confirms the other does allow divergence to take place without fragmenting the narrative into isolated parts. But it does so at a cost. As we have seen, the relationship between Bernard's characters involves so close a match that in one sense there is hardly any allegorical *action* at all. In the entire *Cosmographia*, there is only one true exchange of even so much as conversation between two allegorical characters: the opening plea on Silva's behalf by Nature, answered by Noys. It is understandable that allegorically this is the most successful part of the poem. Other speeches by Bernard's characters are answered only with polite nods and gestures, as if to indicate that in so close a fit, there is nothing more to say. Thus, after Noys responds to Nature's appeal, Nature simply throws herself at Noys' feet, 'grateful' in mind and countenance alike ('tam mente quam vultu gratiosa,' *Meg.* II, iii, 3-5). Similarly, at the beginning of Book II, when Noys tells Nature to seek out Urania and Physis, Nature leaves at once, 'her countenance equally expressive of gratitude and eagerness' ('gratulantis vultu pariter et volentis,' *Mic.* III, iv, 1-2). When Nature reaches Urania, as we have noted, her attempt to speak is cut short, so that what might have been an illuminating exchange is simply one more confirmation that the question has already been answered before it is asked. The agreement is so general in this text that the *Cosmographia*, in its *allegorical* action, is basically a dumb show, while in its doctrinal exposition, it is effusive. The reason for this tight fit between characters is not only a kind of celestial decorum about subordinating lower principles to higher ones. Later allegory, like the *Romance of the Rose*, recognizes hierarchies, too, but develops an energetic interplay between its figures. It is rather a sign that allegory, for all its breakthroughs in this poem, has not yet fully learned to draw out its action in an expansive way. When Bernard does try to generate decisive action, a certain awkwardness takes over, as when Urania, Nature, and Physis are finally assembled, and suddenly, without warning, Noys 'brings on her own presence' ('et ecce Noys presenciam intulit,' *Mic.* IX, viii, 9–10), and takes control of the event. We know what Bernard is trying to express, but we smile at the result. The awkwardness here arises from the attempt to show that Noys, the divine Mind, is the background that controls the activity of Urania, Nature, and Physis; now that the component parts are assembled, God's plan, as it were, leaps into the foreground. In effect, Noys' abrupt entrance dramatizes the old problem of specifying causes, which allegory never completely solves. For all the interlocking action of the *Romance of the Rose*, the narrative sometimes lurches, as 'God' suddenly intervenes, only to withdraw in the same motion, after introducing a new character onstage.[34] In the *Cosmographia*, while allegorical maneuvers display far greater finesse than the brusque encounters of Prudentius or the volatile flights of Martianus, they do not yet exhibit the kind of suppleness and flexibility that fully diversifies the allegorical method.

In part as a result of such formal limitations, much of the story depends upon action that is allegorical only in a restricted sense. Bernard's real amplification comes when he describes the world in its own right, as in the great catalogue poem of *Megacosmos* (III), where the universe unfolds in a magnificent variety of starscapes, landscapes, animals, and plants, or in the cosmic panoramas of *Microcosmos* (III and V), which provide the framework for Nature's ascent to Urania and their descent together to earth. This is not to say that the inclusion of such 'literal' elements is a flaw in allegorical writing. As we have argued from the start, even the most radical form of allegory, personification, is viable only insofar as it diversifies a concept in tangible terms.[35] Further, the very notion of a multileveled universe highlights the fact that the 'literal' and the 'allegorical' are relative categories, admitting of degrees. By the same token, however, the internal consistency of an allegory depends upon the controlled modulation between different levels of discourse. When a late medieval allegory like *Piers Plowman*

---

[34] See *Le Roman de la Rose*, ed. Félix Lecoy, 3 vols. (Paris, 1965–70), ll. 3232 and 15455.

[35] See Ch. I, above. My sense of this interplay has been deepened by the exchange of views with Professor Winthrop Wetherbee and the late Professor Irvin Ehrenpreis.

keeps restlessly, abruptly shifting in perspective, it is self-consciously calling into question such modes of language—as well as the theological categories underlying them.[36] While that kind of extreme ambivalence is still far from the smoothly articulated universe of the *Cosmographia*, even Bernard's work does not always negotiate easily between the allegorical and literal modes. Thus, in one sense the spectacle of Urania descending to earth, alongside a Nature that has ascended to her, is an allegory on a grand scale of the soul's passage into a body.[37] In itself this strategy is evocative and appealing; while for a twelfth-century Christian the soul does not actually 'descend'—any more than does the principle of celestial understanding at large or, to take our earliest example, Wisdom—it can legitimately 'descend' in allegory, as a figurative expression of the divine informing the human. Both on the way up and down, however, these allegorical travellers encounter a host of actual souls ('vulgus . . . animarum'), about to 'descend' from 'heaven to the kingdom of Dis' ('de celo Ditis ad imperium . . . fuerant descensure').[38] It may well be true that Bernard is not here claiming that the soul actually slips from heaven, a Neoplatonic and Origenist doctrine fundamentally revised by Christians already in the late antique world.[39] But his oscillation between the 'descent' of an allegorical figure—'descensus eo michi non levis,' worries Urania (*Mic.* IV, 22)—and the 'descent' of the soul itself leaves uncertain the precise status of his discourse, and with it, the exact meaning of the soul's embodiment.

More broadly, such a linguistic and philosophic ambivalence about the soul's 'descent' recalls the long medieval controversy among commentators on Plato and Boethius over the extent to

---

[36] See, e.g., John Burrow, 'The Action of Langland's Second Vision,' *Essays in Criticism*, 15 (1965), 247–68; repr. in *Style and Symbolism in* Piers Plowman, ed. Blanch, cited above in Ch. II, n. 38, pp. 209–27; Priscilla Jenkins, 'Conscience: The Frustration of Allegory,' in Piers Plowman: *Critical Approaches*, ed. S. S. Hussey (London, 1969), pp. 125–42.

[37] See Stock, pp. 163–4.

[38] See *Mic.* III, viii, and V, viii, with my discussion below.

[39] See the discussions above corresponding to Ch. III, nn. 8, 18, 40–3, and 73–4, with the refs. in the notes. For the treatment of the soul's 'descent' in the twelfth-century *Aeneid* commentary ascribed to Bernard, which includes a specific ref. to Macrobius and the constellation of Cancer, see the Jones edn. cited in Ch. III, n. 56, pp. 28–30, 67.

which the soul's 'astral chariot,' wheeling from heaven to earth, might be understood metaphorically (Ch. V, n. 6). Seeking in effect to save the appearances, the boldest of these commentators in the twelfth century, William of Conches, argues that the astral chariot is an *integumentum* for astral *influence* upon the animated body: stars are thus the 'vehicles' of souls 'causaliter, non localiter.'[40] In a sense, Bernard's soul is divided between these two possibilities. 'Causally,' an allegorical agent, Urania, descends from heaven to earth. But 'locally,' the souls are themselves in heaven, awaiting their actual descent.[41] If the elusiveness of Bernard's language has its appeal, it also exhibits a problem we have seen throughout the allegorical tradition, the difficulty of specifying the precise relation between the abstract agent of a phenomenon and an instance of the phenomenon, of gaining a perspective on an object without either wholly parting from it or merging with it.

The most striking case of this dilemma is the treatment of Nature herself, and in considering her for a moment, we can see the fulfillment of the paradox we noted at the start, that even in allegory which has come of age, its very growth tends to sow the seeds of its own destruction. We have already observed that whereas in *Megacosmos* Nature is the grand cosmic intermediary between Silva and Noys, in *Microcosmos* she becomes a groping spirit, learning how to make man. This split in her roles is due in part to a distinction we have seen central to the emergence of allegory, the fact that 'nature' has more than one side. It may refer to the natural world as a whole, or to a particular reference point within that world, such as human nature. By exploiting this split, Bernard was able to solve in some measure a problem that had been complicating the possibilities of personification since Plato, the cycle of receding causes. Bernard needed a figure who could help generate the action of the poem, but who could yet assess that very action, who could act as the *standpoint* from which to see it.

[40] See *Glosae*, p. 212, with the variants and discussions in Gregory, *Anima*, pp. 160–4, and Jeauneau, 'Macrobe,' cited in Ch. III, n. 43, 16–20.

[41] Revealingly, as Bernard shifts his mode of discourse, it becomes difficult to specify their 'location': initially seen waiting in the galaxy at the constellation of Cancer (III, viii), they are later seen waiting in the sphere of Jupiter (V, viii), as 'Jove' oscillates between its status as a heavenly body and its allegorization as master of the universe.

That is, he needed a figure who could be both inside and outside the story, a character within the narrative who was yet the perspective on that narrative.

This excruciating problem he solved by creating a character who was one of the actors, yet at the same time the context for action. In *Megacosmos*, it is via Nature that Silva's appeal reaches Noys and so sets in motion the creation of the greater world. In *Microcosmos*, it is via Nature's ascent and descent that earthly nature aspires toward heaven in the very act of being inspired by it. The other characters of Bernard's drama, for all their two-sidedness, were not quite suited for such a central role. In themselves, they were either too lofty, like Noys, or too lowly, like Silva, to mediate between the two extremes. In interacting, on the other hand, they tended to *become* their counterparts, and thus to collapse the distance necessary for such a comprehensive perspective. The more Silva desired being, the more her 'desire' suggested that she already had being. Conversely, the more Noys was 'sad' about Silva's wretchedness, the more she herself tended to become wretched, since there is no separation between the divine disposition and divine nature. Such convergences reflect the fact that all these causal forces are really instruments of a single truth, into which they must eventually recede. As we have seen, Bernard partially solved this problem by creating a 'third thing,' by making these philosophic principles *characters* who could change their faces while remaining in truth the same persons. But this in itself was not a sufficient safeguard against the coalescences which tended to collapse his text, and so Bernard created Nature, a comprehensive 'third thing,' who traverses the whole range of allegorical transactions, yet remains somewhat separate from each of them. In Nature, Bernard created a kind of standpoint who remains outside the action even while being part of it.

This notion of an external perspective, a *consciousness*, becomes increasingly important in later allegory, as it comes to grips with the problem of evaluating action as well as expressing it, assessing causes as well as generating them. In some respects, Bernard's Nature is the ancestress not only of Alan of Lille's Nature, but of the *humana natura* that serves as its counterpart, the gradually perceiving narrator of the *Complaint*, and more broadly, of the vaguely articulated 'I' who wanders through late medieval allegory, the 'lover' who stalks the garden of the *Romance of the Rose*, the Dante who walks through his own potentialities in the *Divine Comedy*.[42] Already by the time of Dante, however, that vague consciousness is taking on its own substantial existence, and by the time of the spectator who watches the Parliament of Fowls, this literal consciousness, turning events over in its own mind, has become the focus of the story. When the 'I' becomes the source of narrative action, controlling events under the guise of merely responding to them, medieval allegory finally passes into more diffusive forms. In Bernard, of course, that stage has not arrived. It is important to observe, though, even while we admire his insight, that in creating the perspective of 'Nature,' he also developed a rival to allegorical writing within the form itself, and so compromised traditional allegory in the very act of enhancing it.

At the same time, perhaps the keenest insight of Bernard's poem is that such problems are inseparable from the promise of allegorical writing, that allegory advances only by constantly transforming its own designs. If that is a dilemma for his allegory, it is also the dilemma of his world, perpetually in need of transformation from a provisional condition to a final one. For the matter of that world is as oblique as any allegory; it is the very principle of ambiguity—'the diverse' ('diversum'), Bernard calls it—an otherness always at some remove from the One ('unitas').[43] Bernard never denies this problematic disparity; at times it seems to stymie the most determined efforts of reconciliation. Yet for all the evil he associates with the material world, for all the pessimism he sometimes expresses about it, he seeks to resolve its ambiguous condition not by escaping it, but by engaging it. Probing its constituent parts and playing them off each other until they generate a sense of

[42] On the early depiction of individual consciousness in allegorical writing, see Muscatine, 'The Emergence of Psychological Allegory,' cited above in Ch. I, n. 2; Jauss, 'Form,' pp. 191–206; 'Transformation,' pp. 123–40; and 'Entstehung' (with Uda Ebel), pp. 205–20, 231–4. I am indebted to Dr Jerome Singerman for the phrase about Dante walking through his potentialities.

[43] See *Mic.* XIII, i. Cf. *Thierry*, p. 81. 86–8, quoted above in Ch. V, on 'unitas' and 'alteritas.' For the broad development of this tradition in antiquity and the Middle Ages, see the refs. in my article, 'From the *Cosmographia* to the *Divine Comedy*,' pp. 67–8, n. 4. Bernard's distinction is to implicate the philosophic issue with the imaginative one in a systematic narrative framework.

the whole, he finally makes a virtue of 'Necessity.' In the end, he suggests that the very process of exploiting the diversities of a divided world and a divided language leads toward an integrity beyond them.

The most striking expression of this strategy occurs in the great vision at the midpoint of the poem's action, when the greater universe is complete, and the smaller universe is about to begin: the final chapter of *Megacosmos*. The chapter recapitulates all that has gone before, but also anticipates all that is to come, the eternal transformation of diversity into coherence. Like briefer retrospectives elsewhere in the *Cosmographia*, the passage thus acts like a kind of Eriugenist *recapitulatio*, 'reintegrating' the cosmic and formal dialectic of the poem—only at the same time it gives that intensive process an expansive, imaginative dimension in its own right.[44] We have already seen the complementary interaction of the constituents of Bernard's universe. Nature's ascent toward celestial understanding is the other side of her descent with it. Even at the extremes of the universe, Silva is but the other side of Noys. Yet in Bernard's central vision, such analogous relationships finally have an anagogic force, as all component parts radically converge into a comprehensive whole:

The life and well-being of the universe consists in sovereign and ancient causes: spirit, sentience, agitation, order. Noys lives, the exemplars live, without life the visible creation would not live everlastingly. Hyle preexisted, preexisted in matter, preexisted in the spirit of eternal life. For it is not to be believed that the wise creator of insensate matter did not first establish a foundation for it in a living source.

Rerum incolumitas vitaque mundi causis quidem principalibus et antiquis—spiritu, sensu, agitatione, ordinatione—consistit. Vivit Noys, vivunt exemplaria: sine vita non viveret rerum species eviterna. Preiacebat Yle: preiacebat in materia, preiacebat in spiritu vivacitatis eterne. Neque enim credibile est sapientem opificem insensate materie nec viventis originis fundamina prelocasse. (*Meg.* IV, viii, 1-7)

If once we thought that Hyle and Noys were at extreme ends of the cosmos, the distance between them seems to have collapsed.

[44] For other 'retrospectives' in the *Cosm.*, see, e.g., *Mic.* XIII, i and XIV, 171-8, with my discussion below; for the Eriugenist 'recapitulatio,' see the discussion corresponding to Ch. IV, n. 62, above, and the refs. in the note.

In one breath, Bernard derives the life of the universe from agitation and order, from matter and spirit, from Hyle and Noys, life springing from—life. As we observed earlier, this passage is suggestive of the *Asclepius* author, with his matter inseparable from a pervasive 'spiritus,' and of Eriugena, with his matter preexisting in the divine causes.[45] Yet Bernard's matter is drawn into an all-encompassing 'life' more fundamentally than the 'ungenerated' matter of the *Asclepius*, while conversely, his 'life' seems to permeate all things even more immanently than the divine source of the *Periphyseon*. The reciprocal operations of the universe are turning into radical continuities.

In such a cosmos, each turn of the circumference seems only to display the center.

Thus, from the life of Mind, from the spirit of Silva, from the World Soul, from the very quick of created life, the eternity of things grows together. . . . For the universe is a continuum, a chain in which nothing may be dispersed or broken off. Thus, roundness, the perfect form, determines its shape.

Ex Mentis igitur vita, Silve spiritu, Anima mundi, mundialium vegetatione, rerum eternitas coalescit. . . . Mundus enim quiddam continuum, et in ea cathena nichil dis/sipabile vel abruptum. Unde illum rotunditas, forma perfectior, circumscribit. (*Meg.* IV, viii, 10–12; ix, 5–8)

In this circularity, it is difficult to tell just what is the source of life: Mind, Silva, the World Soul—or all of them at once. It is a cosmos bursting on all sides with vitality, where characters and causes merge with each other, where ultimately there is no up or down, in a striking transformation of the old pattern of ascent and descent.[46] The eternity of things, says Bernard in that

---

[45] See *Asc.*, ch. 14, and *Periph.* III, 636BC, cited in Ch. V, with the refs. to Lucentini and d'Onofrio in Ch. V, n. 1. Cf. Remigius on the *reditus* in which 'Yle enim ad Deum reuertitur,' noted by d'Onofrio, 689, n. 341, and a twelfth-century Boethius commentary on the principle that 'Erit itaque Deus pater aeternus et *nous* et *hylē*,' noted in *Cosm.* (tr.), p. 154, n. 133, both passages ed. by Silk, *Saecvli*, cited in Ch. V, n. 90, pp. 320 and 158, with pp. 157, 177. On 'vita,' see *Meg.* IV, iv, 8–9; a number of Boethius commentaries displaying an overlap with Eriugenist views identify the 'vita' of John 1 : 3–4 with the divine ideas; see (with *Periph.* III, 640A–642D) the commentaries cited by Lucentini, pp. 34–5, n. 91, and d'Onofrio, 664–5, and *Saecvli*, p. 156. While these parallels to Bernard's conception are suggestive, none quite displays his orientation.

[46] Stock valuably points out that the drama of the *Cosm.* has both active and passive dimensions, that the life of the universe springs from below, as well as descending from

extraordinary verb, does not merely preside over all: it 'grows together,' it 'coalesces' ('coalescit'). The predicate suggests the 'coalescent' (*symphyes*) whole of Stoic physics,[47] but together with its subject, 'eternitas,' it reveals a world at once more expansive and more contractive than that earlier cosmos. For as the preceding plot has shown, the constituents of this new whole have acquired by this time a more distinct sense of their own physical, temporal, and imaginative dimensions, while as the recapitulation confirms, those very distinctions are forever assimilated into an eternal presence that is itself 'growing together' at every turn, composing the 'rotunditas' of perfect form.

Even eternity, after all, is divided, divided into time, and yet this very division recoils upon itself and returns to eternity.

Setting out from eternity, time, wearied by its long circuit, is resolved into the bosom of eternity. From oneness it separates into number, from the unmoving into movement. . . . The point at which times end is the point from which they are renewed . . .

Ab eternitate tempus initians in eternitatis resolvitur gremium, longiore circulo fatigatum. De unitate ad numerum, de stabilitate digreditur ad momentum. . . . Quod ubi finiunt inde tempora renascuntur . . . (*Meg.* IV, xi, 4–13)

above; see pp. 93, 108, 125, 144–50, 159, 169, 175, 222–6, 231–3, 280–1. It is important, however, to clarify the function of this two-sidedness in the allegorical structure of the poem. First, the action emerging from below, like all the activity of this allegory, is oblique action; this should qualify statements like 'God is both the One and the Many' (pp. 149–50). Second, the movement away from allegory in this passage is not exactly a movement toward rational exposition. This is perhaps difficult to see from a perspective in which allegory is considered the 'myth,' a kind of covering over the scientific structure (pp. 9, 19–20, 274), and a passage like *Meg.* IV a 'demythologization' (pp. 119, 173). The point is rather that Bernard makes allegory *itself* an analytic instrument, as opposed to the decorative, rhetorical covering of the earlier trope. It is the allegorical drama itself that acts out the 'scientific' analysis of the causes of creation. The section quoted above, far from a movement toward clear, rational exposition, is precisely the opposite, moving away from differentiation toward unification, away from analysis, toward vision. I make these comments because it is essential to realize the momentous changes allegory is undergoing in such passages: the *allegory* is analytic, dealing with the causes of things; the *breakage* of allegory is synthetic, reverting to non-differentiation. It is a reversal appropriate to a literary form that depends for its very vitality upon reversal.

[47] See Sambursky, p. 41, and Hahm, pp. 183, n. 80 and 194, works cited above in Ch. II, nn. 30 and 29.

The sentiment is not new;[48] its function here is striking. For as we have seen, the *Cosmographia* is preeminently about division, about breaking up the instantaneous act of creation into component parts. The display of time returning upon itself, of temporal division flowing into eternal vision, is the goal of Bernard's whole allegory, which exploits factions to show the integrity underlying them, which deploys the others to approach the One. How unlike the compositional allegory of Prudentius, in which Queen Humility had to stand still in order to win her victory! How unlike the interpretive allegory of Raban Maur, in which the seasonal course of time had to be suspended in order to reveal the eternal principle behind it! In the *Cosmographia*, Bernard exploits the transitional, the 'other,' the duality of allegory, in order to reconstitute the permanent, the integral, the whole.

Under the pressure of this movement, Bernard's very language tends to strain against the old divisions. In the act of partition, his diction aims toward consolidation.

From the intelligible universe was born the sensible universe, the perfect from the perfect.

Ex mundo intelligibili mundus sensibilis perfectus natus est, ex perfecto. (*Meg.* IV, xi, 1-2)

It is as if Bernard had cleaved in two not only the cosmos, but the word 'perfectus,' only to show the two halves cleaving to each other. Boethius had applied the term 'perfectus' to both the created world ('perfectum') and to its parts ('perfectasque,' *Consolation* III, m. ix, l. 9); Bernard applies it at once to the creation and to its Creator, stressing by its split reference the integrity that ultimately consolidates the 'intelligible' realm with the 'sensible' one.

In such language, divine plenitude itself is divided only to enhance its own plenitude:

Plentiful, therefore, was he who produced the plenum formed by plenitude.

[48] For some of its diverse formulations, see *Asc.*, ch. 31; Proclus, discussed in Courcelle, *Tradition*, pp. 203-7; Boethius, *Consolation* IV, pr. vi; for its transformation in Dante, see Dronke, 'Boethius, Alanus and Dante,' cited above in Ch. III, n. 81, 124-5, and in our own century, see Eliot, *Four Quartets*.

Plenus erat igitur qui genuit plenumque constituit plenitudo. (*Meg.* IV, xi, 2-3)[49]

The movement of the sentence almost seems to enact the 'rotunditas' of the cosmos. The first half of the sentence begins in a straightforward manner:

Plenus erat igitur qui genuit plenum . . .

Plentiful, therefore, was he who produced the plenum . . .

but the suffix attached to 'plenum' ('que') indicates continuation, and the active verb that follows, 'constituit,' seems to turn the earthly plenum into the subject for the rest of the sentence. By the end of the sentence, however, 'plenum' turns out to be not the subject of the verb, but the object:

. . . plenumque constituit plenitudo.

. . . and plenitude formed the plenum.

The earthly plenum that seems for a moment to act is now seen to be that which is acted upon, the object surrounded on both sides by the plenitude of God. Like Silva's yearning at the beginning of the *Cosmographia*, the earth's aspiration to fullness is shown to be, in strict truth, heaven's condescension to fulfill it.

Yet because of this understanding, the world is finally free to act without compromising the power of God.

For just as the sensible universe grows whole from the whole, and grows beautiful from the beautiful, so it is made eternal by its eternal exemplar.

Sicut enim integrascit ex integro, pulcrescit ex pulcro, sic exemplari suo eternatur eterno. (*Meg.* IV, xi, 3-4)

In effect, it is no longer an Augustinian world, passively receiving the divine light. Or rather, it is a world which finally realizes the Augustinian vision, which shows that, from the other side, to receive the light is to reach up toward it, to be made is to become. Those verbs of growth—'integrascit,' 'pulcrescit'—emerge not only from the great world as a whole,

---

[49] I have omitted the editor's punctuation in this passage and translated it to suggest a sense of its initial, forward 'momentum,' which is progressively qualified at each point after 'genuit' and finally revised in a retrospective reading of the sentence; see, e.g., Dronke's comma after 'genuit' and my discussion below.

but from its humblest inhabitants. As Bernard earlier describes the quickening of life in the cosmic catalogue of *Megacosmos*, the crocus pales ('Pallescitque') beside the purple hyacinth, and the scent of mace 'competes' ('certat') with beds of cassia (*Meg.* III, 329–30). Such animating techniques, long part of the stock in trade of the rhetoricians, become rather flamboyant in the poetic manuals of the late twelfth and early thirteenth centuries,[50] but for Bernard they seem to display a deeper philosophic point, as if to suggest, with Clarembald of Arras, that even the meanest flowers that blow do have a potentiality to act. That potentiality is displayed in the central vision of the poem by the whole sensible universe, growing whole ('integrascit') from below, even as it is integrated from above ('ex integro').

Such is the process of perpetual transfiguration envisioned at the center of the *Cosmographia*, a passage where the story is suspended for a moment, as if the allegory were taking account of itself. The language has a certain self-consciousness about it, a sense that in composing the words, the poet is also criticizing them—'weaving' and 'unweaving' the texture of his world ('texit et retexit,' *Meg.* IV, xiv, 7–8), in the closing words of the vision itself.[51] In merging the compositional and critical traditions of allegory, it is true, Bernard gives new vitality to the allegorical tradition. But in the paradox we have encountered throughout this study, the movement toward allegory is the beginning of the movement away from it. The central vision of the *Cosmographia*, where the allegory tries to assess itself, and in so doing, points away from itself toward the truth, is the ancestor of the great 'internal explications' of later medieval allegory: the self-evaluation that Alan of Lille inserts at the very midpoint of the *Anticlaudianus* (V, 265–77); the criticism of

[50] See, e.g., the vivid verbs exhibited by Geoffrey of Vinsauf, *Poetria Nova* IV ('Ornaments of Style'), ed. Edmond Faral in *Les Arts poétiques,* cited (above) in Ch. III, n.70; for Bernard's general influence upon Matthew of Vendôme and Geoffrey, see *Cosm.* (tr), p. 57, with p. 59. Cf. the kinetic effect of a tapestry on the creation described in an earlier poem by Baudri of Bourgueil to Adela, Countess of Blois, a selection from which is printed as poem 155 in *Oxford Book*, cited above in Ch. IV, n. 41.

[51] For this translation of 'texit et retexit,' see the n. in *Cosm.*, p. 167. The parallel cited by Dronke and Wetherbee should be supplemented by the Remigius commentary ed. by Silk, *Saecvli*, p. 320, which suggests how such an unraveling is a *reditus* to God, a 'resolution' from bodies into elements, from elements into Hyle, from Hyle to God.

Nature that Nature's own priest delivers in the extended discourse on the 'heavenly park' in the *Romance of the Rose*; the professorial explication that occupies the middle book of Chaucer's *House of Fame*. Such passages are critical comments on the poetic composition, breakages within the very literary form that depends on breakage, the turning of division against itself that ceaselessly transforms allegory as it passes into the later Middle Ages.[52]

In this sense, it seems almost as if the final passage of the *Cosmographia* were not only a retrospective on its own dynamic processes, but an anticipation of the perpetual transfiguration to come.

The nature of the universe flows back into itself, and so survives itself; it abides, nourished by its very flowing away. For that which is cast outward runs back into the sum of things, and dies not once that it may die often.

> Influit ipsa sibi mundi natura, superstes,
> Permanet et fluxu pascitur usque suo:
> Scilicet ad summam rerum iactura recurrit,
> Nec semel ut possit sepe perire perit.
> (*Mic.* XIV, 171–4)[53]

It is a kind of *exstasis*, a standing outside itself, as the universe survives its own destruction ('superstes'), becomes a bystander of its own participation, like Nature ascending through nature itself, making itself its own object. The universe's centrifugal tendencies ('iactura') are but the other side of its centripetal ones ('recurrit'). It expands and contracts at once. 'Not once, that it may often' ('Nec semel ut possit sepe'), the last phrase begins, as if to suggest continuing activity, like the cycle just described. But then the last two words of the phrase come crashing in on this activity—'it dies to die' ('perire perit')—only to cancel themselves out in turn, by doubling up upon themselves. Like the universe as a whole, the text contradicts

---

[52] As in the case of the *Cosm.*, this broad process extends beyond specific passages to the dynamics of such sophisticated allegories as a whole; for some of its later medieval aspects, see Maureen Quilligan, 'Allegory, Allegoresis, and the Deallegorization of Language: The *Roman de la rose*, the *De planctu naturae*, and the *Parlement of Foules*,' in *Allegory, Myth, and Symbol*, ed. Bloomfield, pp. 163–86.

[53] In the last line I have omitted the editor's punctuation; see my discussion below, and cf. n. 49 above.

the act of death in the very process of asserting it. Death is made permanent because even it continues to die, so that life may continue to live.

At the same time, this transfiguration has its darker consequences. In the perpetual flux, all composite things, including man himself, must dissolve. 'With the slippage of his body, the whole man flows away.' ('Effluit occiduo corpore totus homo,' *Mic.* XIV, 176.)[54] Nothing divided by nature, whether the constituents of the cosmos or the categories of allegory, can exhibit in its own right the integrity of the whole. All that is available to man is to explore those dualities, to manipulate the divided world with his own faculties and powers—and it is with these that Bernard concludes the poem, ending with man's 'all-capable hands' ('omnificasque manus,' *Mic.* XIV, 179–82).[55] It seems a comment on both the liabilities and the possibilities of his own work that Bernard concludes with the need to engage the world in its own right. Such a process cannot resolve the disparities of a divided world, but as the allegories of experience to come will show beyond Bernard's own still-limited program, it can begin to comprehend the world's dynamics, and thus exhibit on the human level that 'manifold faculty or spirit' ('multiplex . . . sensus vel spiritus,' *Meg.* IV, ix, 8–11) which organizes matter itself. In this sense, the multiplicity of human discourse, whatever its limitations, has its own potentiality, testifying to the creativity of God. In a famous comparison, Augustine had said that God 'enriched the course of world history by the kind of antithesis that gives beauty to a poem':

The opposition of such contraries ('contraria contrariis opposita') gives an added beauty to speech; and in the same way there is beauty in the composition of the world's history arising from the antithesis of contraries—a kind of eloquence in events, instead of in words.[56]

---

[54] Dronke, *Cosm.*, pp. 48–9, argues that even in this passage there are wordplays suggesting the perpetual generation of new life; cf. Wetherbee, *Cosm.* (tr.), pp. 51–2, on the tone here.

[55] On human engagement with the world as a source of cultural progress and cosmic reform in the *Cosm.*, see Stock, pp. 77–82, 122, 147, 161–2, 234–7.

[56] See *De Civ. Dei* XI, 18; *PL* 41, 332; translation based on *The City of God*, tr. Henry Bettenson (Harmondsworth, 1972).

Such a divine act is not available in its full propriety to a man composing in words, living in a world that is itself but an image —the image of a better world ('mundi melioris ymago,' *Mic.* X, 9). Yet it is only by delving into the figurative world of which he is part, like the figures of this very drama, learning to find their way about the universe, that he can begin to discover the substantive world at its source.

In the end, this perspective both complicates and enriches the original program of Noys (*Mic.* X), as she directs her charges to complete the world with man—the very model of division and consolidation. 'He shall draw his mind from heaven, his body from the elements,' she proclaims. 'Though of diverse natures,' these shall be 'joined into one.' 'Divine shall he be, earthly shall he be,' capable of 'conforming to his two natures' ('Naturis . . . duabus'). 'With his very figure testifying' to the majesty of his mind ('maiestatem mentis testante figura'), he shall 'lift up his head to the stars,' making their courses the 'pattern' for his own life. 'He shall behold in light the causes immersed in darkness' ('mersas caligine causas'), 'so that Nature may keep nothing concealed.' As in so much of Bernard's poem, the thought itself is ancient, but it is transformed by its deployment.[57] As the actual creative process preceding and following this proclamation shows, these dualities of matter and spirit produce critical tensions, requiring the constant adjustment of one force to another. At the same time, though, these very tensions provoke the drive to turn the old formulas into new potentialities. Already in the *Cosmographia*, 'heaven' and the 'elements' are not merely categories framing man according to 'mind' and 'body'; they are themselves becoming objects of his own systematic investigation. If in one sense, then, man's 'diverse natures' are a problematic duality, in another sense they provide an opportunity for him to see both sides of things; they thus make him the kind of figure ('figura') that not only constitutes a double reference, but comprehends it—both that which it appears to be, and that to which it refers. 'Non simplex natura hominis'—the nature of man is twofold. With these words,

---

[57] On the general thought, see the refs. cited in *Cosm.* (tr.), p. 162, nn. 69–73, esp. Silverstein, 97, n. 28; on its qualification, see Wetherbee, pp. 179–86; Stock, pp. 200–2; and my discussion below.

Prudentius had ended his allegory of man, consigning him to perpetual war, until, as he put it, God himself comes to bring peace (*Psychomachia*, ll. 904, 910). It is a measure of how far allegory—and the world—have changed, that Bernard uses this very twofold nature ('Naturis . . . duabus') not to withhold salvation until God comes, but to show that he comes only as we depart toward him. The principle of that movement, as in every allegory, is the study of causes ('causas'), which even when wrapped in the *involucra* of dark conceits, eventually unfold into the light of truth.

It is in this way that the *Cosmographia* reveals a tendency central to the 'renaissance of the twelfth century,' the period in which allegory finally comes of age. When we speak about a new 'this-worldliness' in that era, we mean not that it denied the other world, not that it ignored it, not even that it deemphasized it. Rather, we mean precisely the opposite, that because the twelfth century truly valued the other world, it revalued this one; that because it truly believed that heaven was the goal, it cultivated the means to reach it; that it no longer merely quoted the famous text of Romans 1: 20, in which invisible things are to be understood by the things that are made, *invisibilia* by *visibilia*, but rather demonstrated it, acted it out, for the first time in the Christian West.

Indeed, the *Cosmographia* showed that in a two-sided universe, our task is precisely to fulfill the oblique side of the transaction, not to seek escape from it. If the direct is the property of the divine, then the oblique is its proper counterpart on earth. Far from being sinful to cultivate this world, then, it was presumptuous to pretend we were not in it. Only by aspiring from below could we receive the light from above. This insight underlies the whole *Cosmographia*. The passivity of mere matter is passivity only from the perspective of *God*. From *our* perspective, the reception of the divine form *is* our passion for it, *is* the active struggle. It is not a sequential act, where we aspire and God rewards. It is a reciprocal one, where the very meaning of God's search for us is, from our point of view, our search for him.

Yet even while we celebrate our obliquity and fashion our allegories, the celebration is tempered by the knowledge that fiction is only a beautiful consolation for exile. We remain at some remove from the truth, and the best we can do, as Augustine pointed out, is remove those removals, turn things into signs, until all signs end in God. The *Cosmographia* is the first full allegorical articulation of this dilemma, and it is a mark of its wisdom that even in demonstrating the great powers of oblique language, it found them wanting. At the same time, it displayed the other side of that want, the active yearning for integrity. The sentiment had long affected the interpretive and compositional traditions, but the *Cosmographia* infused it into the very dynamics of a philosophic and imaginative technique, into the obliquity of allegorical discourse, which yearned, like Matter itself, to escape from otherness, and, in Bernard's words, to be born again.

Bernard Silvestris thus confirmed the problem and the promise with which we began this study, that the deeper we penetrate into the center of things, the more we consign our language obliquely to the circumference. He wrote a poem on that circumference, and in so doing, turned allegory into a full-scale, sophisticated narrative. Occasionally, it is true, he tried too hard to reach the center, to imitate the divine 'complication' of things, and his poem, even where it is not obscure, remains desperately complicated. On the whole, however, the *Cosmographia* remains true to the weaknesses and strengths of the allegorical tradition; indeed, it finally places them in relief. It demonstrates that allegory—like all fiction—remains powerless to prevent the self-exposure of its own deficiencies. The exploitation of that powerlessness, however, is itself a kind of power. For in the process, allegory not only shows what the truth is not; it shows, from the other side, what it is.

AFTERWORD

Across the great sea we pursue a fleeing Italy. (Virgil,
Aeneid V, 628–9.)

During the periods explored in this study, it seems at times as if
the technique of allegory itself 'dies not once that it may die
often'—regenerating itself in the process. No broad investigation of certain aspects of that technique can do more than offer
a few perspectives on its complex development. Even in a
single major work, the dynamics of allegory are far more intricate than any provisional category of our own analysis, and
the movement of allegory as a whole is inseparable from
changes in orientation far beyond the scope of this book.

Two thousand years, after all, separate that primal episode in
the *Iliad*, where a man is poised between disruptive 'anger' and
the goddess Athena, from the primal episode in the *Cosmographia*, where a Nature is poised between a 'hostile
coalescence' and the 'divine Mind.' Whatever the traces—
many times removed—of that original configuration, the new
opening belongs to a radically different world. By the time of
the *Cosmographia*, Athena has not just been interpreted in terms
of wisdom; Wisdom itself has been incorporated into a
transcendent God who yet projects himself dramatically into
his own work. Anger has not just been conceptualized in terms
of *thymos;* passion itself has been drawn into a single psychic
continuum, so that it can act as a figure aspiring toward
reason, as well as disrupting it. The framework for the encounter between reason and passion is not just man, but
Nature as a whole, a figure who exhibits at once God's implication with the very physics of matter and matter's inherent
potentiality for the divine. If the allegorical tradition begins in
some respects with Homer's suggestive moment of individual
revelation, it requires the most expansive philosophic and imaginative strategies to produce Bernard's extended allegory of
cosmic creation.

At the same time, however far removed from its origins,
allegory seems always to be returning toward them—returning

with a difference. As the figures of the *Cosmographia* move up and down the universe, they enact not only the program of God, but the possibilities of man, who by the close of the allegory is about to emerge as an individual in his own right, confronting the very dualities which compose him. A generation later, in the *Complaint of Nature*, the individual himself is the central witness to the allegorical plot, which plays out before him his own moral and imaginative dilemmas. By the time of the *Anticlaudianus,* the man *in propria persona* begins (somewhat tentatively) to enter the allegorical action itself, helping to organize the closing *psychomachia*. Still, as the individual personality thus begins to return to the narrative foreground, the result is not quite some new Achilles, but a consciousness interacting with an array of abstract possibilities, systematically deployed on their own terms. In trying to coordinate such figures, that consciousness is seeking at the same time to order itself; the very operation of the allegory thus depends increasingly on the modulations of the human mind. With the *Romance of the Rose* and the *Divine Comedy*, the individual's constant movement outward to explore the figurative world coincides with his constant movement inward to compose himself—a center that seems forever to recede with each advance.

If such systematic developments await the future, they are inseparable from the diverging and converging tendencies displayed in allegory from the start. At once slipping away from its object and toward it, allegory is always seeking to come to terms with the disparities of its world and its own technique. It is true that the increasing interaction between the two allegorical traditions gradually integrates these problems, but it never fully resolves them. It rather produces increasingly sophisticated ways to refine and articulate its own dilemmas, no sooner generating figures than displacing them, while simultaneously turning that critique into a new starting point for its own creations. In this dynamic process, the technique of allegory seems almost to make a comment not only upon itself, but upon those who explore it—and finally, upon every search for the causes of things. Such explorations are forever aspiring toward a fulfillment that lies beyond them. They may point the way toward an end; in themselves, they remain always a beginning.

APPENDIX I

On the History of the Term 'Allegory'

The history of the word tells us much about its nature. *Allēgoria* has two component parts in Greek. The first of these parts, coming from the word *allos*, means 'other'; it inverts the sense of the second component. This second component is the verb *agoreuein*, originally meaning 'to speak in the assembly,' in the *agora*. Though already in Homer this verb has the general meaning 'to speak,' throughout its history it retained the original sense of discoursing in public, speaking in the open.

The 'open assembly,' or *agora*, however, which lies at the heart of the verb, developed at an early stage two quite different connotations. On the one hand, it referred to an official assembly. Thus, the verb *agoreuein*, in its simple form, is found above all in political and legal contexts, and in the Athenian legislative assembly, the phrase *Tis agoreuein bouletai?* means 'Who wishes to address the house?' On the other hand, the word *agora* also referred to the open market. Accordingly, its derivatives sometimes had the sense of 'common' or 'low,' such as the adjective *agoraios*.

The second component of the word 'allegory' thus had historical connections both with official, political address and with everyday, common speech. When this component was combined with the inverting word *allos,* the resulting composite connoted both that which was said in *secret*, and that which was *unworthy* of the *crowd*. These two connotations of the word 'allegory'—guarded language and elite language—became explicit parts of allegorical theory and practice. The sense of secretive, guarded language had special importance for political allegory, in which the allegorist spoke, as it were, other than in the official assembly. The sense of elite, superior language had particular point in religious and philosophic contexts, in which the allegorist spoke other than in the common market place. Such connotations, however, as with all general characterizations about the word, apply only at particular times and in different degrees in the history of allegorical writing.

The composition of the word also helps to explain the two distinct traditions of allegory, which are inverse in procedure. *Allos* combined with *agoreuein* by dropping its *os* suffix, as was common before words beginning with *a* + guttural, such as *agoreuein*. The composite word thus means to 'speak otherwise,' to 'say other things,' to say other than that which is meant. Insofar as the emphasis is placed on *saying* other than what is meant, allegorical theory and practice is largely a grammatical or rhetorical matter, concentrating on the *compositional* technique of creating an allegorical text. This is the focus of one of the two traditions of allegory, allegorical composition. Insofar as the emphasis is placed on *meaning* other than what is said, allegorical theory and practice is largely a philosophic or exegetical matter, stressing the *interpretive* technique of extracting meaning from a text already written. This is the focus of the other tradition of allegory, allegorical interpretation.

The word itself first appears in the Hellenistic period, with reference to the grammatical or rhetorical tradition. If the rhetorician whom we call 'Demetrius' wrote his *On Style (De Elocutione)* as early as 270 BC, as G. M. A. Grube argues in *A Greek Critic: Demetrius on Style, The Phoenix*, Supplementary Volume IV (Toronto, 1961), 56, his use of the noun *allēgoria*—along with its verbal, adverbial, and adjectival forms—may be the first extant appearance of the word. Here it has the restricted sense of a trope, like the brief figure of speech Aristotle defined as 'to mean something other than what one says' (*to mē ho phēsi legein*)—though Aristotle did not use the word 'allegory.' The treatise *On Style*, however, may be as late as the first century AD; this was the view of W. Rhys Roberts, ed. and tr., *Demetrius on Style* (Cambridge, 1902), p. 64. For recent discussions of the treatise's date, see Grube, 'The Date of Demetrius *On Style*,' *Phoenix*, 18 (1964), 294–302 (third century BC); D. M. Schenkeveld, *Studies in Demetrius* On Style (Amsterdam, 1964), pp. 135–48 (first century AD); and Grube, 'Greek Historians and Greek Critics,' *The Phoenix*, 28 (1974), 75 (again, an argument for the third century BC). The only other extant case in which the word may appear this early is the statement attributed to the third-century BC Stoic, Cleanthes, where the adverbial form, 'allegorically' (*allēgorikōs*), occurs. The presence of the word in this quotation, however, may be due to the writer of the report, who lived centuries after Cleanthes himself. In any case, here the word is used as an interpretive, not a rhetorical, term. See R. P. C. Hanson, *Allegory and Event: A Study of the Sources and Significance of Origen's Interpretation of Scripture* (Richmond, Va., 1959), pp. 37–8, and Reinhart Hahn, *Die Allegorie in der antiken Rhetorik*, Diss. Tübingen 1967 (Tübingen, 1967), pp. 15–16. The word's first certain extant appearance in a Greek rhetorical treatise is in Philodemus, about 60 BC. See *Philodemi Volumina Rhetorica*, ed. Siegfried Sudhaus (Leipzig, 1892), 164. 122, 174. 24 and 181. 25, where the word is treated as a familiar trope (*tropos*) and linked with metaphor. A generation earlier than Philodemus' treatise, this trope is translated into Latin as 'permutatio' by the author of the *Rhetorica ad Herennium*, and classified among the 'figures of diction' ('exornationes verborum'), as opposed to the 'figures of thought' ('exornationes sententiarum'). See the edition by H. Caplan (Cambridge, Mass., 1954), IV, xxxiv, 46, and see p. xxvi for the date of the treatise, 86–82 BC. It was Cicero who first used the Greek word *allēgoria* in a Latin rhetorical treatise, and who also gave it, at times, the sense of a continued *series* of metaphors, rather than a restricted figure of speech. See his *De Oratore*, ed. and tr. H. Rackham (Cambridge, Mass., 1948), III, xli, 166, and his *Orator*, ed. and tr. H. M. Hubbell (Cambridge, Mass., 1939), xxvii, 94: 'a continuous stream of metaphors' ('cum fluxerunt continuae plures tralationes [= translationes]'). This was the sense that Quintilian, in the first century AD, canonized in his *Institutio Oratoria*. See the edition of H. E. Butler, 4 vols. (London, 1920–2), IX, ii, 46: 'A continuous metaphor makes an allegory' (*'allēgorian* facit continua *metaphora'*); see also VIII, vi, 44–7, for Quintilian's example of a sustained allegory by Horace. While the earlier, restricted sense of the word appears elsewhere both in Cicero and in Quintilian, and continues throughout the rhetorical tradition, the sense of a sustained rhetorical composition retains a firm hold on rhetorical theory after Quintilian. Cicero considered allegory a metaphor, or 'tralatio,' while Quintilian also referred to it as 'inversio,' a word that is coupled with *allegoria* in one of the earliest English appearances of the word in a rhetorical context, Thomas Elyot's *Dictionary*: '*Allegoria*—a figure called inversion, where it is one in woordes, and an other in sentence or meaning'; quoted in Angus Fletcher, *Allegory: The Theory of a Symbolic Mode* (Ithaca, N.Y., 1964), p. 2, n. 1. This definition, in fact, is a direct translation of Quintilian's *Inst. Orat.* VIII, vi, 44.

The word *allēgoria* does not appear in the other tradition of allegory, allegorical interpretation, until the first centuries BC and AD. (A possible exception is its attribution to the third-century BC philosopher, Cleanthes; see above.) The actual practice of allegorical interpretation, however, began systematically in the sixth century BC, with the philosophic interpretation of Homer; see Ch. II. Until the first century BC, the word *hyponoia*, 'under-sense,' was used to designate that which was meant (the philosophic meaning), as opposed to that which was said (the literal meaning). Strabo, writing near the turn of the first centuries BC and AD, may have been the first to use the grammatical term *allēgoria* (as a participle) in reference to the allegorical *interpretation* of Homer; see Buffière, p.46. In any case, the word rapidly gains currency in this exegetical sense by the first century AD. This may be the result in part of the increasing interest of grammarians in such exegetical speculations; see J. Tate, 'Plato and Allegorical Interpretation,' *The Classical Quarterly*, 24 (1930), 2. The rhetorician Heraclitus uses both *hyponoia* and *allēgoria* to describe his interpretation of Homer. So does the great Jewish exegete Philo, at about the same period, only with reference to the Bible, not Homer. Plutarch, in a work from the late first or early second century AD, is the first to note consciously the substitution of terms. 'Long ago,' he writes in De Audiendis Poetis iv, 19, these underlying meanings were called hyponoiai; 'now' they are called allēgoriai; see Pépin, pp. 87–8. The older word, however, remained current for centuries after Plutarch. The word allēgoria appears once in the New Testament, as a participle, in Galatians 4:24, translated into the Vulgate as 'quae sunt per allegoriam dicta' ('which things are said by an allegory'). Paul's application of the word here to the relation between Old and New Covenants helps to pose for early Christian exegesis the question of shifts in history, as well as in linguistic reference; see my account and notes in Chs. III and IV. In the early fifth century, Augustine, drawing upon the rhetorical tradition along with the exegetical one, cites the gloss of the phrase from Galatians as 'which things signify one thing by another' ('quae sunt aliud ex alio significantia'); see De Trinitate XV, 9; PL 42, 1068. After Augustine, related definitions of allegory in an interpretive context are frequent. See, e.g., Cassiodorus (sixth century), Expositio in Psalterium, Psal. XXXI, PL 70, 223B: 'Allegory is . . . when one thing is said, and another thing is signified' ('Allegoria est . . . quando aliud dicitur, et aliud significatur'); Raban Maur (early ninth century), commenting on the Galatians verse, in Ennar. in Epp. Pauli Lib. XV, in Epist. ad Galat., PL 112, 330C: 'Allegory is, properly speaking, a technique of grammar . . . It alleges one thing in words, and signifies another thing in meaning' ('Allegoria proprie de arte grammatica est . . . Aliud praetendit in verbis, aliud significat in sensu'); Hugh of St. Victor (twelfth century), De Scripturis et Scriptoribus Sacris, c. 3, PL 175, 12B: 'Allegory is a kind of "other-speaking" ("alieniloquium"), since one thing is said and another thing is signified' ('Dicitur allegoria quasi alieniloquium, quia aliud dicitur et aliud significatur'). In the early seventh century, Isidore of Seville had used the word 'alieniloquium' to describe the grammatical technique of allegory; it is the Latin equivalent of the Greek composite allos + agoreuein. See Isidore's Etymologiae I, xxxvii, 22, in the edition of W. M. Lindsay, Isidori Hispalensis Episcopi: Etymologiarum sive Originum Libri XX, 2 vols. (Oxford, 1911). The first use of the word 'allegory' in English is, predictably, the translation of the Galatians verse in the 'Wycliffite' Bible, c.1384: 'The whiche thingis ben seid by allegorie, or goostly vndirstondinge.' See Middle English Dictionary, ed. Hans Kurath and Sherman M. Kuhn (Ann Arbor, Mich., 1956–   ), s.v. 'allegorie.'

In both traditions of allegory, then, the basis for the word, its theory, and its practice, is obliquity. While it shares this characteristic with other metaphorical techniques, such as the broad technique of 'irony,' defined by both Cicero (*De Oratore* III, liii, 203) and Quintilian (*Inst. Orat.* IX, ii, 44) as 'saying one thing and meaning another,' allegory is the preeminently oblique way of writing. See, e.g., Quintilian's distinction in *Inst. Orat.* VIII, vi, 58. Among the variations on the procedure, particularly *obscure* allegory has been called 'enigma' ('aenigma') since Quintilian; see *Inst. Orat.* VIII, vi, 52; Augustine, *De Trin.* XV, 9, in *PL* 42, 1068–9; and Isidore, *Et.* I, xxxvii, 26. The word *allegoria* also refers frequently in Christian exegesis to one particular transfer among a series of allegorical transfers from the literal sense: the 'allegorical' meaning, the 'tropological' or 'moral' meaning, and the 'anagogic' meaning. Even among exegetes who specified this use of the term, however, the word *allegoria* was often used to include the general system of such transfers; see de Lubac, I, i, 139–57, and I, ii, 373–83, 403–6, 416–23; Jean Pépin, *Dante et la tradition de l'allégorie* (Montreal, 1970), pp. 45–50, 88–9, 129, n. 11; and my discussion in Chs. III and IV. The widespread distinction between 'allegory' and 'symbol,' which varies from theorist to theorist and remains problematic in both practical and conceptual terms, is in many respects a development of the Romantic period. See Pépin, pp. 58–61, for Schelling and other German theorists; Graham Hough, *A Preface to* The Faerie Queene (London, 1962), pp. 100–2, and Edward A. Bloom, 'The Allegorical Principle,' *English Literary History*, 18 (1951), 185, for Blake, Coleridge, and the English view. Even among the Romantics, the terminological distinction may obscure the literary practice; see, e.g., Michael Murrin, *The Veil of Allegory: Some Notes toward a Theory of Allegorical Rhetoric in the English Renaissance* (Chicago, 1969), pp. 199–212, on Wordsworth and Shelley. In its early history, the word 'symbol' (*symbolon*) is often used in Neoplatonic and Neopythagorean criticism to suggest a particularly mysterious shift of reference, although the term sometimes converges with the word 'icon' (*eikōn*), which designates a more straightforward kind of correlation, and the two procedures themselves, which are not always clearly distinguished, overlap with the broad exegetical strategy of *allegoria*. See Buffière, p. 59; Hahn, *Die Allegorie*, p. 31, n. 34, and p. 146; Pépin, *Dante et la tradition de l'allégorie*, pp. 15–19; Coulter, pp. 32–72; John Dillon, 'Image, Symbol and Analogy: Three Basic Concepts of Neoplatonic Allegorical Exegesis,' in *The Significance of Neoplatonism,* ed. R. Baine Harris (Norfolk, Va., 1976), pp. 247–62; Wesley Trimpi, *Muses of One Mind* (Princeton, 1983), pp. 164–240; and my discussion in Ch. III. For the 'symbol' in medieval Christian writing, see, e.g., Gerhart B. Ladner, 'Medieval and Modern Understanding of Symbolism: A Comparison,' *Speculum*, 54 (1979), and my discussion and notes in Ch. IV. The use of the word 'allegory' in non-verbal contexts, such as art, as well as the broad definitions the word sometimes receives today, are developments which occur long after the early history of allegory, and should not be applied indiscriminately to this early period.

In constructing this sketch of the history of the word, I have found particularly useful the summaries of Grube, *A Greek Critic*, pp. 85, 124-5, 134-5; Buffière, pp. 45-59; Pépin, pp. 85-92; Hahn, *Die Allegorie*, pp. 15-16 and 127-30; and Henri de Lubac, ' "Typologie" et "allégorisme," ' *Recherches de science religieuse*, 34 (1947), 180-226. For a concise, learned overview of the two allegorical traditions, see Pépin's *Dante et la tradition de l'allégorie*. My account of the word's etymological history and early development is based in part on articles by Pierre Chantraine, *Dictionnaire Étymologique de la Langue Grecque*, I (Paris, 1968), s.v. *agora*; J. C. Joosen and J. H. Waszink, in *Reallexikon für Antike und Christentum*, s.v. 'allegorese'; Konrad Müller, in *Paulys Realencyclopädie der classischen Altertumswissenschaft*, Supplementband IV, 16-22, s.v. 'allegorische dichtererklärung'; H. G. Liddell and R. Scott (eds.), rev. H. J. Jones, *A Greek-English Lexicon* (Oxford, 1968), s.v. *agora*, *agoreuō*, and *allēgoreō*; and J. Geffcken, in *Encyclopaedia of Religion and Ethics*, I (1908), s.v. 'Allegory, Allegorical Interpretation.' While the focus of this study is the investigation of allegory itself, rather than the analysis of a word, the one is not entirely possible without the other.

APPENDIX II

On the History of the Term 'Personification'

The word 'personification' is a composite of the Latin words *persona*, meaning 'mask' or 'person,' and *facere*, meaning 'to make.' This term corresponds to the original Greek composite *prosōpopoiia*, which was transliterated in Roman times as *prosopopoeia*, and which still has currency alongside the word 'personification.' The first element of the Greek word, *prosōpon*, refers originally to the face or countenance of a person, later to a façade in general. This sense of a front or façade affects the whole history of the word and its derivatives, and accounts in part for the rhetorical consensus that 'personification' is a verbal front, a literary façade masking something else underneath it. Indeed, by the time of Greek tragedy, the word *prosōpon* refers explicitly to the mask worn by a character on stage, and later to the character itself, the 'person.' Combining the word with the verb, *poiein*, 'to make,' the composite word *prosōpo-poiein* means to compose by means of *prosōpa*. Accordingly, the noun *prosōpo-poiia* means 'the composing of speeches for characters,' or 'dramatization.' Like the word *allēgoria*, this word is a creation of the Hellenistic period. In the early first-century BC *Rhetorica ad Herennium*, IV, liii, *prosōpopoiia* is expressed as 'conformatio,' grouped among the 'figures of thought' ('exornationes sententiarum'—but see Caplan's note on p. 399 of his edition), and applied to the rhetorical practice of either fashioning a presence for a person who is absent, or attributing form and language to that which is mute, formless, or inanimate. Cicero, *De Oratore* III, liii, 205, calls it the 'introduction of fictitious persons' ('personarum ficta inductio'), and considers it one of the methods of amplification in skillful oratory. It is Quintilian who transliterates the Greek word into Latin as *prosopopoeia;* see *Inst. Orat.* I, viii, 3; IV, i, 69; and XI, i, 41). At times he echoes Cicero's description of the technique; thus, in *Inst. Orat.* VI, i, 25, he writes: 'And by such impersonations I mean fictitious speeches supposed to be uttered, such as an advocate puts in the mouth of his client' ('Prosopopoeiae, id est fictae alienarum personarum orationes, quales litigatorum ore dicit patronus'; tr. Butler). In his full discussion of *prosopopoeia*, though (*Inst. Orat.* IX, ii, 29–37), he presents it as a very broad technique, including the fashioning of conversations between ourselves and others, as well as the giving of speeches to the dead, to cities, or to abstractions ('formae'). In the Middle Ages, the word normally has the general sense in which

Isidore of Seville defines it: 'the fashioning of a character and speech for inanimate things' ('cum inanimalium et persona et sermo fingitur,' *Et.* II, xiii, 1). While the affiliation of the word with 'allegory' is a late development, the incipient technique itself is called *allēgoria* as early as the first century AD; see Heraclitus' *Homeric Problems*, ed. and tr. Félix Buffière in *Héraclite: Allégories d'Homère* (Paris, 1962), ch. 29, pp. 35–6, on Homer's 'Strife' (*Eris*), and Hahn, *Die Allegorie*, pp. 51 and 130. In a larger sense, the whole history of the word demonstrates a close connection with the creative technique of saying something in fiction and meaning something else in fact; cf. Pépin, *Dante et la tradition de l'allégorie*, p. 14. For this account of the word's etymology and early history, see esp. Pierre Chantraine, *Dictionnaire Étymologique de la Langue Grecque*, III (Paris, 1974), s.v. *prosōpon*; H. G. Liddell and R. Scott (eds.), rev. H. J. Jones, *A Greek-English Lexicon* (Oxford, 1968), s.v. *prosōpon* and *prosōpo-poieō*; and Karl Reinhardt, *Vermächtnis der Antike: Gesammelte Essays zur Philosophie und Geschichtsschreibung*, ed. Carl Becker (Göttingen, 1960), pp. 8–9.

The technique of personification, in its broad sense, is extremely old. In the traditional account, it arises from the ancient practice of elevating abstract concepts to the condition of personalized gods. Such abstractions appear already in Canaanite and Hittite mythological stories. See, e.g., the Canaanite *Poem of Baal*, translated and discussed in Theodore Gaster's *Thespis: Ritual, Myth, and Drama in the Ancient Near East*, rev. edn. (New York, 1961), pp. 114–24, which includes such figures as 'Sir Sea' (p. 155), 'Sir Adroit-and-Cunning' (p. 161), and 'Sir Holy-and-Blessed' (p. 181). Among the Greeks, too, natural phenomena like 'Ocean' (*Ōkeanos*) were often anthropomorphized while remaining physical conditions, and altars were erected to such abstractions as *Phēmē* (Fame or Rumor) and *Eirēnē* (Peace); see T. B. L. Webster, 'Personification as a Mode of Greek Thought,' *Journal of the Warburg and Courtauld Institutes*, 17 (1954), 10 and 14. Among the earliest Roman gods were abstractions such as 'Public Faith' ('Fides Publica'), 'Fortune' ('Fortuna'), and 'Concord' ('Concordia'). These 'deified abstracts' were apparently brought to Rome from the cult practices of the Italic peoples, and it has been argued that the practice is part of the inheritance of Indo-European civilization; see L. R. Lind, 'Roman Religion and Ethical Thought: Abstraction and Personification,' *The Classical Journal*, 69 (Dec. 1973–Jan. 1974), 117, and 'Primitivity and Roman Ideas: The Survivals,' *Latomus*, 35 (1976), 258. In such abstract deification, 'the personal god,' writes Lind ('Primitivity,' 250), 'develops from an impersonal force.'

Reinhardt, on the other hand, argued forcefully against the notion, which he traced to Grimm, that the gods emerge from the 'personification' of abstract concepts. On the contrary, he claimed, abstract personifications emerge from the gods (*Vermächtnis*, pp. 7–11). Arguing that the Hellenistic term *prosōpopoiia* means the technique of putting a mask on a thing or condition (pp. 8–9), Reinhardt found the origins of the process in the progressive association of the Olympians with human conditions. Thus, for example, a goddess like 'Themis' ('Justice'), who was in Homer the minister of the Olympian Zeus, eventually became associated so closely with the *human* condition of 'justice' that in Aeschylus' *Prometheus* she opposed Zeus himself (*Vermächtnis*, pp. 26–32). It was a similar transformation of the god into a personified human condition, in Reinhardt's view, that accounted for the 'Eros' of Plato's *Symposium*, who was 'young' because 'Eros' dwells in young hearts; the 'Lyssa,' or madness, who in Aeschylus was an actual demon, but who in Euripides was a personified state of mind; and the figures of 'Agnoia' (Ignorance) and 'Elenkhos' (Argument) in Menander's comedies (pp. 8–9).

Here, as in so many discussions about a broadly defined word, the conflict over the origins of 'personification' may be largely a terminological problem. The deified abstracts worshipped in Greece and Rome undeniably emerged from the practice of making an abstract condition a personal god; but these gods were not 'personifications' in the literary sense that Reinhardt tried to explain. Literary personification requires a *fictional* personality—as Cicero put it, 'the introduction of fictitious persons'—and the early gods of Rome were too literal for that status. Lind himself ('Roman Religion,' 109) distinguishes between the gods of religious cult and 'the personifications of Old Comedy,' which are 'dramatic allegory.'

In short, it is necessary to distinguish two meanings of the term 'personification.' One refers to the practice of giving an *actual* personality to an abstraction. This practice has its origins in animism and ancient religion, and is called 'personification' by modern theorists of religion and anthropology. Reinhardt's claim that Grimm was the 'scientific founder' of this theory is questionable. Herder, Heyne, and other German theorists had argued earlier that the names (*nomina*) originally given to abstract conditions gradually took on the powers (*numina*) of gods; see Pépin, pp. 39–40. For that matter, in some respects the argument appears already in Stoic thought; see Cicero's *De Natura Deorum* II, xxiii–xxviii, 59–72.

The other meaning of 'personification,' the one used throughout this study, is the historical sense of *prosopopoeia*. This refers to the practice of giving a consciously *fictional* personality to an abstraction, 'impersonating' it. This rhetorical practice requires a separation between the literary pretense of a personality, and the actual state of affairs. Thus, we cannot properly speak of literary 'personification' when Homer calls 'fire' by the name of 'Hephaestus' (*Iliad* II, 426), who is also described as a personal god. As J. Geffcken puts it, *Encyclopaedia of Religion and Ethics*, I (1908), pp. 327–8, this usage 'is neither allegory nor a conscious substitution of the gift of the god for his name (Plutarch), but a direct identification of the god with his earliest form of earthly manifestation.' Conversely, it is only when the 'personality' is a literary fiction separate from the actual condition that we have literary 'personification.' The history of personification bears out the fact. 'Fortuna' the actual deity may have been brought to Rome as early as the seventh or sixth century BC (Lind, 'Roman Religion,' 110), but the full-scale personification of 'Fortuna' did not occur until the Middle Ages, when 'the personified figure' no longer had 'a basis in fact,' as Howard R. Patch puts it in *The Goddess Fortuna in Mediaeval Literature* (1927; repr. London, 1967), p. 16; cf. also pp. 4 and 26. Reinhardt was right to point to drama and the Hellenistic period as turning points in this rhetorical tradition, but it is possible to find something of both the duality of perspective he associated with it and the actual practice of such 'impersonation' before Hellenism and outside drama; see, for example, Otto Seel, 'Antike und Frühchristliche Allegorik,' in *Festschrift für Peter Metz*, ed. Ursula Schlegel and Claus Zoege von Manteuffel (Berlin, 1965), pp. 11–23, and Webster, 'Personification,' 12 and 15. The broad technique in fact occurs briefly in the form of rhetorical flourishes in any sophisticated language; see, e.g., Charles Forster Smith, 'Personification in Thucydides,' *Classical Philology*, 13 (1918), 241–50.

There is, however, a major characteristic shared by the 'personifications' of Webster, Lind, and Reinhardt. Whether as gods or as fictions, they emerge from an emphasis on *human* conditions. See, for example, Webster, 'Personification,' 13, on Greek 'personifications of abstracts . . . at moments of great and compelling emotion,' and 14, on 'the giving of a hymn or cult to abstract ideas which are felt to be of extreme importance at some particular moment.' Compare Lind, 'Primitivity,' 258, on the Roman concern for 'what the gods could do for the Romans,' and 260, on Rome's 'functional and specialized' view of religion. Finally, compare Reinhardt, *Vermächtnis*, p. 25, on Hesiod's concern for 'the situation of men,' and p. 19, on the reconciliation of the eternal Olympians with 'the here and now' of spatial and temporal restrictions. While the rapport between personifications and persons is impressive, it remains imperfect. In its literary form, this disparity produces pressures to reconcile the fictional personification with the human personality. As in allegory as a whole, the self-consciousness of a distinction between fiction and fact increasingly preoccupies the technique.

INDEX

A note is normally indexed only if the topic for which it is cited is not mentioned in the corresponding discussion in the body of the text.